武井宏之

My younger brother made this (papier-mâché)
Hiroyuki Takei for my 32nd birthday. His
eyes are a little crazy, but at times like this
I feel I'm really blessed.

—*Hiroyuki Takei*

Unconventional author/artist Hiroyuki Takei began his career
by winning the Osamu Tezuka Cultural Prize (named after
the famous artist of the same name). After working as an
assistant to famed artist Nobuhiro Watsuki, Takei debuted in
Weekly Shonen Jump in 1997 with **Butsu Zone**, an action
series based on Buddhist mythology. His multicultural
adventure manga **Shaman King**, which debuted in 1998,
became a hit and was adapted into an anime TV series. His
new series **Ultimo** (*Karakuri Dôji Ultimo*) is currently being
serialized in the U.S. in **SHONEN JUMP**. Takei lists Osamu
Tezuka, American comics and robot anime among his many
influences.

SHAMAN KING VOL. 30
SHONEN JUMP Manga Edition

STORY AND ART BY
HIROYUKI TAKEI

English Adaptation/Lance Caselman
Translation/Lillian Olsen
Touch-up Art & Lettering/John Hunt
Design/Nozomi Akashi
Editor/Eric Searleman

VP, Production/Alvin Lu
VP, Sales & Product Marketing/Gonzalo Ferreyra
VP, Creative/Linda Espinosa
Publisher/Hyoe Narita

Printed in Canada

Published by VIZ Media, LLC
P.O. Box 77010
San Francisco, CA 94107

10 9 8 7 6 5 4 3 2 1
First printing, September 2010

PARENTAL ADVISORY
SHAMAN KING is rated T for Teen and is
recommended for ages 13 and up. This
volume contains violence.
ratings.viz.com

SHONEN JUMP MANGA

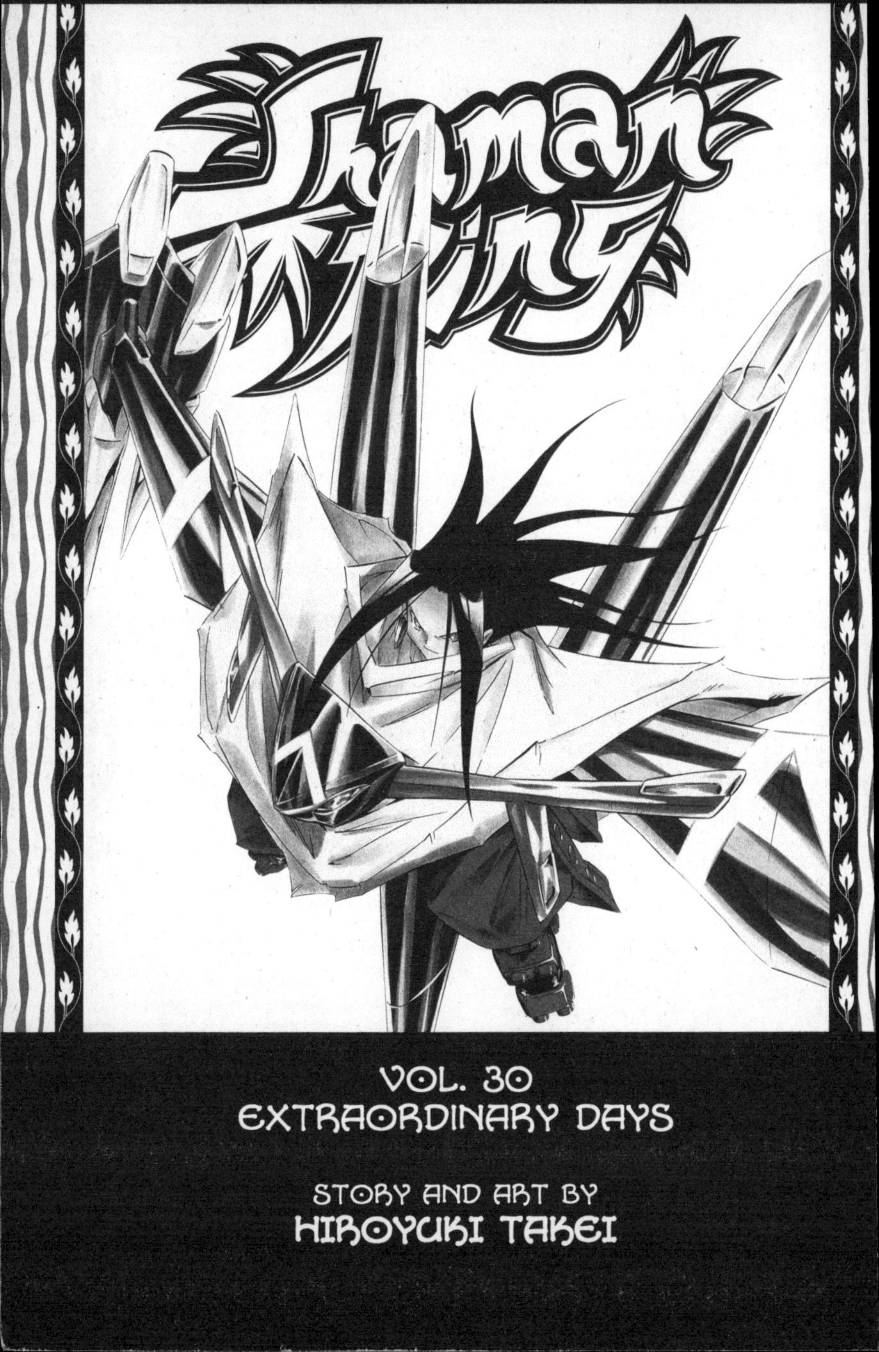
Shaman King

VOL. 30

EXTRAORDINARY DAYS

STORY AND ART BY

HIROYUKI TAKEI

CHARACTERS

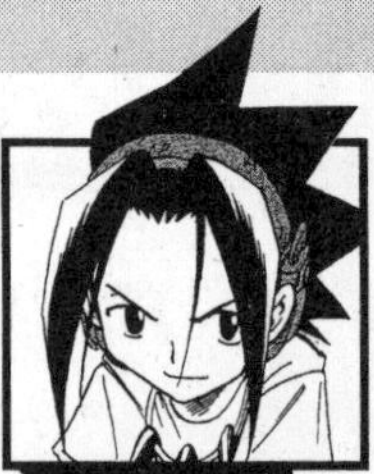

Yoh Asakura
Outwardly carefree and easygoing, Yoh bears a great responsibility as heir to a long line of Japanese shamans.

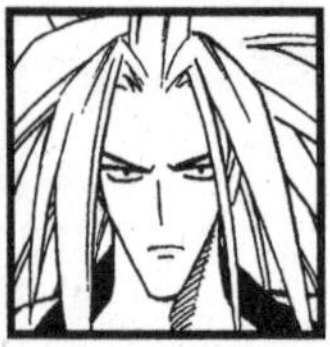

Amidamaru
"The Fiend" Amidamaru was, in life, a samurai of such skill and ferocity that he was a veritable one-man army. Now he is Yoh's loyal, and formidable, spirit ally.

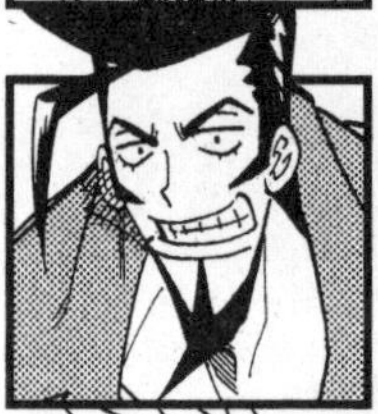

"Wooden Sword" Ryu
On a quest to find his Happy Place. Along the way, he became a shaman.

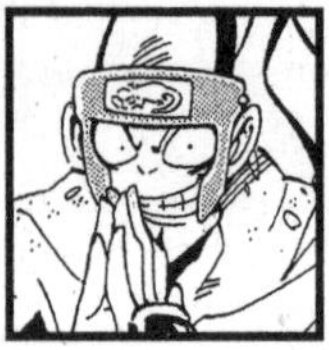

Tokagero
The ghost of a bandit slain by Amidamaru. He is now Ryu's spirit ally.

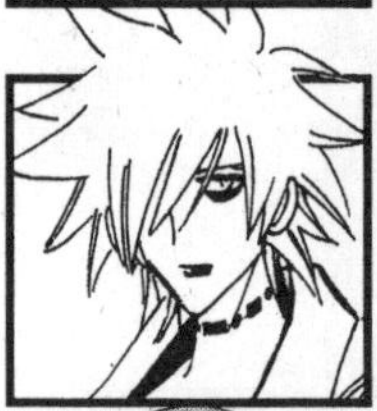

Faust VIII
A creepy German doctor and necromancer who is now Yoh's ally.

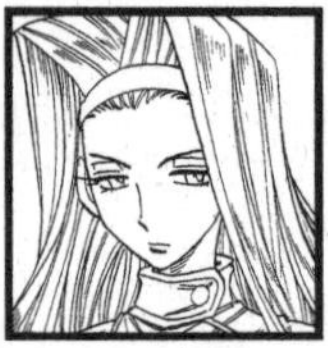

Eliza
Faust's late wife.

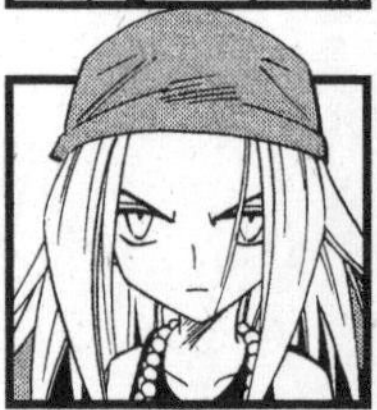

Anna Kyoyama
Yoh's butt-kicking fiancée. Anna is an itako, a traditional Japanese village shaman.

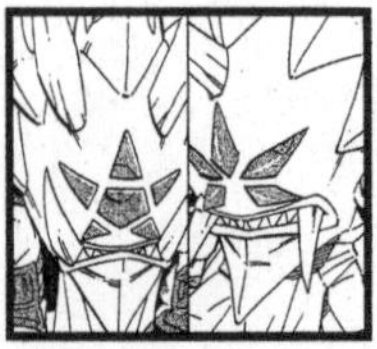

Zenki & Goki
Spirits who formerly served Hao but now serve Anna.

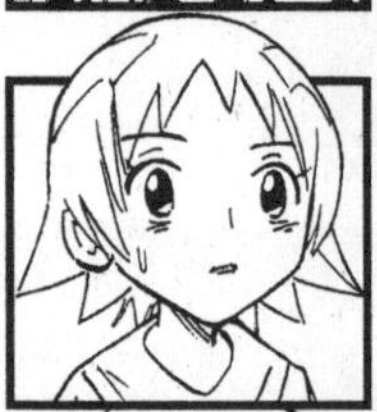

Tamao Tamamura
A shaman in training who uses a kokkuri board. She's in love with Yoh.

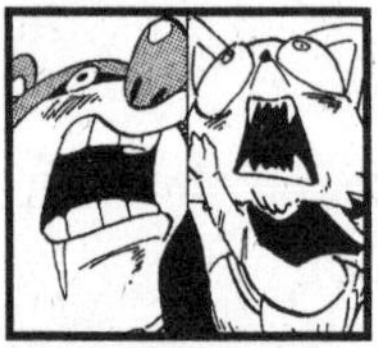

Ponchi & Konchi
Tamao's spirit allies. Not known for their genteel ways.

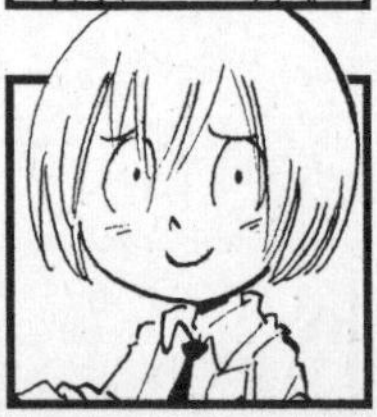

Manta Oyamada
A high-strung boy with a huge dictionary. He has enough sixth sense to see ghosts, but not enough to control them.

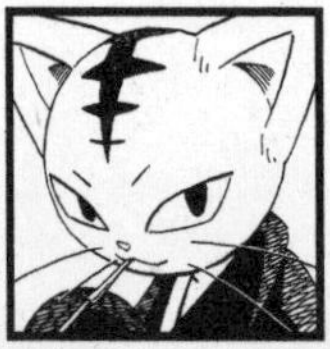

Matamune
A split-tailed cat who helped Yoh save Anna from her own powers.

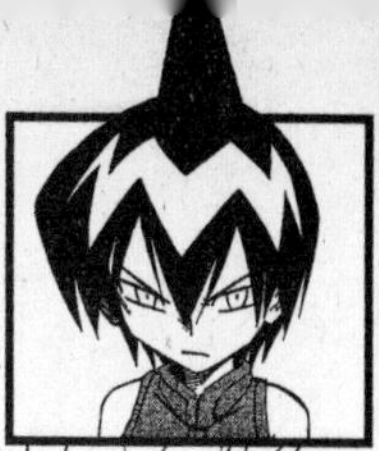

Tao Ren
A powerful shaman and the scion of the ruthless Tao Family.

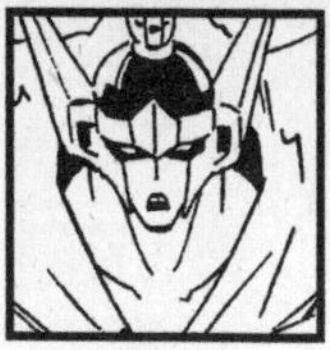

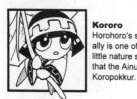

Bason
Ren's spirit ally is the ghost of a fearsome warlord from ancient China.

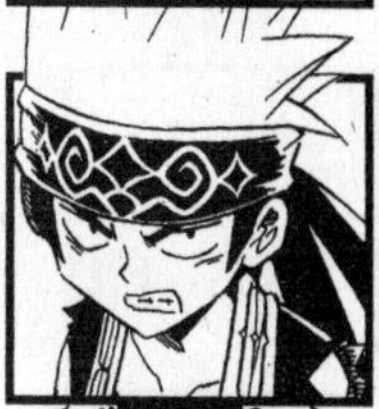

Horohoro
An Ainu shaman whose Over Soul looks like a snowboard.

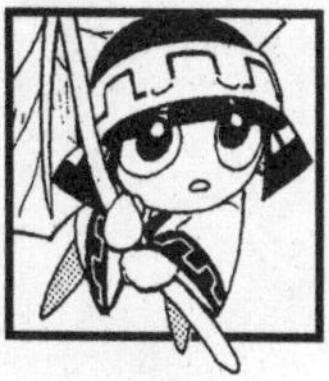

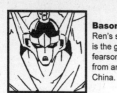

Kororo
Horohoro's spirit ally is one of the little nature spirits that the Ainu call Koropokkur.

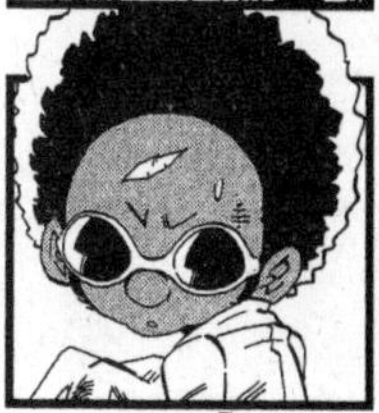

Joco
A shaman who uses humor as a weapon. Or tries to.

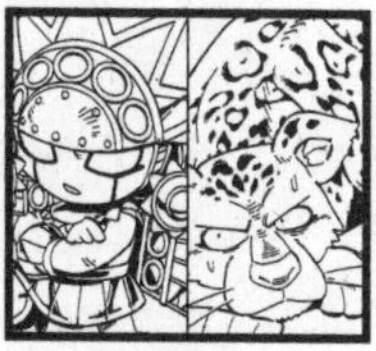

Mic & Pascual Abaj
Joco's jaguar spirit ally and the ghost of an Indio shaman.

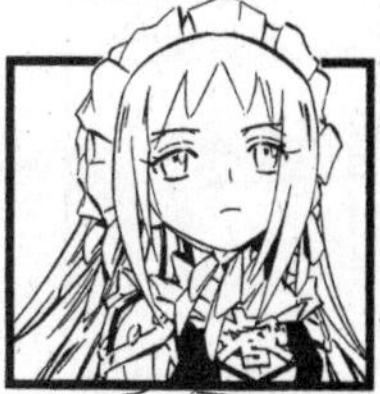

Jeanne, the Iron Maiden
The nominal leader of the X-LAWS. Spends most of her time in a medieval torture cabinet.

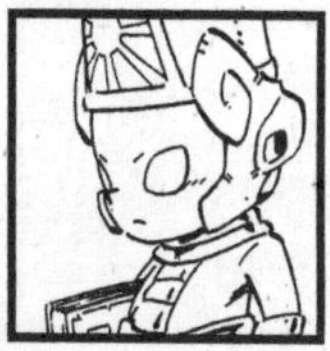

Shamash
Jeanne's spirit ally, a Babylonian god.

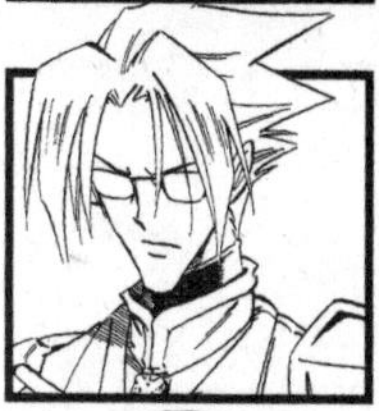

Marco
The true leader of the X-LAWS.

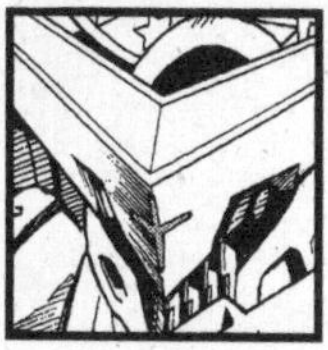

Michael
Marco's Archangel.

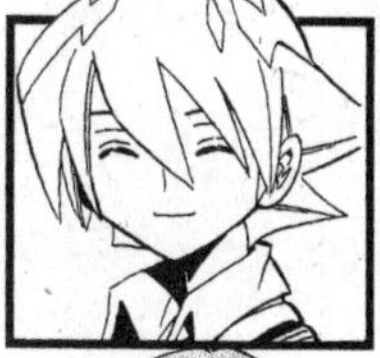

Lyserg
A young shaman with a vendetta against Hao.

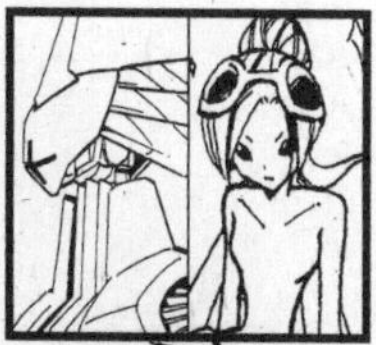

Morphea & Zeruel
Lyserg's poppy fairy and his new Angel.

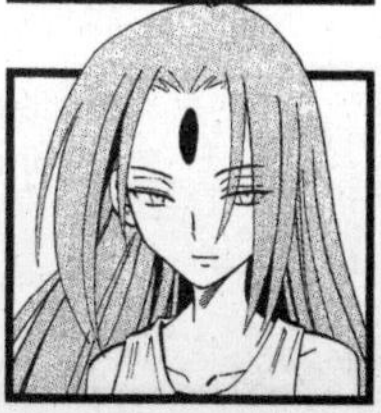

Sati
The leader of Gandala. She brought Ryu and Joco back from the dead.

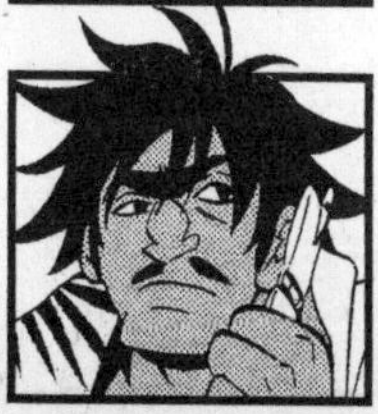

Kadu
A member of Gandala with Ragaraja.

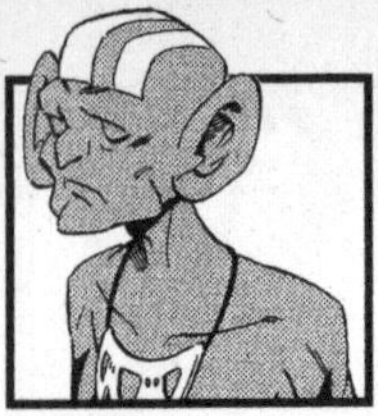

Yainage
A member of Gandala with Kundali.

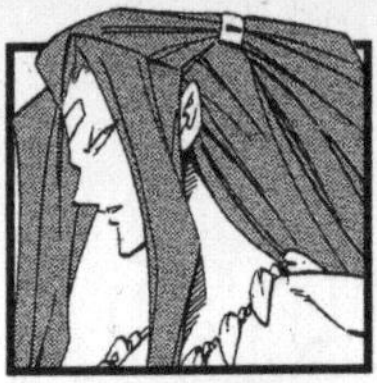

Jackson
A member of Gandala with Acala.

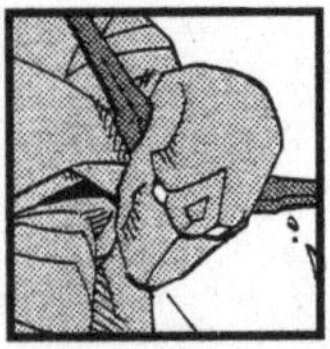

Spirit of Fire
One of the five High Spirits that belonged to the Patch.

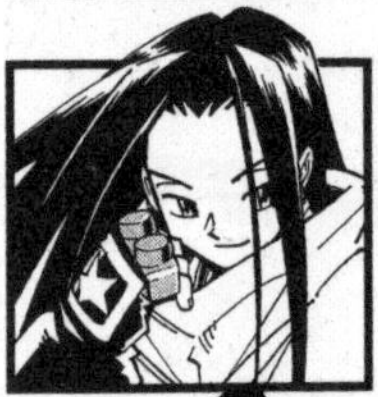

Hao
An enigmatic figure who calls himself the "Future King."

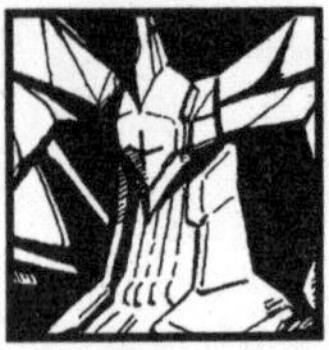

Lucifer
The first Angel, controlled by Luchist.

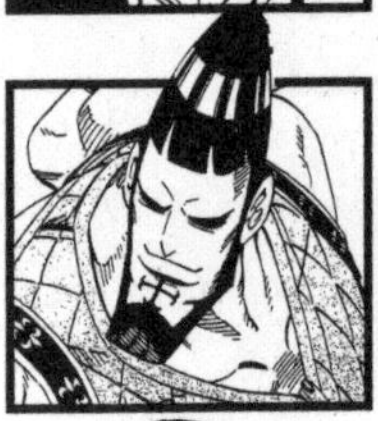

Luchist
The founder of the X-LAWS who now wants to destroy them for his master, Hao.

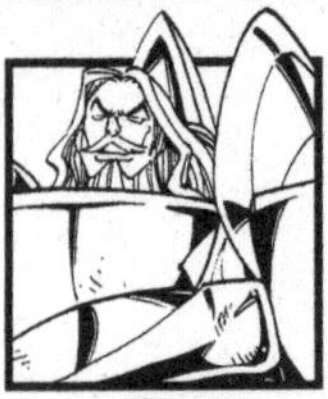

Ashcroft
Canna's spirit, an aged knight who seems chivalrous but actually has a foul mouth and a worse temper.

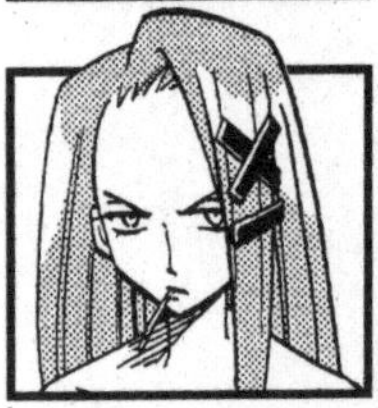

Canna Bismarck
A member of Hana-gumi, one of Hao's teams.

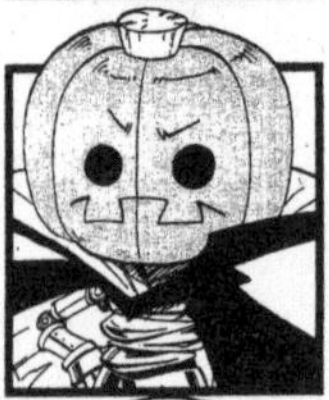

Jack
Mattie's pumpkin doll, which uses knives as weapons.

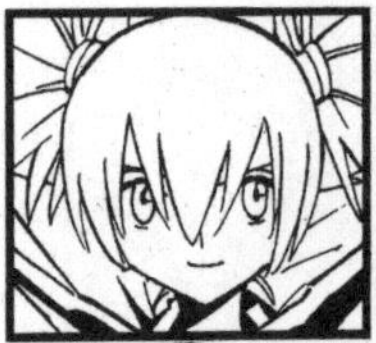

Mathilda
Nicknamed "Mattie," she's a druid with Hana-gumi.

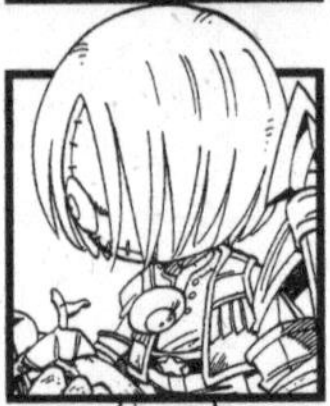

Chuck
Marie's cowboy gunslinger doll.

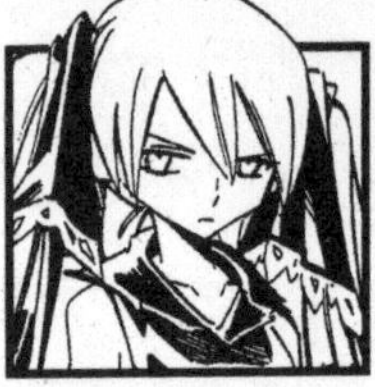

Marion Fauna
Nicknamed "Marie," she's a quiet doll-master with Hana-gumi.

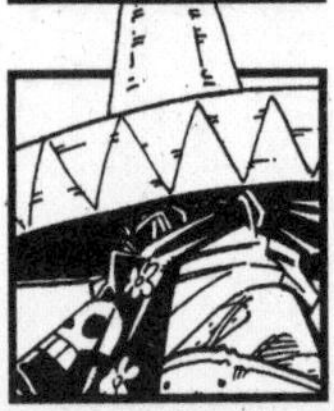

Peyote
Formerly with Tsuchi-gumi. He was defeated by Team Ren but continues to work for Hao.

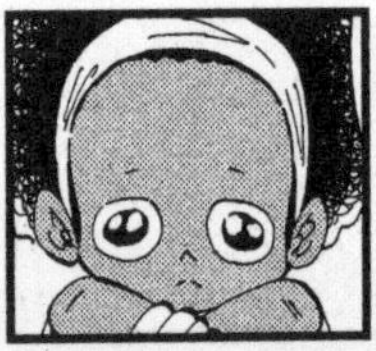

Opacho
Hao's devoted minion who has the power to see the future.

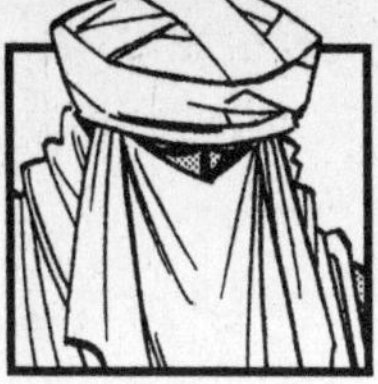

Turbine
A minion of Hao's who hides his face behind a turban and a veil.

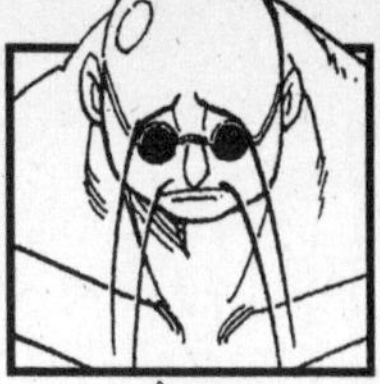

Zang Ching
A minion of Hao's whose spirit ally is a panda ghost called Xiong Xiong.

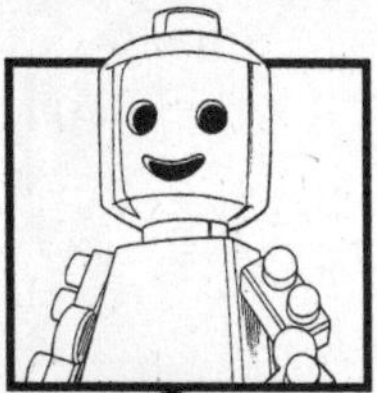

Blocken
A minion of Hao's whose body is made of toy building blocks.

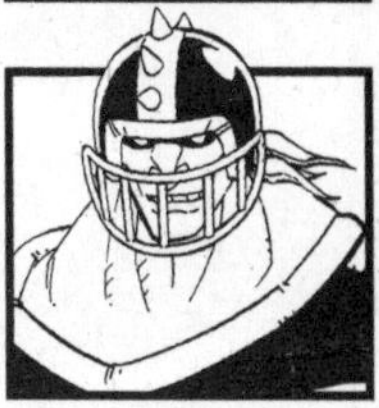

Big Guy Bill
Hao's minion, a football player whose spirit allies are his 21 former teammates.

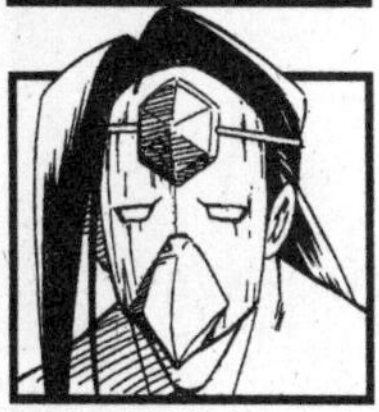

Mickey Asakura
Yoh's father. He wears a tengu mask.

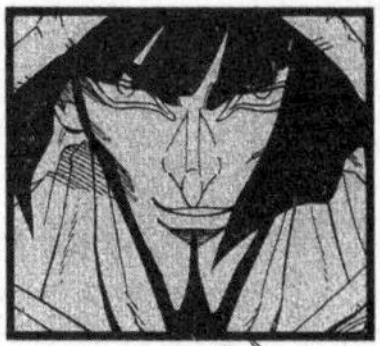

Anahol
A minion of Hao's whose brother, Anatel, was killed by the X-LAWS.

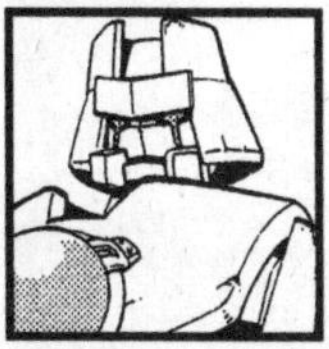

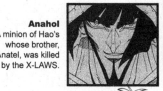

Golem
A robotic creature constructed by Dr. Munzer, Salerm and Ludsev's father.

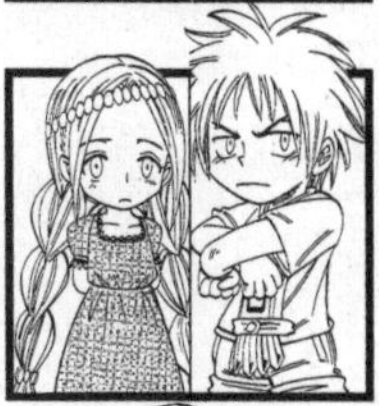

Salerm & Ludsev
A brother and sister who own the Golem.

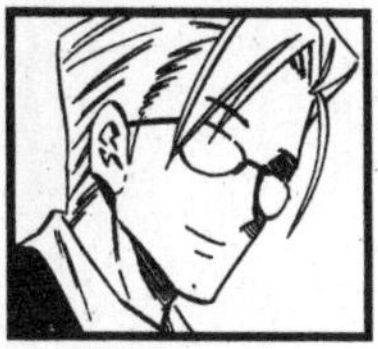

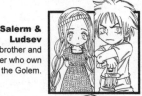

Tamurazaki
Secretary to Mansumi, Manta's father. After the Great Spirit.

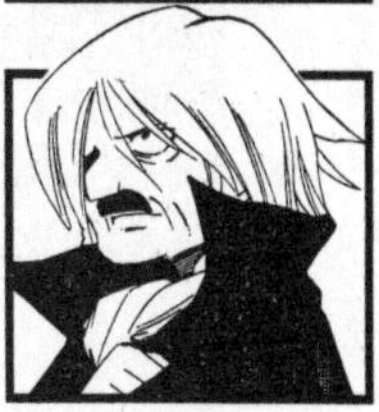

Mansumi Oyamada
Manta's father and the President of the Oyamada Company. He has his sights on the Great Spirit.

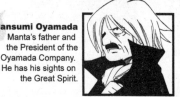

THE STORY THUS FAR

Yoh Asakura not only sees dead people, he talks and fights with them too. That's because Yoh is a shaman, a traditional holy man able to interact with the spirit world. Yoh is now a competitor in the Shaman Fight, a tournament held every 500 years to decide who will become the Shaman King and shape humanity's future.

Hao continues to prey upon the other shamans, including his own minions, who are less than delighted to discover that their master can read their minds. Knowing that Hao is too powerful to defeat in a fair fight, Sati of Gandala hatches a plan. Yoh, Ren, Horohoro, Joco and Lyserg will acquire the five elemental spirits of the Patch and attack Hao at his one moment of weakness—when he is becoming one with the Great Spirit. But before they can put their plan into action, the five warriors must survive what remains of the Shaman Fight.

SHAMAN KING 30

「非日常さん」

目次 CONTENTS

VOL. 30 EXTRAORDINARY DAYS

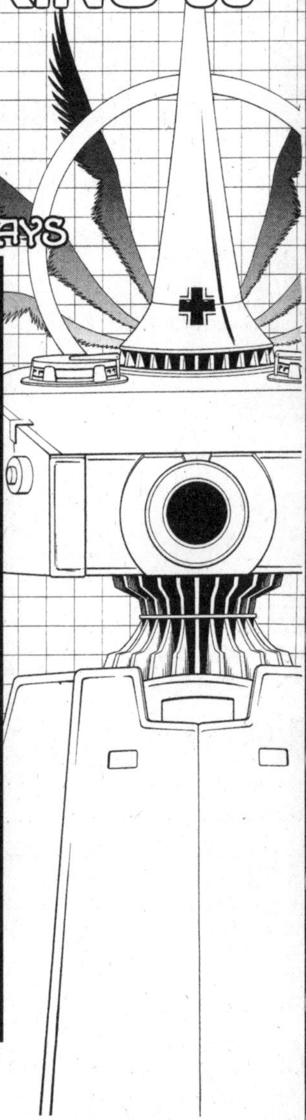

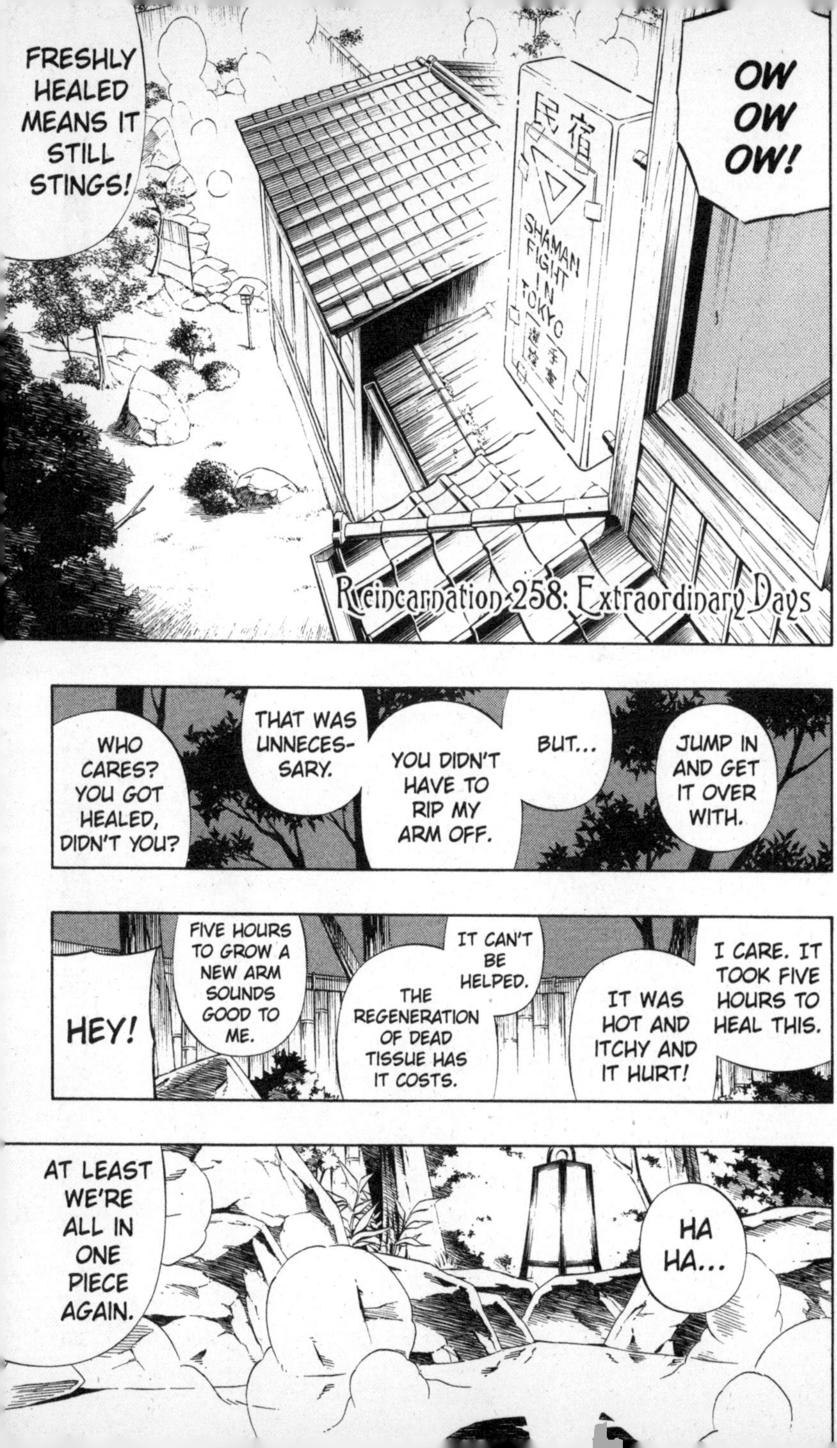
OW OW OW!
民宿
SHAMAN FIGHT IN TOKYO
FRESHLY HEALED MEANS IT STILL STINGS!
Reincarnation 258: Extraordinary Days
JUMP IN AND GET IT OVER WITH.
BUT...
YOU DIDN'T HAVE TO RIP MY ARM OFF.
THAT WAS UNNECES-SARY.
WHO CARES? YOU GOT HEALED, DIDN'T YOU?
I CARE. IT TOOK FIVE HOURS TO HEAL THIS.
IT WAS HOT AND ITCHY AND IT HURT!
IT CAN'T BE HELPED.
THE REGENERATION OF DEAD TISSUE HAS IT COSTS.
FIVE HOURS TO GROW A NEW ARM SOUNDS GOOD TO ME.
HEY!
HA HA...
AT LEAST WE'RE ALL IN ONE PIECE AGAIN.

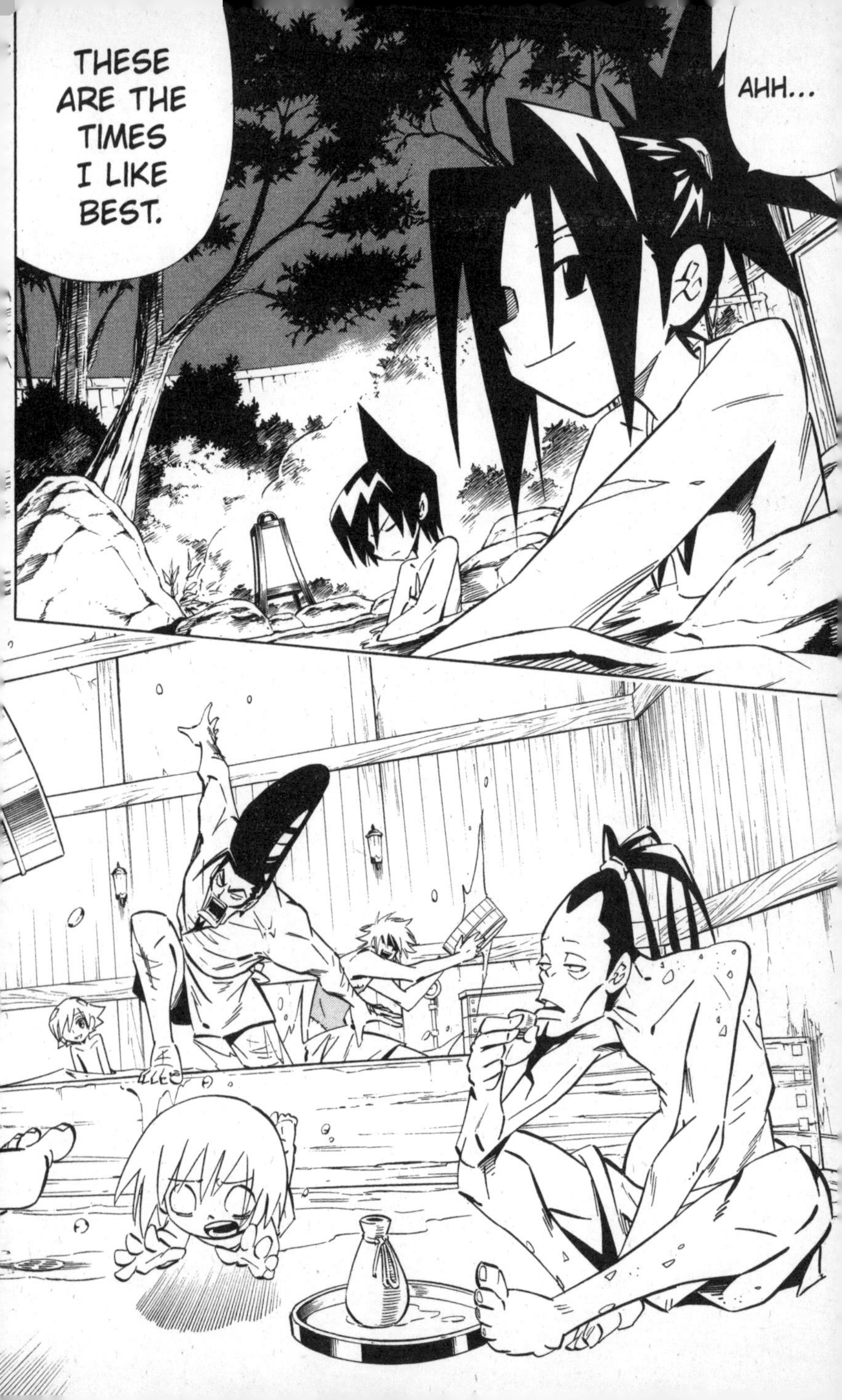
AHH...
THESE ARE THE TIMES I LIKE BEST.

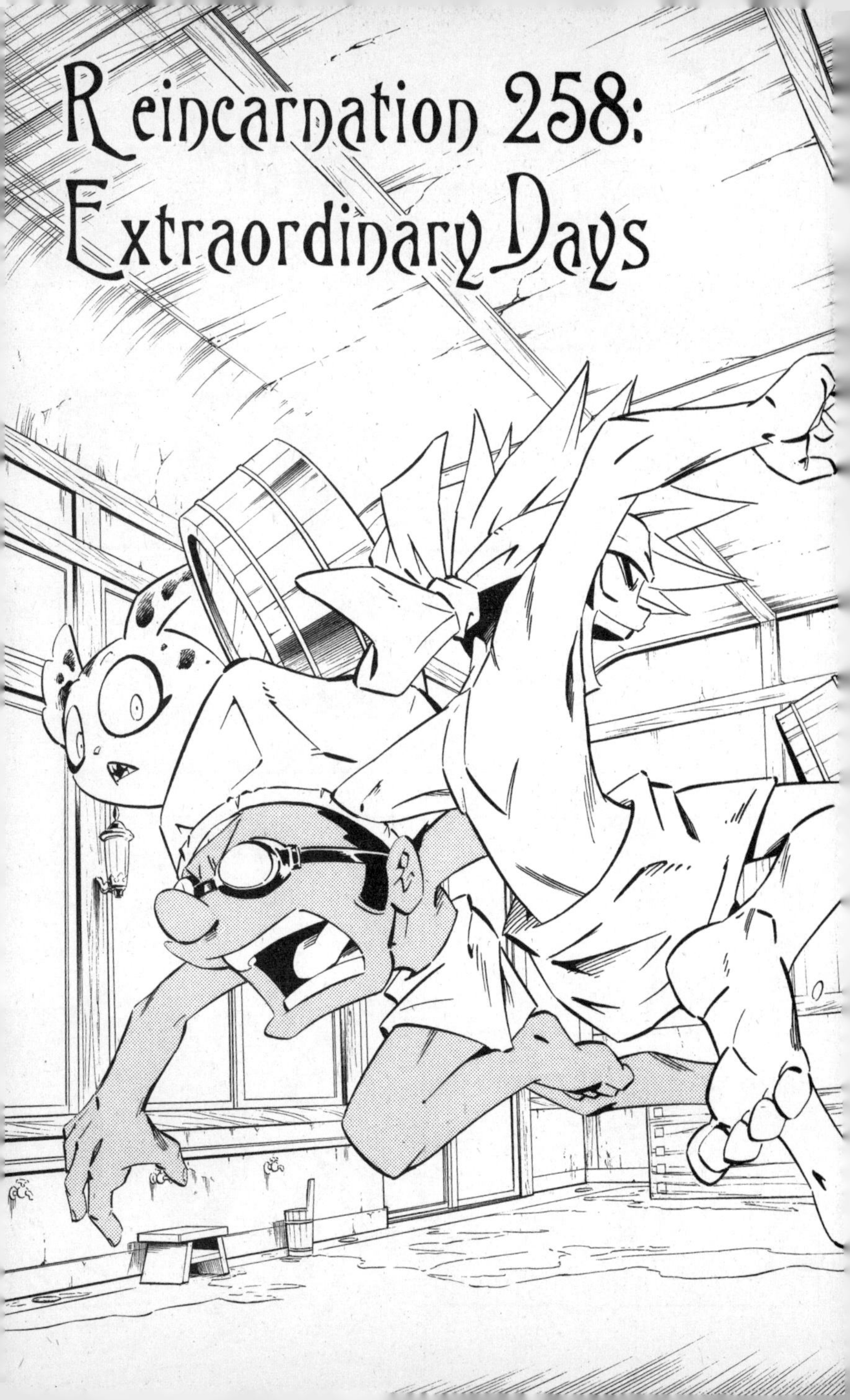
Reincarnation 258:
Extraordinary Days

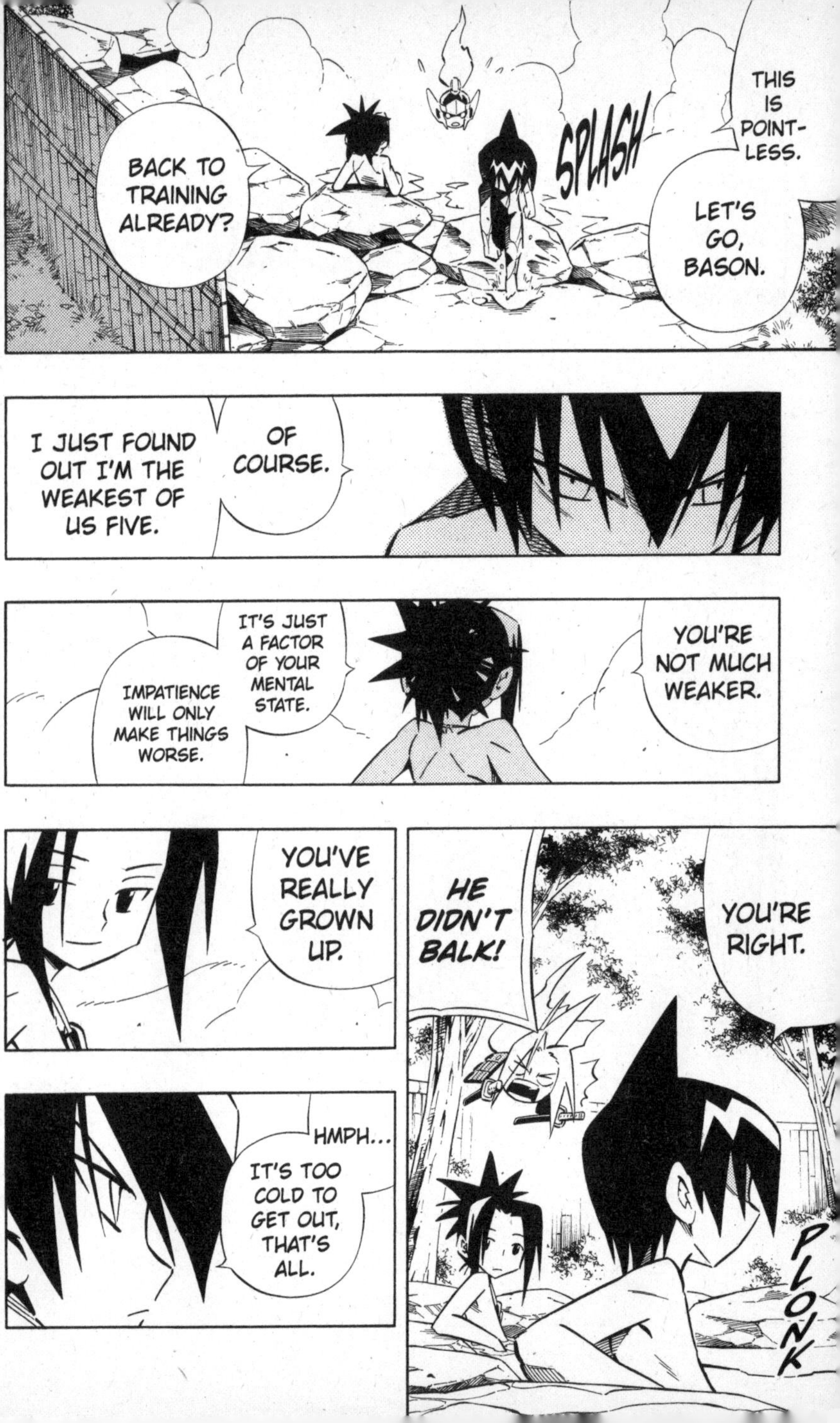
THIS IS POINT-LESS.
LET'S GO, BASON.
SPLASH
BACK TO TRAINING ALREADY?
OF COURSE.
I JUST FOUND OUT I'M THE WEAKEST OF US FIVE.
YOU'RE NOT MUCH WEAKER.
IT'S JUST A FACTOR OF YOUR MENTAL STATE.
IMPATIENCE WILL ONLY MAKE THINGS WORSE.
YOU'RE RIGHT.
HE DIDN'T BALK!
PLONK
YOU'VE REALLY GROWN UP.
HMPH...
IT'S TOO COLD TO GET OUT, THAT'S ALL.

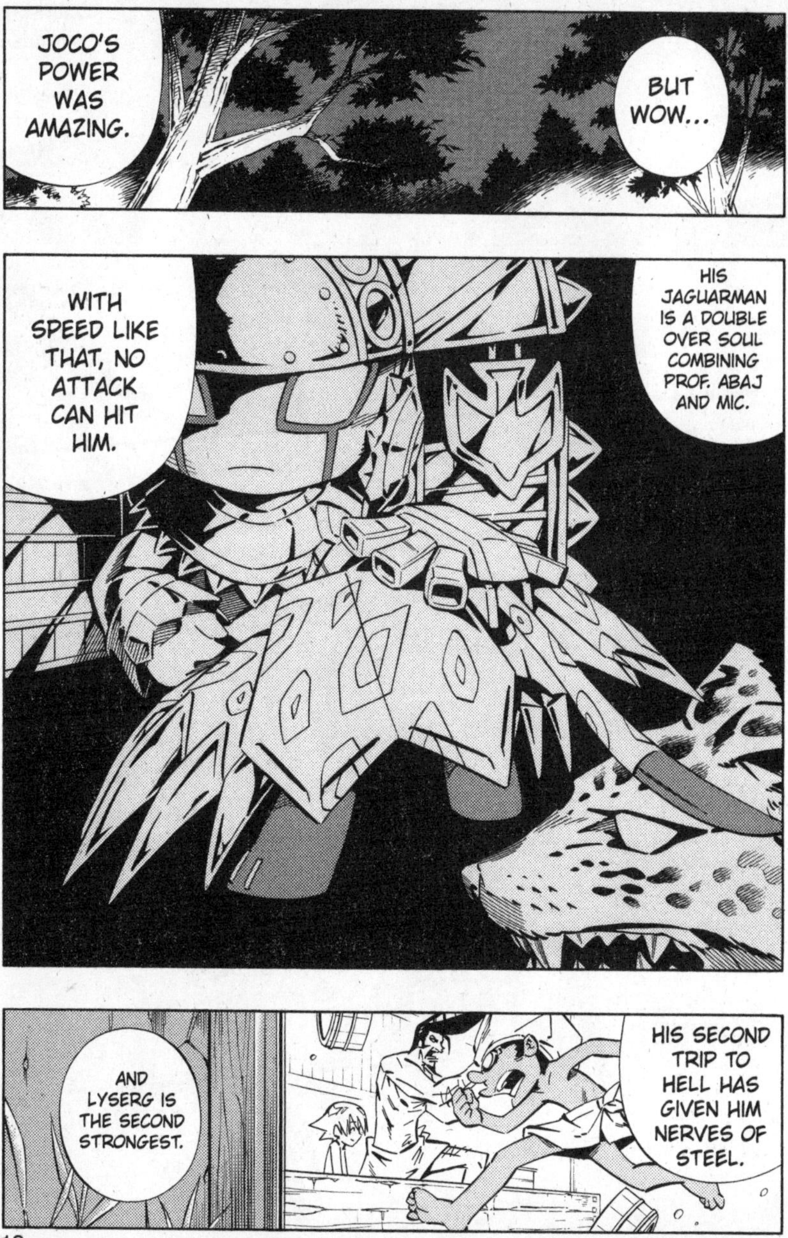
BUT WOW...
JOCO'S POWER WAS AMAZING.
HIS JAGUARMAN IS A DOUBLE OVER SOUL COMBINING PROF. ABAJ AND MIC.
WITH SPEED LIKE THAT, NO ATTACK CAN HIT HIM.
HIS SECOND TRIP TO HELL HAS GIVEN HIM NERVES OF STEEL.
AND LYSERG IS THE SECOND STRONGEST.

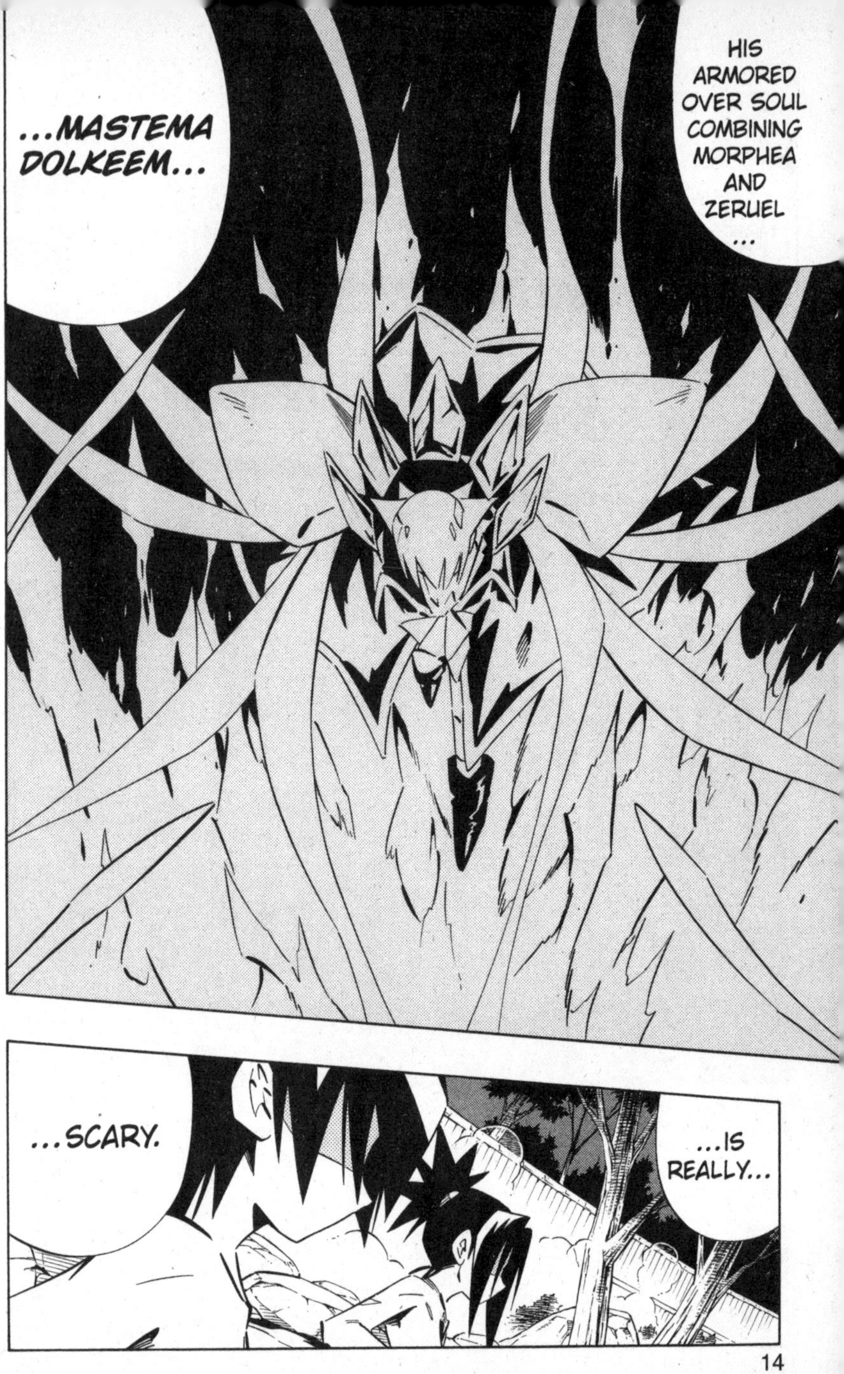
HIS ARMORED OVER SOUL COMBINING MORPHEA AND ZERUEL ...
...MASTEMA DOLKEEM...
...IS REALLY...
...SCARY.

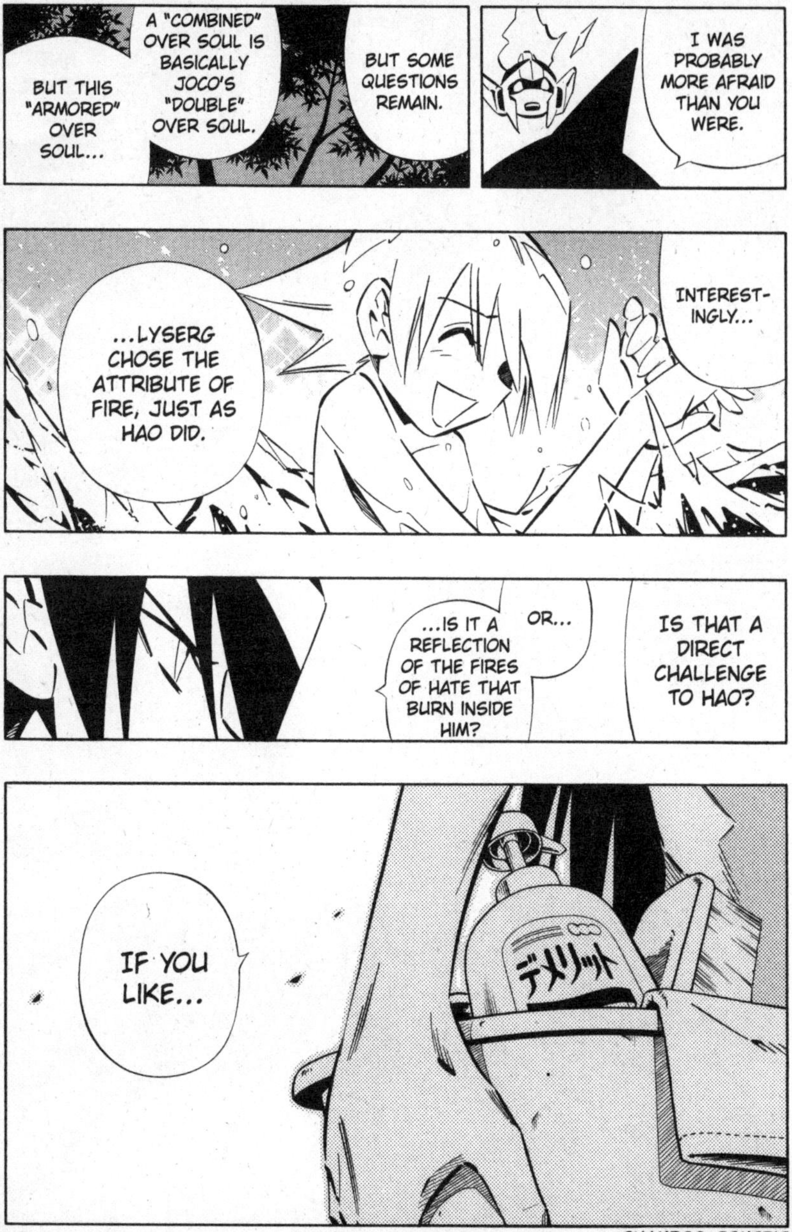
I WAS PROBABLY MORE AFRAID THAN YOU WERE.
BUT SOME QUESTIONS REMAIN.
A "COMBINED" OVER SOUL IS BASICALLY JOCO'S "DOUBLE" OVER SOUL.
BUT THIS "ARMORED" OVER SOUL...
INTEREST-INGLY...
...LYSERG CHOSE THE ATTRIBUTE OF FIRE, JUST AS HAO DID.
IS THAT A DIRECT CHALLENGE TO HAO?
OR...
...IS IT A REFLECTION OF THE FIRES OF HATE THAT BURN INSIDE HIM?
デメリット
IF YOU LIKE...

SHAMPOO: DEMERIT

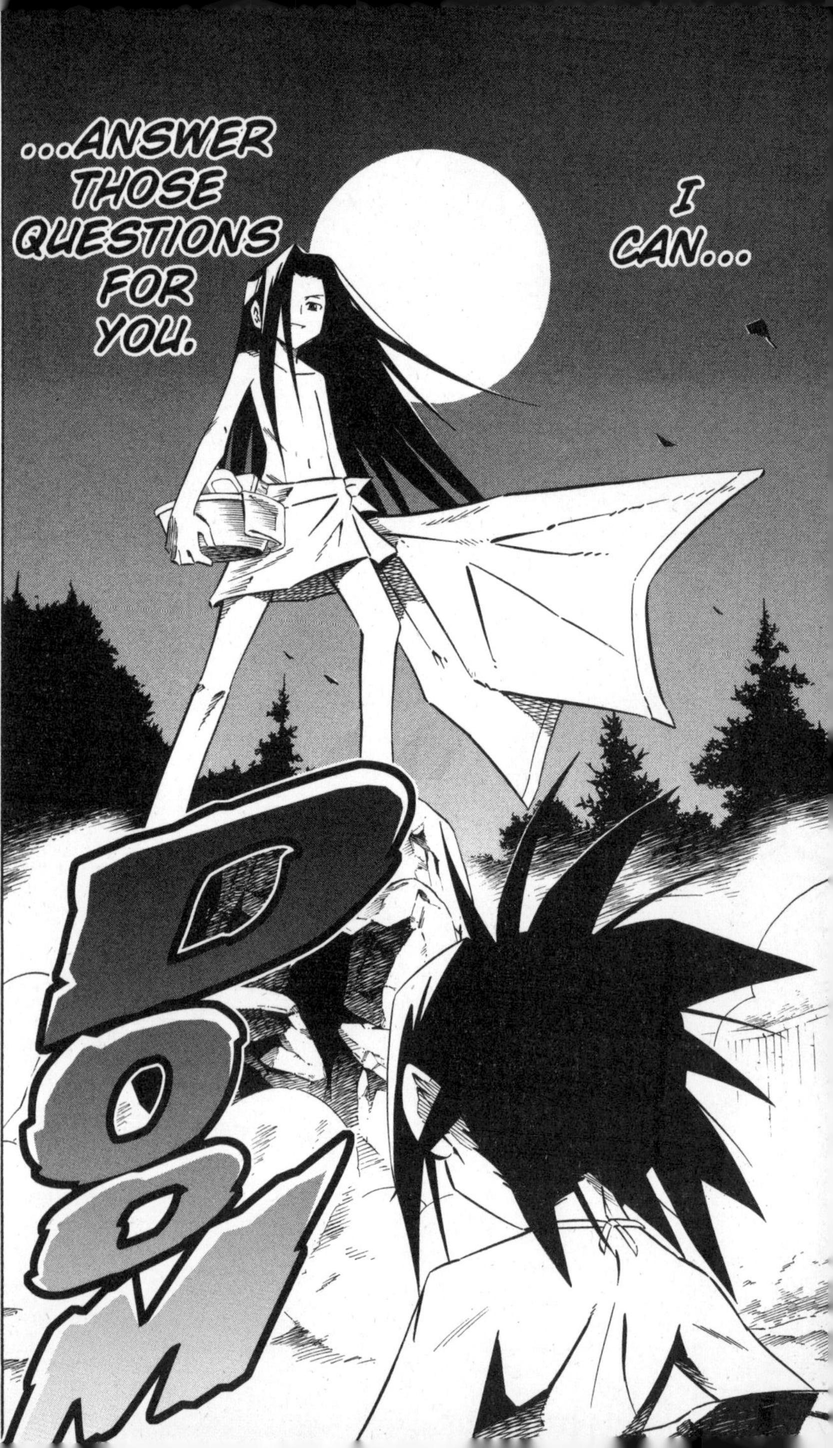
I CAN...
...ANSWER THOSE QUESTIONS FOR YOU.
DOOM

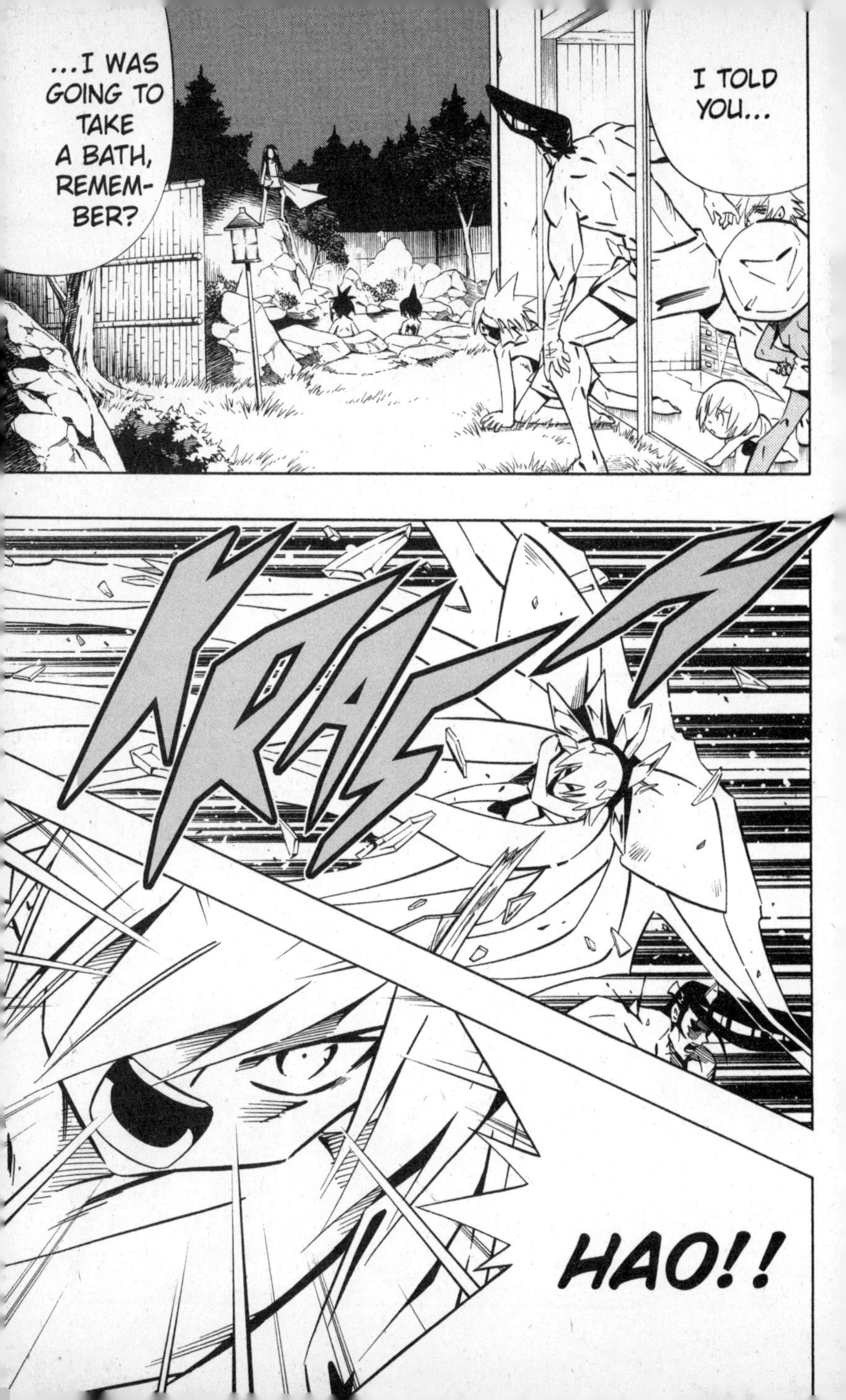
I TOLD YOU...
...I WAS GOING TO TAKE A BATH, REMEMBER?
KRAK
HAO!!

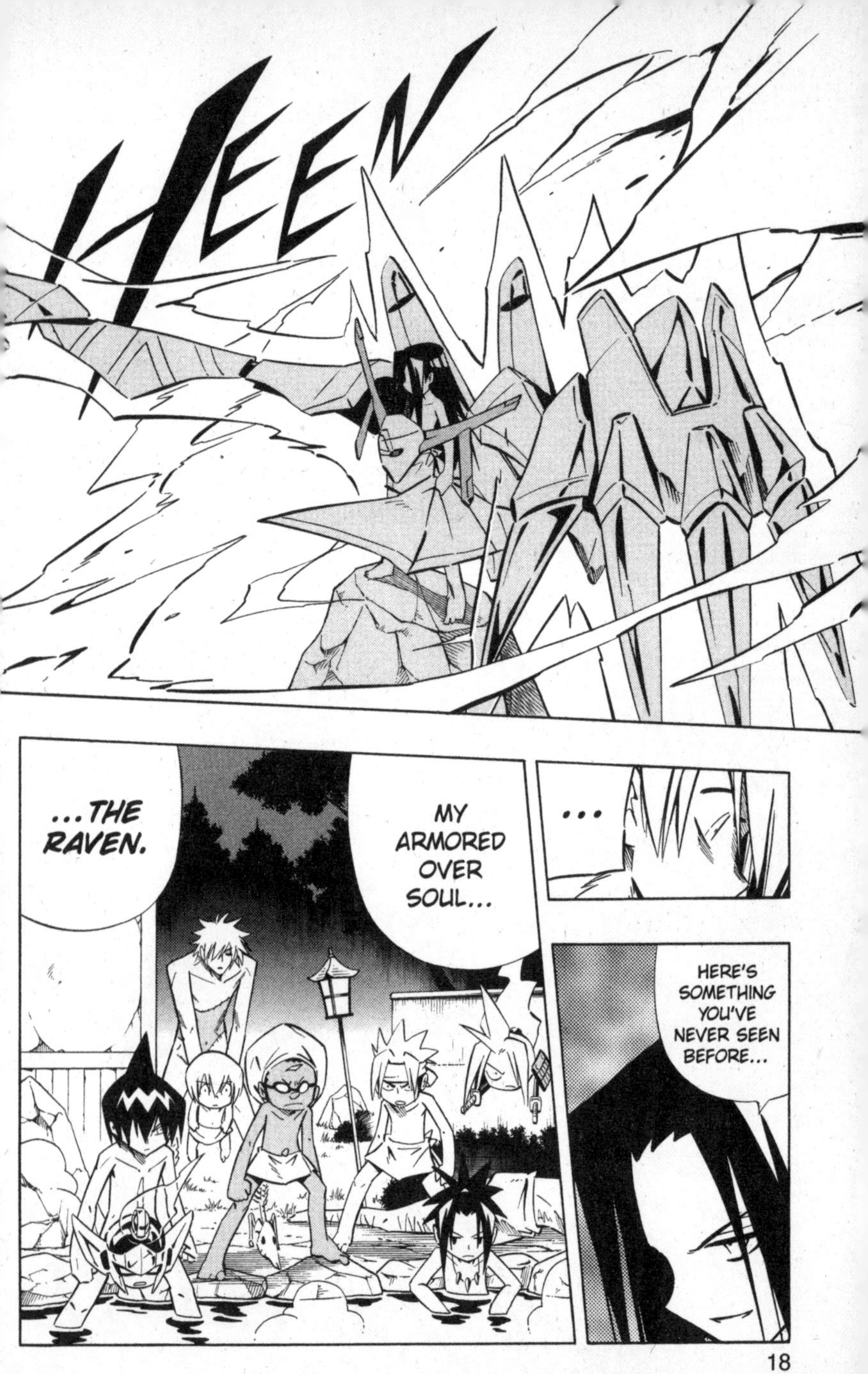
HEEN
...
HERE'S SOMETHING YOU'VE NEVER SEEN BEFORE...
MY ARMORED OVER SOUL...
...THE RAVEN.

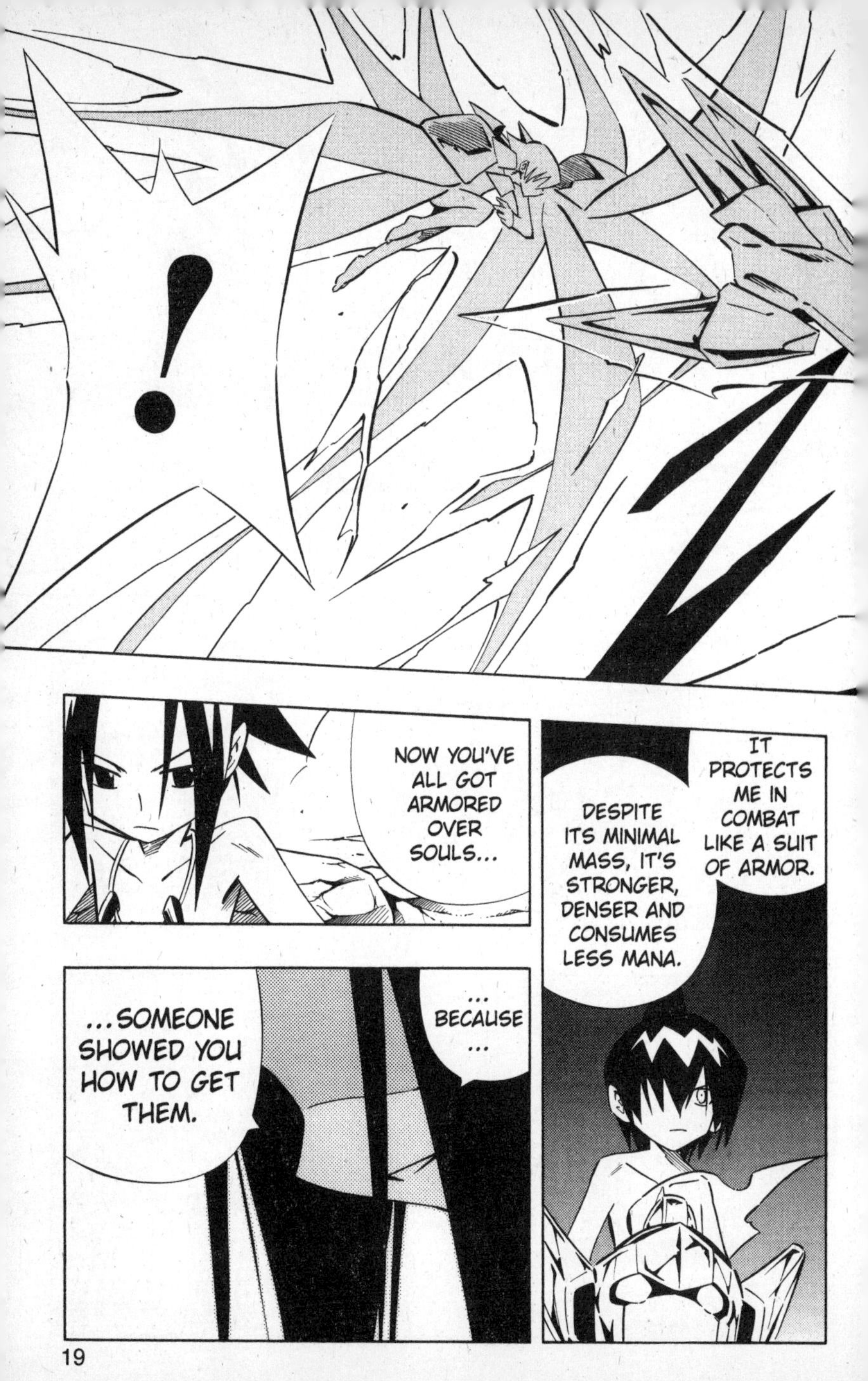
!
IT PROTECTS ME IN COMBAT LIKE A SUIT OF ARMOR.
DESPITE ITS MINIMAL MASS, IT'S STRONGER, DENSER AND CONSUMES LESS MANA.
NOW YOU'VE ALL GOT ARMORED OVER SOULS...
...BECAUSE...
...SOMEONE SHOWED YOU HOW TO GET THEM.

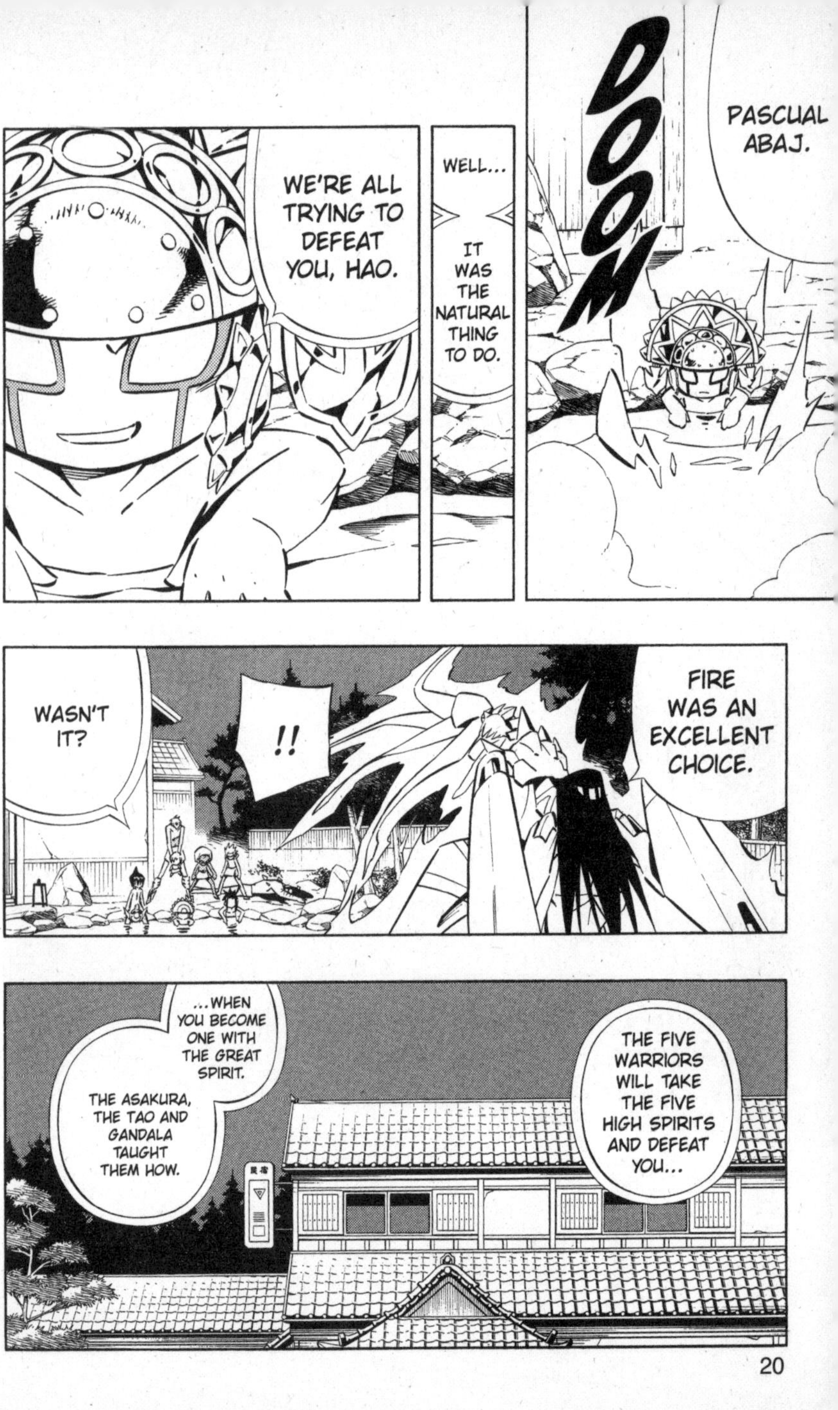

PASCUAL ABAJ.
DOOM
WELL...
IT WAS THE NATURAL THING TO DO.
WE'RE ALL TRYING TO DEFEAT YOU, HAO.
FIRE WAS AN EXCELLENT CHOICE.
!!
WASN'T IT?
THE FIVE WARRIORS WILL TAKE THE FIVE HIGH SPIRITS AND DEFEAT YOU...
...WHEN YOU BECOME ONE WITH THE GREAT SPIRIT.
THE ASAKURA, THE TAO AND GANDALA TAUGHT THEM HOW.

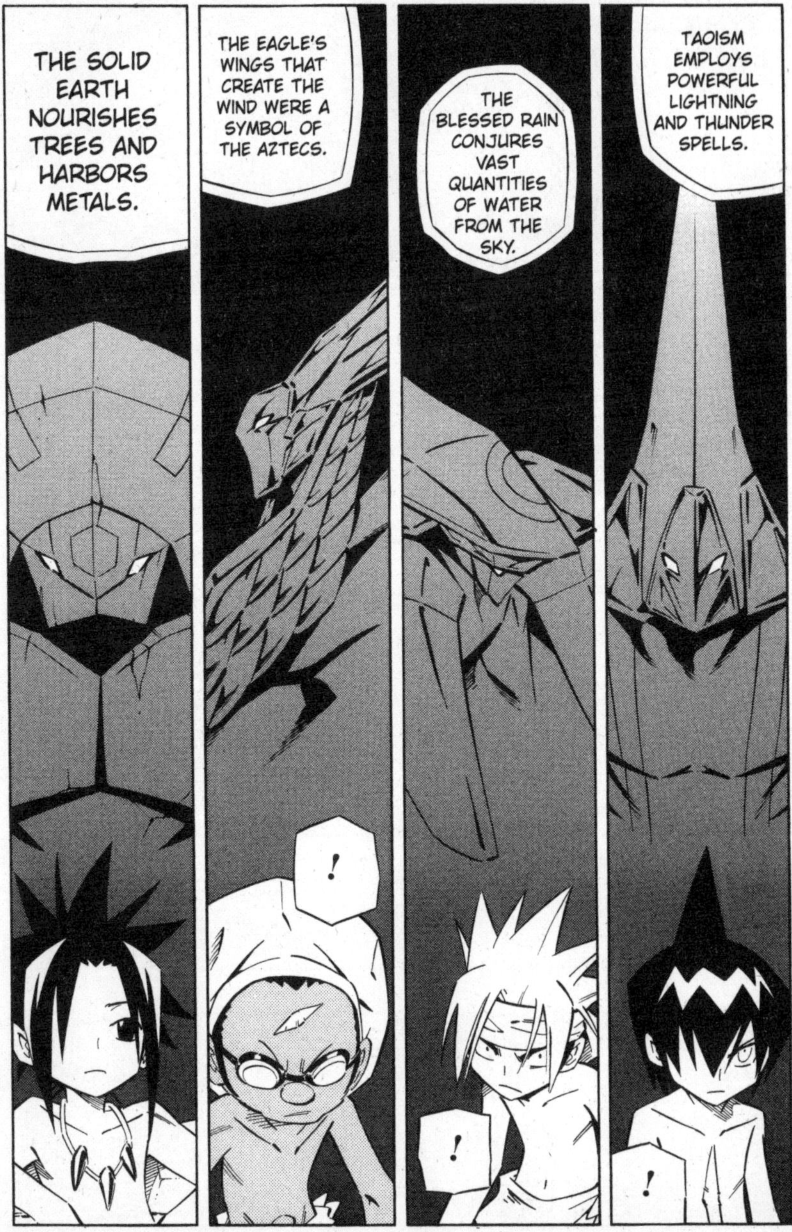
TAOISM EMPLOYS POWERFUL LIGHTNING AND THUNDER SPELLS.
!
THE BLESSED RAIN CONJURES VAST QUANTITIES OF WATER FROM THE SKY.
!
THE EAGLE'S WINGS THAT CREATE THE WIND WERE A SYMBOL OF THE AZTECS.
!
THE SOLID EARTH NOURISHES TREES AND HARBORS METALS.

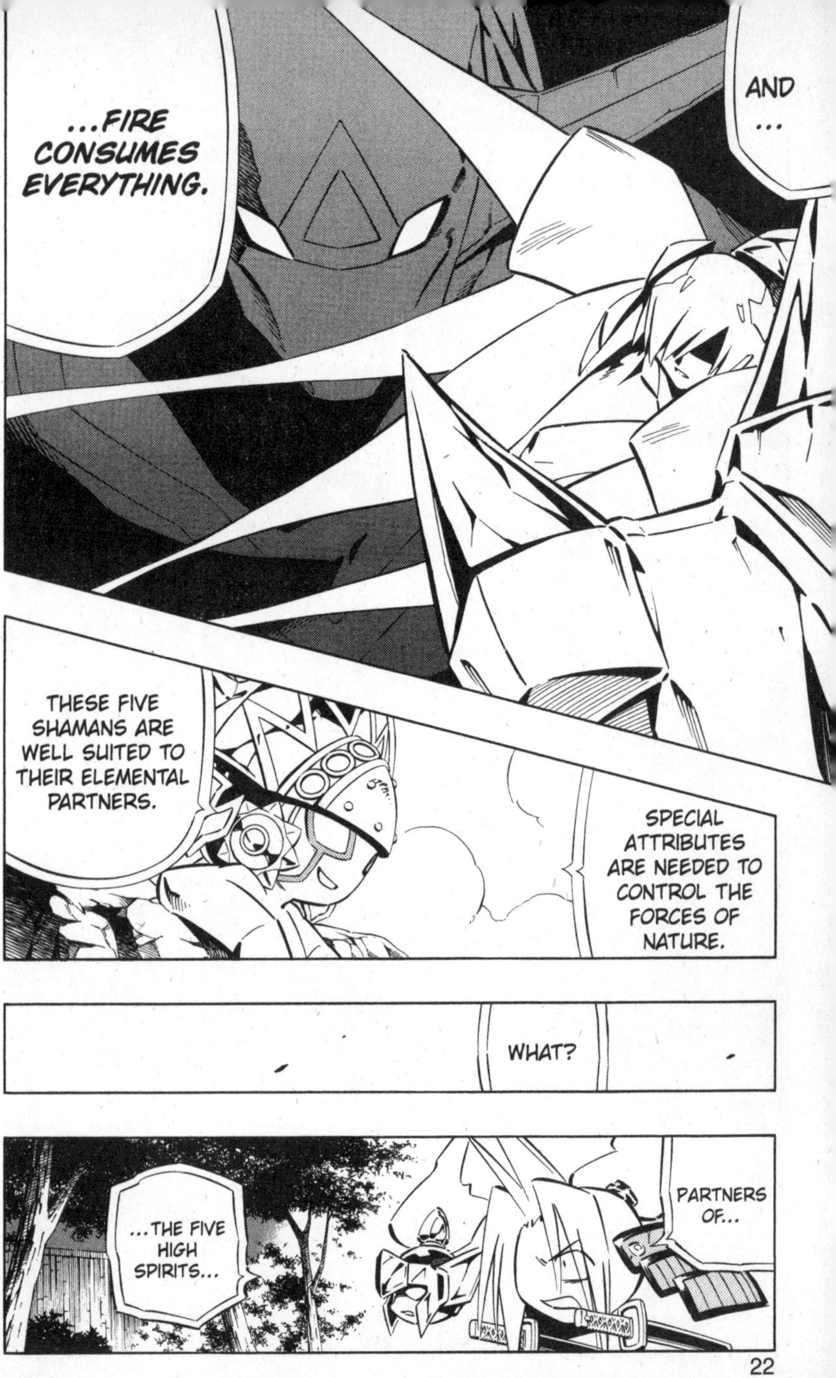
AND ...
...FIRE CONSUMES EVERYTHING.
SPECIAL ATTRIBUTES ARE NEEDED TO CONTROL THE FORCES OF NATURE.
THESE FIVE SHAMANS ARE WELL SUITED TO THEIR ELEMENTAL PARTNERS.
WHAT?
PARTNERS OF...
...THE FIVE HIGH SPIRITS...

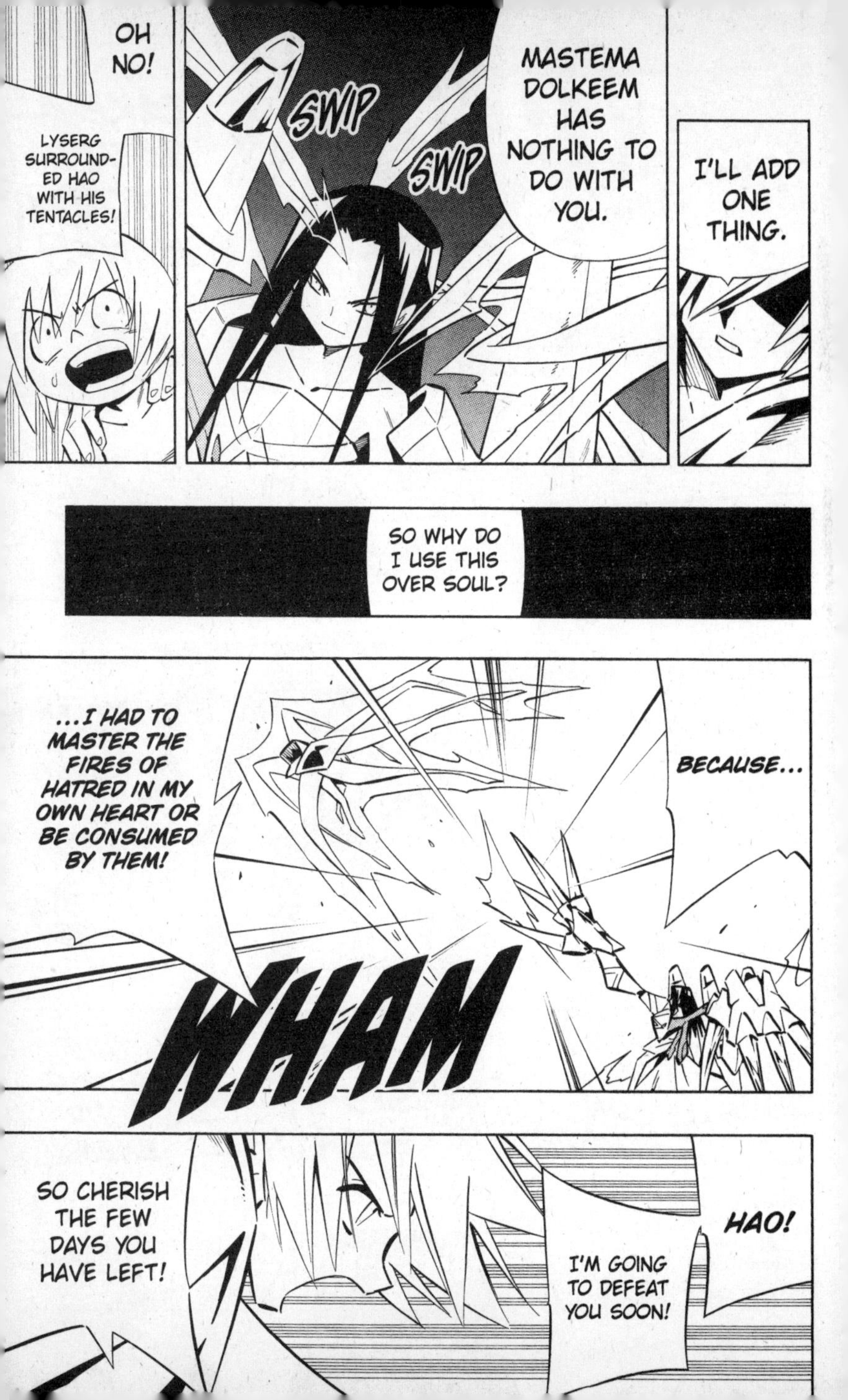
I'LL ADD ONE THING.
MASTEMA DOLKEEM HAS NOTHING TO DO WITH YOU.
SWIP
SWIP
OH NO!
LYSERG SURROUNDED HAO WITH HIS TENTACLES!
SO WHY DO I USE THIS OVER SOUL?
BECAUSE...
...I HAD TO MASTER THE FIRES OF HATRED IN MY OWN HEART OR BE CONSUMED BY THEM!
WHAM
HAO!
I'M GOING TO DEFEAT YOU SOON!
SO CHERISH THE FEW DAYS YOU HAVE LEFT!

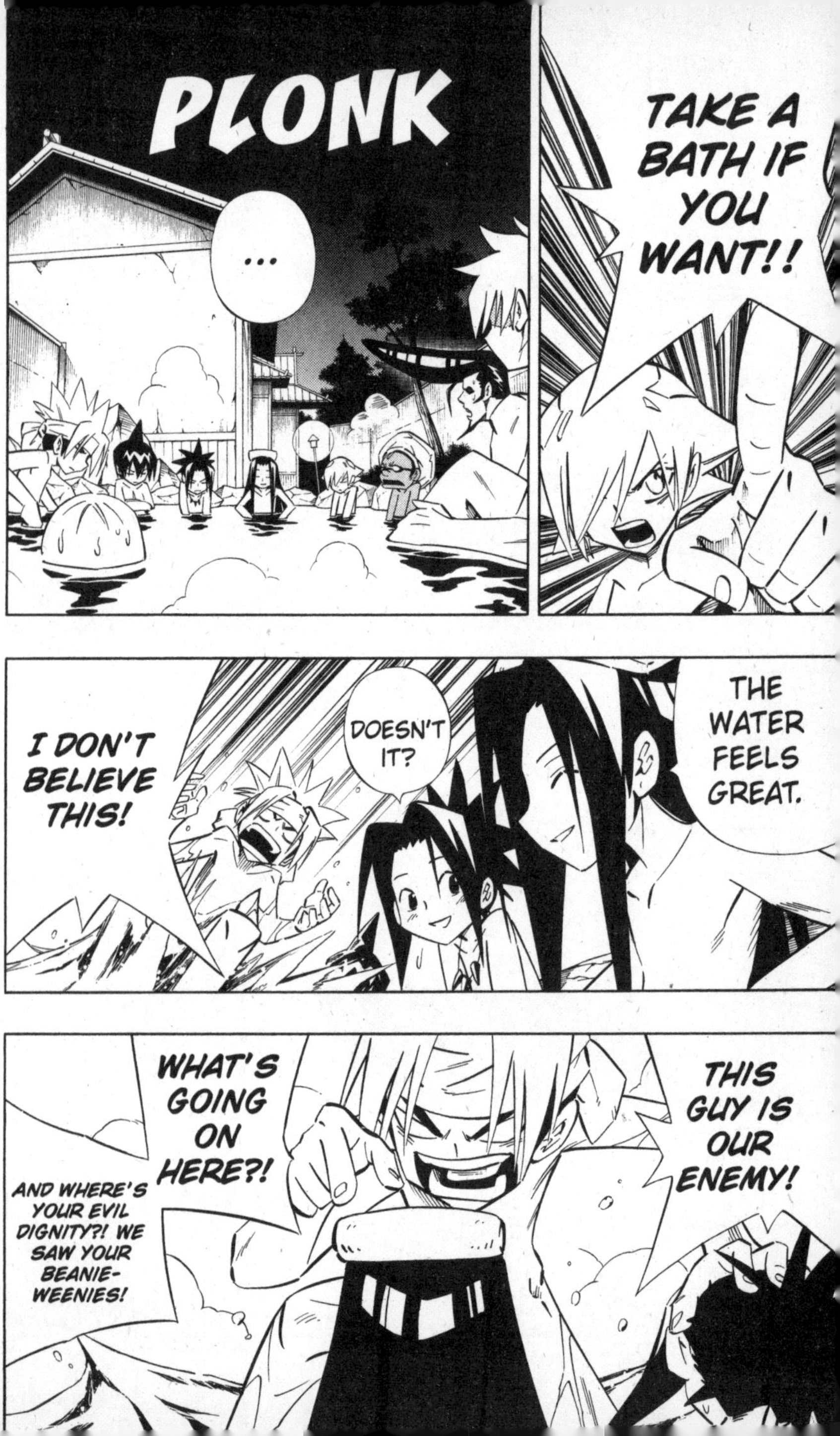
TAKE A BATH IF YOU WANT!!
PLONK
...
THE WATER FEELS GREAT.
DOESN'T IT?
I DON'T BELIEVE THIS!
THIS GUY IS OUR ENEMY!
WHAT'S GOING ON HERE?!
AND WHERE'S YOUR EVIL DIGNITY?! WE SAW YOUR BEANIE-WEENIES!

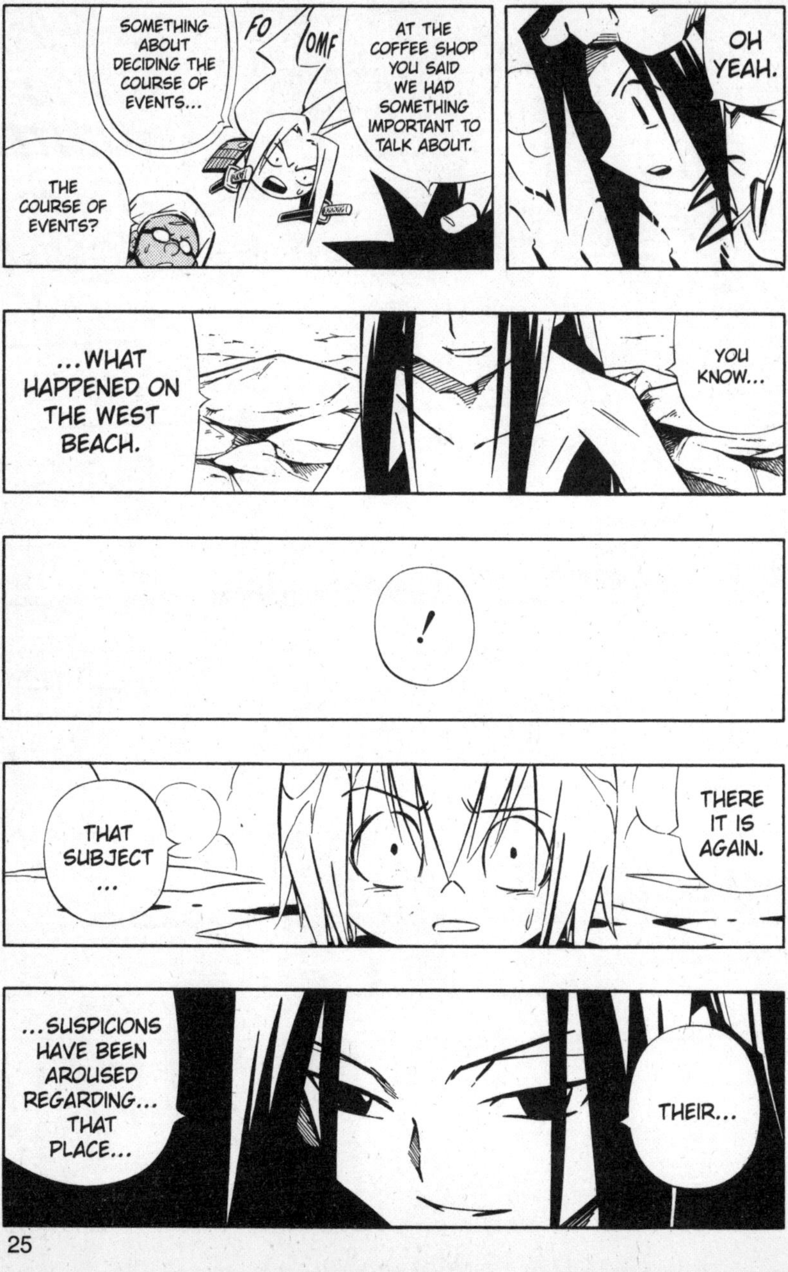
OH YEAH.
AT THE COFFEE SHOP YOU SAID WE HAD SOMETHING IMPORTANT TO TALK ABOUT.
FO OMF
SOMETHING ABOUT DECIDING THE COURSE OF EVENTS...
THE COURSE OF EVENTS?
YOU KNOW...
...WHAT HAPPENED ON THE WEST BEACH.
!
THERE IT IS AGAIN.
THAT SUBJECT ...
THEIR...
...SUSPICIONS HAVE BEEN AROUSED REGARDING... THAT PLACE...

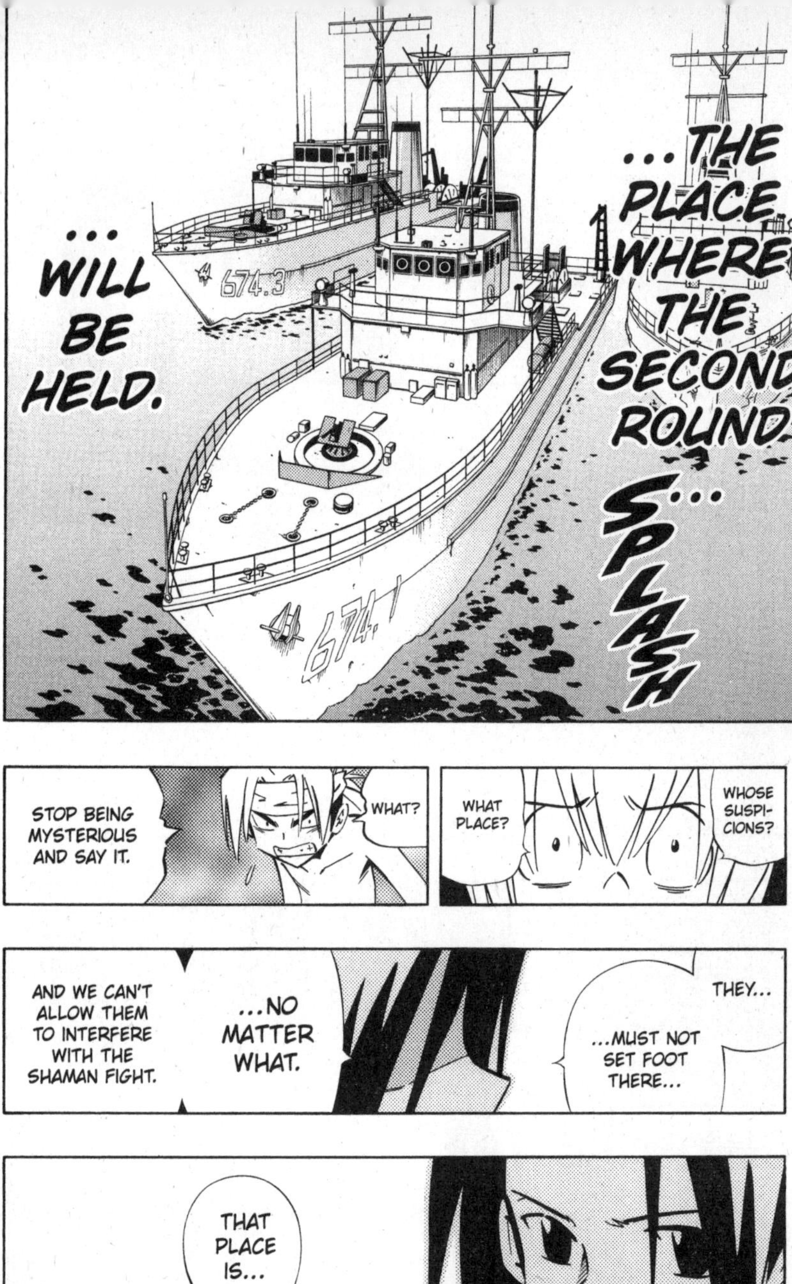
...THE PLACE WHERE THE SECOND ROUND...
...WILL BE HELD.
SPLASH
WHOSE SUSPI-CIONS?
WHAT PLACE?
WHAT?
STOP BEING MYSTERIOUS AND SAY IT.
THEY...
...MUST NOT SET FOOT THERE...
...NO MATTER WHAT.
AND WE CAN'T ALLOW THEM TO INTERFERE WITH THE SHAMAN FIGHT.
THAT PLACE IS...

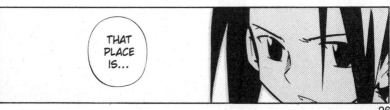

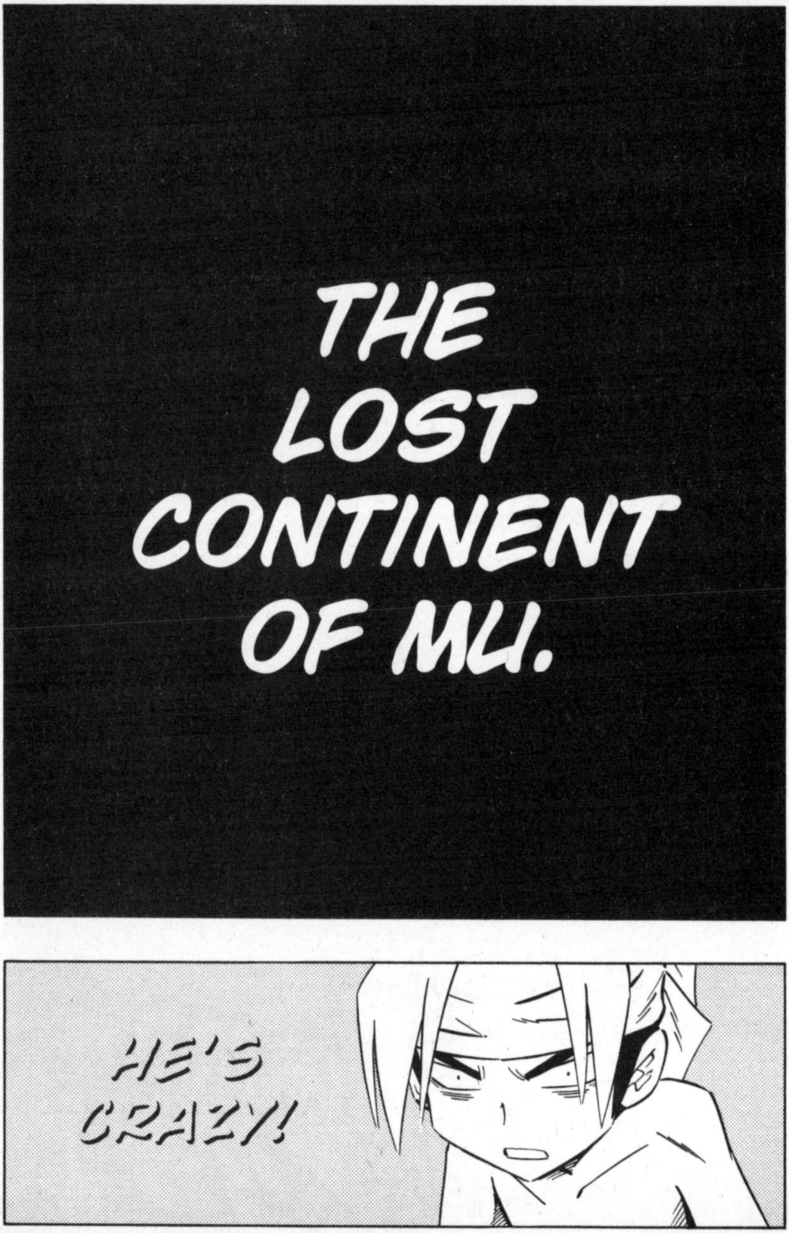
THE LOST CONTINENT OF MU.
HE'S CRAZY!

Shaman King

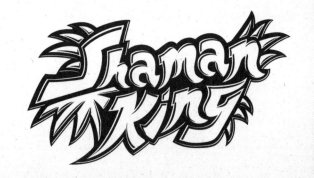

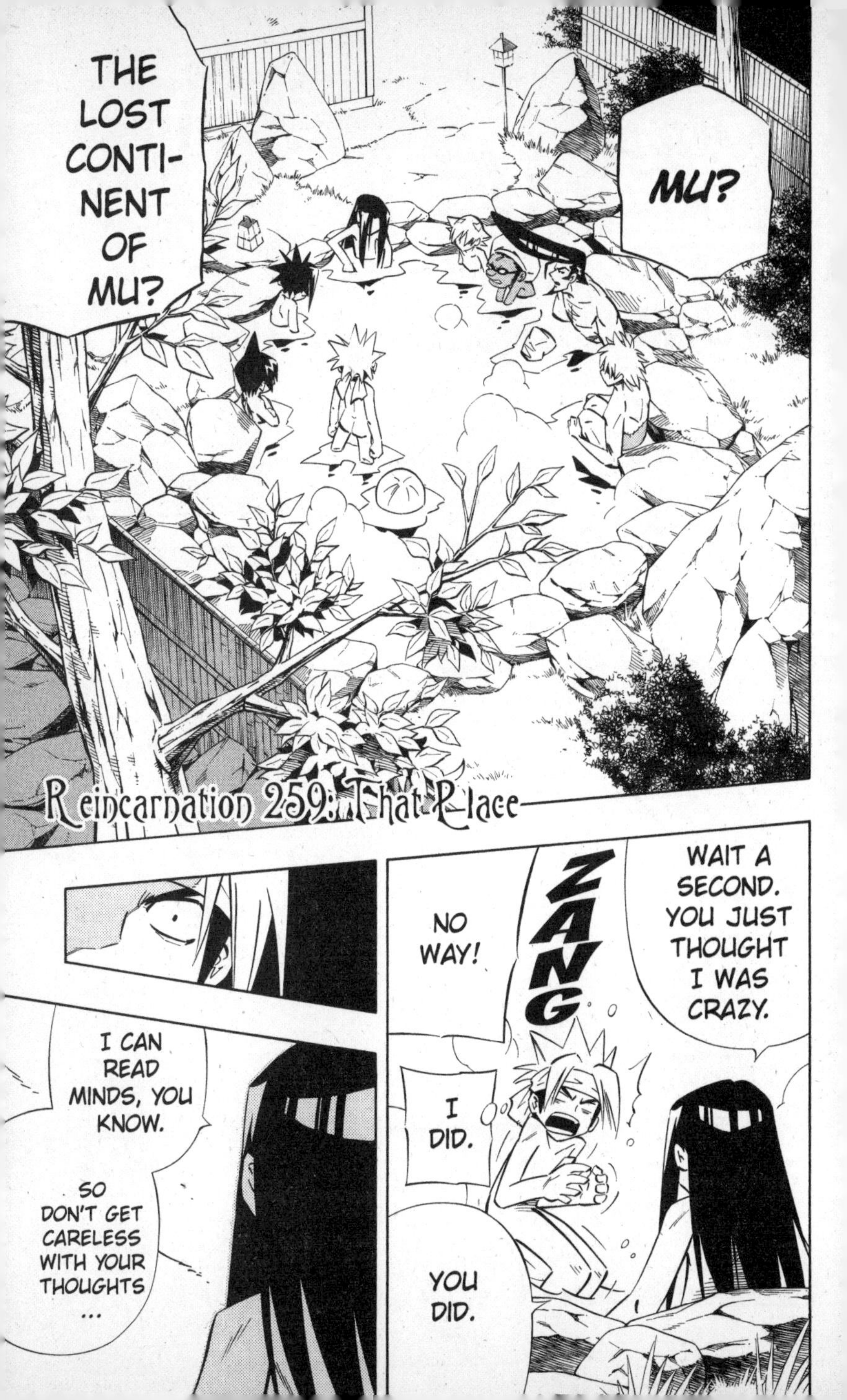
MU?
THE LOST CONTINENT OF MU?
Reincarnation 259: That Place
WAIT A SECOND. YOU JUST THOUGHT I WAS CRAZY.
ZANG
NO WAY!
I DID.
YOU DID.
I CAN READ MINDS, YOU KNOW.
SO DON'T GET CARELESS WITH YOUR THOUGHTS...

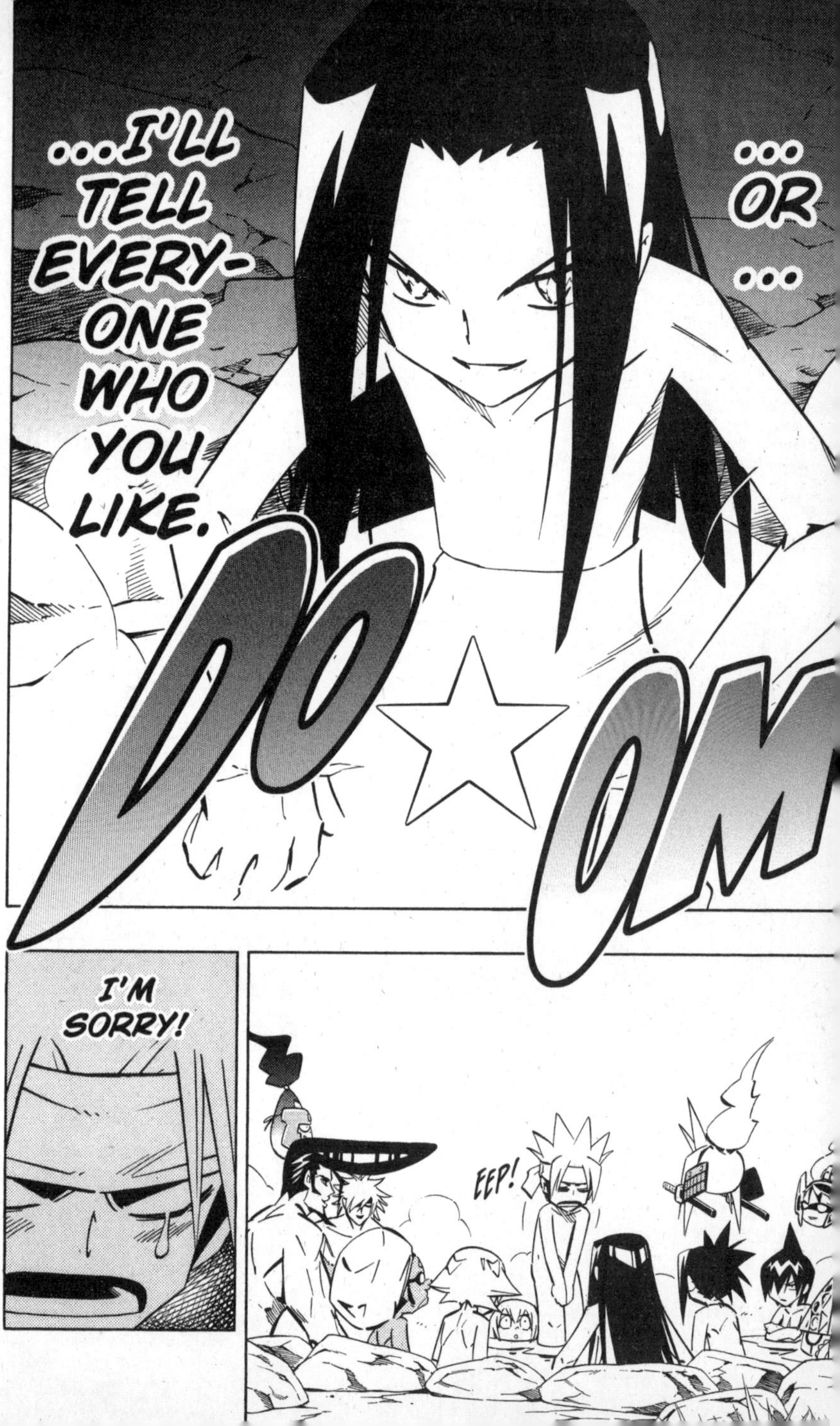
...OR...
...I'LL TELL EVERYONE WHO YOU LIKE.
DO☆OM
EEP!
I'M SORRY!

Reincarnation 259: That Place

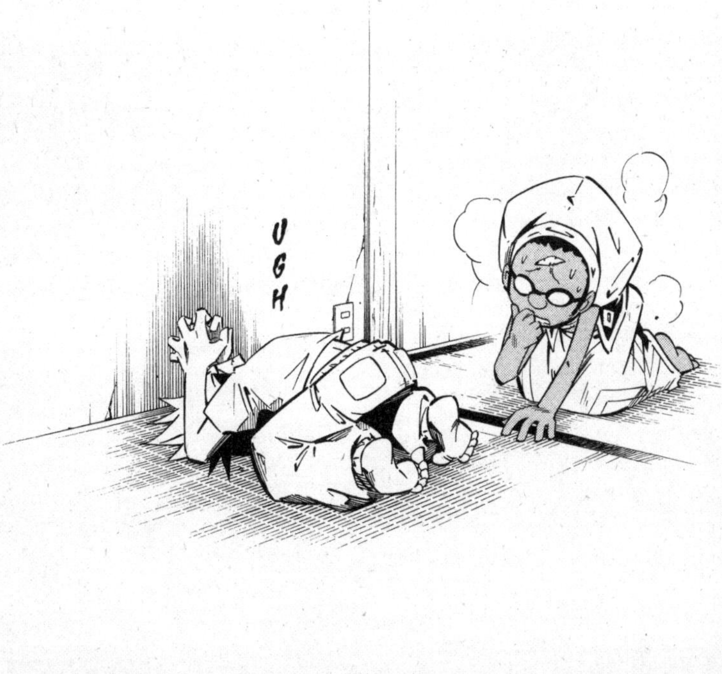
UGH

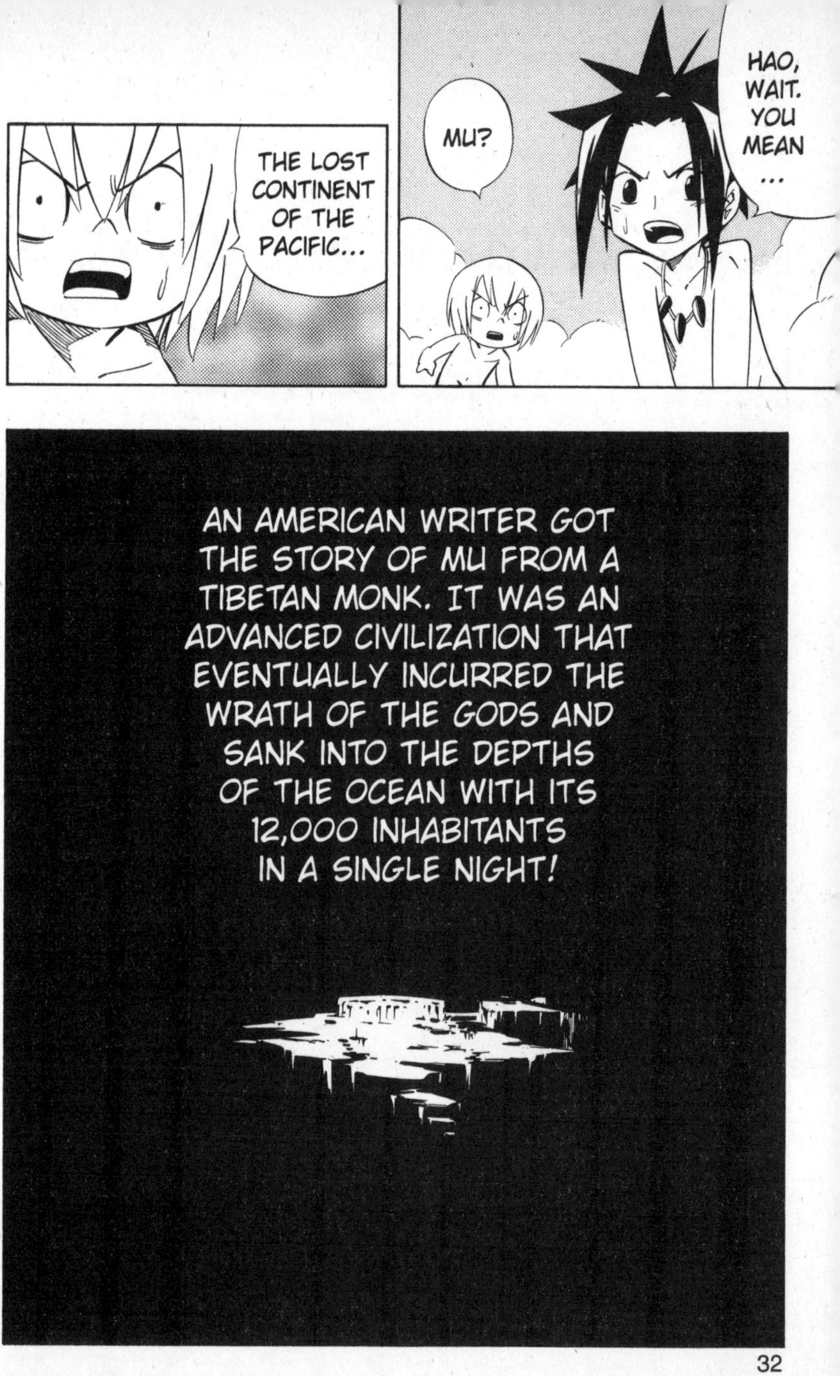
HAO, WAIT. YOU MEAN ...
MU?
THE LOST CONTINENT OF THE PACIFIC...
AN AMERICAN WRITER GOT THE STORY OF MU FROM A TIBETAN MONK. IT WAS AN ADVANCED CIVILIZATION THAT EVENTUALLY INCURRED THE WRATH OF THE GODS AND SANK INTO THE DEPTHS OF THE OCEAN WITH ITS 12,000 INHABITANTS IN A SINGLE NIGHT!

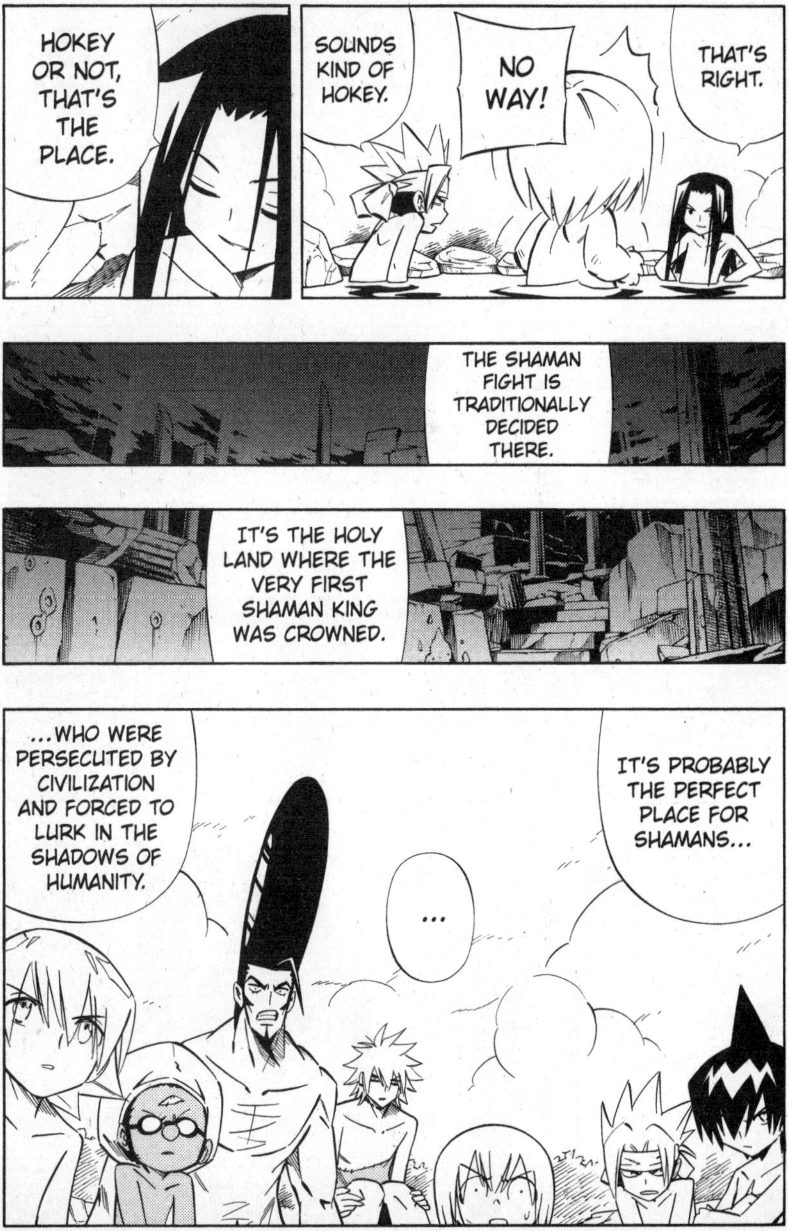
THAT'S RIGHT.
NO WAY!
SOUNDS KIND OF HOKEY.
HOKEY OR NOT, THAT'S THE PLACE.
THE SHAMAN FIGHT IS TRADITIONALLY DECIDED THERE.
IT'S THE HOLY LAND WHERE THE VERY FIRST SHAMAN KING WAS CROWNED.
IT'S PROBABLY THE PERFECT PLACE FOR SHAMANS...
...
...WHO WERE PERSECUTED BY CIVILIZATION AND FORCED TO LURK IN THE SHADOWS OF HUMANITY.

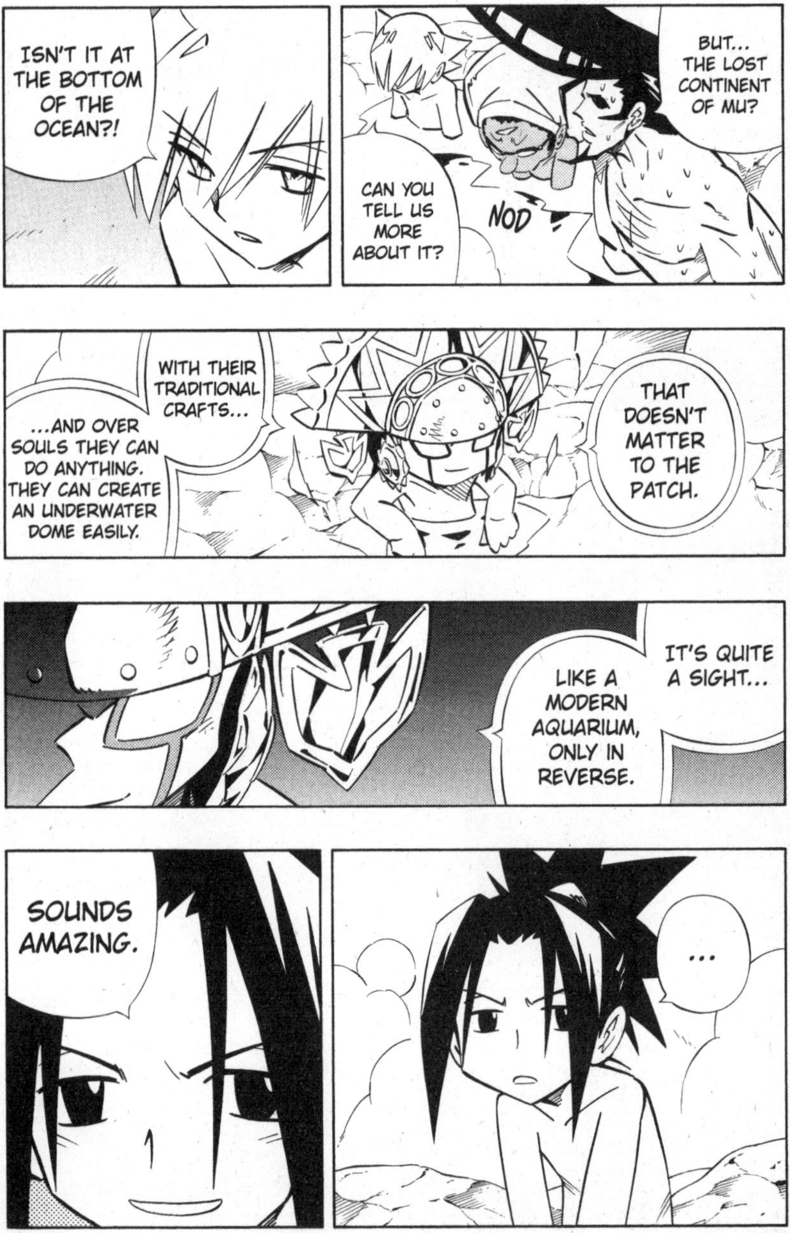
BUT... THE LOST CONTINENT OF MU?
NOD
CAN YOU TELL US MORE ABOUT IT?
ISN'T IT AT THE BOTTOM OF THE OCEAN?!
THAT DOESN'T MATTER TO THE PATCH.
WITH THEIR TRADITIONAL CRAFTS...
...AND OVER SOULS THEY CAN DO ANYTHING. THEY CAN CREATE AN UNDERWATER DOME EASILY.
IT'S QUITE A SIGHT...
LIKE A MODERN AQUARIUM, ONLY IN REVERSE.
...
SOUNDS AMAZING.

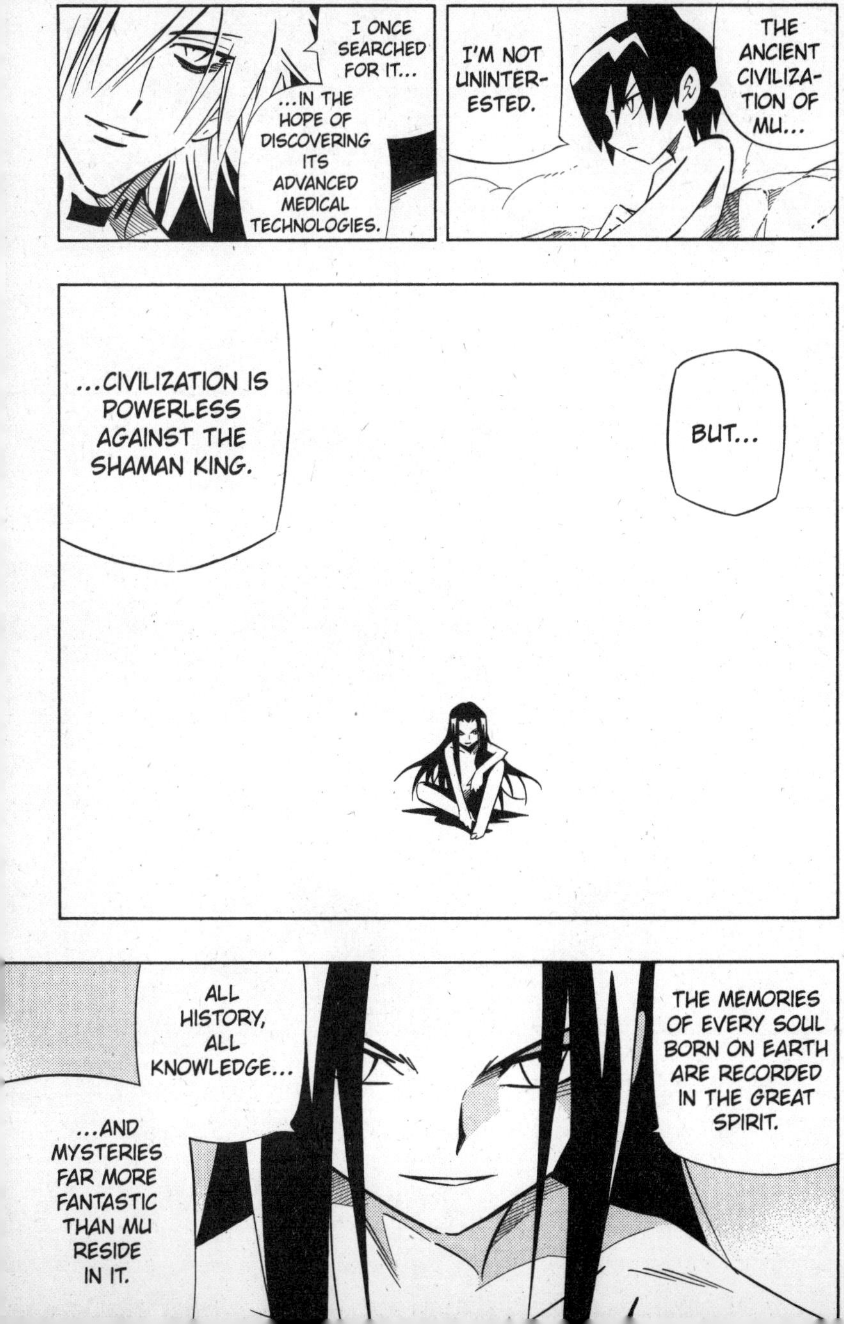
THE ANCIENT CIVILIZATION OF MU...
I'M NOT UNINTERESTED.
I ONCE SEARCHED FOR IT...
...IN THE HOPE OF DISCOVERING ITS ADVANCED MEDICAL TECHNOLOGIES.
BUT...
...CIVILIZATION IS POWERLESS AGAINST THE SHAMAN KING.
THE MEMORIES OF EVERY SOUL BORN ON EARTH ARE RECORDED IN THE GREAT SPIRIT.
ALL HISTORY, ALL KNOWLEDGE...
...AND MYSTERIES FAR MORE FANTASTIC THAN MU RESIDE IN IT.

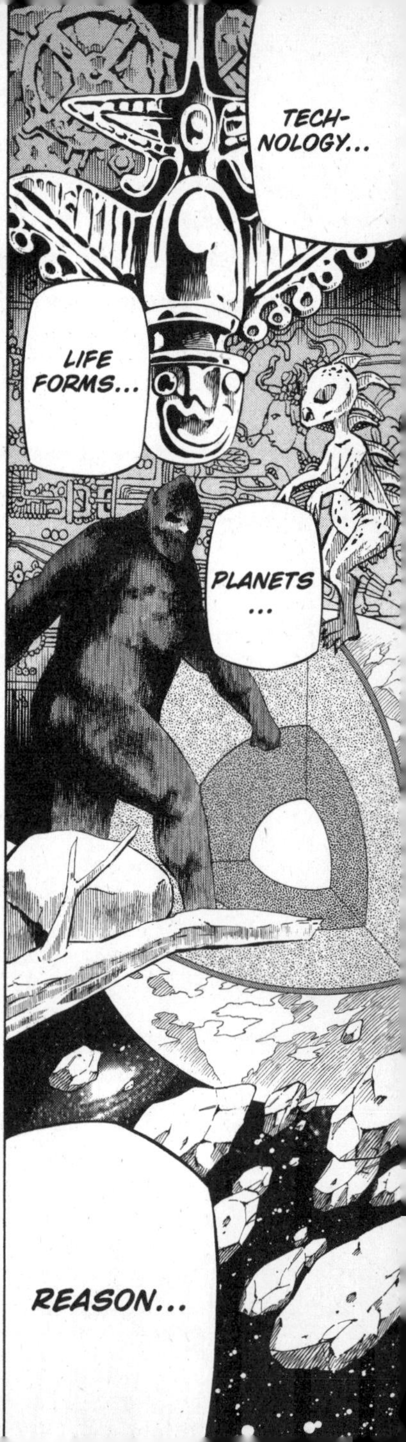
TECH-NOLOGY...
LIFE FORMS...
PLANETS...
REASON...
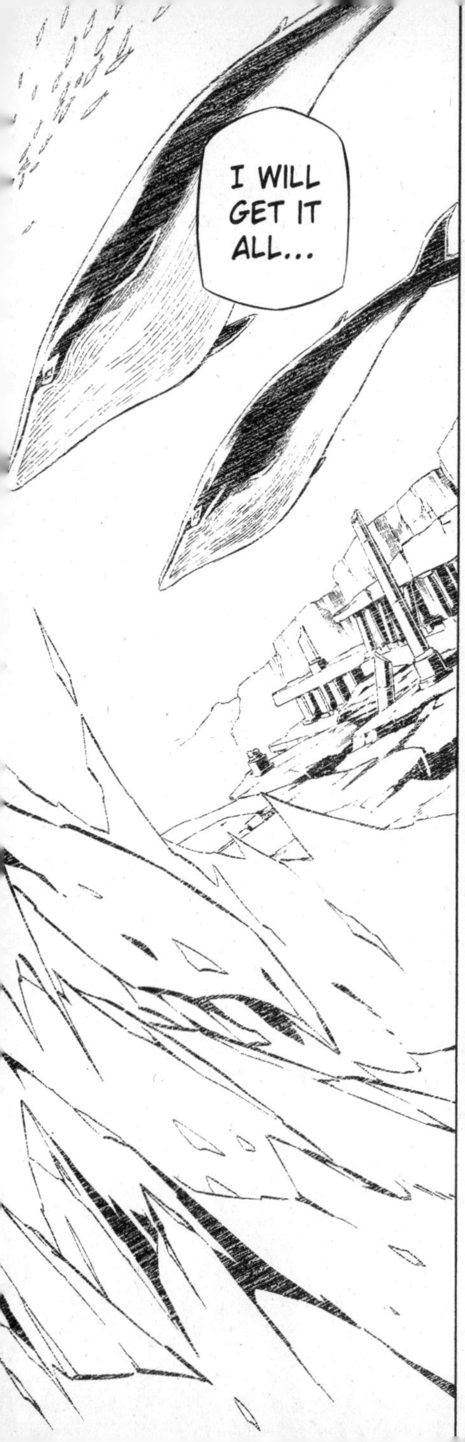
I WILL GET IT ALL...

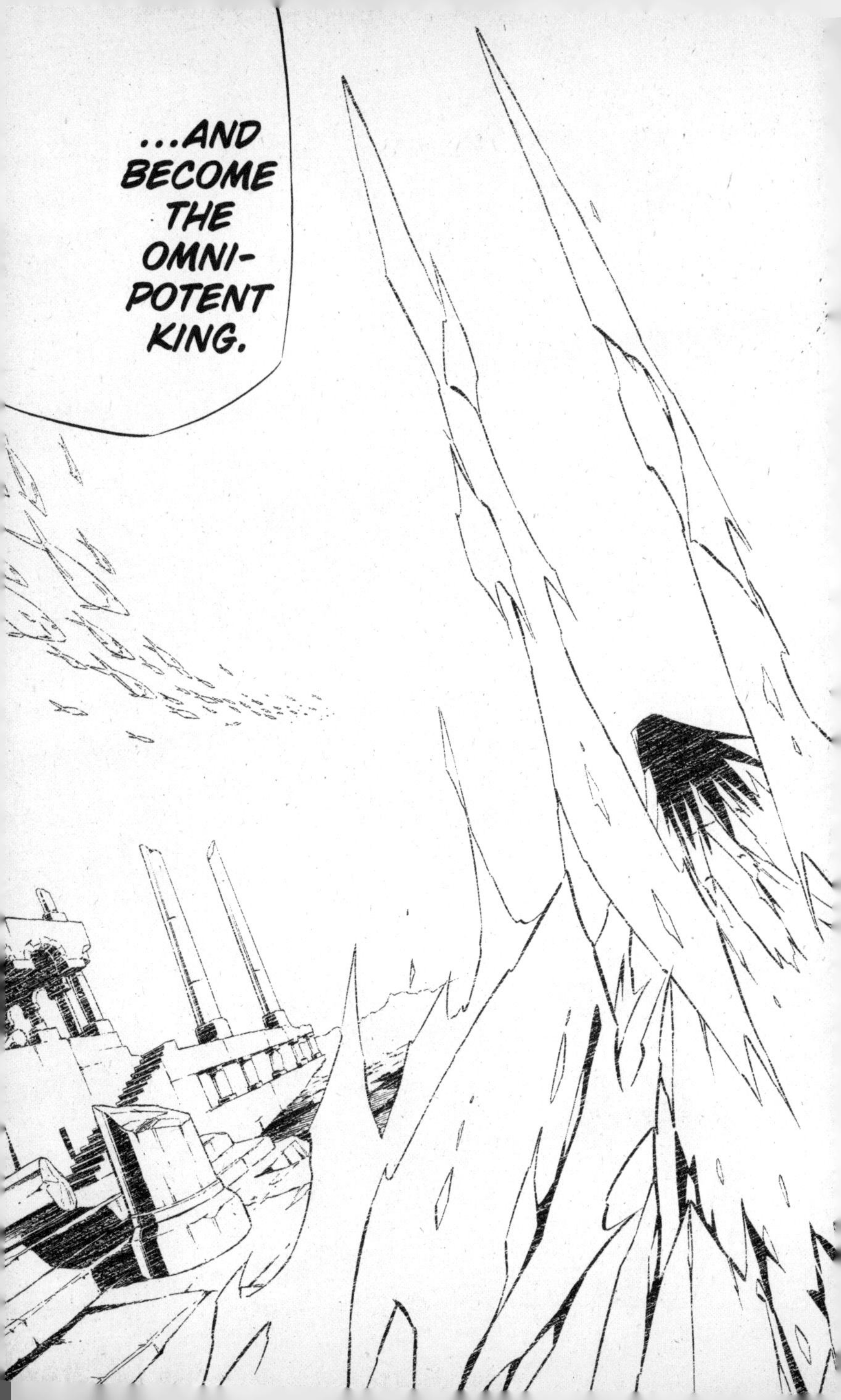
...AND BECOME THE OMNI-POTENT KING.

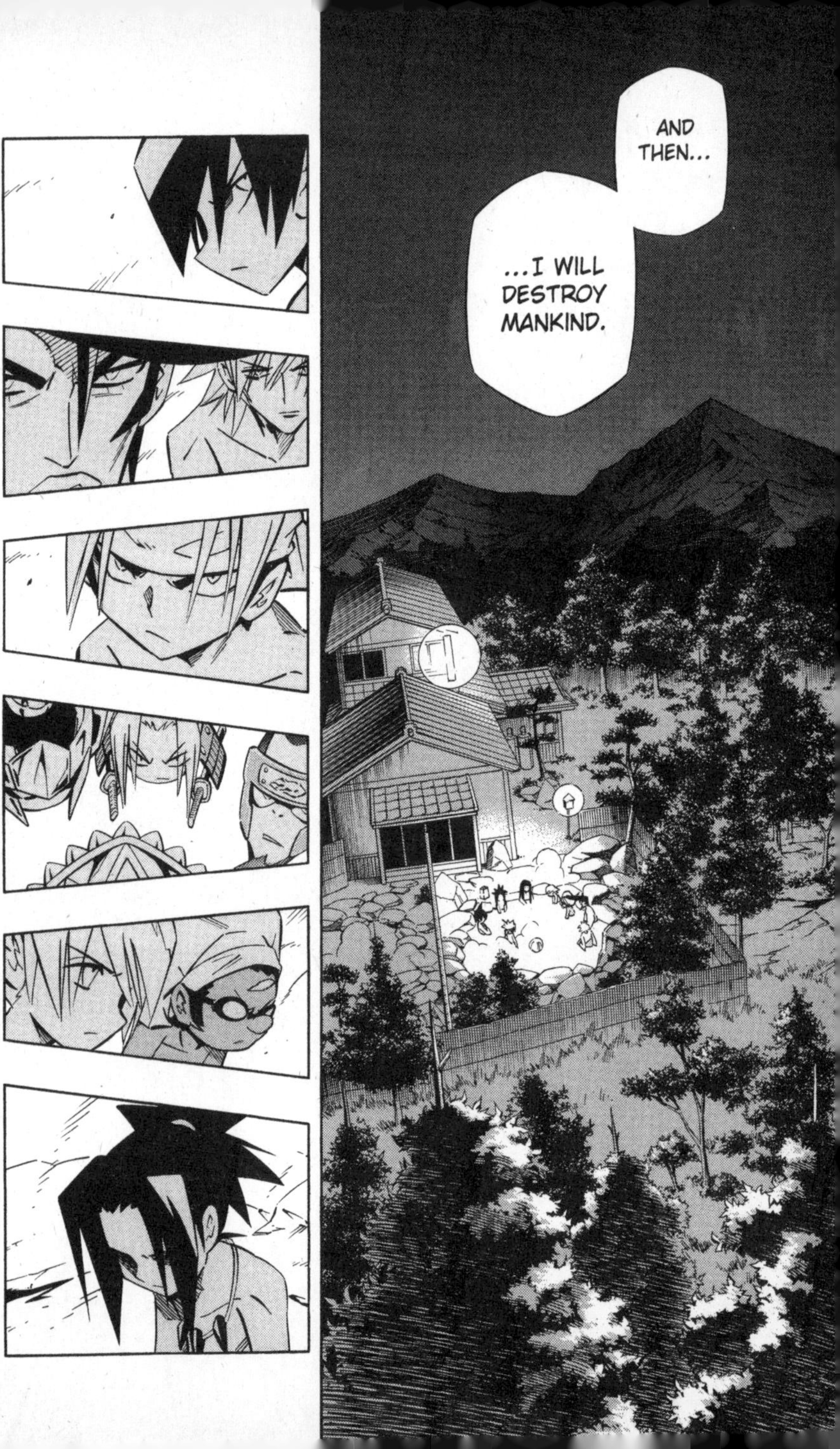
AND THEN...
...I WILL DESTROY MANKIND.

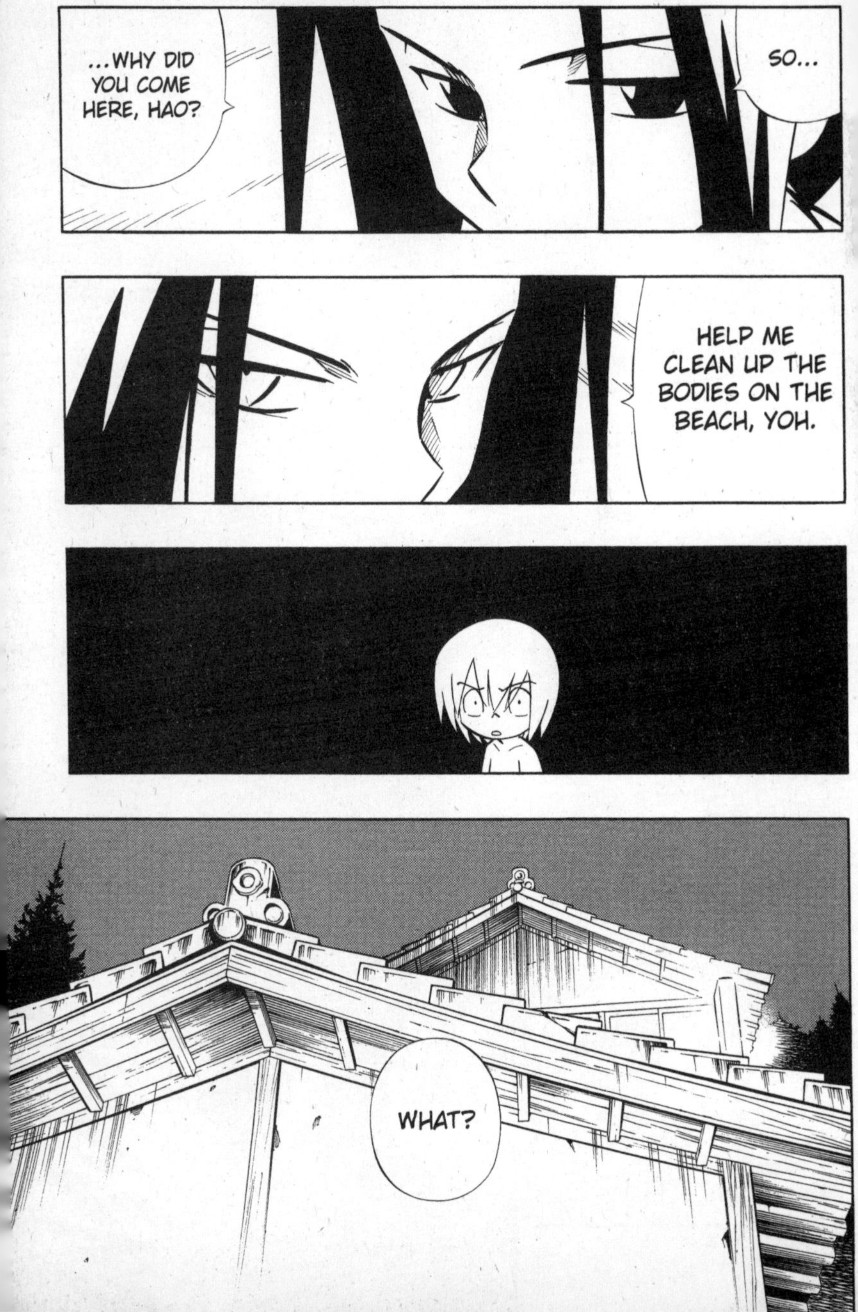
SO...
...WHY DID YOU COME HERE, HAO?
HELP ME CLEAN UP THE BODIES ON THE BEACH, YOH.
WHAT?

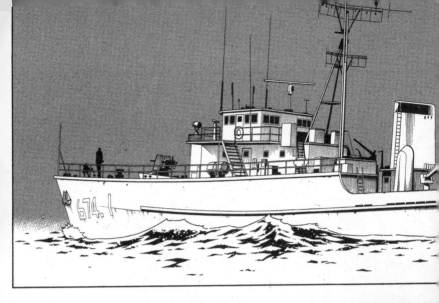

THE LOST CONTINENT OF MU...

IT'S HARD TO BELIEVE, BUT YOU WERE RIGHT, TAMURAZAKI.

IT WAS NOTHING. I JUST STUDIED SOME DOCUMENTS.

SPLASH

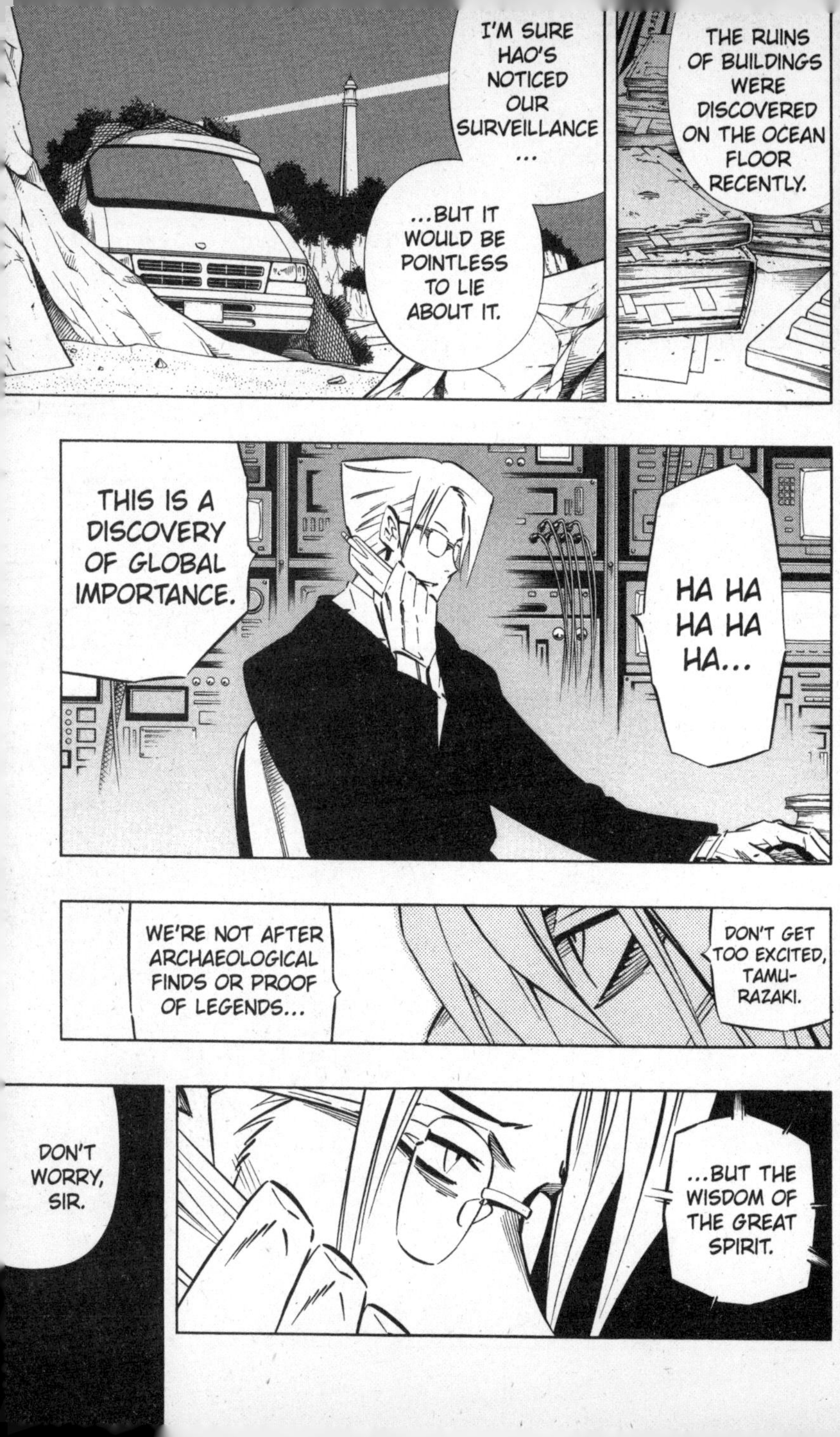
THE RUINS OF BUILDINGS WERE DISCOVERED ON THE OCEAN FLOOR RECENTLY.
I'M SURE HAO'S NOTICED OUR SURVEILLANCE...
...BUT IT WOULD BE POINTLESS TO LIE ABOUT IT.
HA HA HA HA HA...
THIS IS A DISCOVERY OF GLOBAL IMPORTANCE.
DON'T GET TOO EXCITED, TAMU-RAZAKI.
WE'RE NOT AFTER ARCHAEOLOGICAL FINDS OR PROOF OF LEGENDS...
...BUT THE WISDOM OF THE GREAT SPIRIT.
DON'T WORRY, SIR.

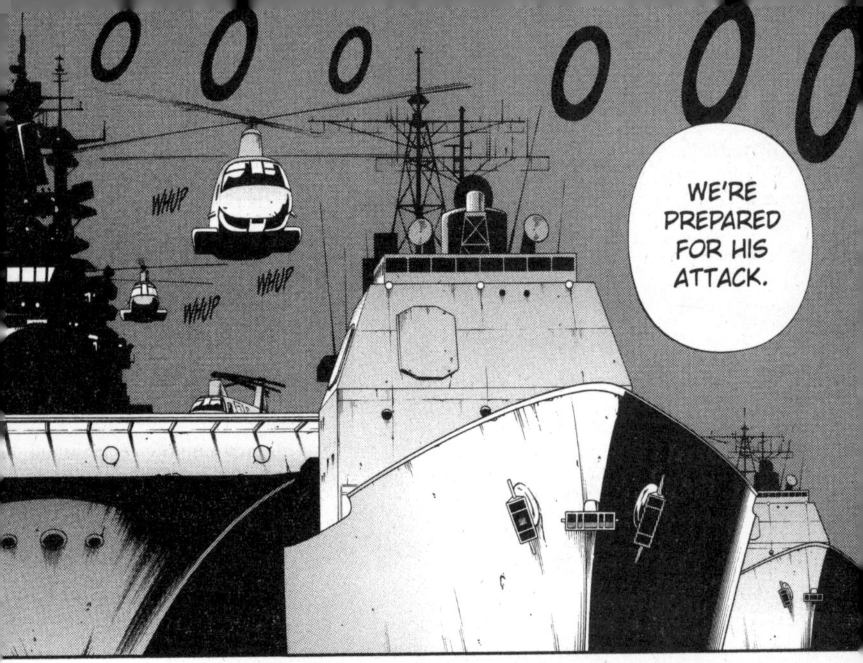
OOOOOO
WE'RE PREPARED FOR HIS ATTACK.
WHUP
WHUP
WHUP

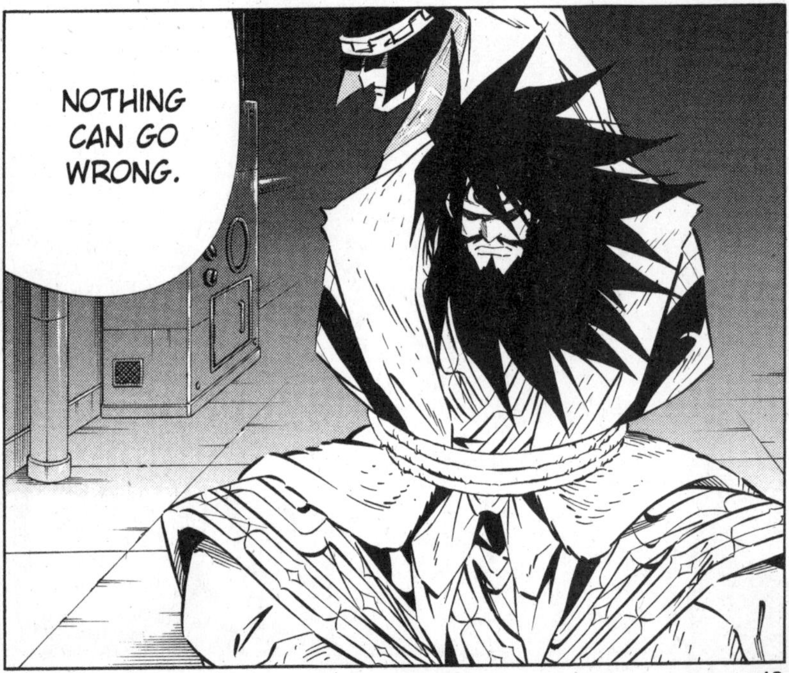
NOTHING CAN GO WRONG.

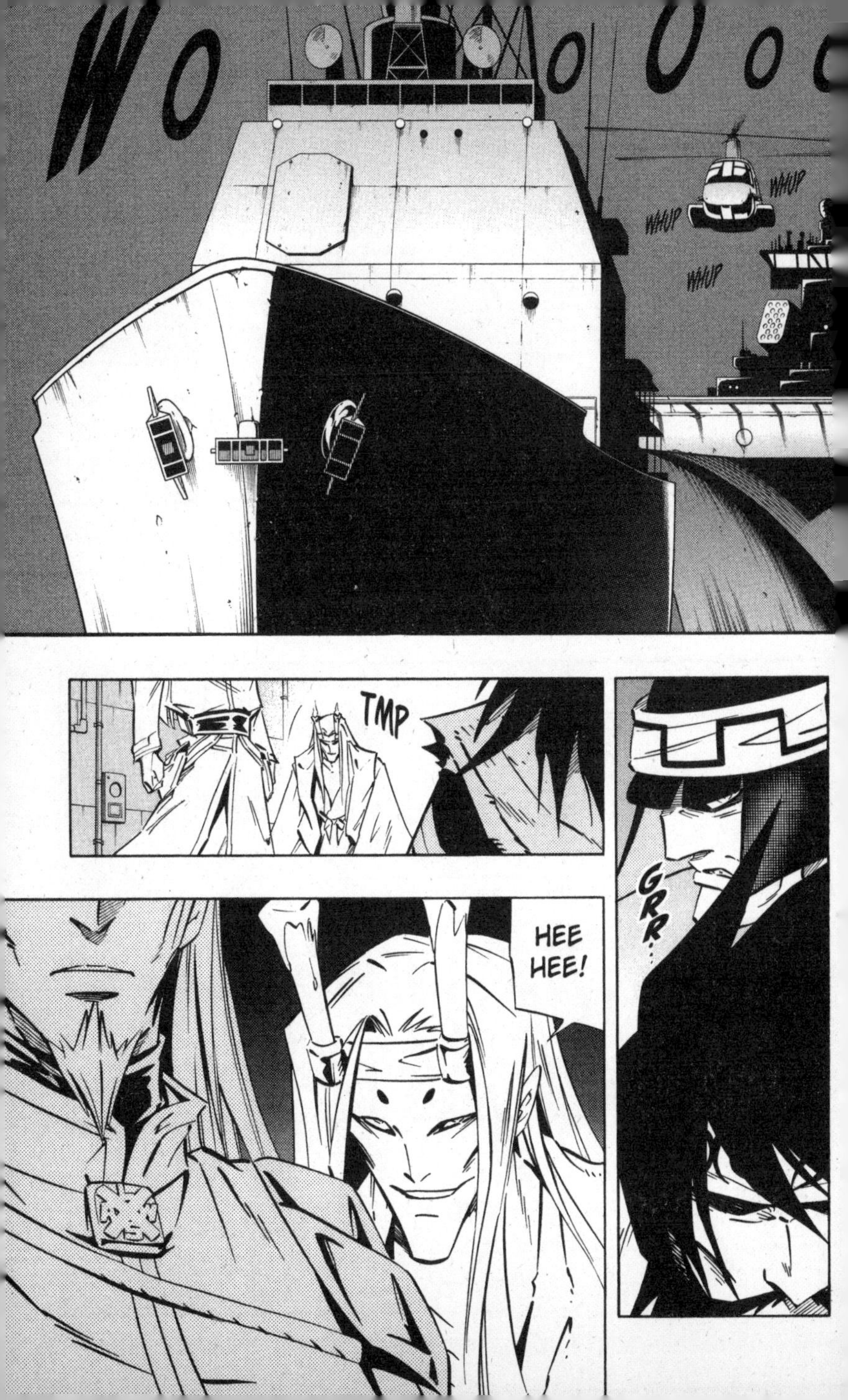
WOOOOO
WHUP
WHUP
WHUP
GRR...
TMP
HEE HEE!

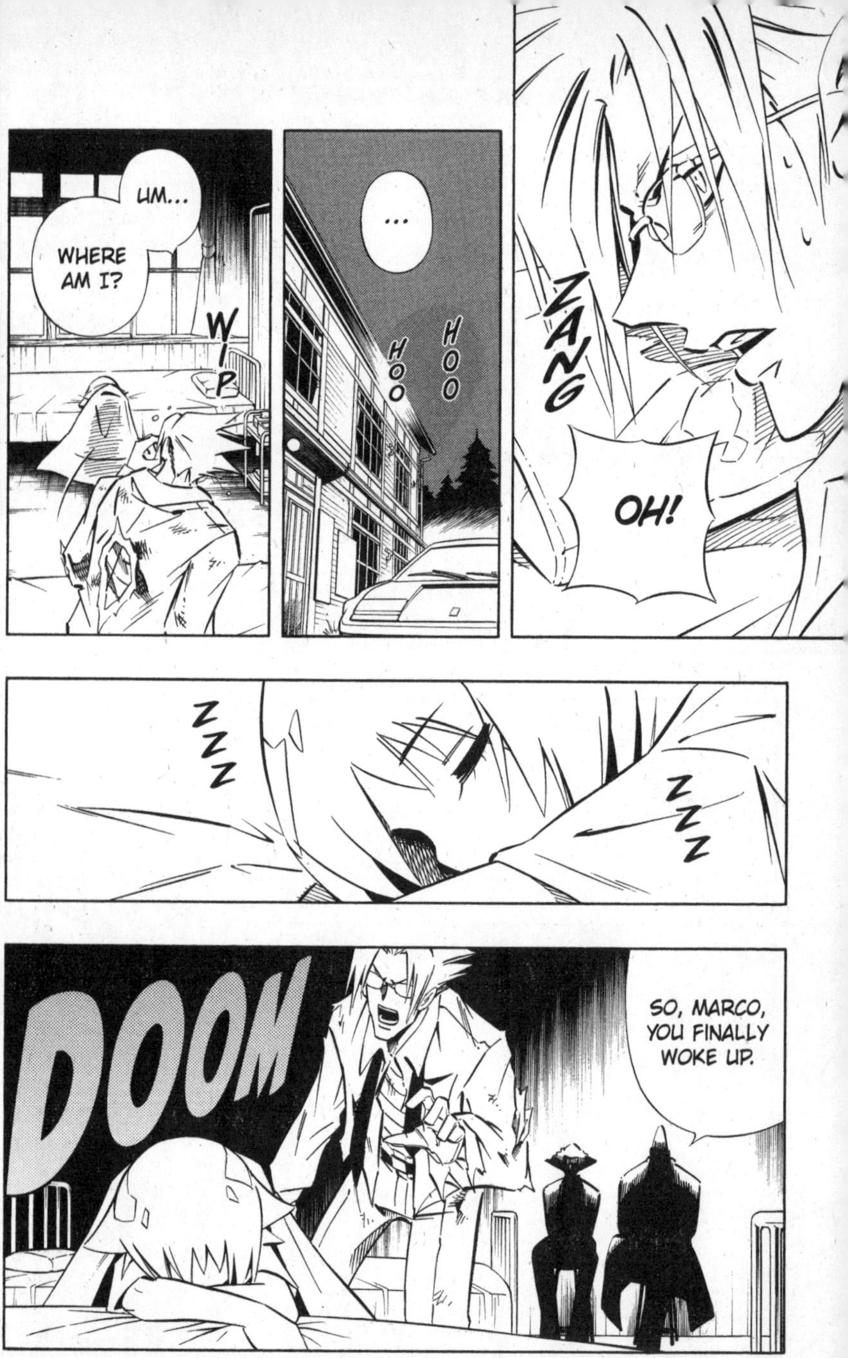
ZANG
OH!
...
HOO
HOO
UM...
WHERE AM I?
WIP
ZZZ
ZZZ
SO, MARCO, YOU FINALLY WOKE UP.
DOOM

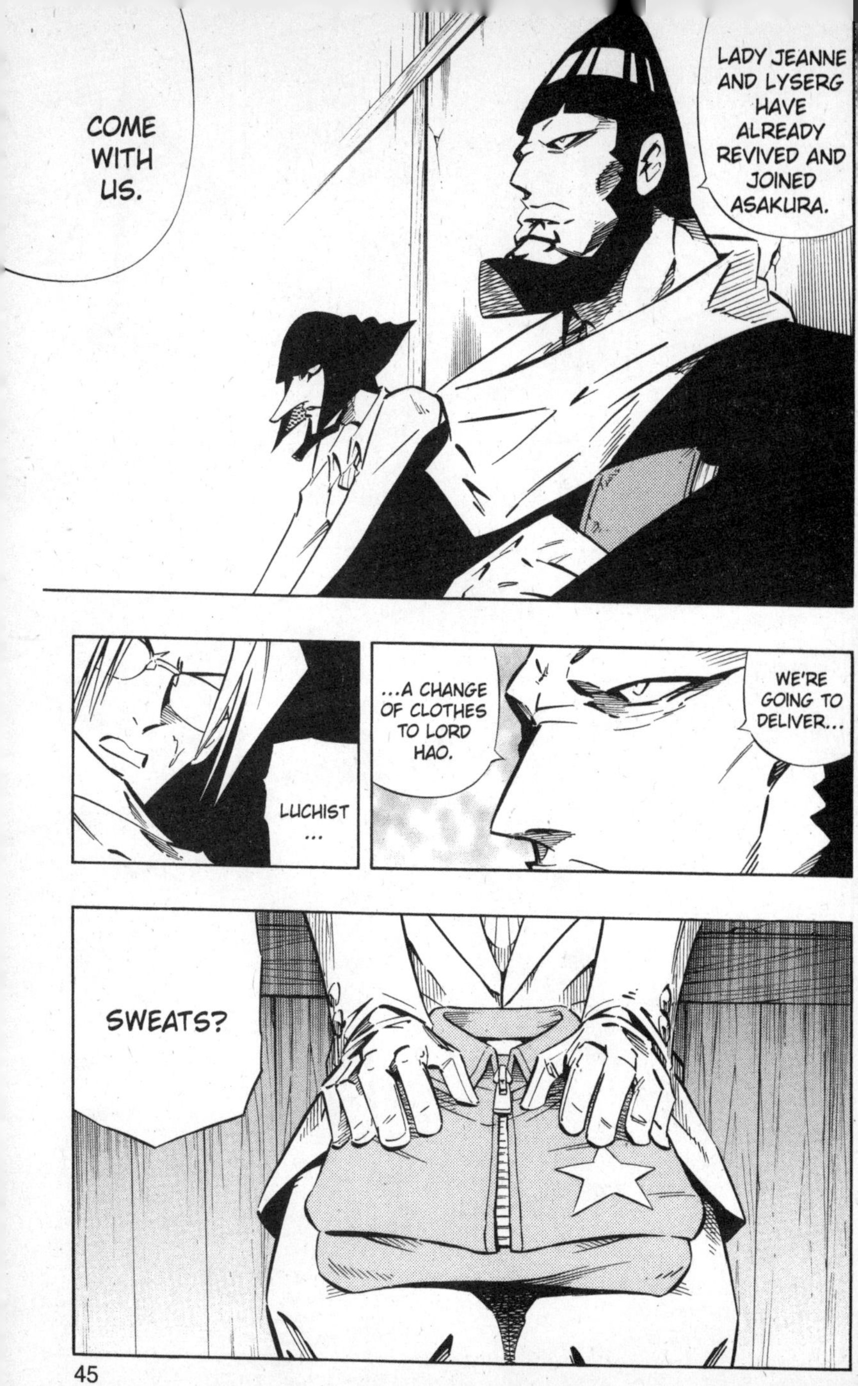
LADY JEANNE AND LYSERG HAVE ALREADY REVIVED AND JOINED ASAKURA.
COME WITH US.
WE'RE GOING TO DELIVER...
...A CHANGE OF CLOTHES TO LORD HAO.
LUCHIST ...
SWEATS?

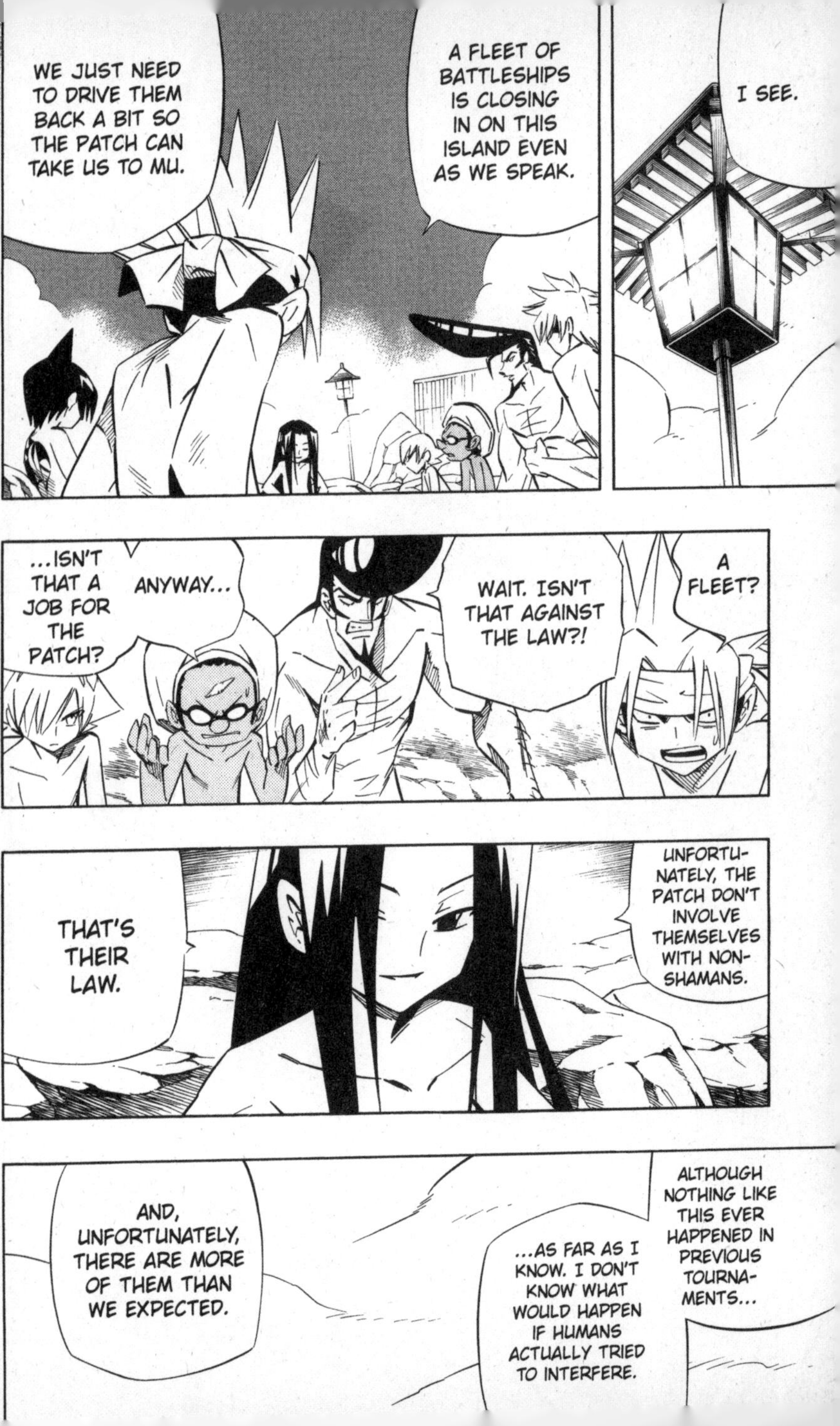
I SEE.
A FLEET OF BATTLESHIPS IS CLOSING IN ON THIS ISLAND EVEN AS WE SPEAK.
WE JUST NEED TO DRIVE THEM BACK A BIT SO THE PATCH CAN TAKE US TO MU.
A FLEET?
WAIT. ISN'T THAT AGAINST THE LAW?!
ANYWAY...
...ISN'T THAT A JOB FOR THE PATCH?
UNFORTUNATELY, THE PATCH DON'T INVOLVE THEMSELVES WITH NON-SHAMANS.
THAT'S THEIR LAW.
ALTHOUGH NOTHING LIKE THIS EVER HAPPENED IN PREVIOUS TOURNAMENTS...
...AS FAR AS I KNOW. I DON'T KNOW WHAT WOULD HAPPEN IF HUMANS ACTUALLY TRIED TO INTERFERE.
AND, UNFORTUNATELY, THERE ARE MORE OF THEM THAN WE EXPECTED.

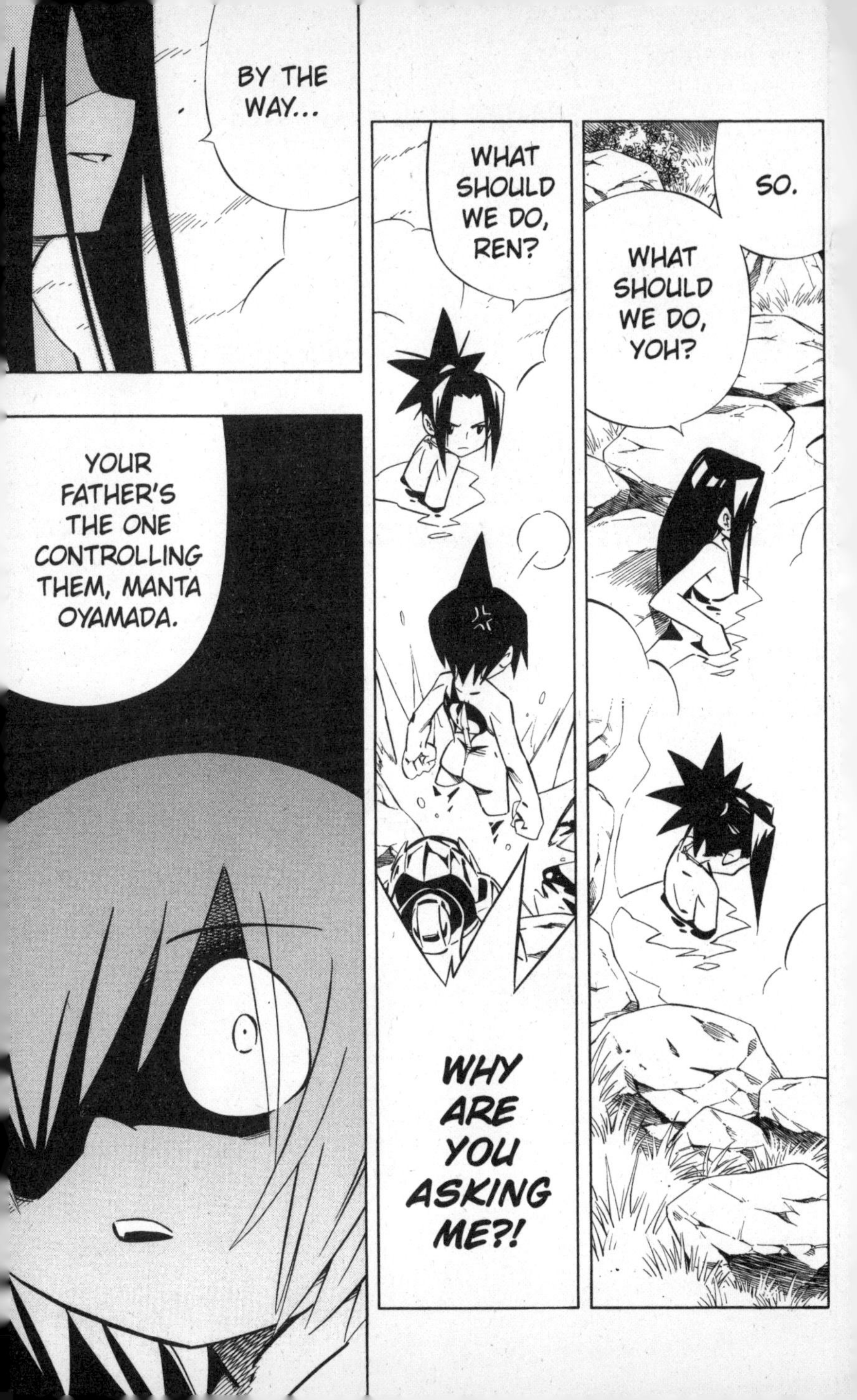
SO.
WHAT SHOULD WE DO, YOH?
WHAT SHOULD WE DO, REN?
WHY ARE YOU ASKING ME?!
BY THE WAY...
YOUR FATHER'S THE ONE CONTROLLING THEM, MANTA OYAMADA.

SHAMAN KING CHARACTER FILE No.152

小山田萬純
MANSUMI OYAMADA

2001
(JAN)

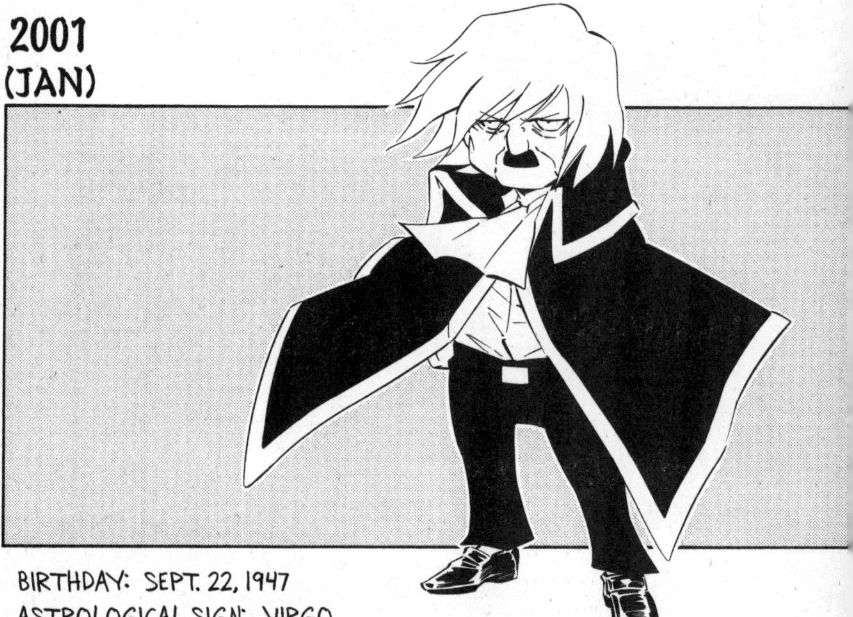

BIRTHDAY: SEPT. 22, 1947
ASTROLOGICAL SIGN: VIRGO
BLOOD TYPE: O
53 YEARS OLD

Reincarnation 260: One Bad Woman

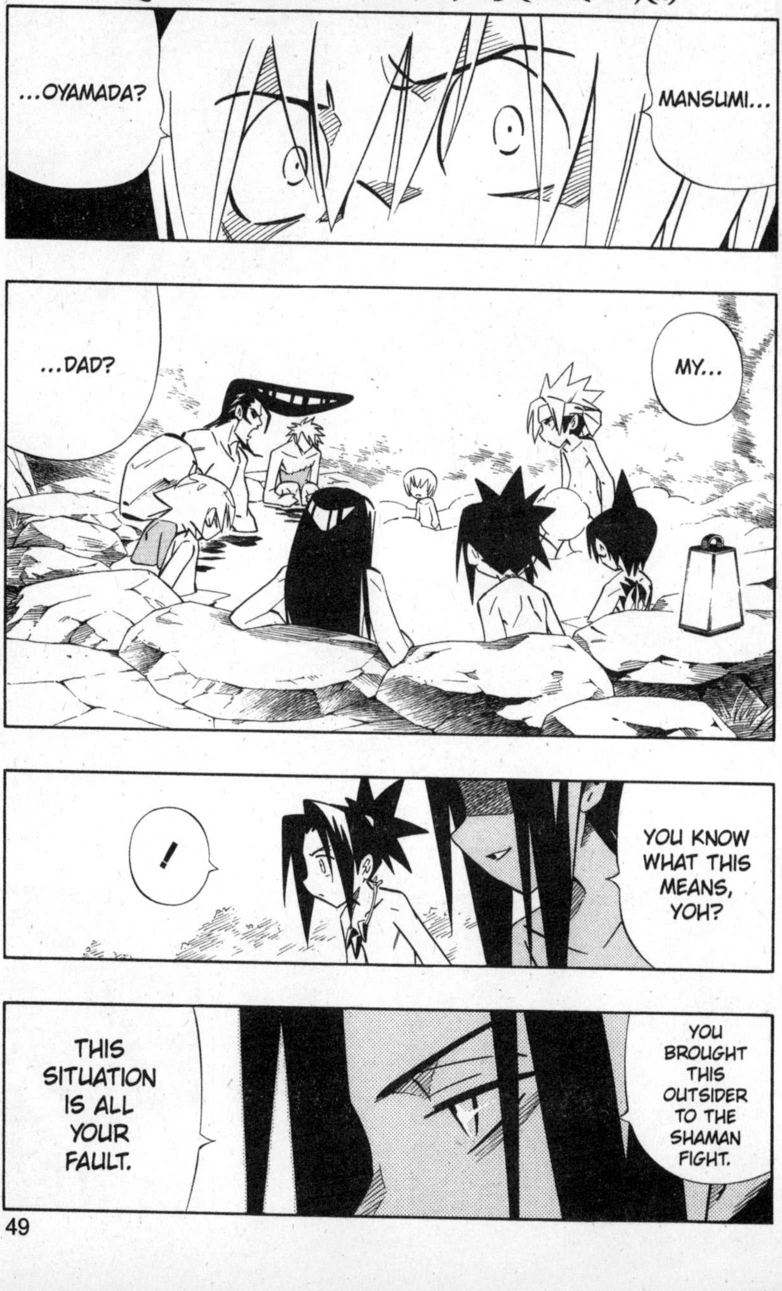
MANSUMI...
...OYAMADA?
MY...
...DAD?
YOU KNOW WHAT THIS MEANS, YOH?
!
YOU BROUGHT THIS OUTSIDER TO THE SHAMAN FIGHT.
THIS SITUATION IS ALL YOUR FAULT.

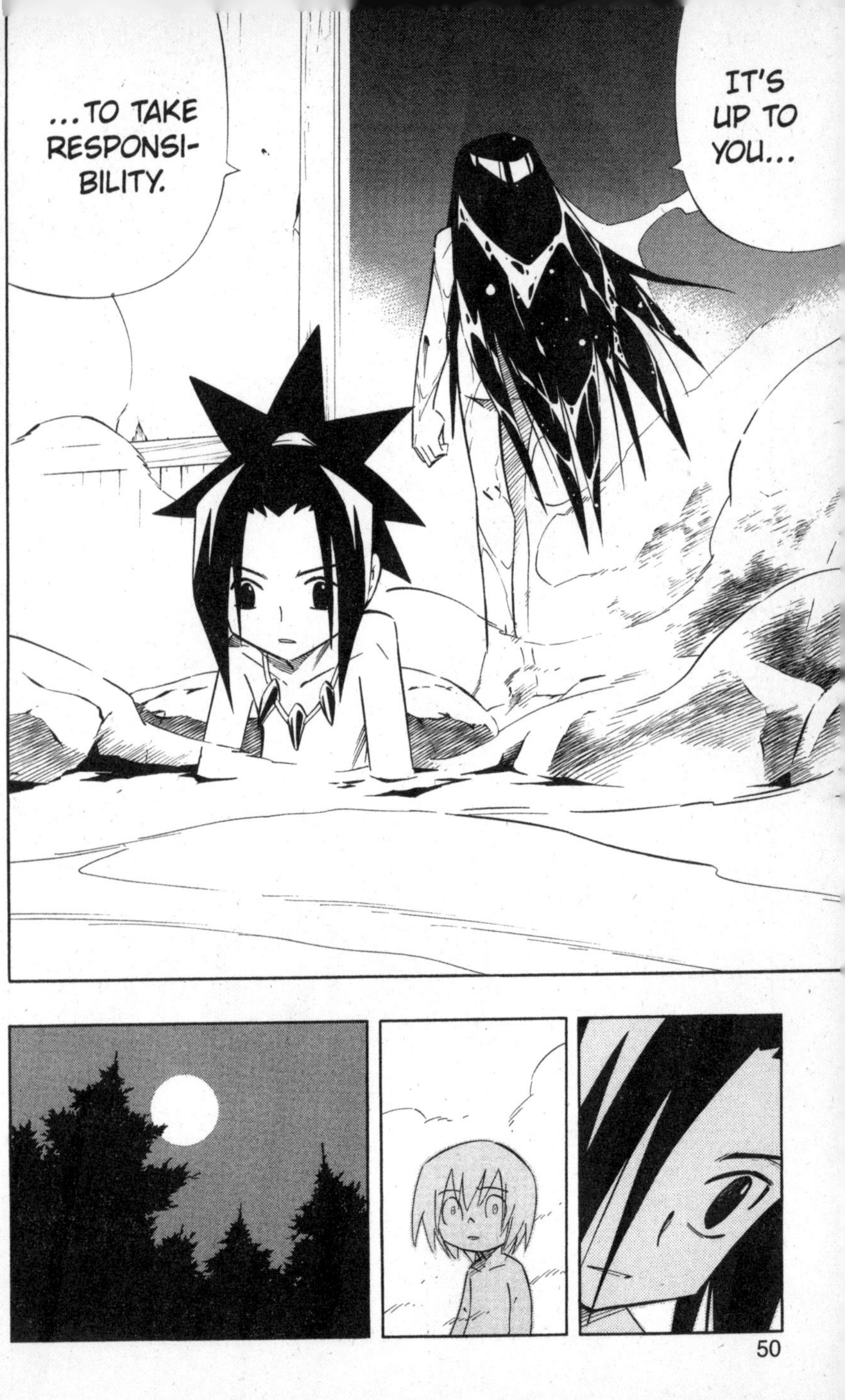
IT'S UP TO YOU...
...TO TAKE RESPONSI- BILITY.

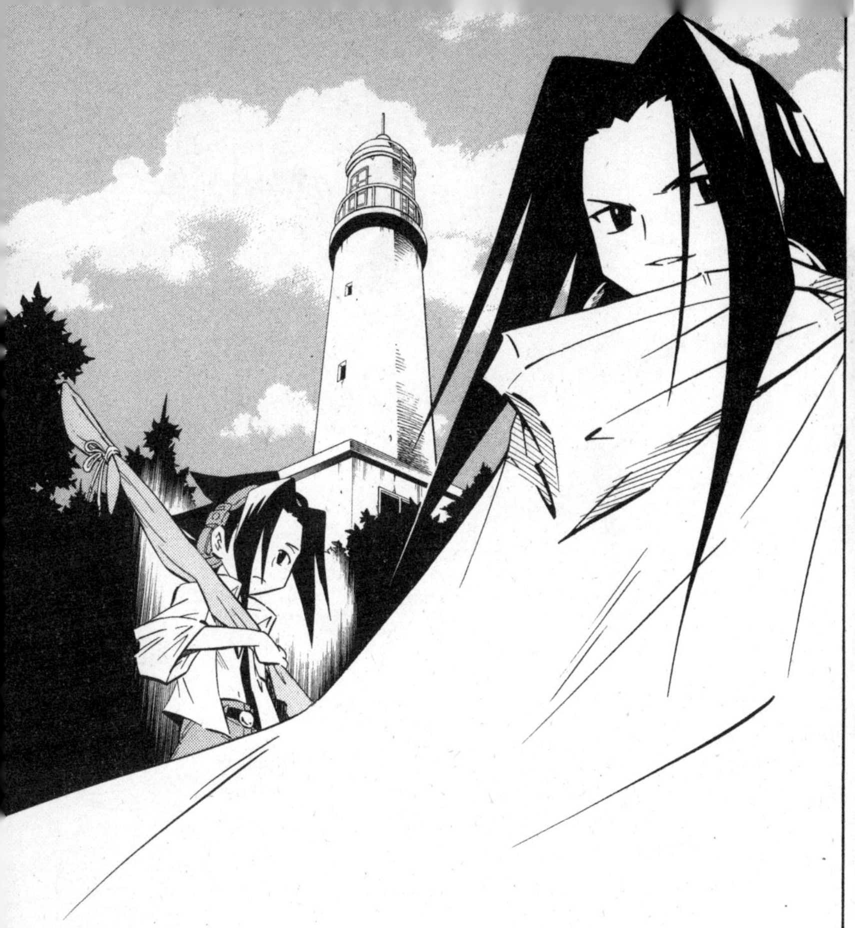

Reincarnation 260: One Bad Woman

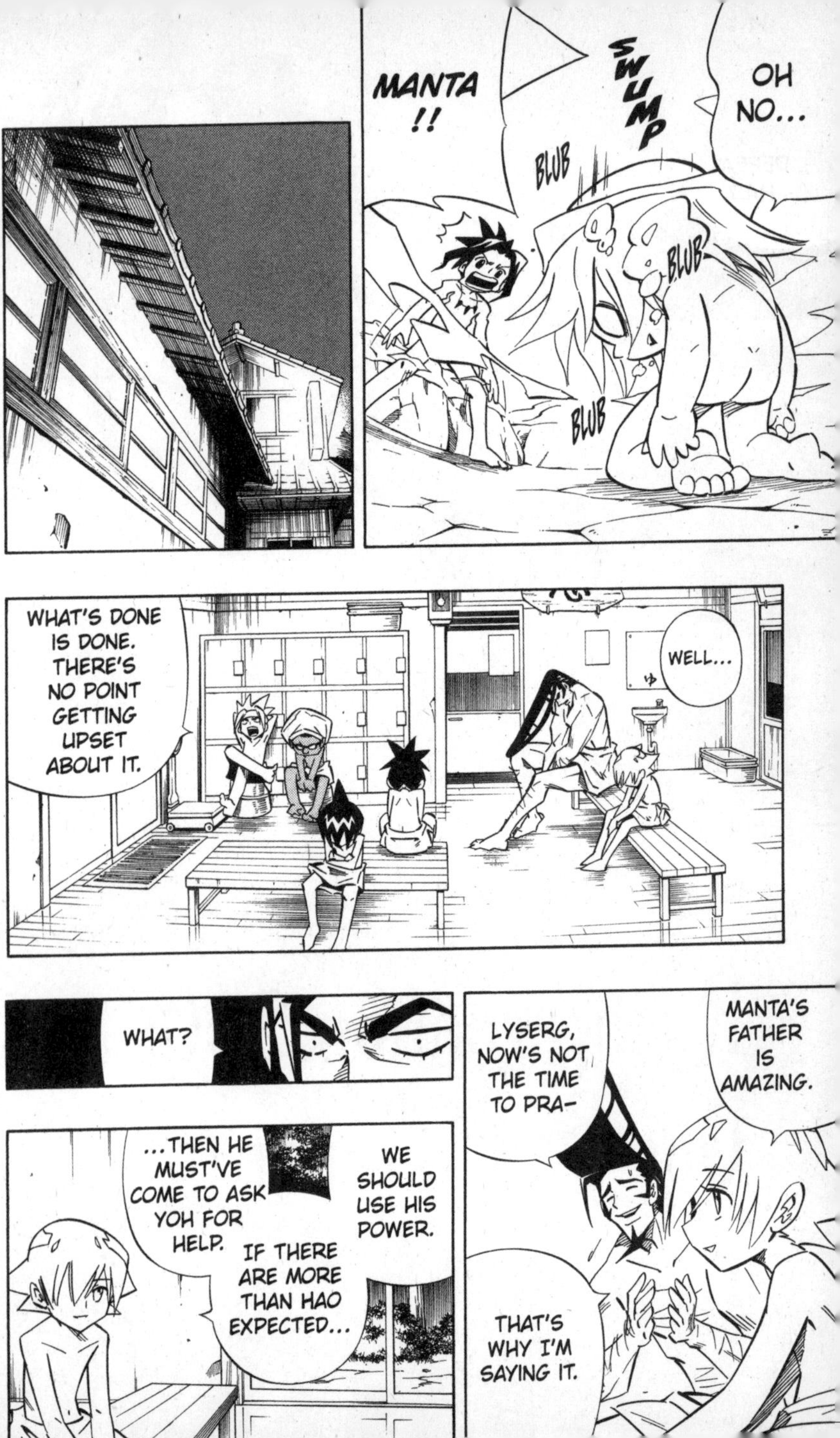
OH NO...
SWUMP
MANTA !!
BLUB
BLUB
BLUB
WELL...
WHAT'S DONE IS DONE. THERE'S NO POINT GETTING UPSET ABOUT IT.
MANTA'S FATHER IS AMAZING.
LYSERG, NOW'S NOT THE TIME TO PRA-
THAT'S WHY I'M SAYING IT.
WHAT?
IF THERE ARE MORE THAN HAO EXPECTED...
...THEN HE MUST'VE COME TO ASK YOH FOR HELP.
WE SHOULD USE HIS POWER.

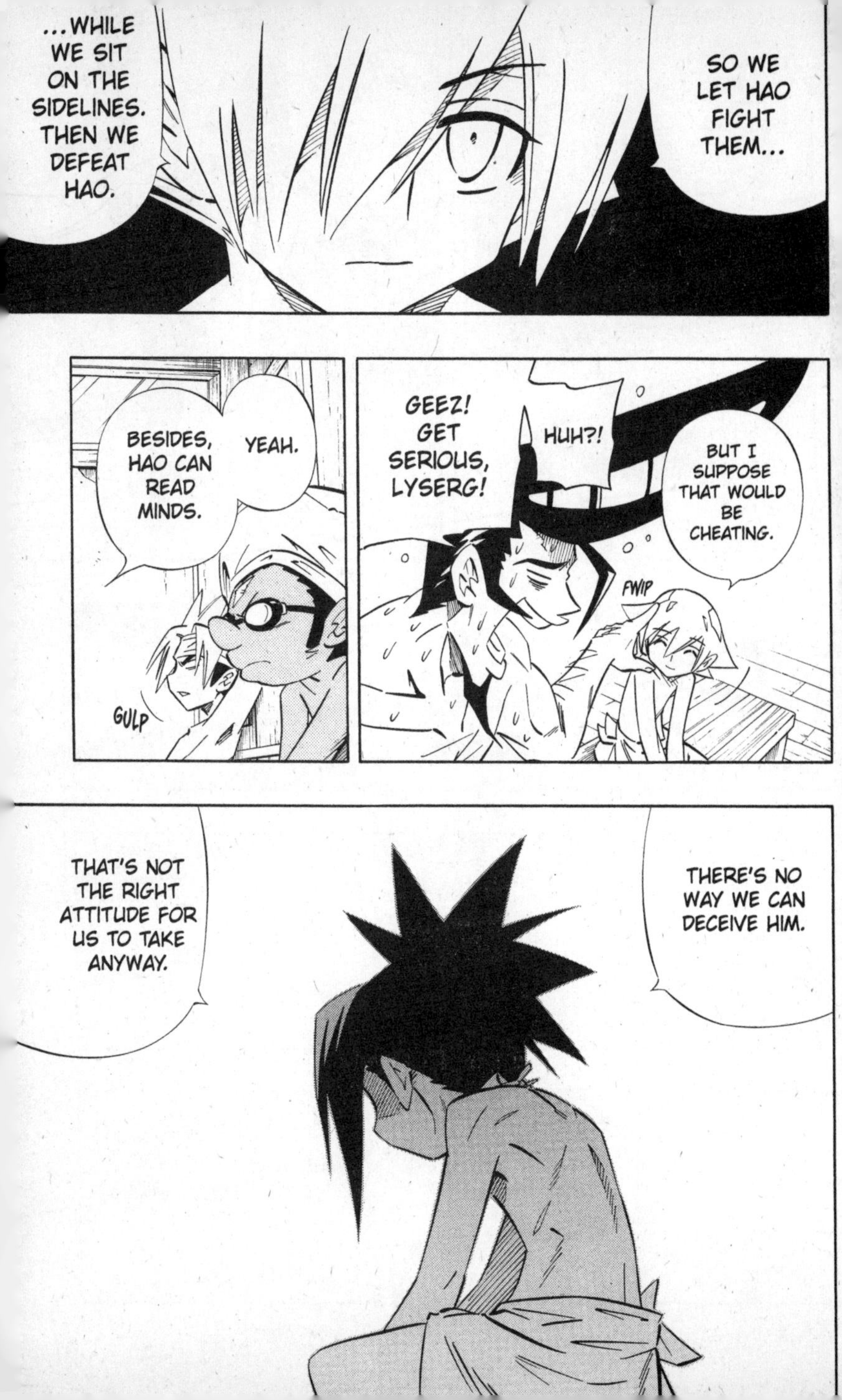
SO WE LET HAO FIGHT THEM...
...WHILE WE SIT ON THE SIDELINES. THEN WE DEFEAT HAO.
BUT I SUPPOSE THAT WOULD BE CHEATING.
FWIP
HUH?!
GEEZ! GET SERIOUS, LYSERG!
YEAH.
BESIDES, HAO CAN READ MINDS.
GULP
THERE'S NO WAY WE CAN DECEIVE HIM.
THAT'S NOT THE RIGHT ATTITUDE FOR US TO TAKE ANYWAY.

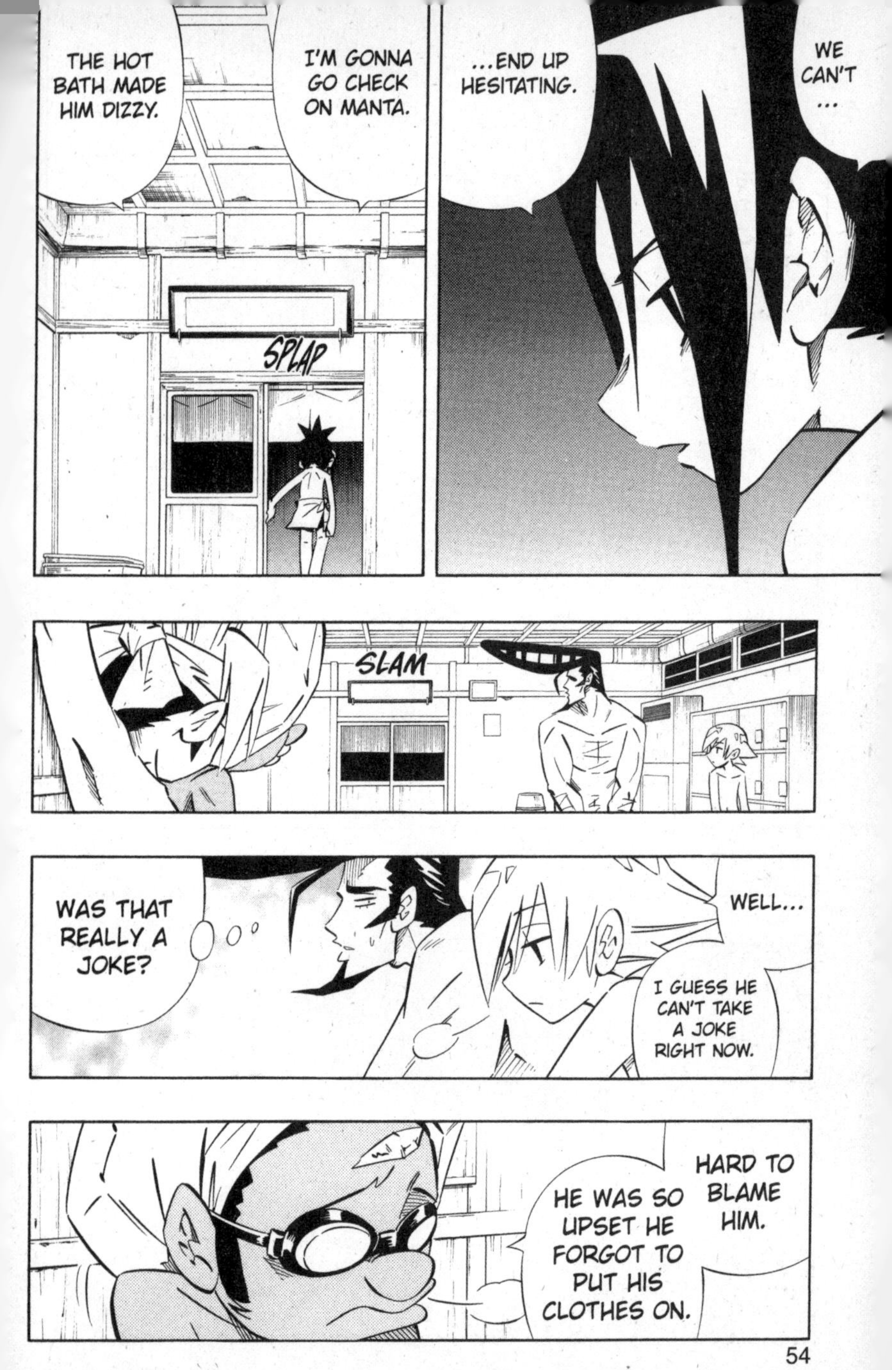
WE CAN'T ...
...END UP HESITATING.
I'M GONNA GO CHECK ON MANTA.
THE HOT BATH MADE HIM DIZZY.
SPLAP
SLAM
WELL...
I GUESS HE CAN'T TAKE A JOKE RIGHT NOW.
WAS THAT REALLY A JOKE?
HARD TO BLAME HIM.
HE WAS SO UPSET HE FORGOT TO PUT HIS CLOTHES ON.

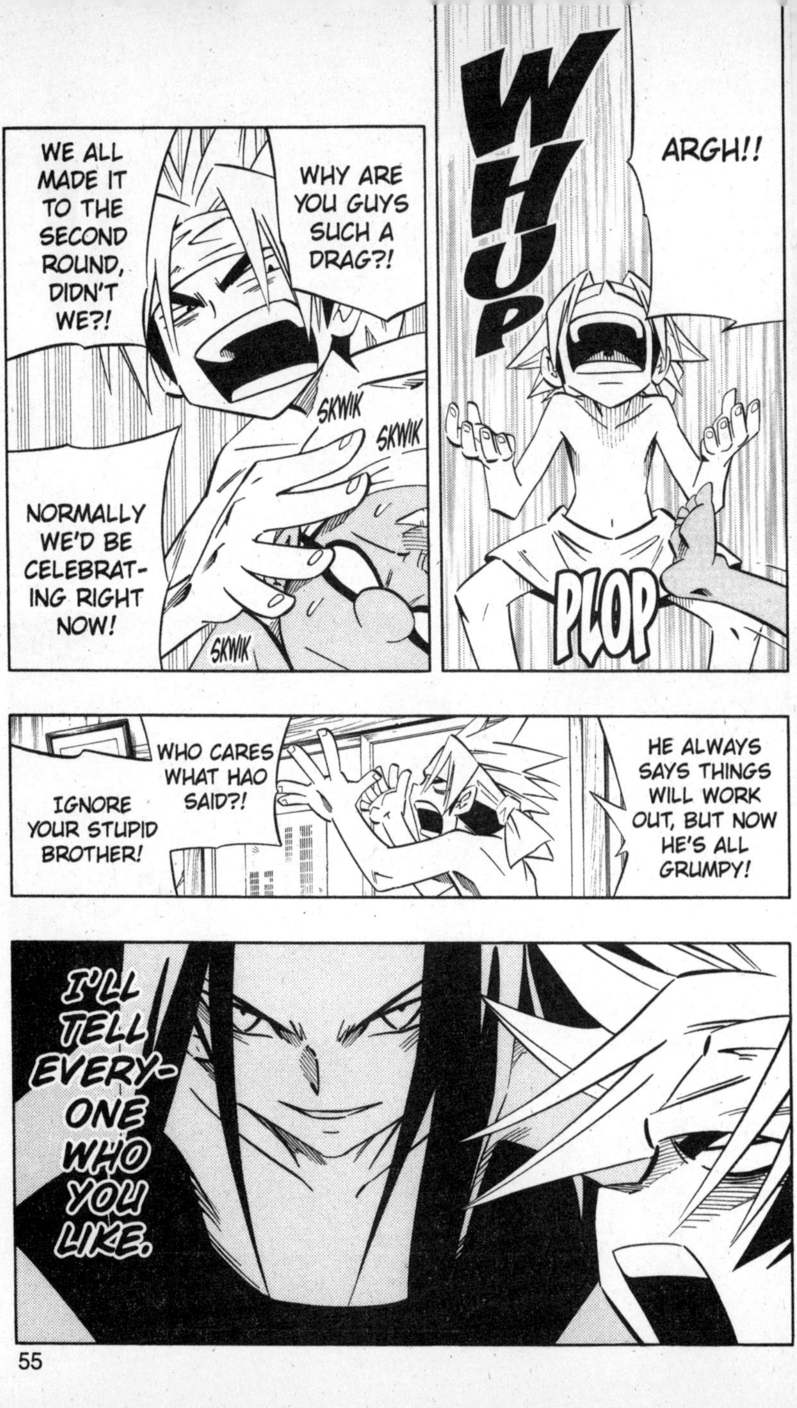
ARGH!!
WHUP
PLOP
WHY ARE YOU GUYS SUCH A DRAG?!
WE ALL MADE IT TO THE SECOND ROUND, DIDN'T WE?!
SKWIK
SKWIK
NORMALLY WE'D BE CELEBRAT-ING RIGHT NOW!
SKWIK
HE ALWAYS SAYS THINGS WILL WORK OUT, BUT NOW HE'S ALL GRUMPY!
WHO CARES WHAT HAO SAID?!
IGNORE YOUR STUPID BROTHER!
I'LL TELL EVERY-ONE WHO YOU LIKE.

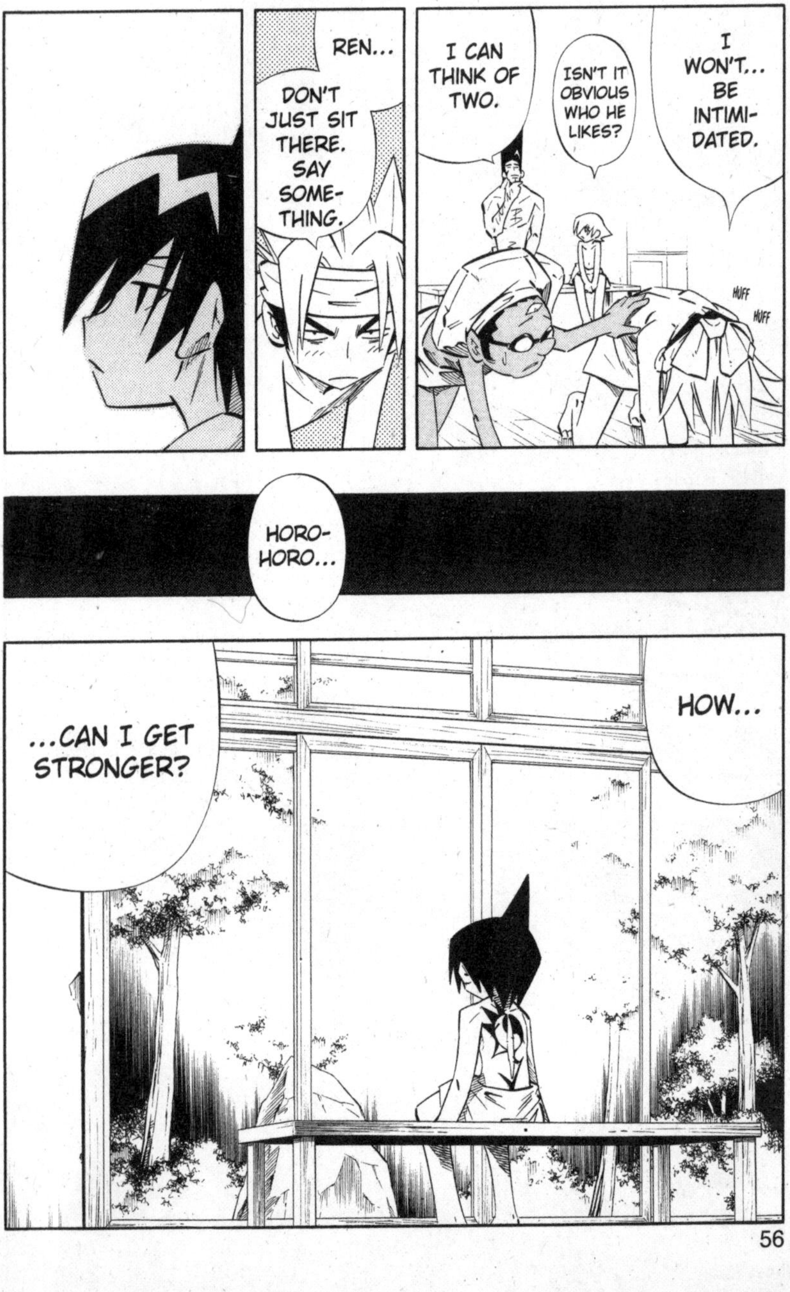
I WON'T... BE INTIMI-DATED.
ISN'T IT OBVIOUS WHO HE LIKES?
I CAN THINK OF TWO.
HUFF
HUFF
REN...
DON'T JUST SIT THERE. SAY SOME-THING.
HORO-HORO...
HOW...
...CAN I GET STRONGER?

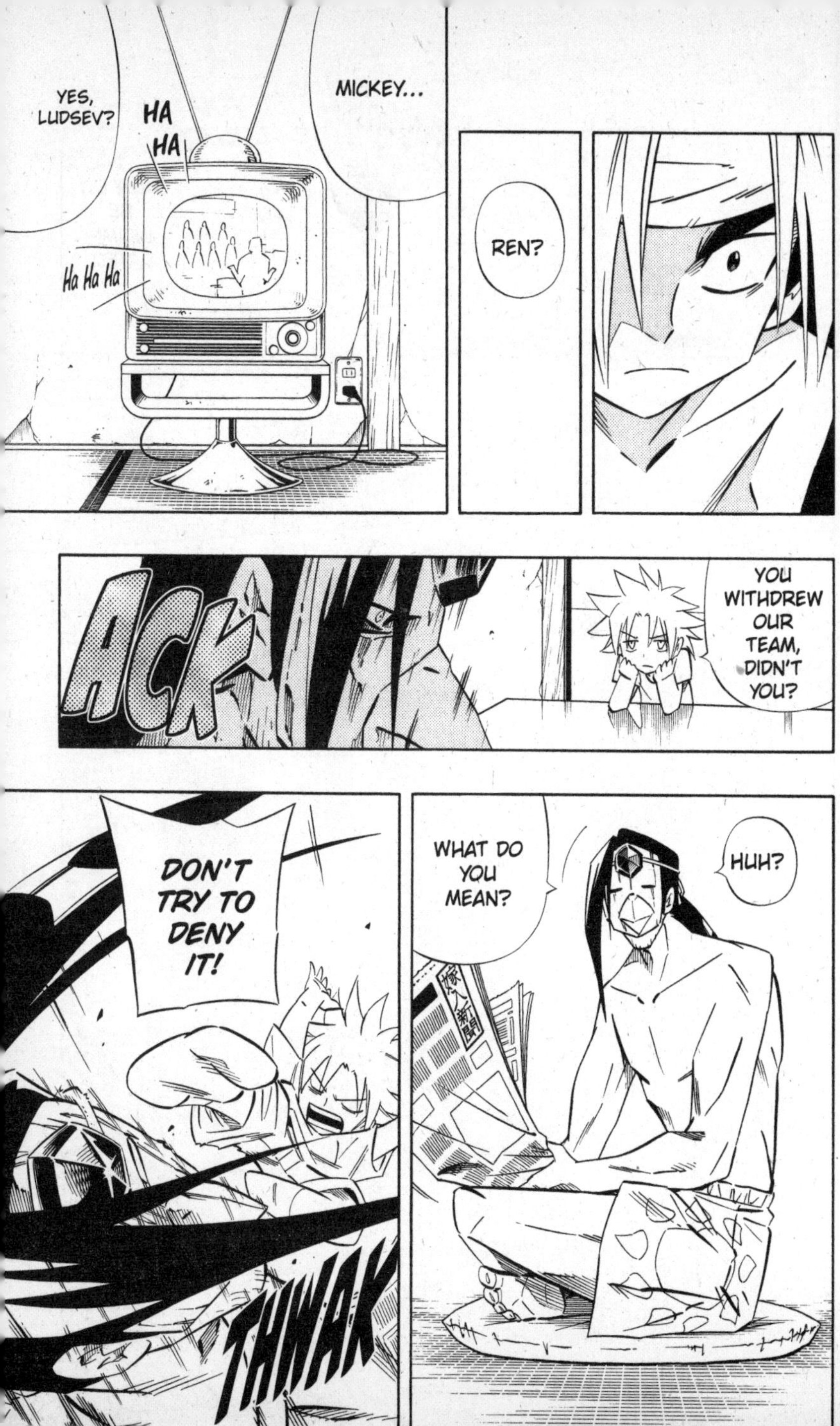
REN?
MICKEY...
YES, LUDSEV?
HA HA
Ha Ha Ha
YOU WITHDREW OUR TEAM, DIDN'T YOU?
ACK
HUH?
WHAT DO YOU MEAN?
DON'T TRY TO DENY IT!
THWAK

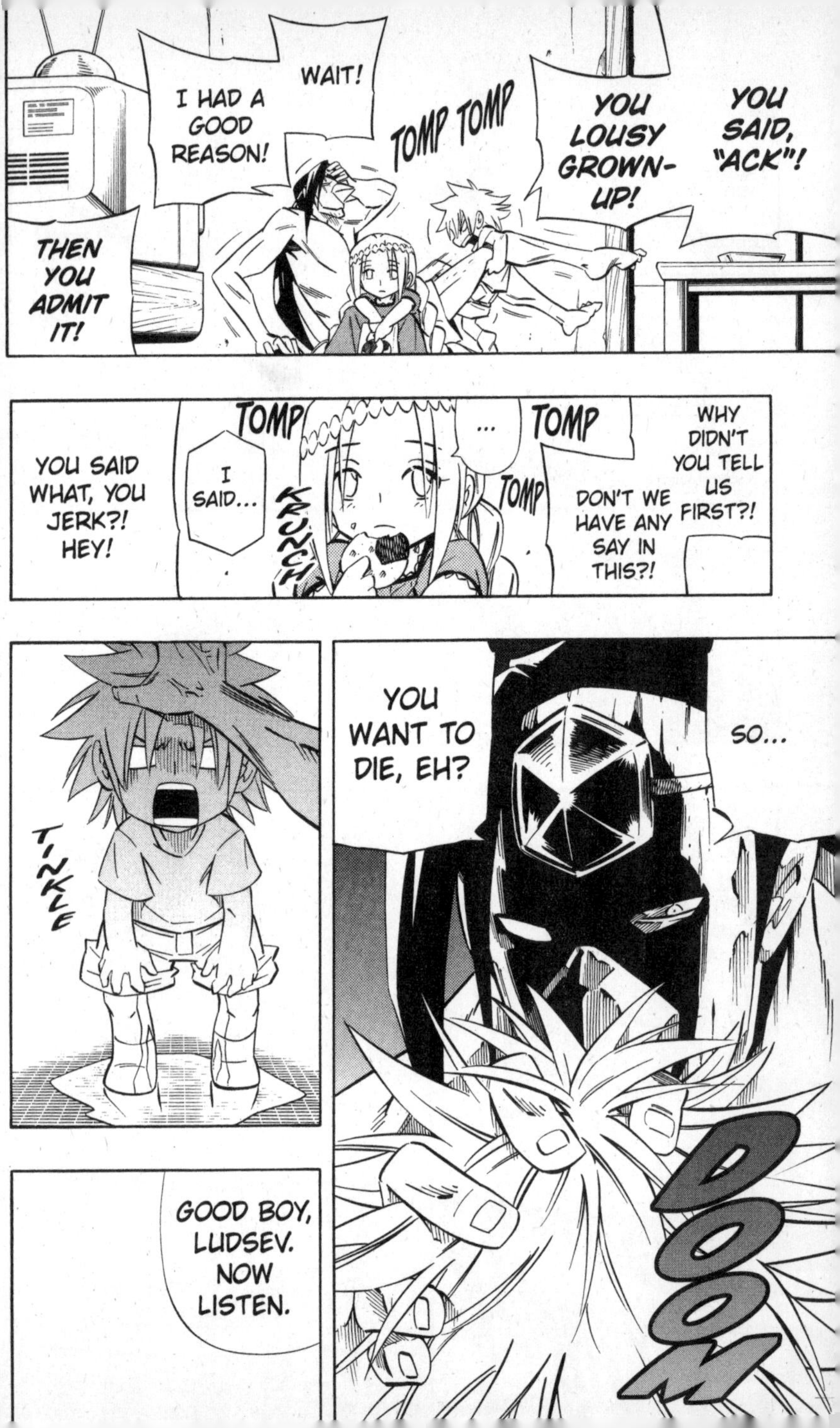
YOU SAID, "ACK"!
YOU LOUSY GROWN-UP!
TOMP TOMP
WAIT!
I HAD A GOOD REASON!
THEN YOU ADMIT IT!
WHY DIDN'T YOU TELL US FIRST?!
TOMP
DON'T WE HAVE ANY SAY IN THIS?!
TOMP
...
TOMP
KRUNCH
I SAID...
YOU SAID WHAT, YOU JERK?! HEY!
SO...
YOU WANT TO DIE, EH?
DOOOM
TINKLE
GOOD BOY, LUDSEV. NOW LISTEN.

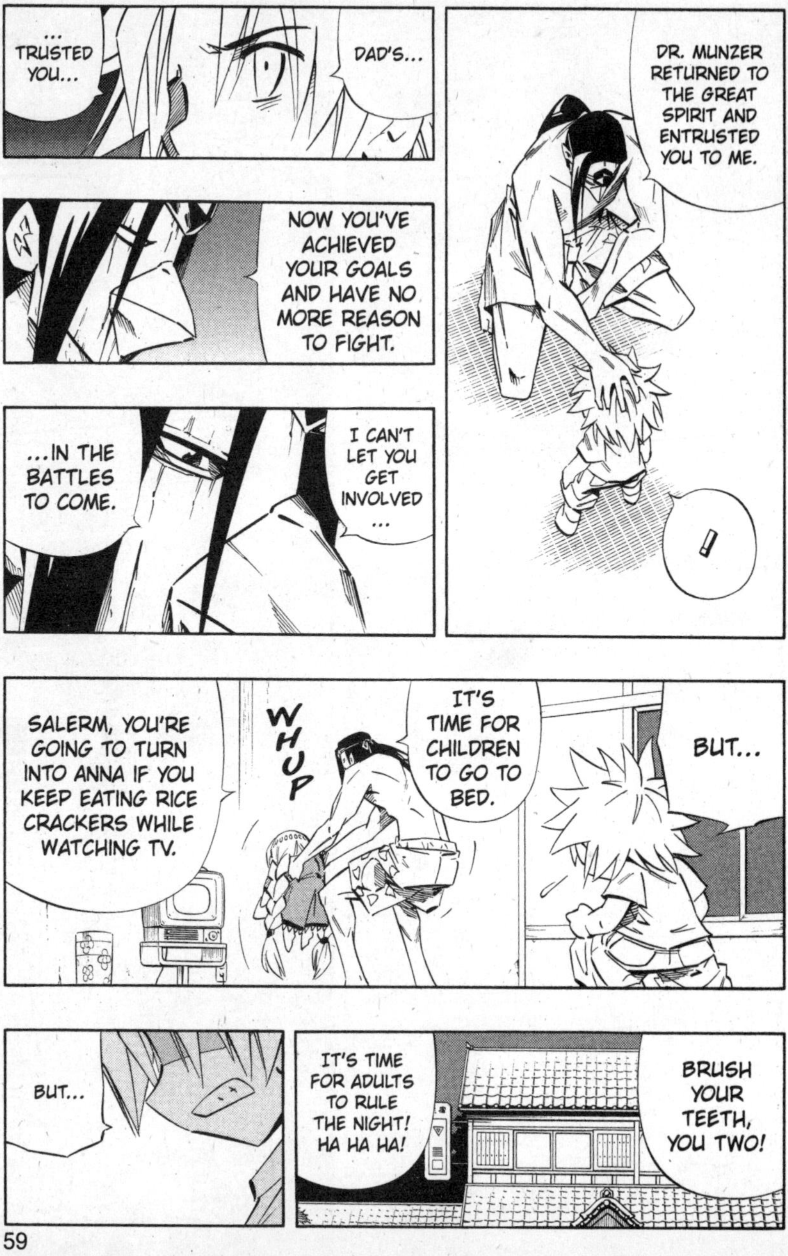
DR. MUNZER RETURNED TO THE GREAT SPIRIT AND ENTRUSTED YOU TO ME.
!
DAD'S...
... TRUSTED YOU...
NOW YOU'VE ACHIEVED YOUR GOALS AND HAVE NO MORE REASON TO FIGHT.
I CAN'T LET YOU GET INVOLVED ...
...IN THE BATTLES TO COME.
BUT...
IT'S TIME FOR CHILDREN TO GO TO BED.
WHUP
SALERM, YOU'RE GOING TO TURN INTO ANNA IF YOU KEEP EATING RICE CRACKERS WHILE WATCHING TV.
BRUSH YOUR TEETH, YOU TWO!
IT'S TIME FOR ADULTS TO RULE THE NIGHT! HA HA HA!
BUT...

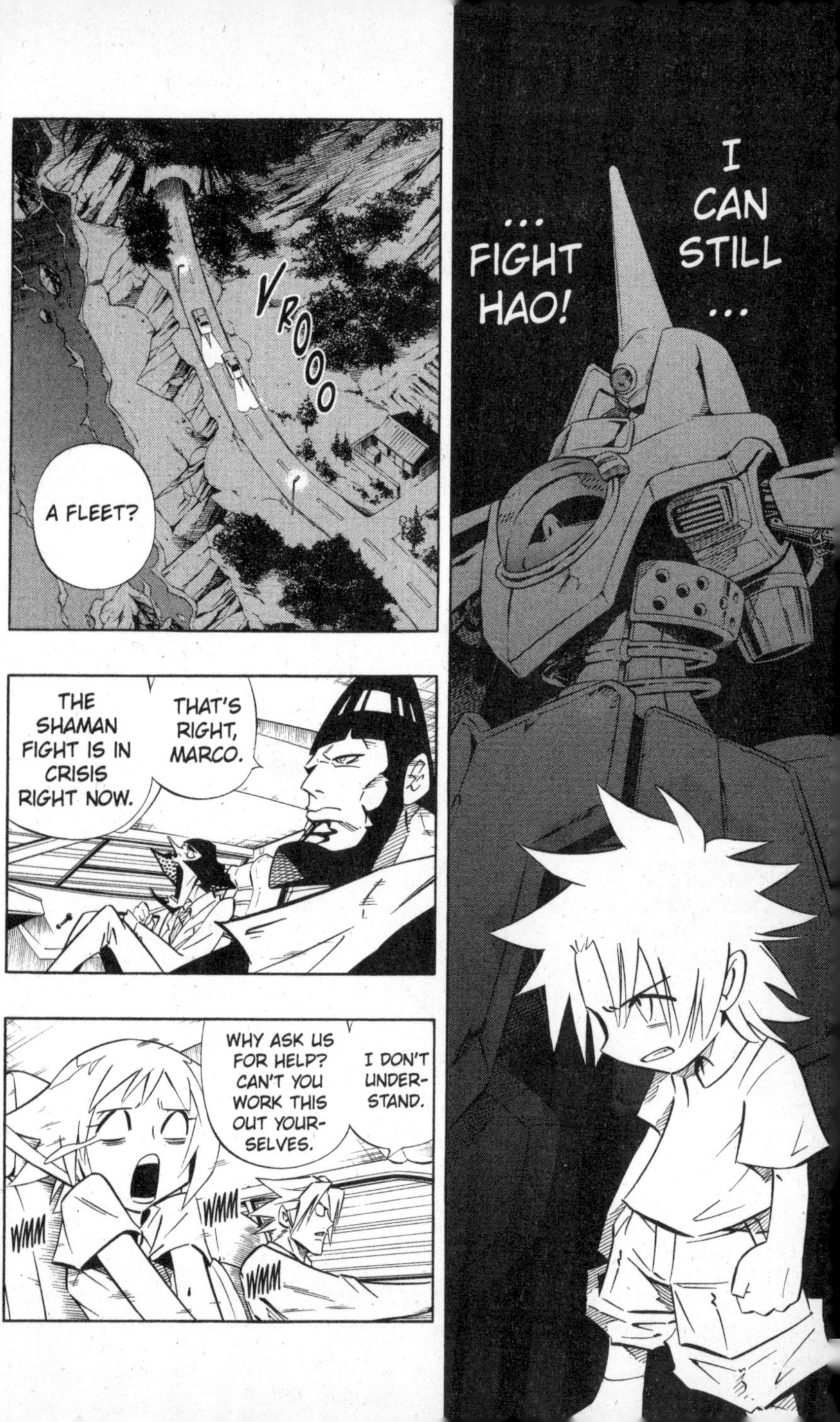
I CAN STILL ...
... FIGHT HAO!
VROOOO
A FLEET?
THAT'S RIGHT, MARCO.
THE SHAMAN FIGHT IS IN CRISIS RIGHT NOW.
I DON'T UNDER-STAND.
WHY ASK US FOR HELP? CAN'T YOU WORK THIS OUT YOUR-SELVES.
WMM
WMM
WMM
WMM

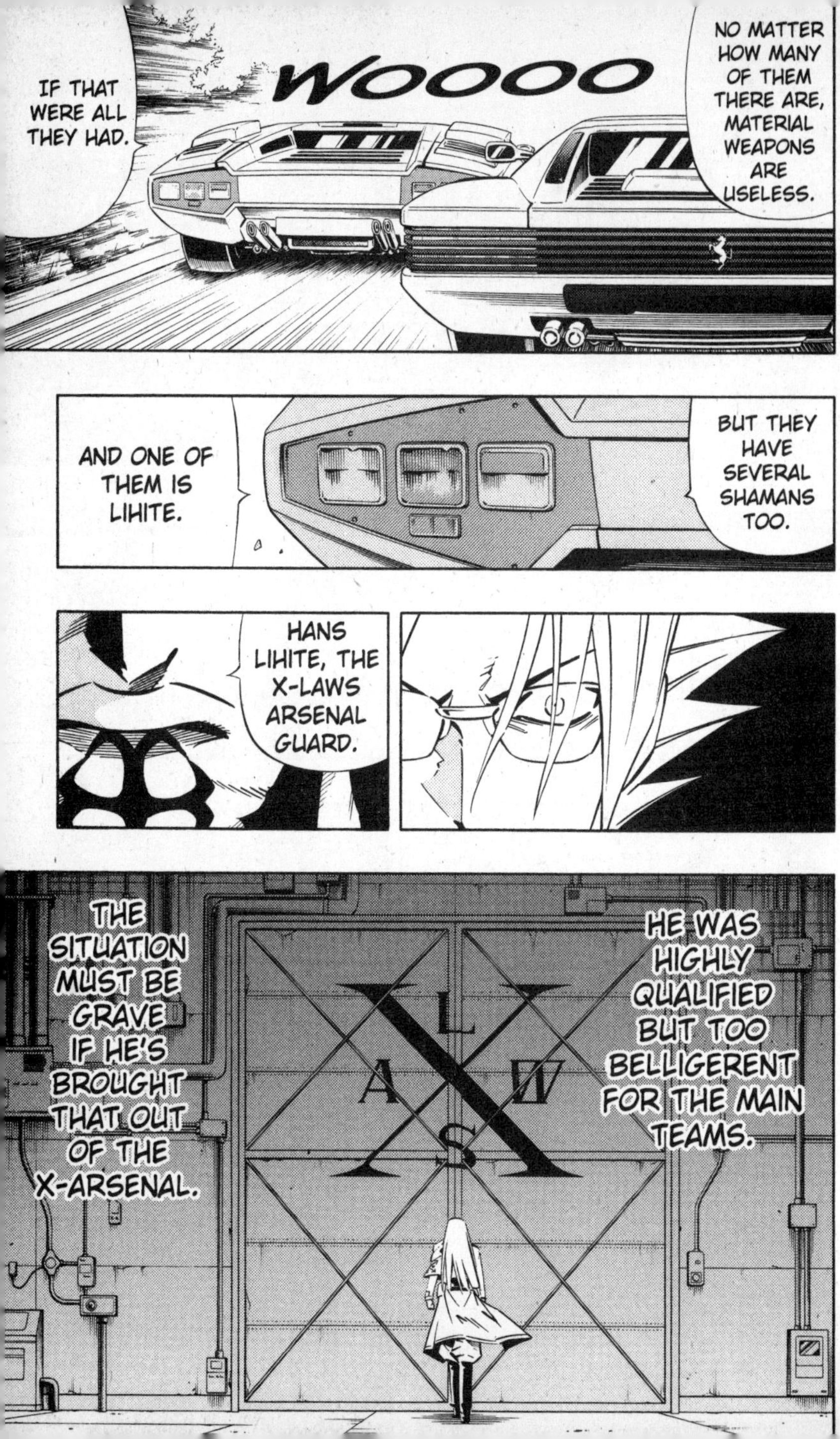
NO MATTER HOW MANY OF THEM THERE ARE, MATERIAL WEAPONS ARE USELESS.
WOOOO
IF THAT WERE ALL THEY HAD.
BUT THEY HAVE SEVERAL SHAMANS TOO.
AND ONE OF THEM IS LIHITE.
HANS LIHITE, THE X-LAWS ARSENAL GUARD.
HE WAS HIGHLY QUALIFIED BUT TOO BELLIGERENT FOR THE MAIN TEAMS.
THE SITUATION MUST BE GRAVE IF HE'S BROUGHT THAT OUT OF THE X-ARSENAL.

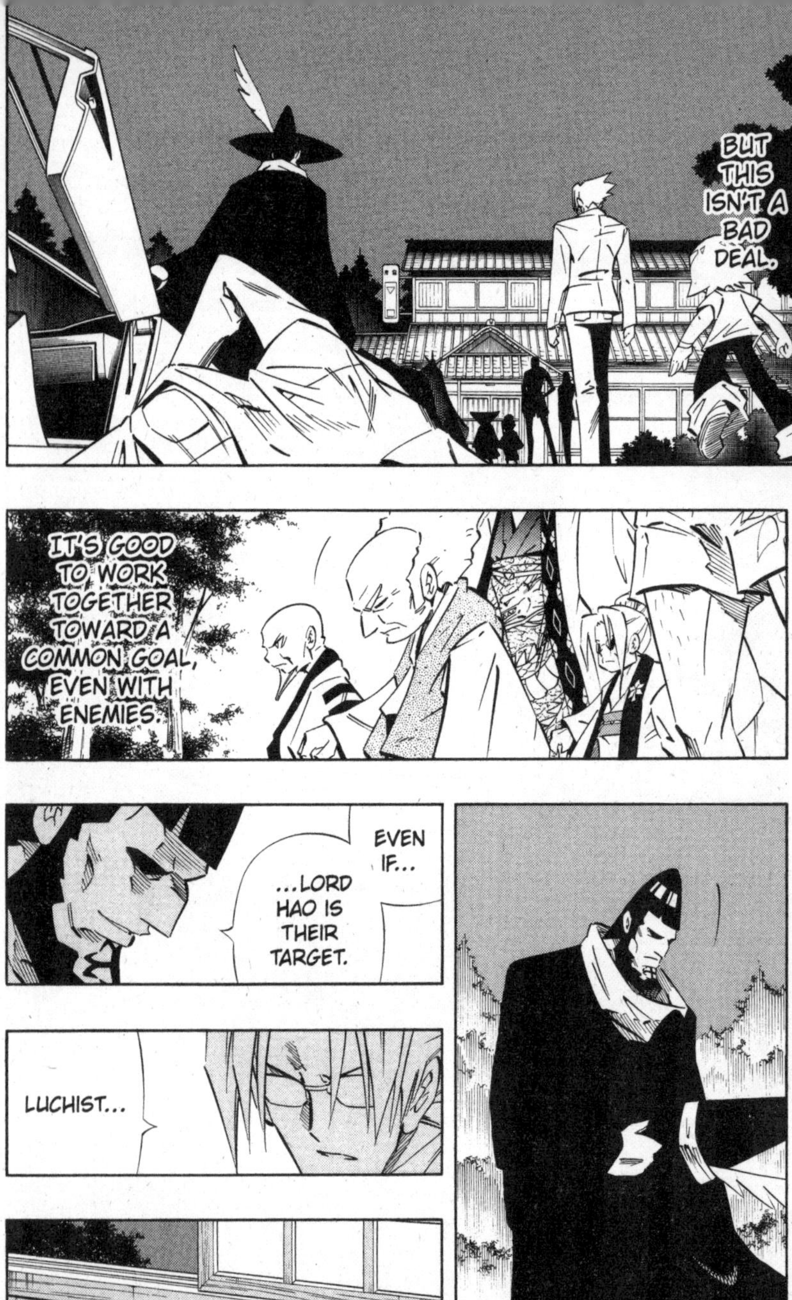
BUT THIS ISN'T A BAD DEAL.
IT'S GOOD TO WORK TOGETHER TOWARD A COMMON GOAL, EVEN WITH ENEMIES.
EVEN IF...
...LORD HAO IS THEIR TARGET.
LUCHIST...

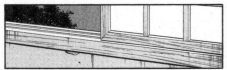

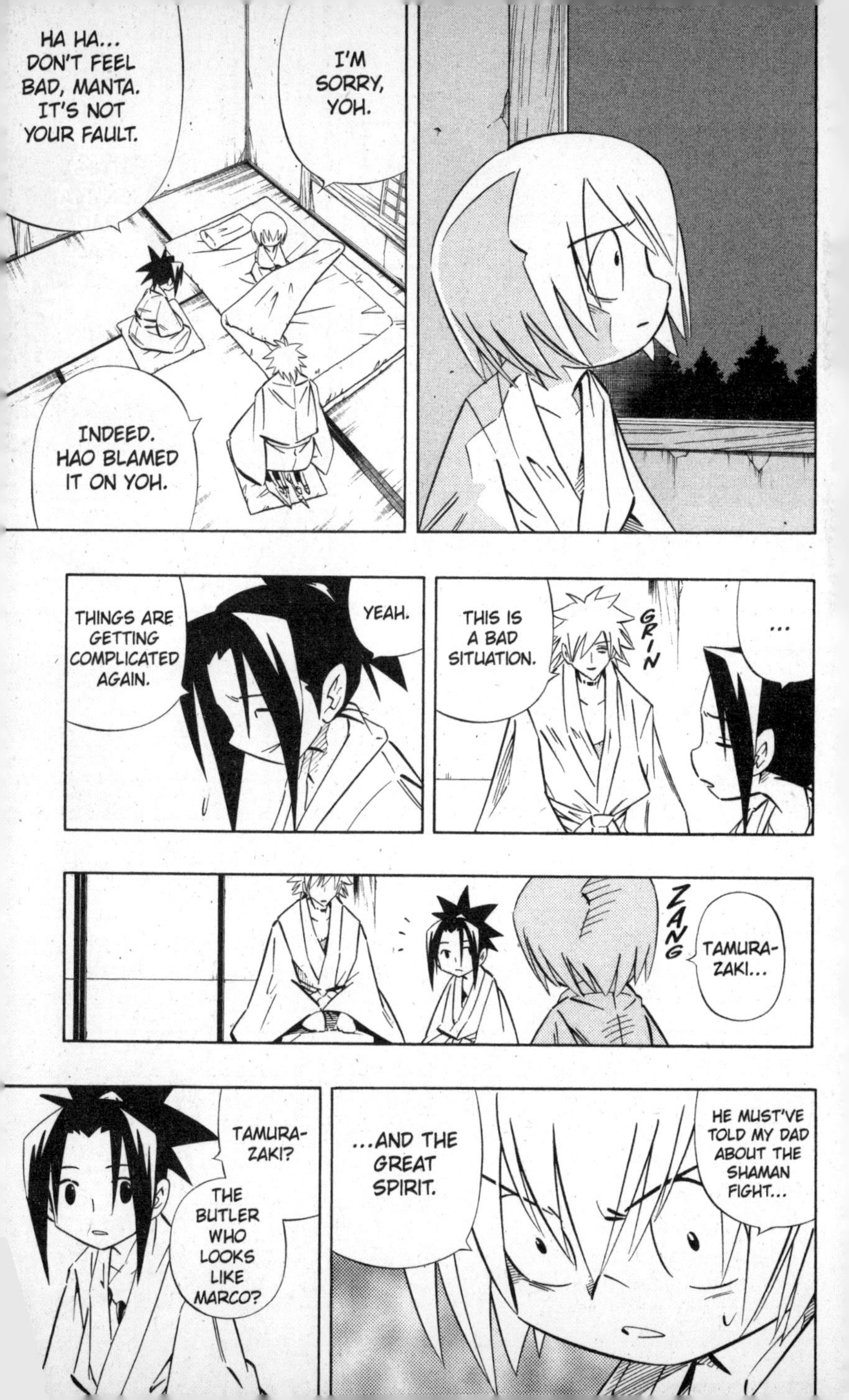
I'M SORRY, YOH.
HA HA... DON'T FEEL BAD, MANTA. IT'S NOT YOUR FAULT.
INDEED. HAO BLAMED IT ON YOH.
...
GRIN
THIS IS A BAD SITUATION.
YEAH.
THINGS ARE GETTING COMPLICATED AGAIN.
ZANG
TAMURA-ZAKI...
HE MUST'VE TOLD MY DAD ABOUT THE SHAMAN FIGHT...
...AND THE GREAT SPIRIT.
TAMURA-ZAKI?
THE BUTLER WHO LOOKS LIKE MARCO?

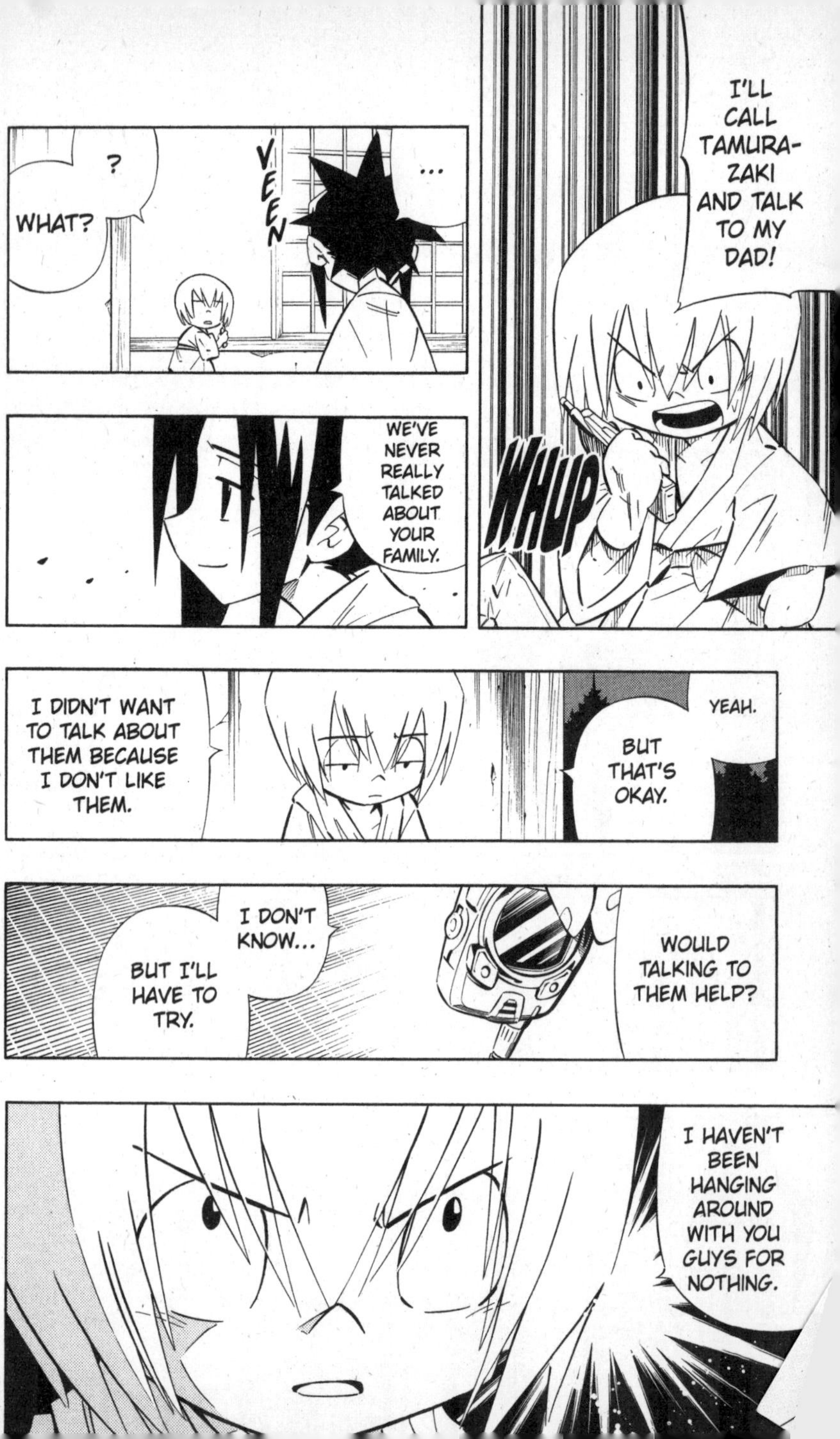
I'LL CALL TAMURA-ZAKI AND TALK TO MY DAD!
WHUP
...
VEEN
?
WHAT?
WE'VE NEVER REALLY TALKED ABOUT YOUR FAMILY.
YEAH.
BUT THAT'S OKAY.
I DIDN'T WANT TO TALK ABOUT THEM BECAUSE I DON'T LIKE THEM.
WOULD TALKING TO THEM HELP?
I DON'T KNOW...
BUT I'LL HAVE TO TRY.
I HAVEN'T BEEN HANGING AROUND WITH YOU GUYS FOR NOTHING.

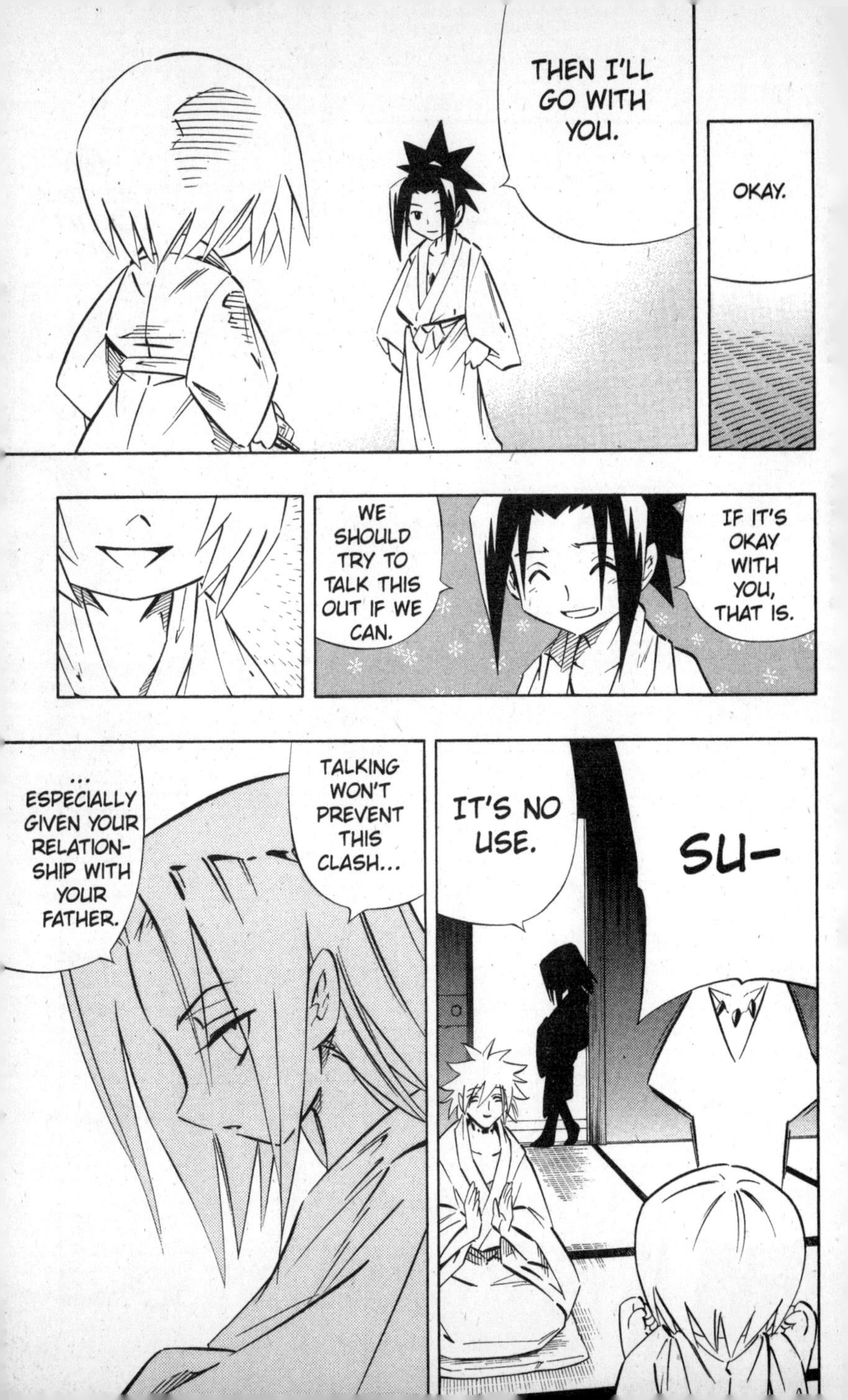
OKAY.
THEN I'LL GO WITH YOU.
IF IT'S OKAY WITH YOU, THAT IS.
WE SHOULD TRY TO TALK THIS OUT IF WE CAN.
SU-
IT'S NO USE.
TALKING WON'T PREVENT THIS CLASH...
...ESPECIALLY GIVEN YOUR RELATION-SHIP WITH YOUR FATHER.

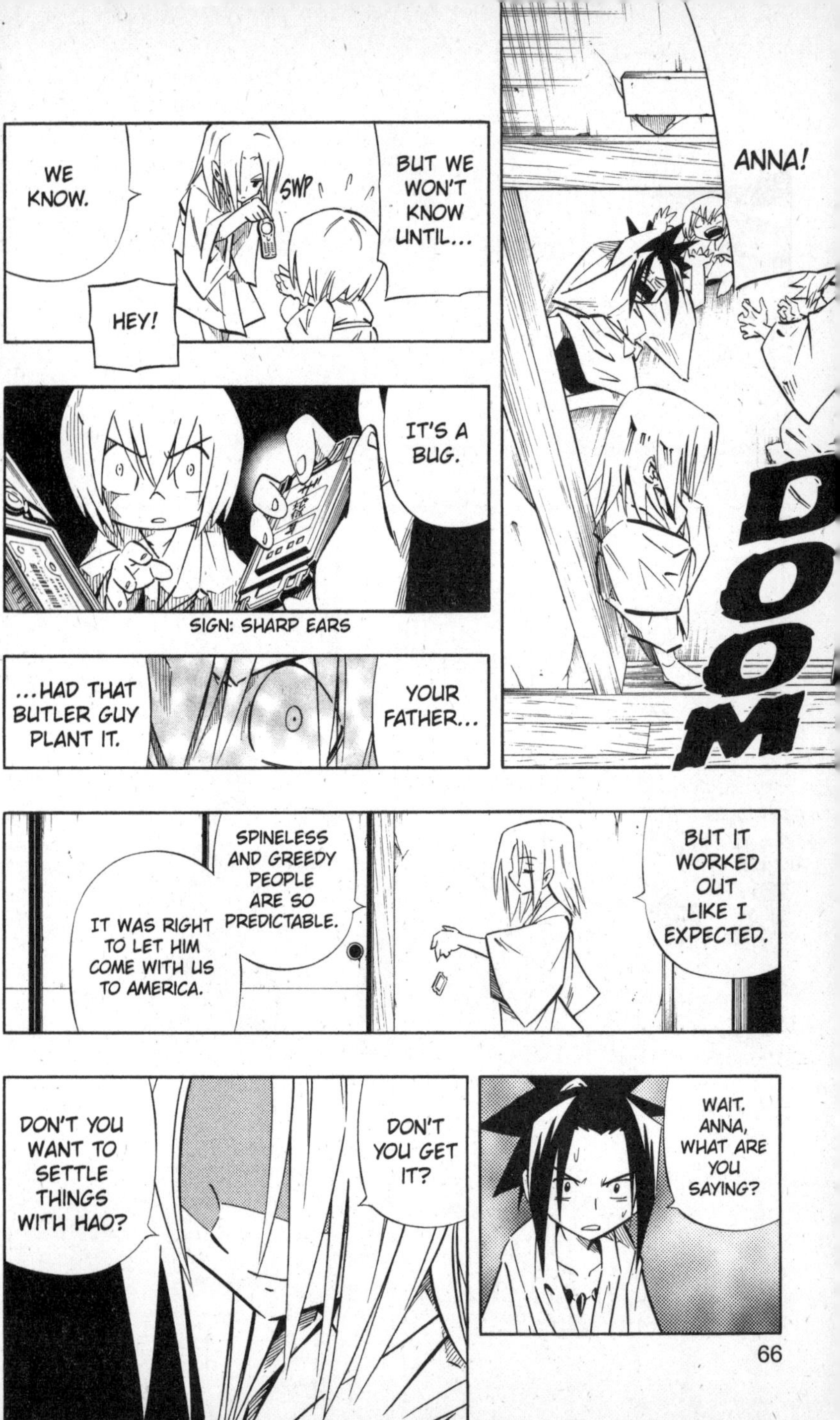
ANNA!
DOOM
BUT WE WON'T KNOW UNTIL...
SWP
WE KNOW.
HEY!
IT'S A BUG.
SIGN: SHARP EARS
YOUR FATHER...
...HAD THAT BUTLER GUY PLANT IT.
BUT IT WORKED OUT LIKE I EXPECTED.
SPINELESS AND GREEDY PEOPLE ARE SO PREDICTABLE.
IT WAS RIGHT TO LET HIM COME WITH US TO AMERICA.
WAIT. ANNA, WHAT ARE YOU SAYING?
DON'T YOU GET IT?
DON'T YOU WANT TO SETTLE THINGS WITH HAO?

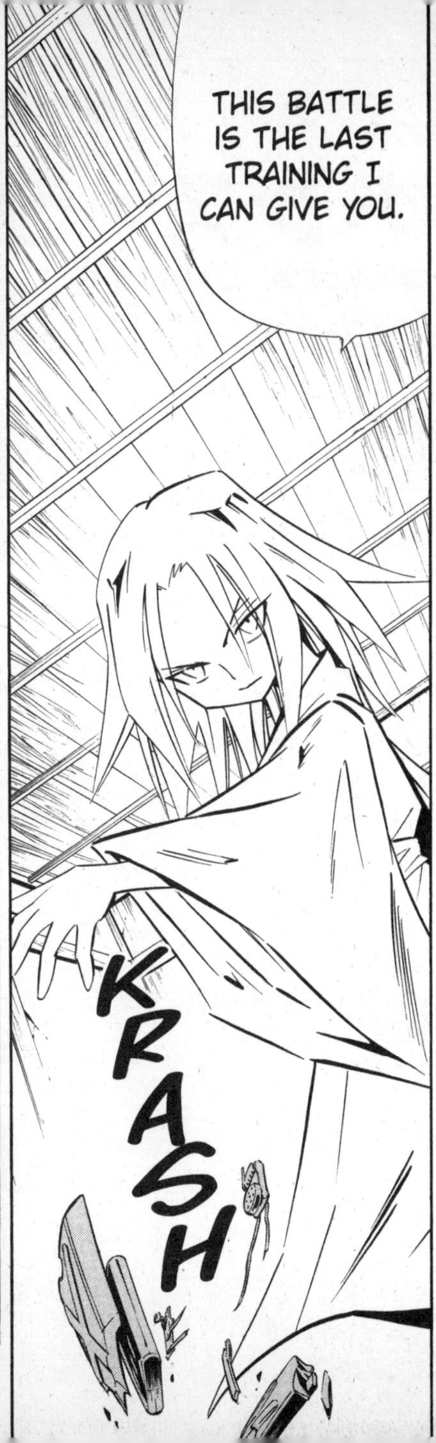
THIS BATTLE IS THE LAST TRAINING I CAN GIVE YOU.
KRASH

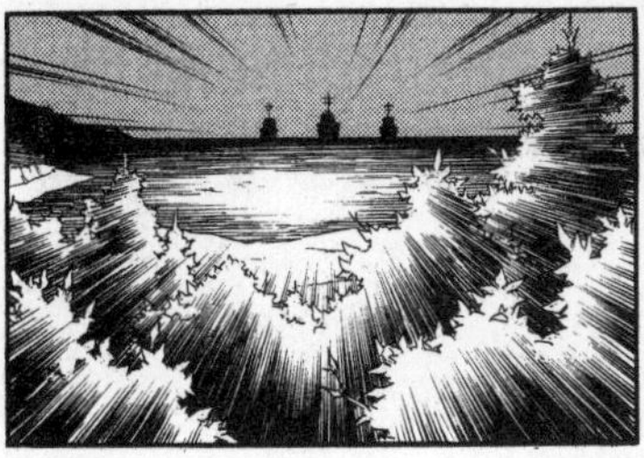

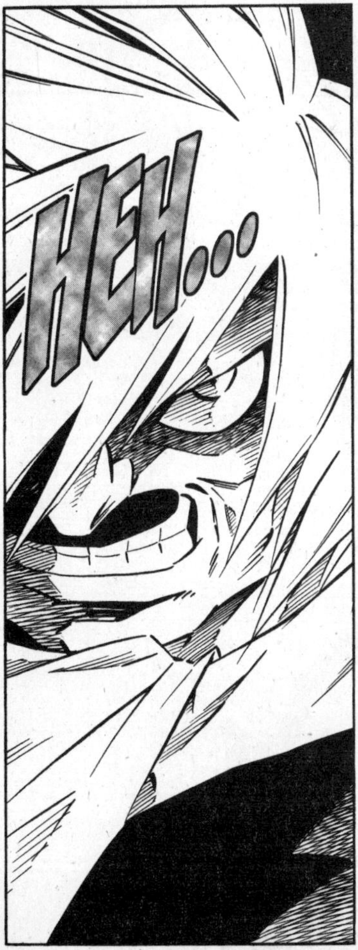
HEH...

SHAMAN KING CHARACTER FILE No.153

ハンス・ライハイト

HANS LIHITE

2001
(JAN)

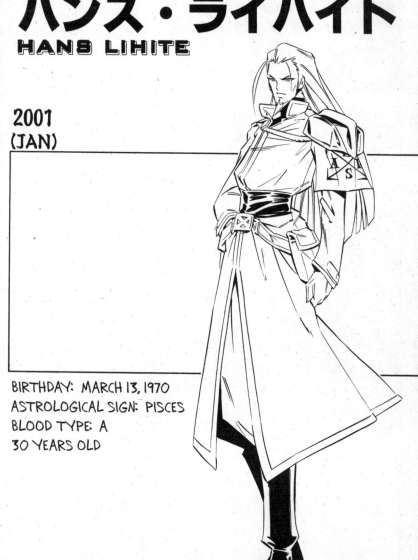

BIRTHDAY: MARCH 13, 1970
ASTROLOGICAL SIGN: PISCES
BLOOD TYPE: A
30 YEARS OLD

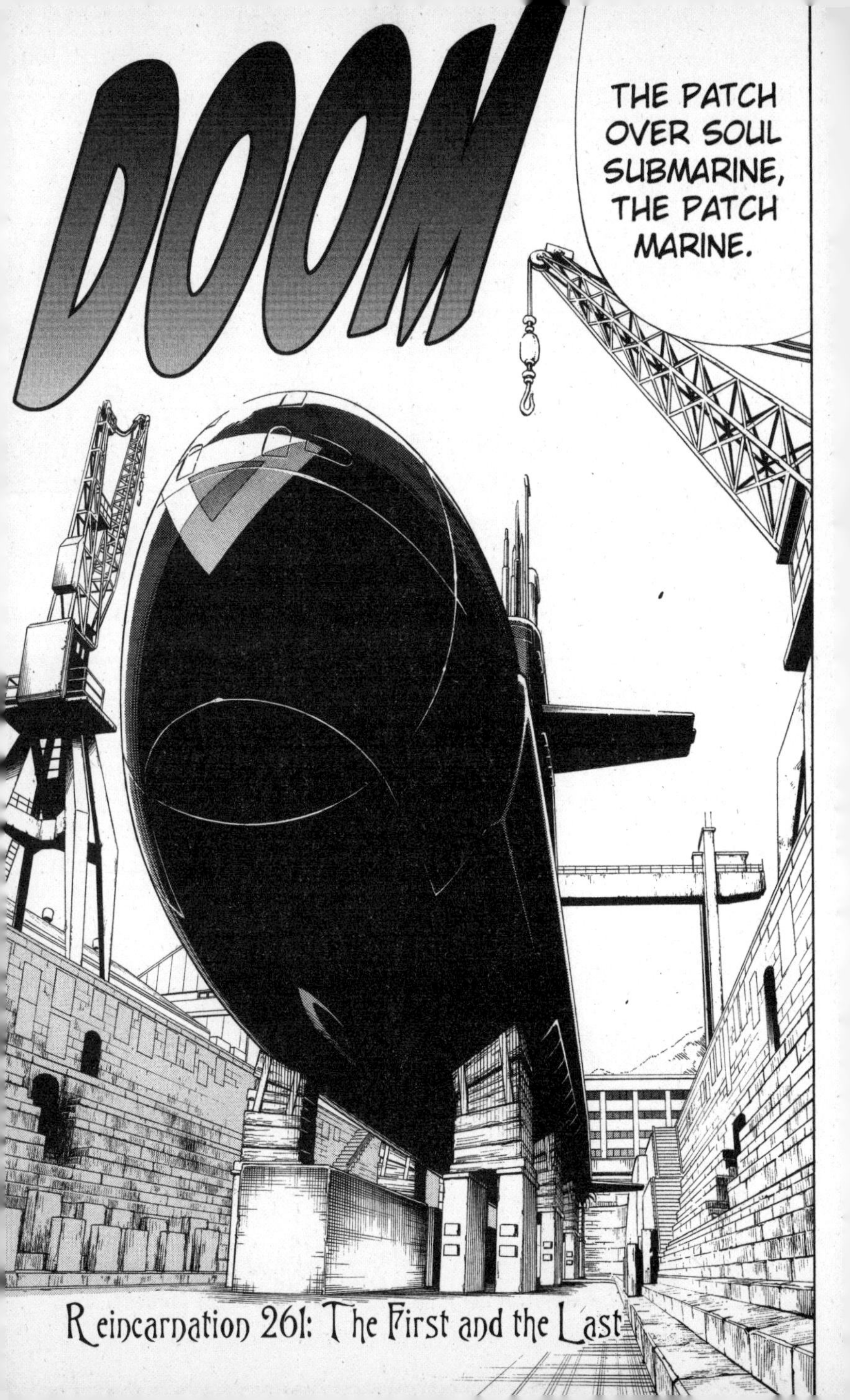
DOOM
THE PATCH OVER SOUL SUBMARINE, THE PATCH MARINE.
Reincarnation 261: The First and the Last

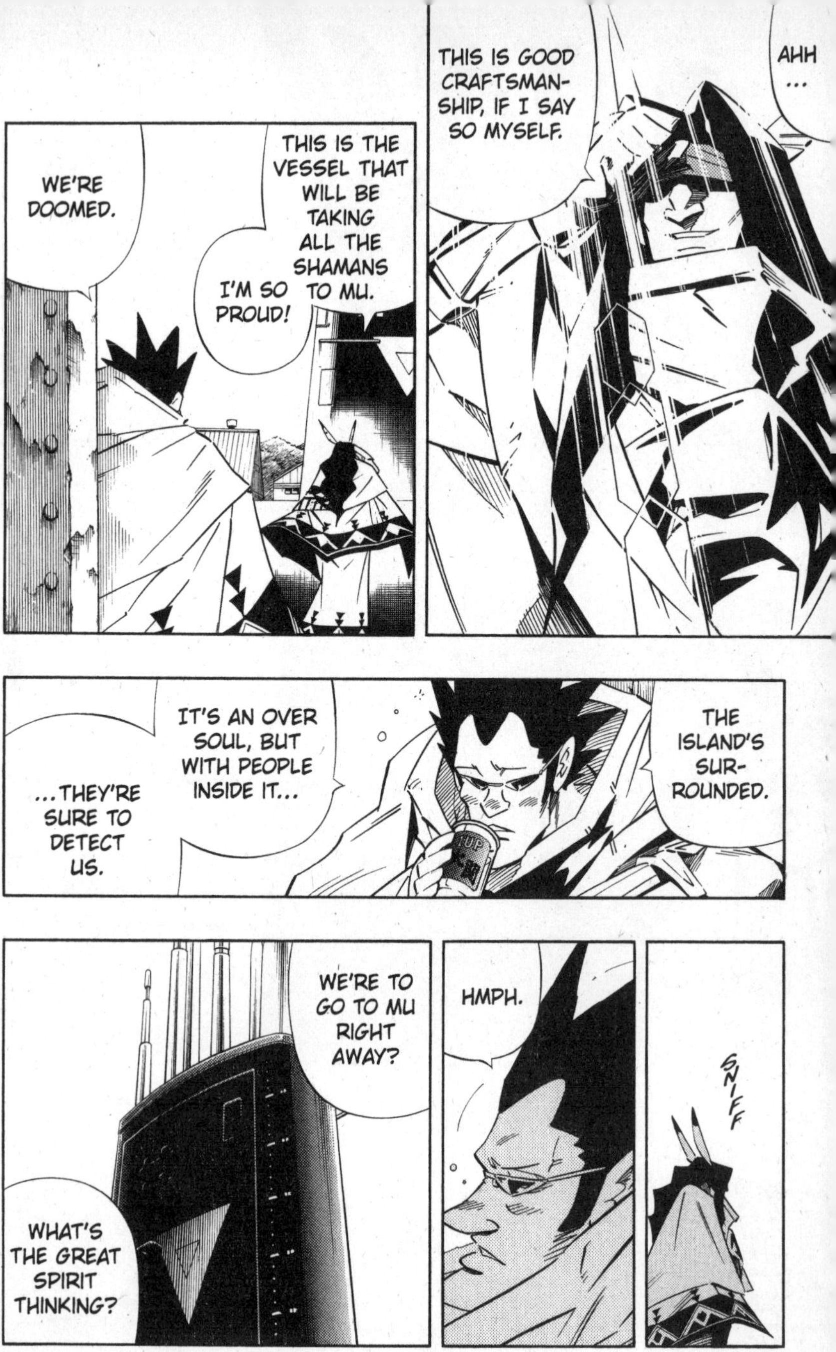
AHH ...
THIS IS GOOD CRAFTSMANSHIP, IF I SAY SO MYSELF.
THIS IS THE VESSEL THAT WILL BE TAKING ALL THE SHAMANS TO MU.
I'M SO PROUD!
WE'RE DOOMED.
THE ISLAND'S SURROUNDED.
IT'S AN OVER SOUL, BUT WITH PEOPLE INSIDE IT...
...THEY'RE SURE TO DETECT US.
SNIFF
HMPH.
WE'RE TO GO TO MU RIGHT AWAY?
WHAT'S THE GREAT SPIRIT THINKING?

Reincarnation 261: The First and the Last

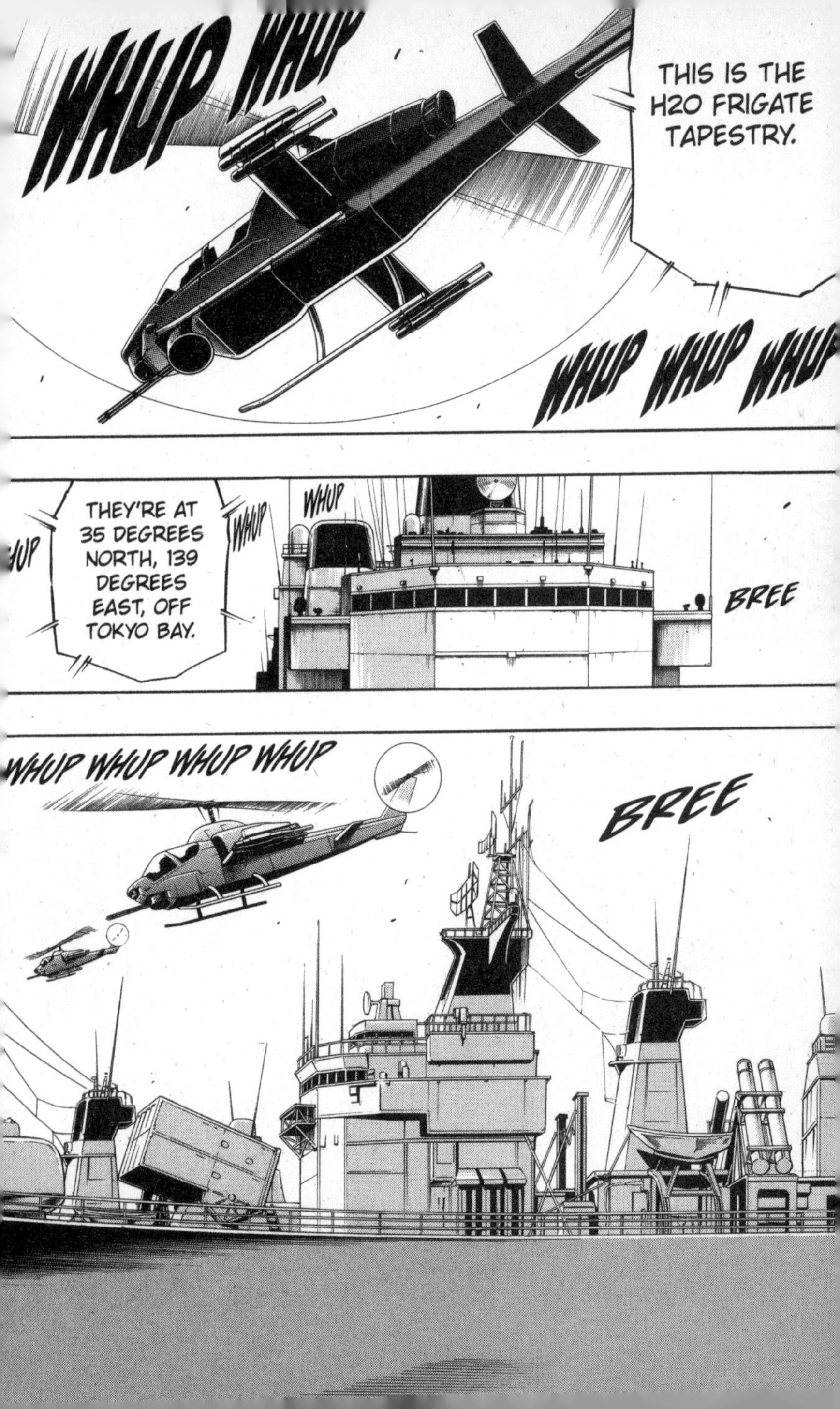
THIS IS THE H2O FRIGATE TAPESTRY.
WHUP WHUP
WHUP WHUP WHUP
BREE
WHUP
WHUP
THEY'RE AT 35 DEGREES NORTH, 139 DEGREES EAST, OFF TOKYO BAY.
BREE
WHUP WHUP WHUP WHUP

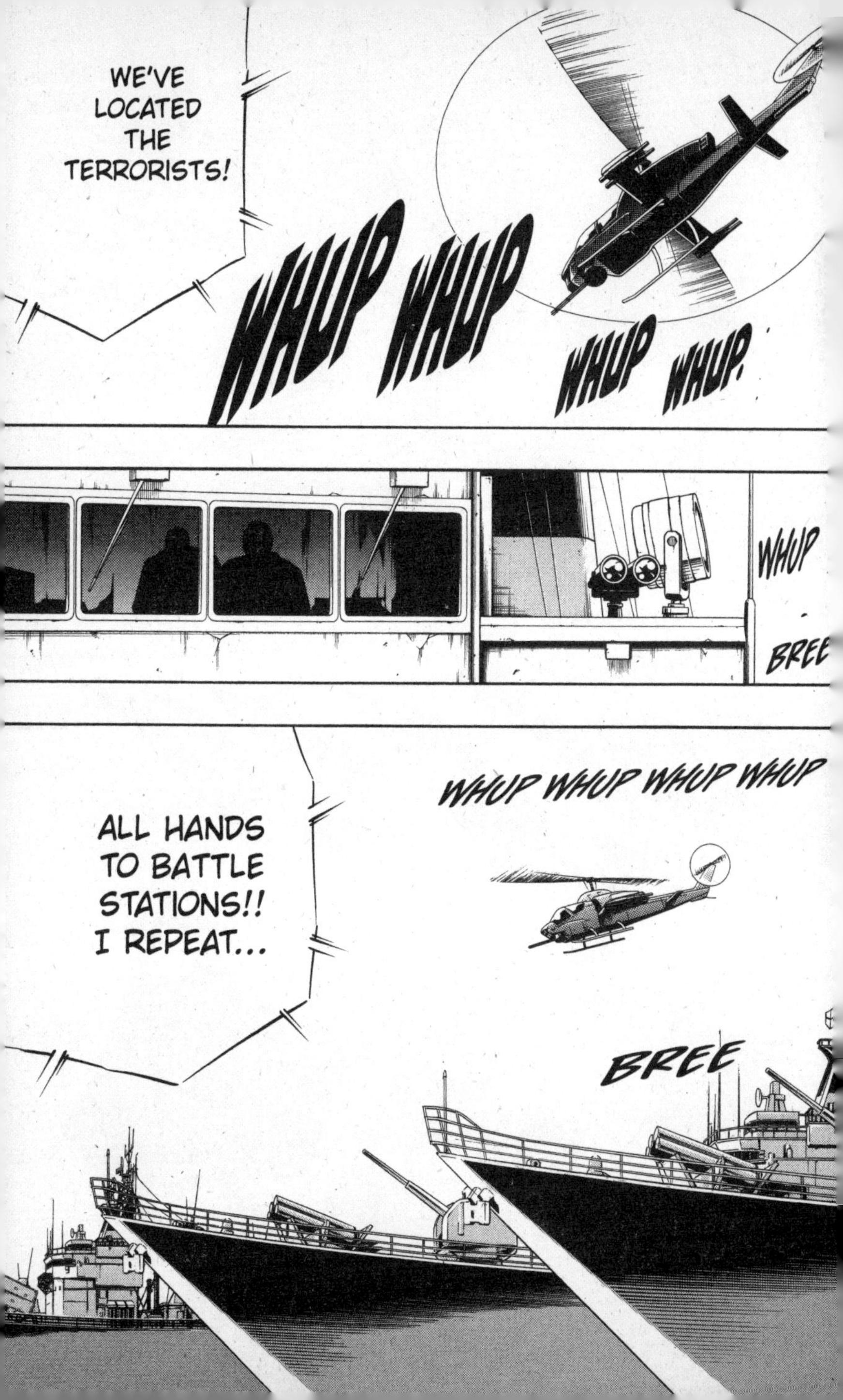
WE'VE LOCATED THE TERRORISTS!
WHUP WHUP
WHUP WHUP.
WHUP
BREE
WHUP WHUP WHUP WHUP
ALL HANDS TO BATTLE STATIONS!! I REPEAT...
BREE

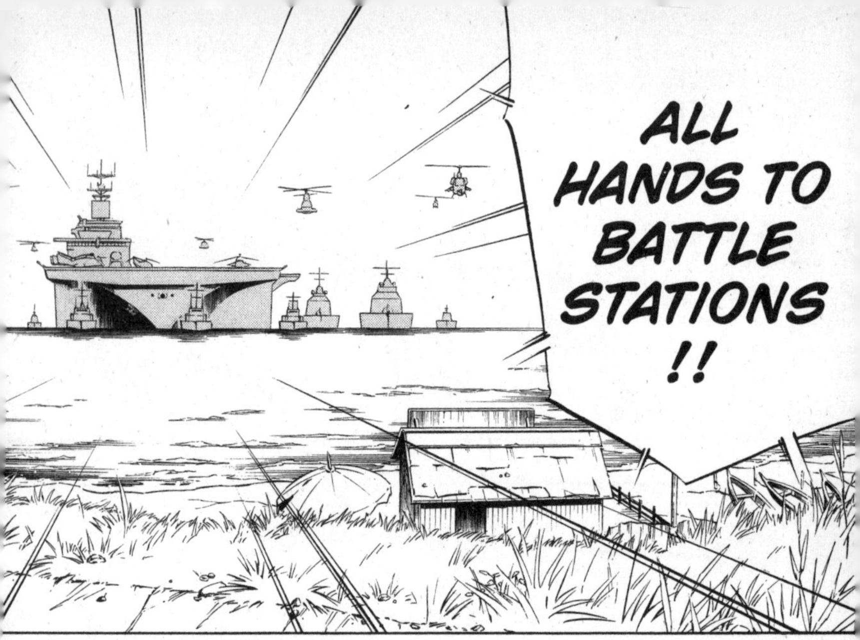
ALL HANDS TO BATTLE STATIONS !!
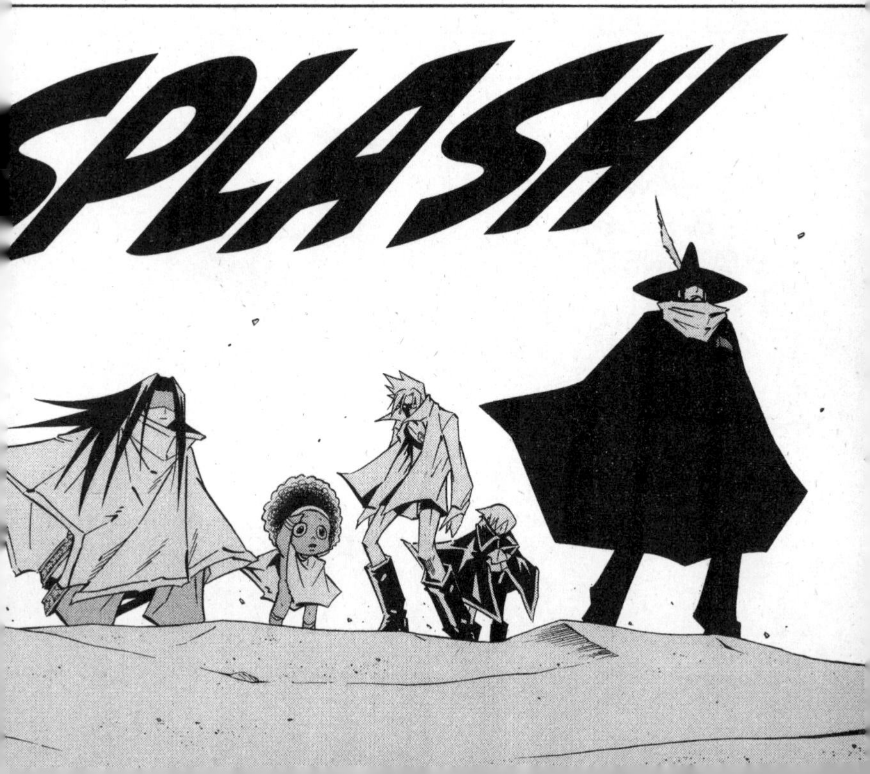
SPLASH

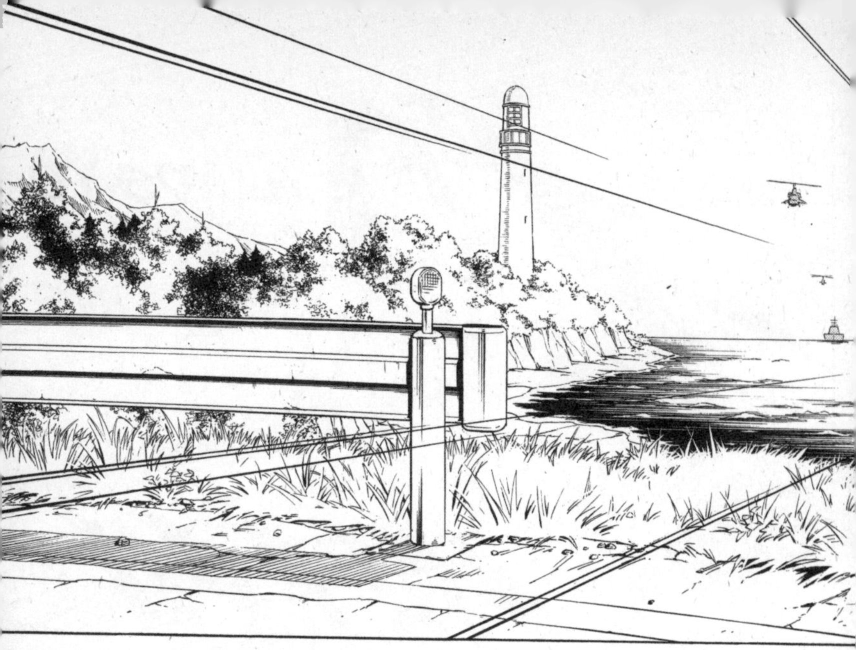
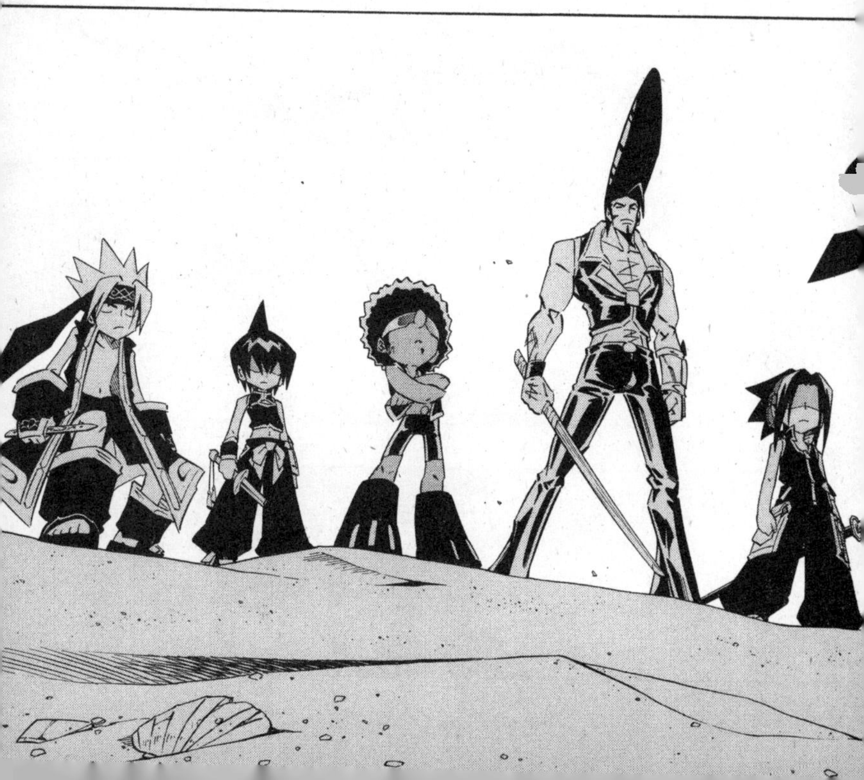

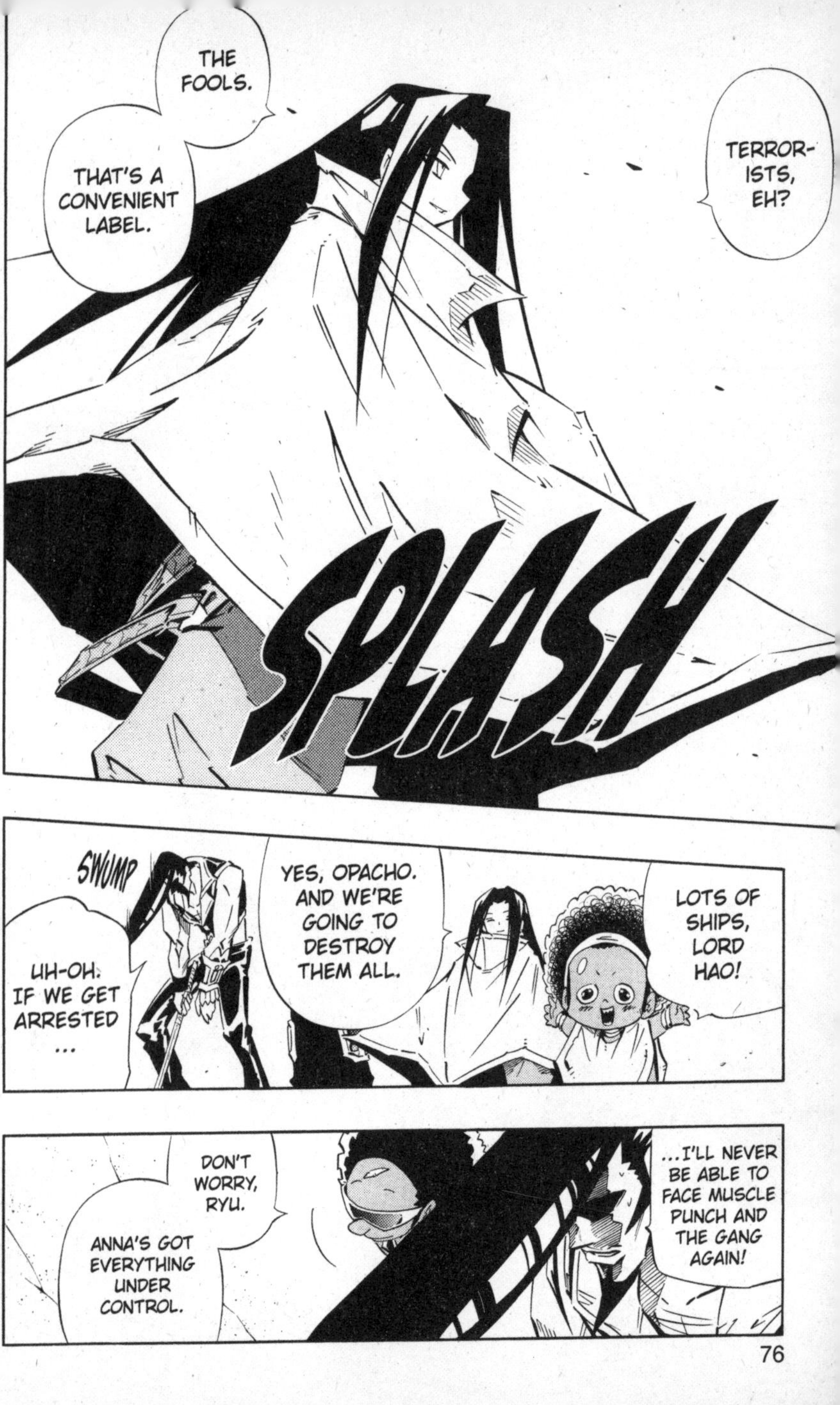
TERRORISTS, EH?
THE FOOLS.
THAT'S A CONVENIENT LABEL.
SPLASH
LOTS OF SHIPS, LORD HAO!
YES, OPACHO. AND WE'RE GOING TO DESTROY THEM ALL.
SWUMP
UH-OH. IF WE GET ARRESTED ...
...I'LL NEVER BE ABLE TO FACE MUSCLE PUNCH AND THE GANG AGAIN!
DON'T WORRY, RYU.
ANNA'S GOT EVERYTHING UNDER CONTROL.

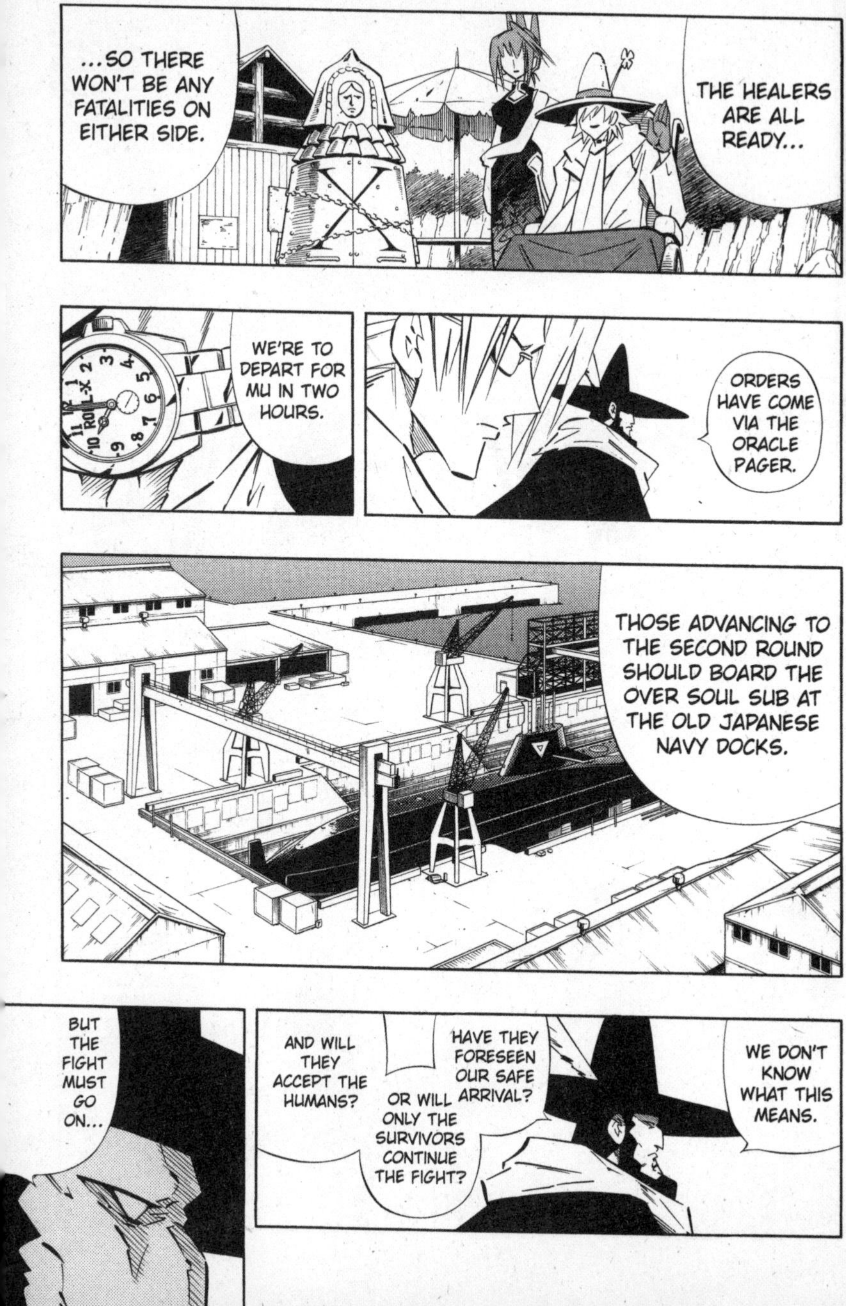
THE HEALERS ARE ALL READY...
...SO THERE WON'T BE ANY FATALITIES ON EITHER SIDE.
ORDERS HAVE COME VIA THE ORACLE PAGER.
WE'RE TO DEPART FOR MU IN TWO HOURS.
THOSE ADVANCING TO THE SECOND ROUND SHOULD BOARD THE OVER SOUL SUB AT THE OLD JAPANESE NAVY DOCKS.
WE DON'T KNOW WHAT THIS MEANS.
HAVE THEY FORESEEN OUR SAFE ARRIVAL?
AND WILL THEY ACCEPT THE HUMANS?
OR WILL ONLY THE SURVIVORS CONTINUE THE FIGHT?
BUT THE FIGHT MUST GO ON...

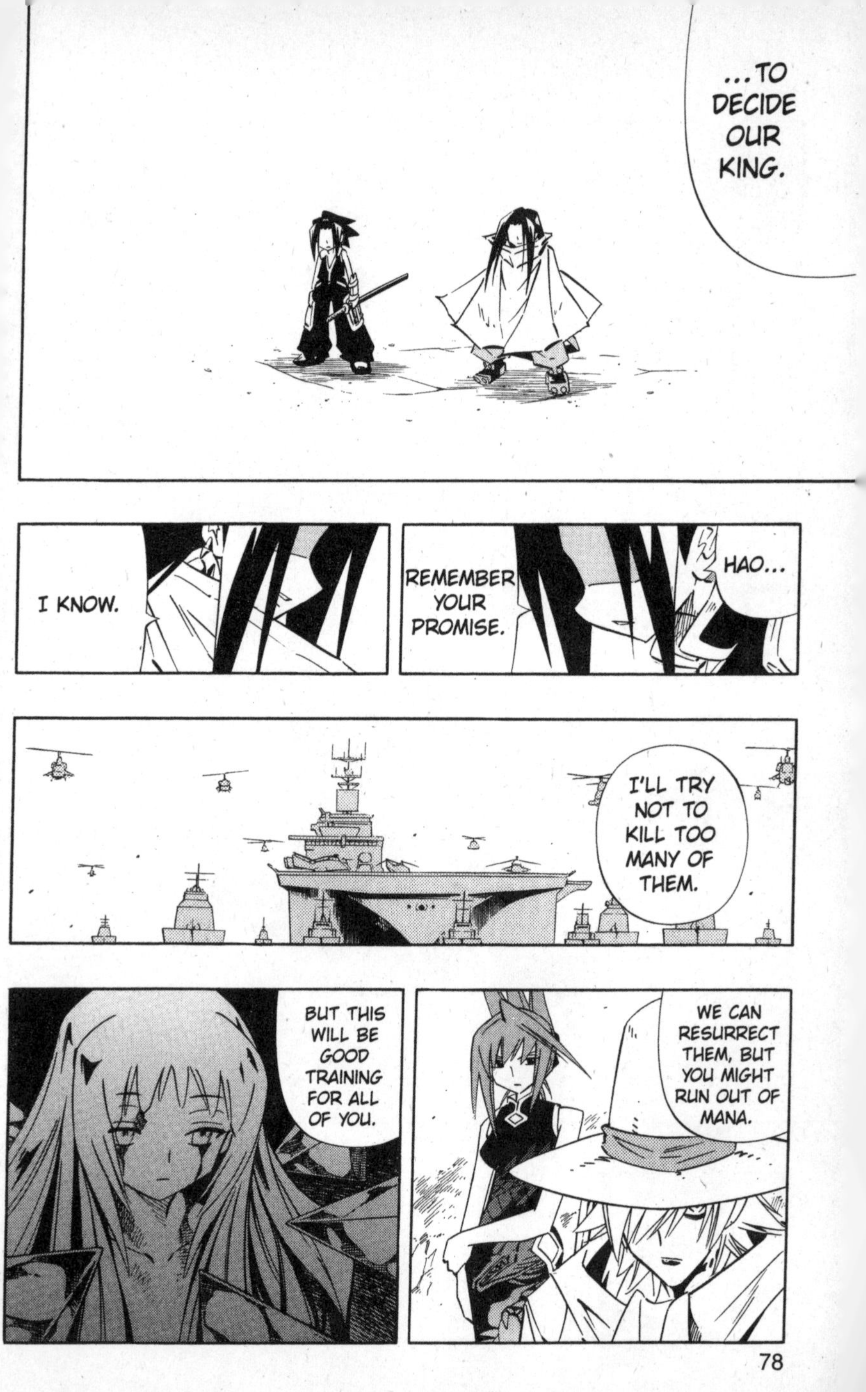
...TO DECIDE OUR KING.
HAO...
REMEMBER YOUR PROMISE.
I KNOW.
I'LL TRY NOT TO KILL TOO MANY OF THEM.
WE CAN RESURRECT THEM, BUT YOU MIGHT RUN OUT OF MANA.
BUT THIS WILL BE GOOD TRAINING FOR ALL OF YOU.

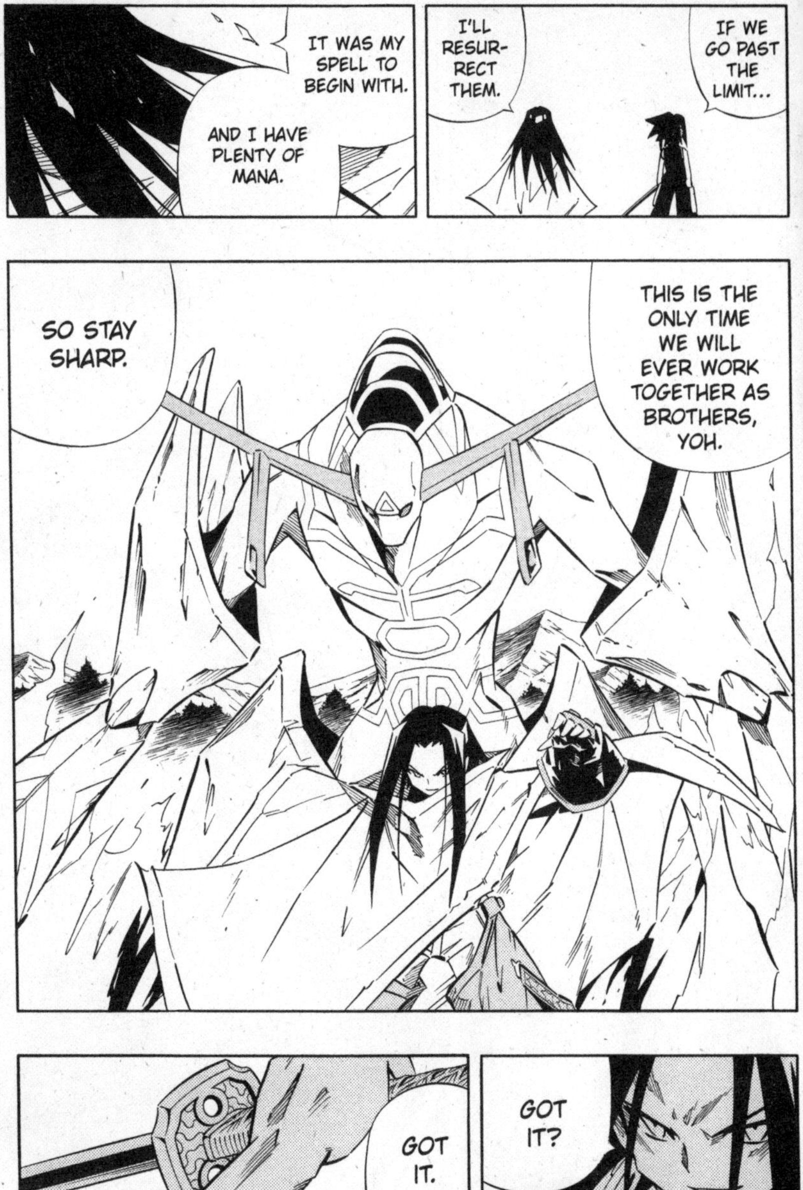
IF WE GO PAST THE LIMIT...
I'LL RESURRECT THEM.
IT WAS MY SPELL TO BEGIN WITH.
AND I HAVE PLENTY OF MANA.
THIS IS THE ONLY TIME WE WILL EVER WORK TOGETHER AS BROTHERS, YOH.
SO STAY SHARP.
GOT IT?
GOT IT.

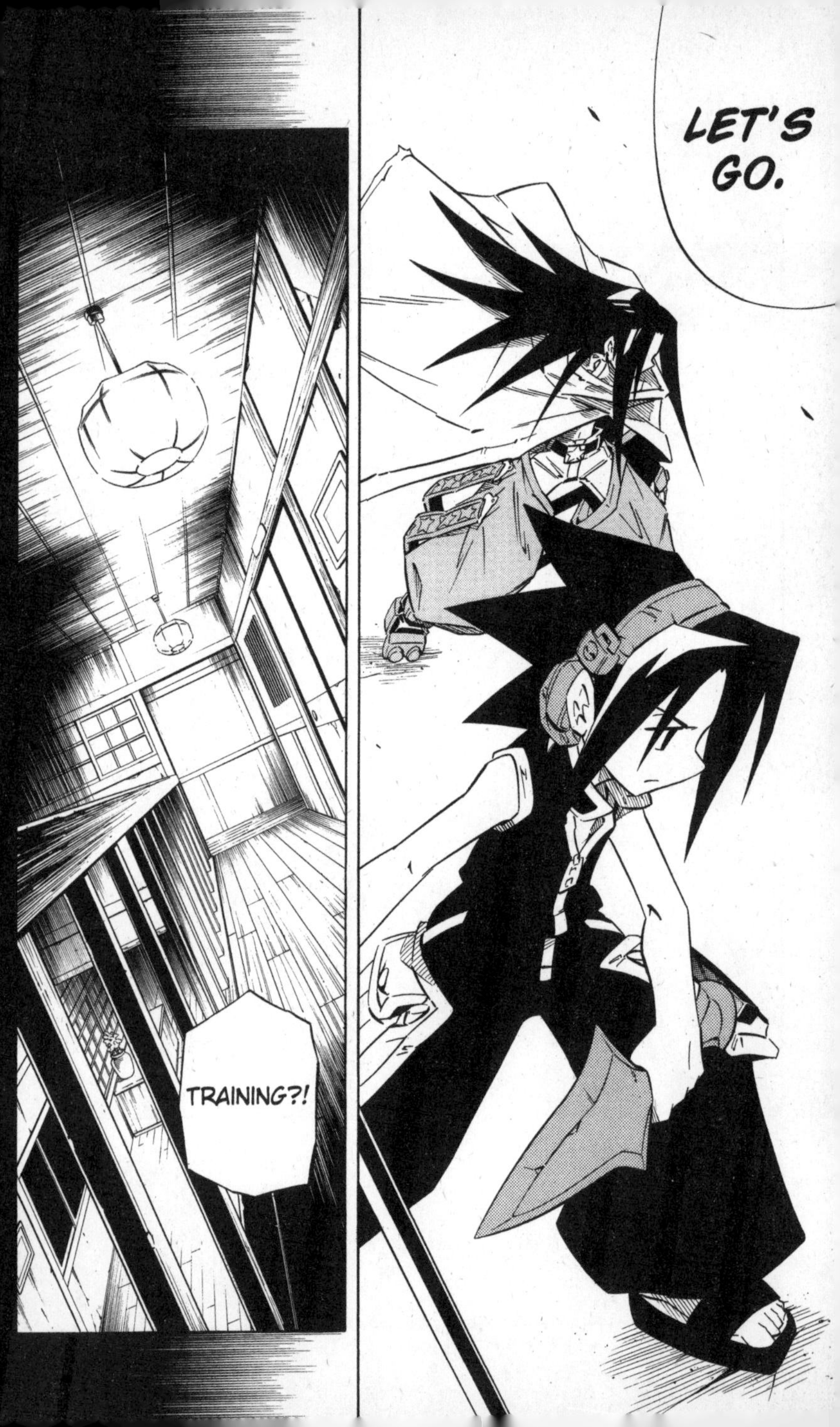
LET'S GO.
TRAINING?!

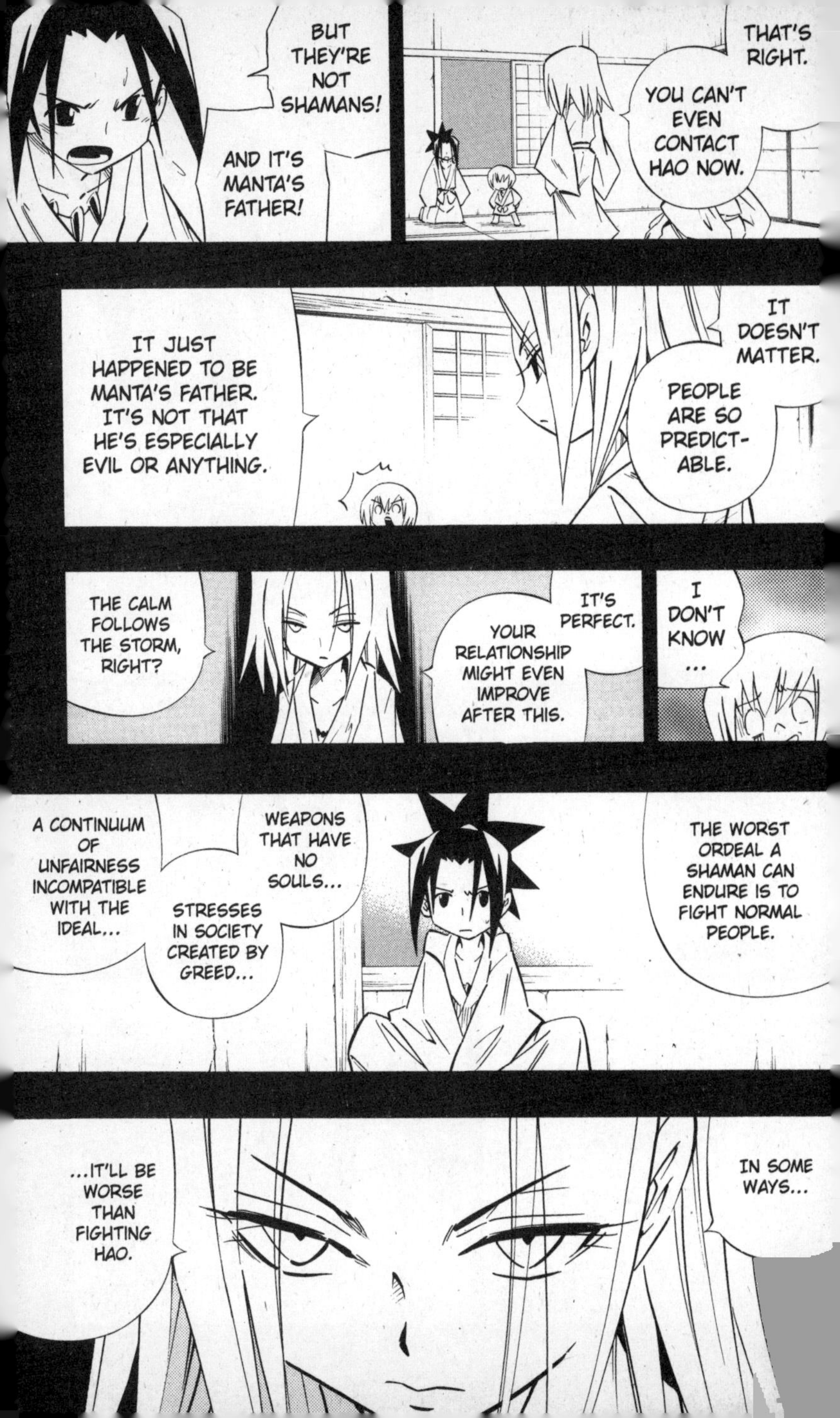
THAT'S RIGHT.
YOU CAN'T EVEN CONTACT HAO NOW.
BUT THEY'RE NOT SHAMANS!
AND IT'S MANTA'S FATHER!
IT DOESN'T MATTER.
PEOPLE ARE SO PREDICT-ABLE.
IT JUST HAPPENED TO BE MANTA'S FATHER. IT'S NOT THAT HE'S ESPECIALLY EVIL OR ANYTHING.
I DON'T KNOW...
IT'S PERFECT.
YOUR RELATIONSHIP MIGHT EVEN IMPROVE AFTER THIS.
THE CALM FOLLOWS THE STORM, RIGHT?
THE WORST ORDEAL A SHAMAN CAN ENDURE IS TO FIGHT NORMAL PEOPLE.
WEAPONS THAT HAVE NO SOULS...
A CONTINUUM OF UNFAIRNESS INCOMPATIBLE WITH THE IDEAL...
STRESSES IN SOCIETY CREATED BY GREED...
IN SOME WAYS...
...IT'LL BE WORSE THAN FIGHTING HAO.

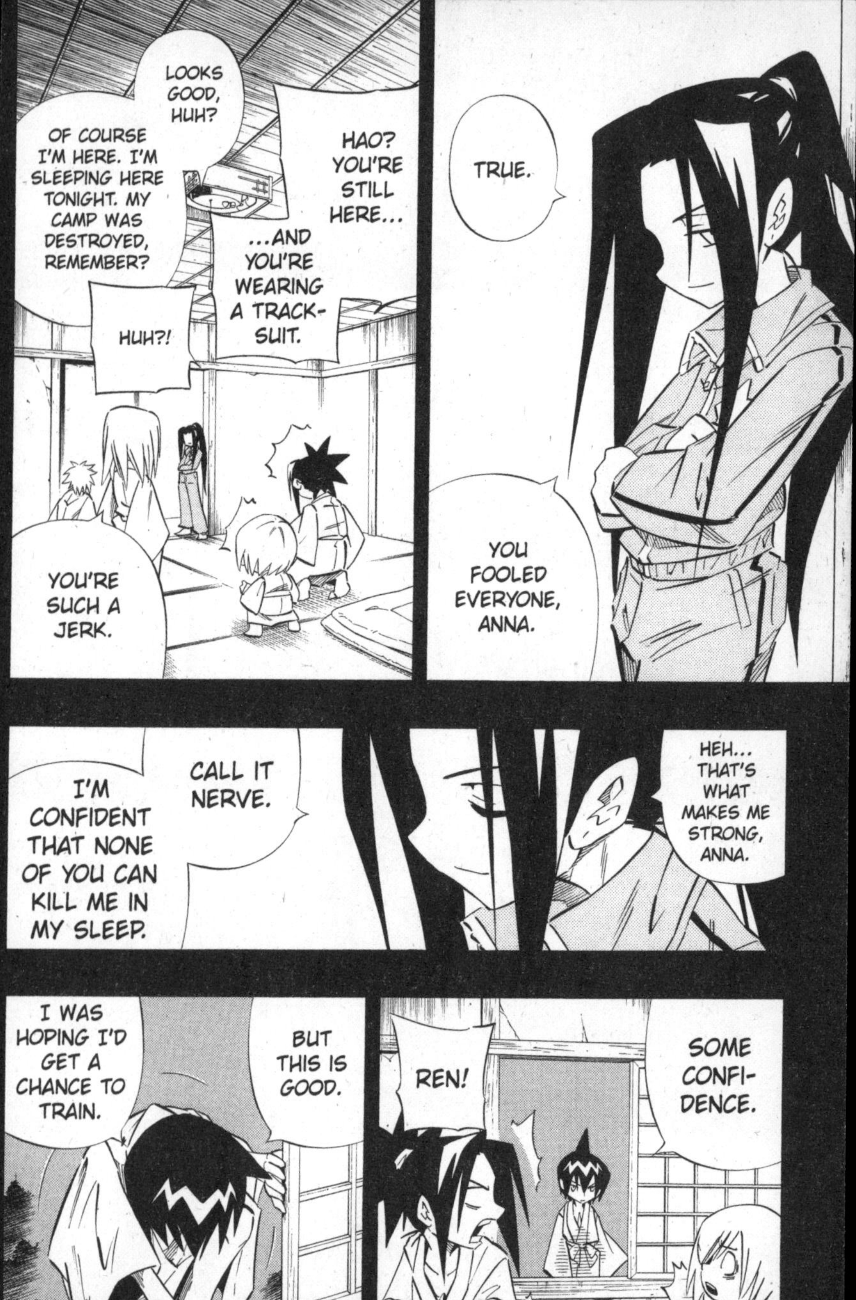
TRUE.
YOU FOOLED EVERYONE, ANNA.
HAO? YOU'RE STILL HERE...
...AND YOU'RE WEARING A TRACK-SUIT.
LOOKS GOOD, HUH?
OF COURSE I'M HERE. I'M SLEEPING HERE TONIGHT. MY CAMP WAS DESTROYED, REMEMBER?
HUH?!
YOU'RE SUCH A JERK.
HEH... THAT'S WHAT MAKES ME STRONG, ANNA.
CALL IT NERVE.
I'M CONFIDENT THAT NONE OF YOU CAN KILL ME IN MY SLEEP.
SOME CONFI-DENCE.
REN!
BUT THIS IS GOOD.
I WAS HOPING I'D GET A CHANCE TO TRAIN.

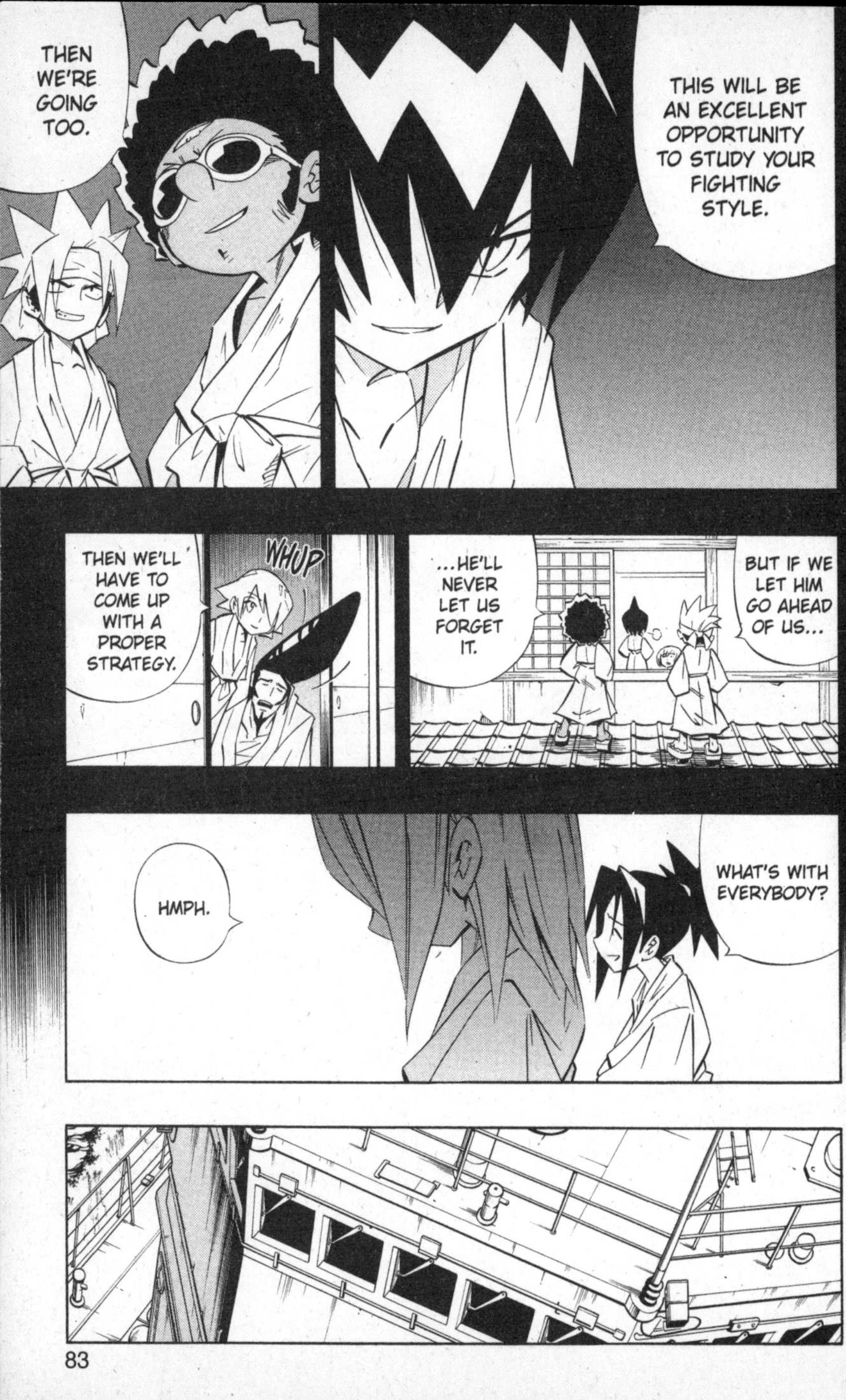
THIS WILL BE AN EXCELLENT OPPORTUNITY TO STUDY YOUR FIGHTING STYLE.
THEN WE'RE GOING TOO.
BUT IF WE LET HIM GO AHEAD OF US...
...HE'LL NEVER LET US FORGET IT.
WHUP
THEN WE'LL HAVE TO COME UP WITH A PROPER STRATEGY.
WHAT'S WITH EVERYBODY?
HMPH.

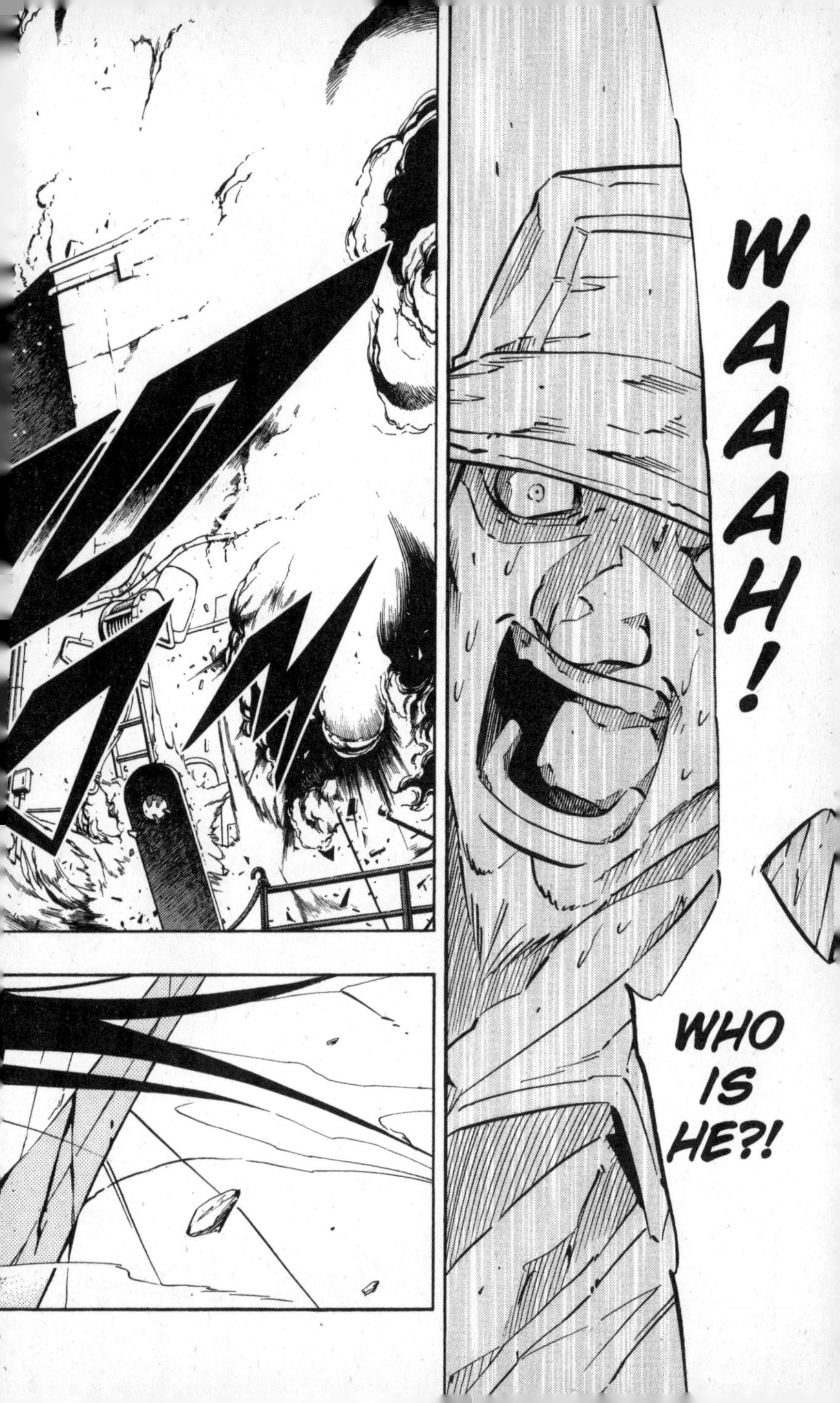
WAAAH!
WHO IS HE?!

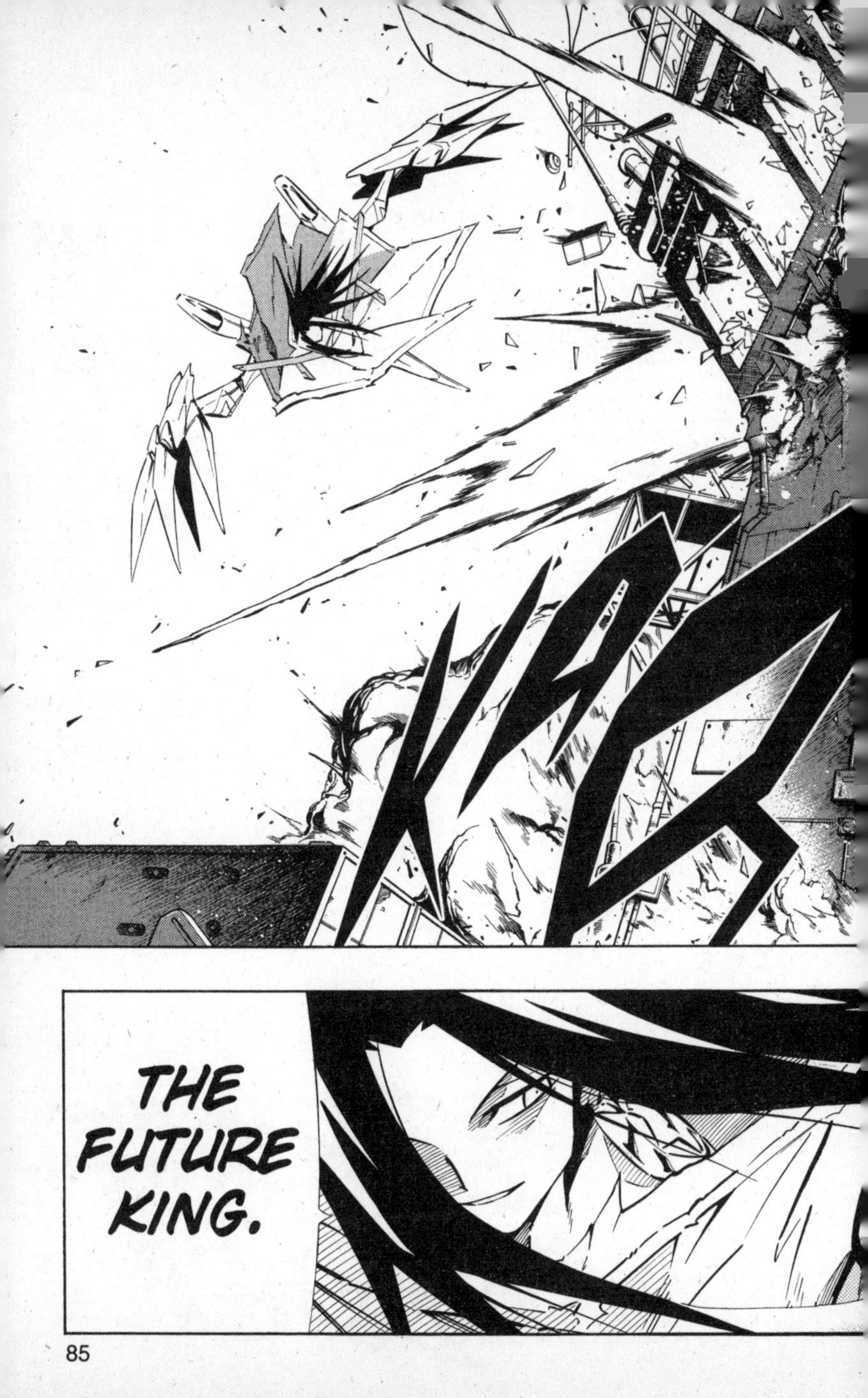
THE FUTURE KING.

Shaman King

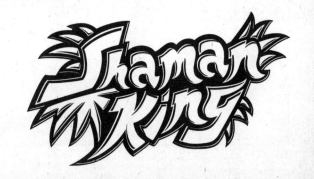

Reincarnation 262: White Scene

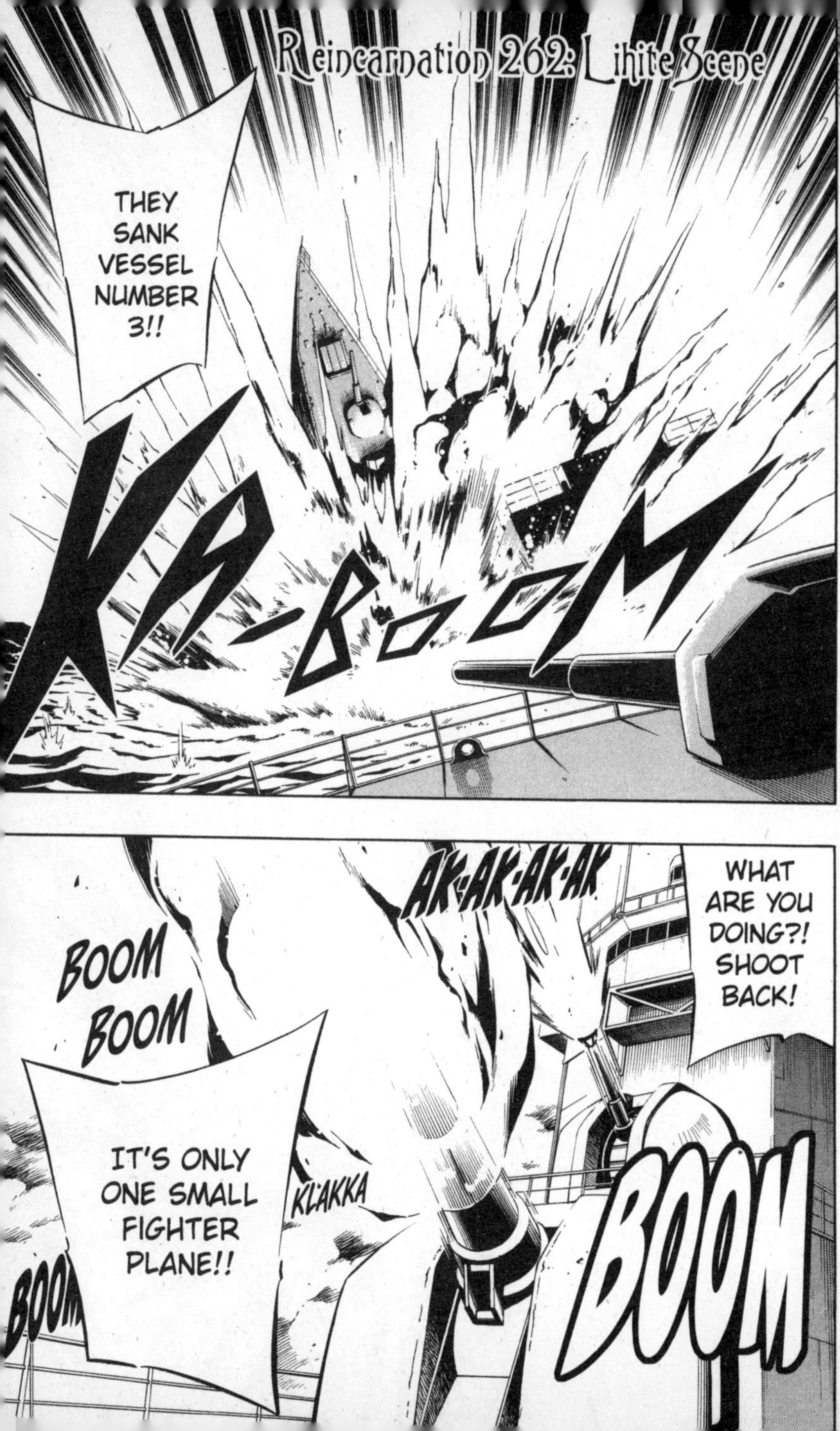
THEY SANK VESSEL NUMBER 3!!
KA-BOOM
WHAT ARE YOU DOING?! SHOOT BACK!
AK-AK-AK-AK
BOOM
KLAKKA
IT'S ONLY ONE SMALL FIGHTER PLANE!!
BOOM BOOM
BOOM

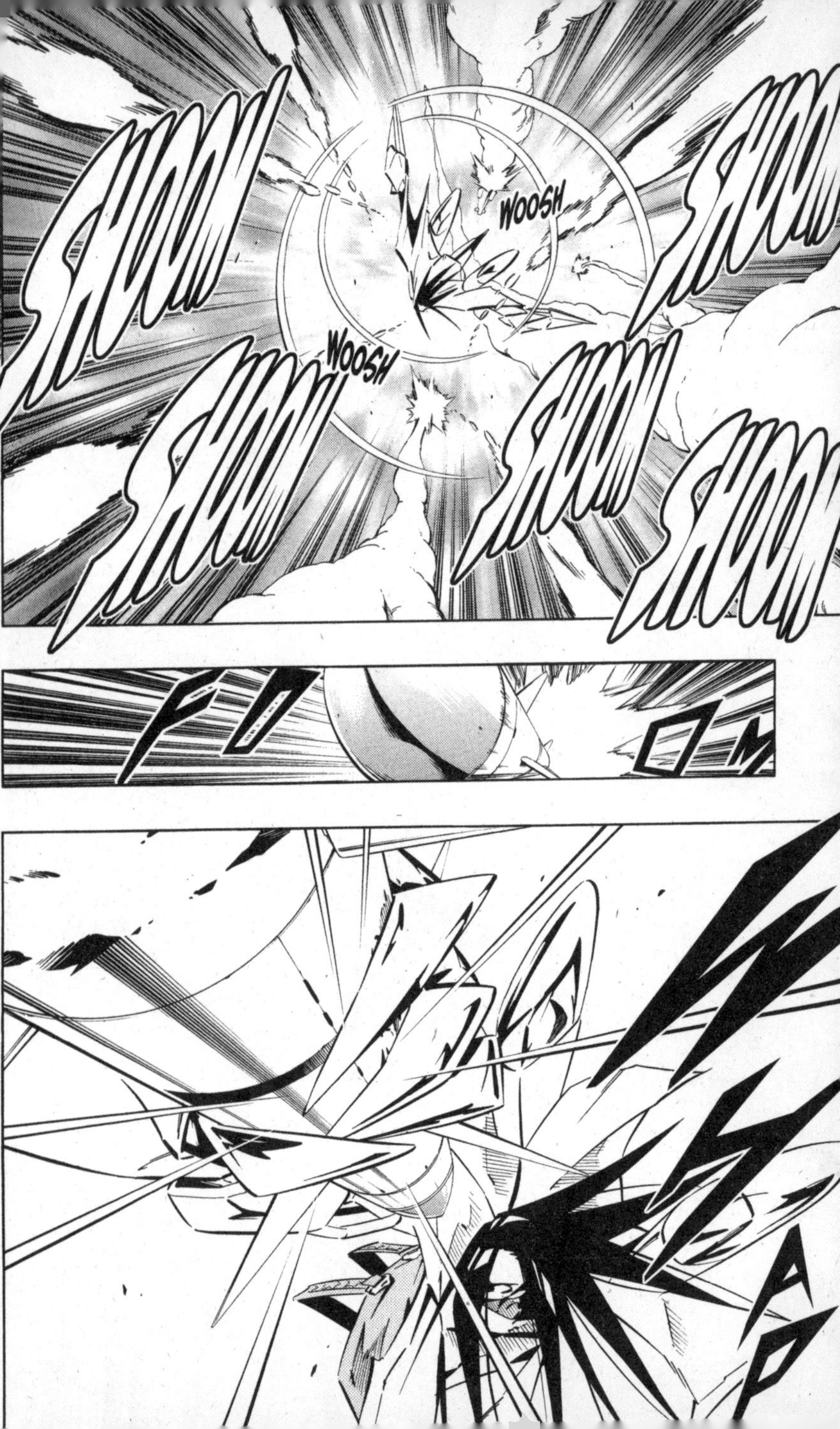
WOOSH
WOOSH

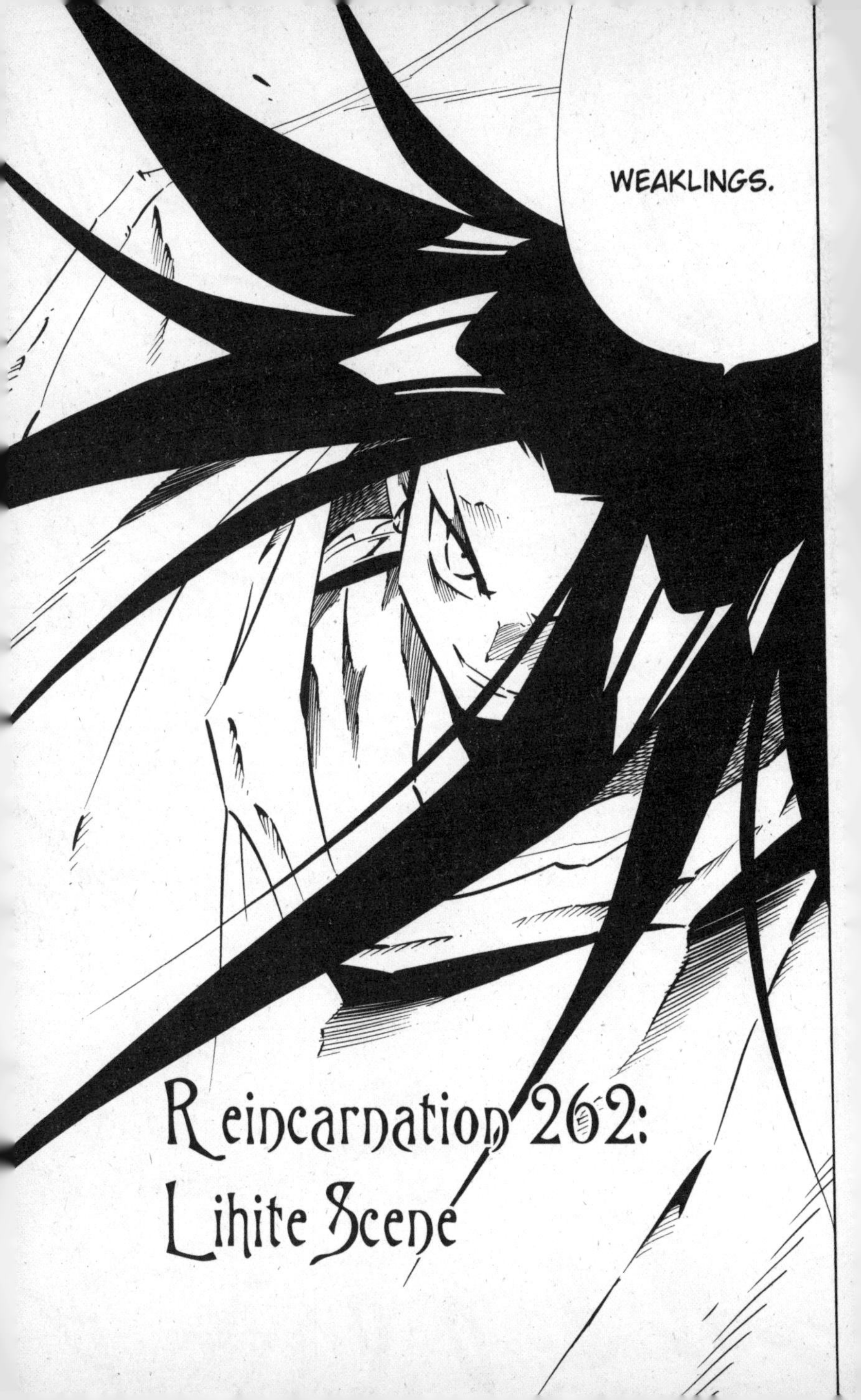
WEAKLINGS.

Reincarnation 262: White Scene

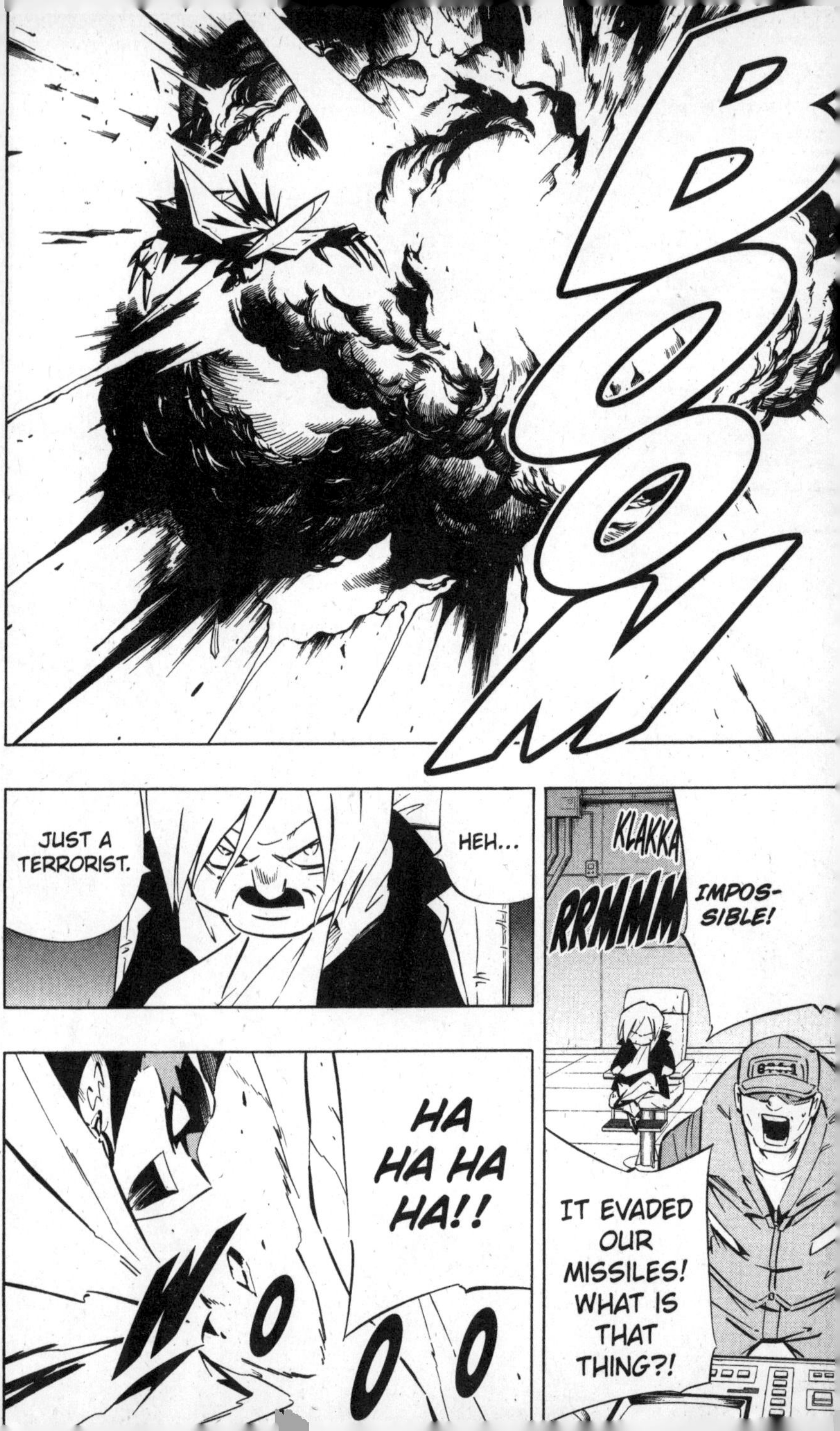
BOOM
KLAKKA
RRMMM
IMPOS-SIBLE!
IT EVADED OUR MISSILES! WHAT IS THAT THING?!
HEH...
JUST A TERRORIST.
HA HA HA HA HA!!
WOOO

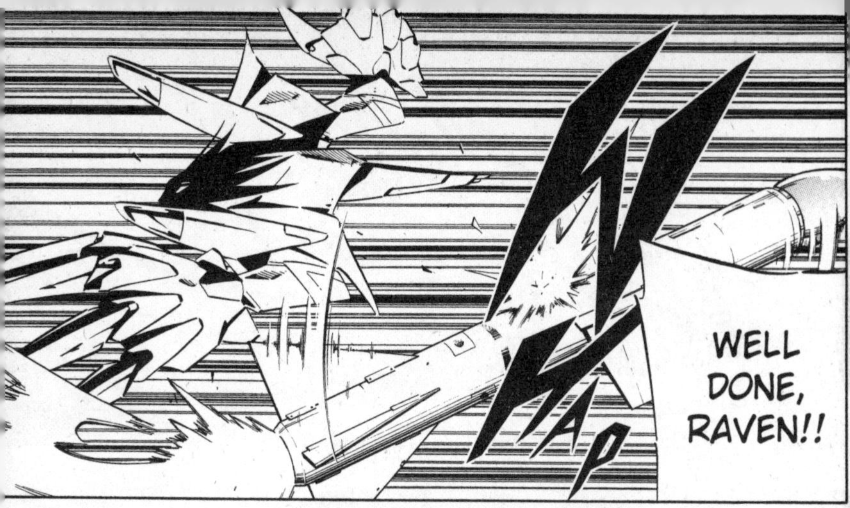
WELL DONE, RAVEN!!

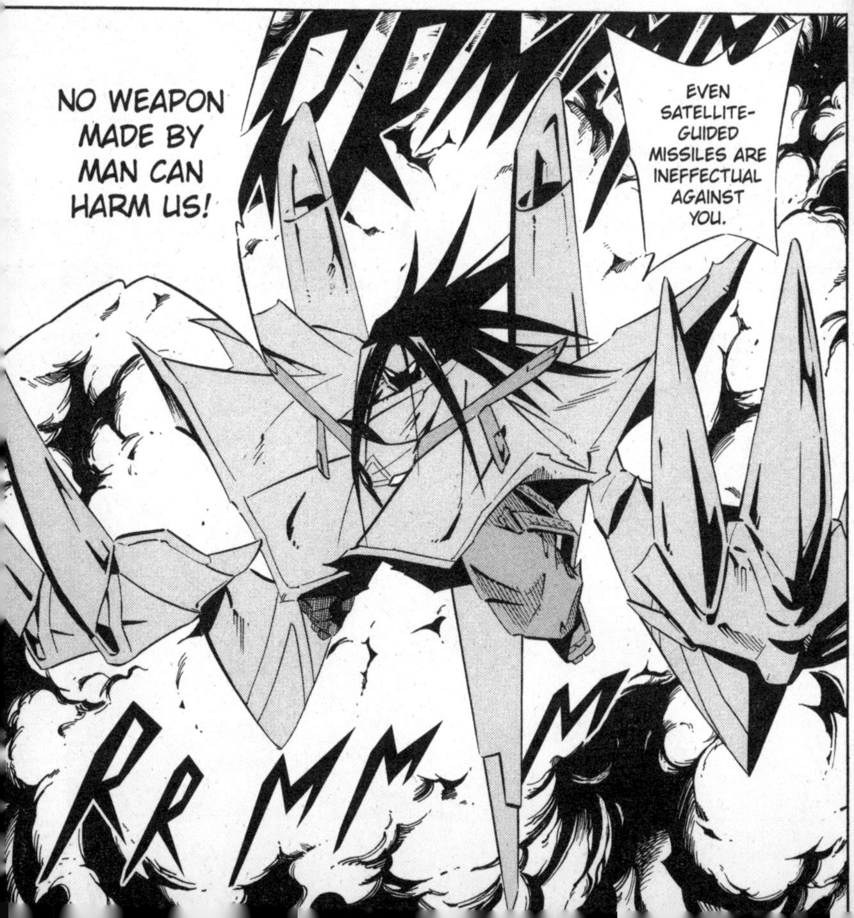
EVEN SATELLITE-GUIDED MISSILES ARE INEFFECTUAL AGAINST YOU.
NO WEAPON MADE BY MAN CAN HARM US!

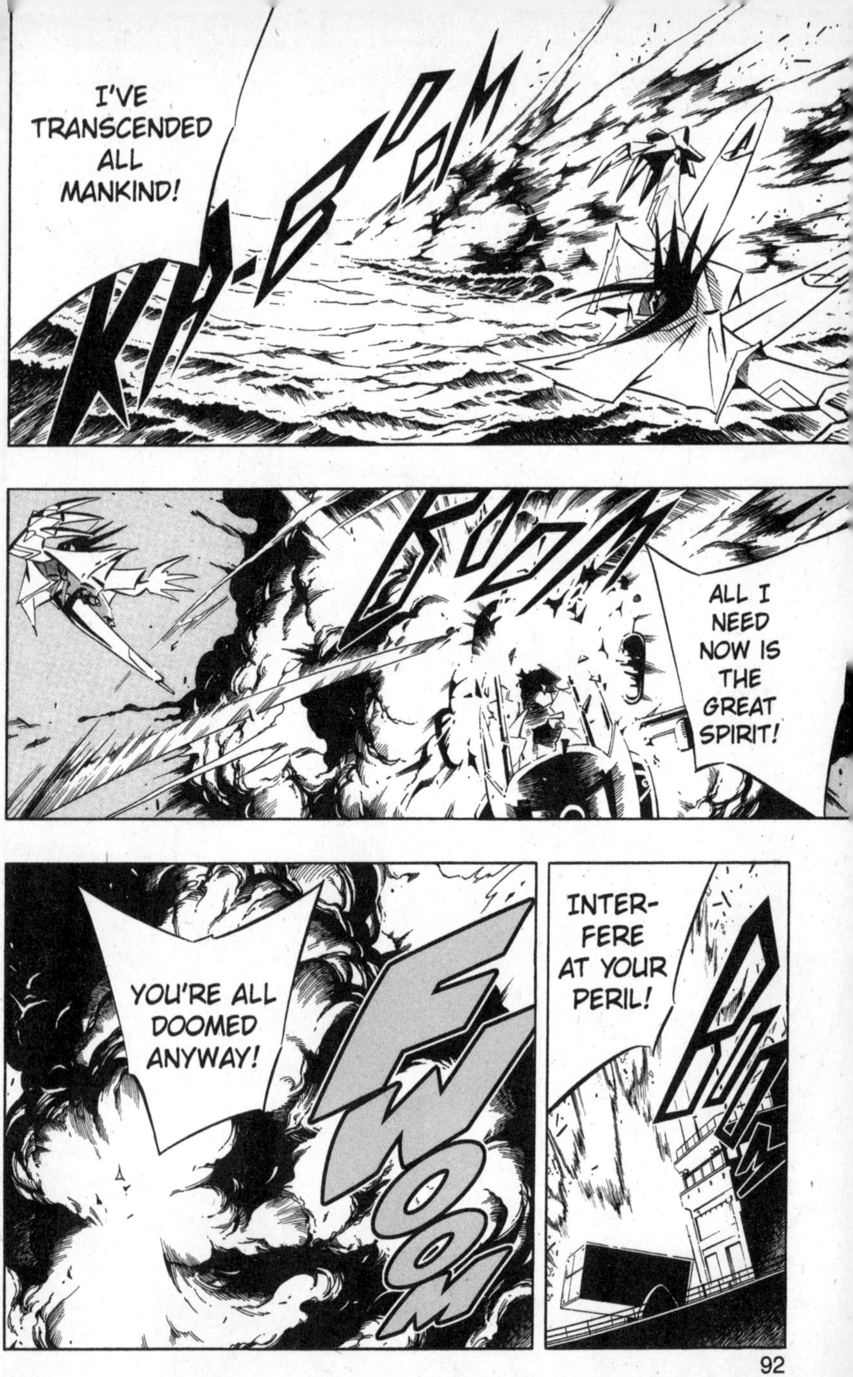
I'VE TRANSCENDED ALL MANKIND!
KA-BOOM
BOOM
ALL I NEED NOW IS THE GREAT SPIRIT!
INTER-FERE AT YOUR PERIL!
YOU'RE ALL DOOMED ANYWAY!

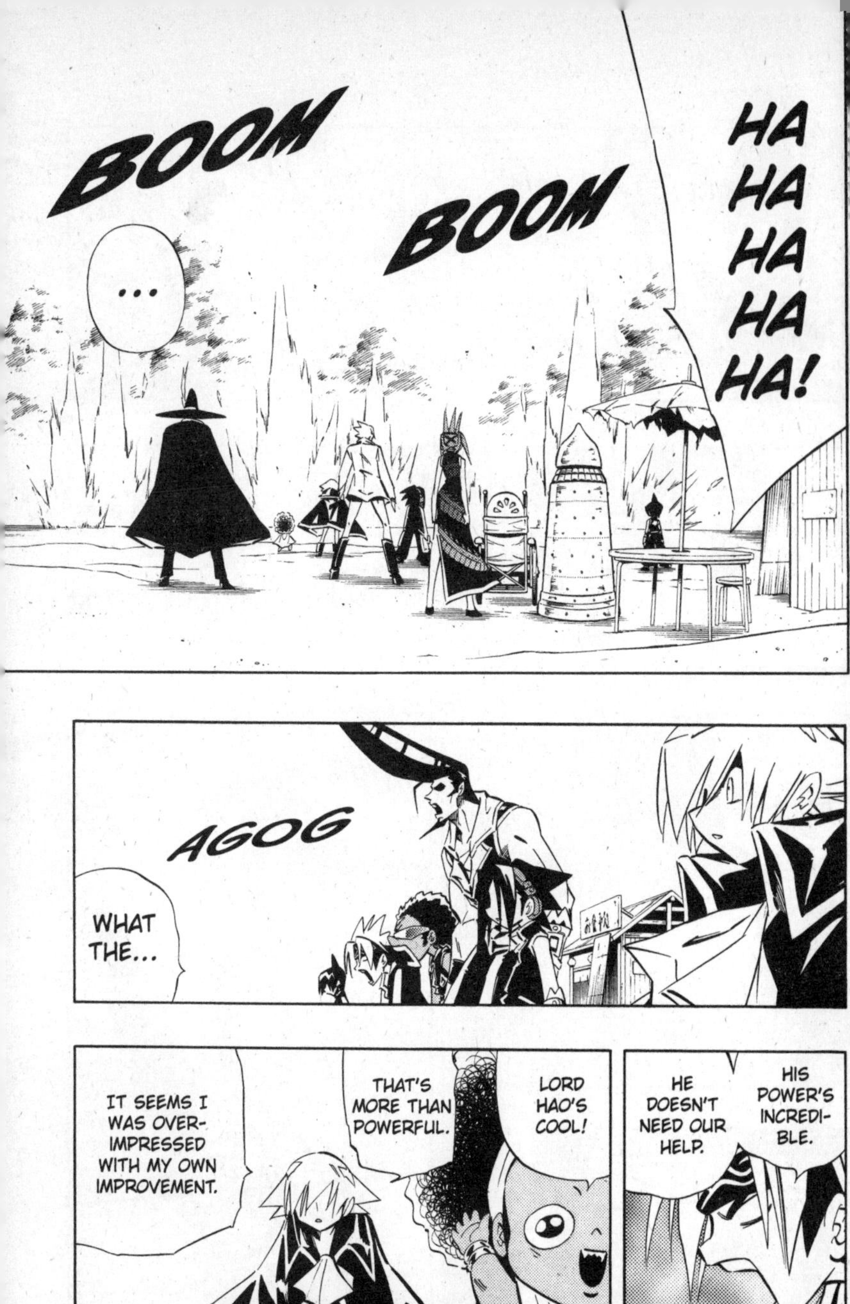
HA HA HA HA HA!
BOOM
BOOM
...
AGOG
WHAT THE...
HIS POWER'S INCREDIBLE.
HE DOESN'T NEED OUR HELP.
LORD HAO'S COOL!
THAT'S MORE THAN POWERFUL.
IT SEEMS I WAS OVER-IMPRESSED WITH MY OWN IMPROVEMENT.

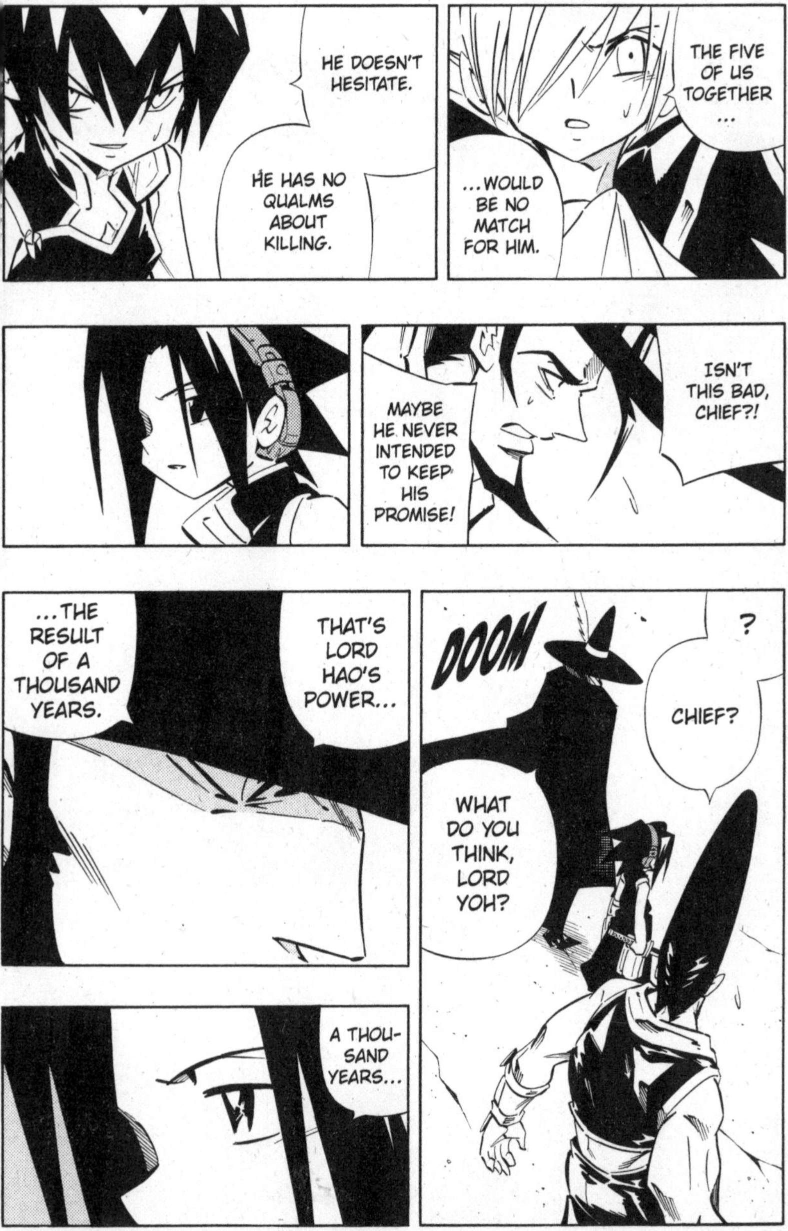
THE FIVE OF US TOGETHER ...
...WOULD BE NO MATCH FOR HIM.
HE DOESN'T HESITATE.
HE HAS NO QUALMS ABOUT KILLING.
ISN'T THIS BAD, CHIEF?!
MAYBE HE NEVER INTENDED TO KEEP HIS PROMISE!
?
CHIEF?
DOOM
WHAT DO YOU THINK, LORD YOH?
THAT'S LORD HAO'S POWER...
...THE RESULT OF A THOUSAND YEARS.
A THOUSAND YEARS...

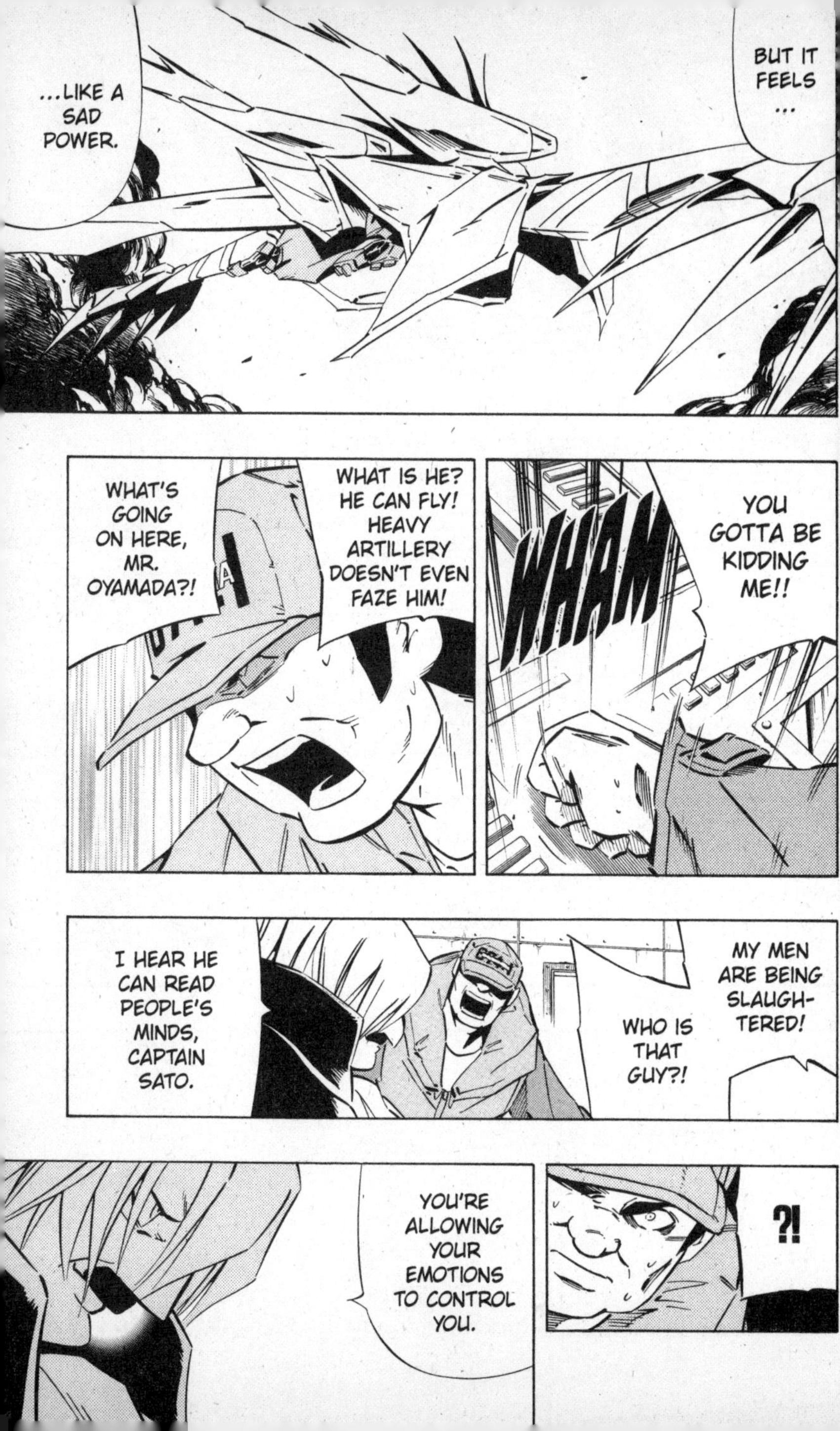
BUT IT FEELS ...
...LIKE A SAD POWER.
YOU GOTTA BE KIDDING ME!!
WHAM
WHAT IS HE? HE CAN FLY! HEAVY ARTILLERY DOESN'T EVEN FAZE HIM!
WHAT'S GOING ON HERE, MR. OYAMADA?!
MY MEN ARE BEING SLAUGH-TERED!
WHO IS THAT GUY?!
I HEAR HE CAN READ PEOPLE'S MINDS, CAPTAIN SATO.
?!
YOU'RE ALLOWING YOUR EMOTIONS TO CONTROL YOU.

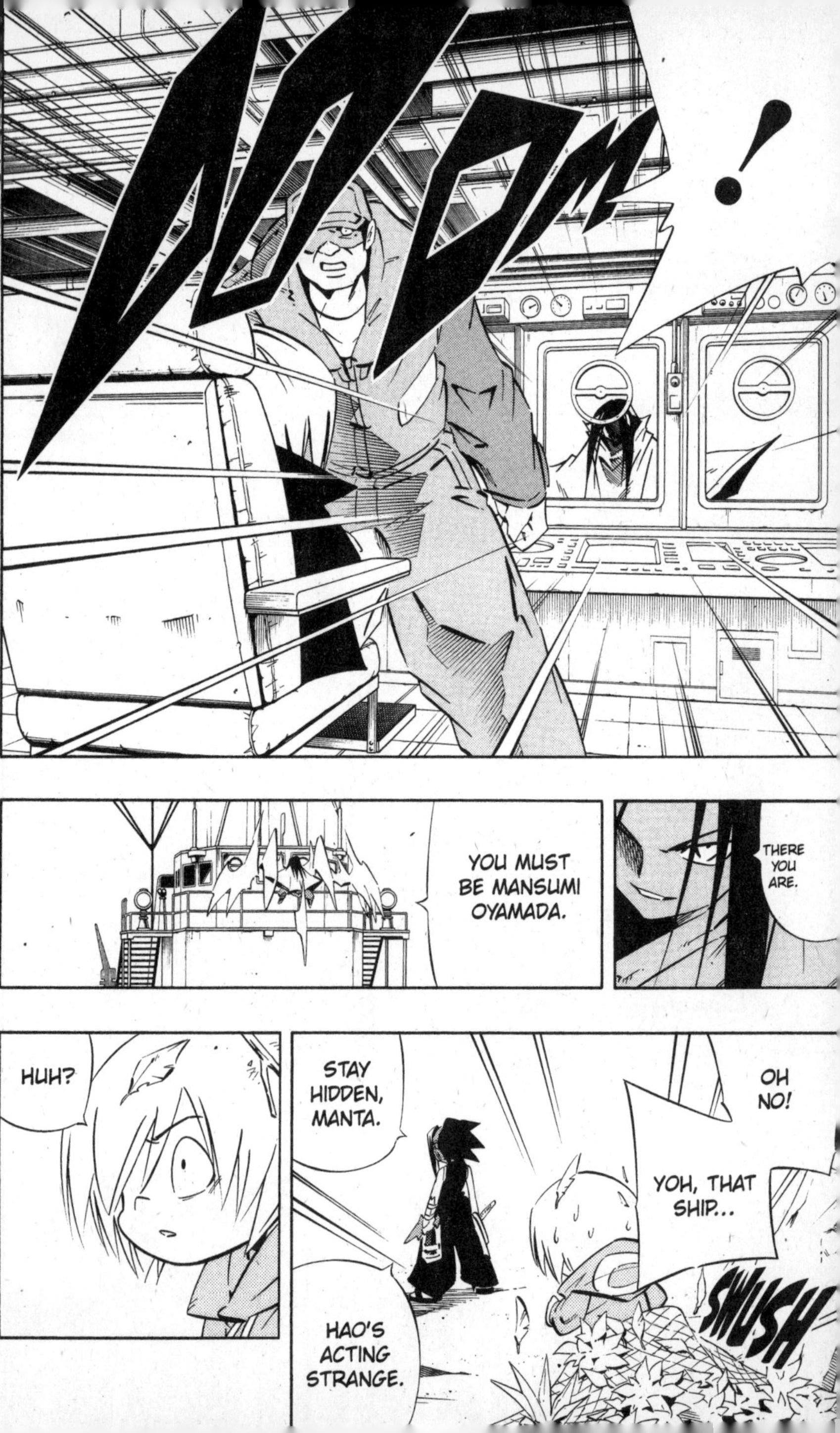
DOOM!
THERE YOU ARE.
YOU MUST BE MANSUMI OYAMADA.
OH NO!
YOH, THAT SHIP...
SHUSH
STAY HIDDEN, MANTA.
HAO'S ACTING STRANGE.
HUH?

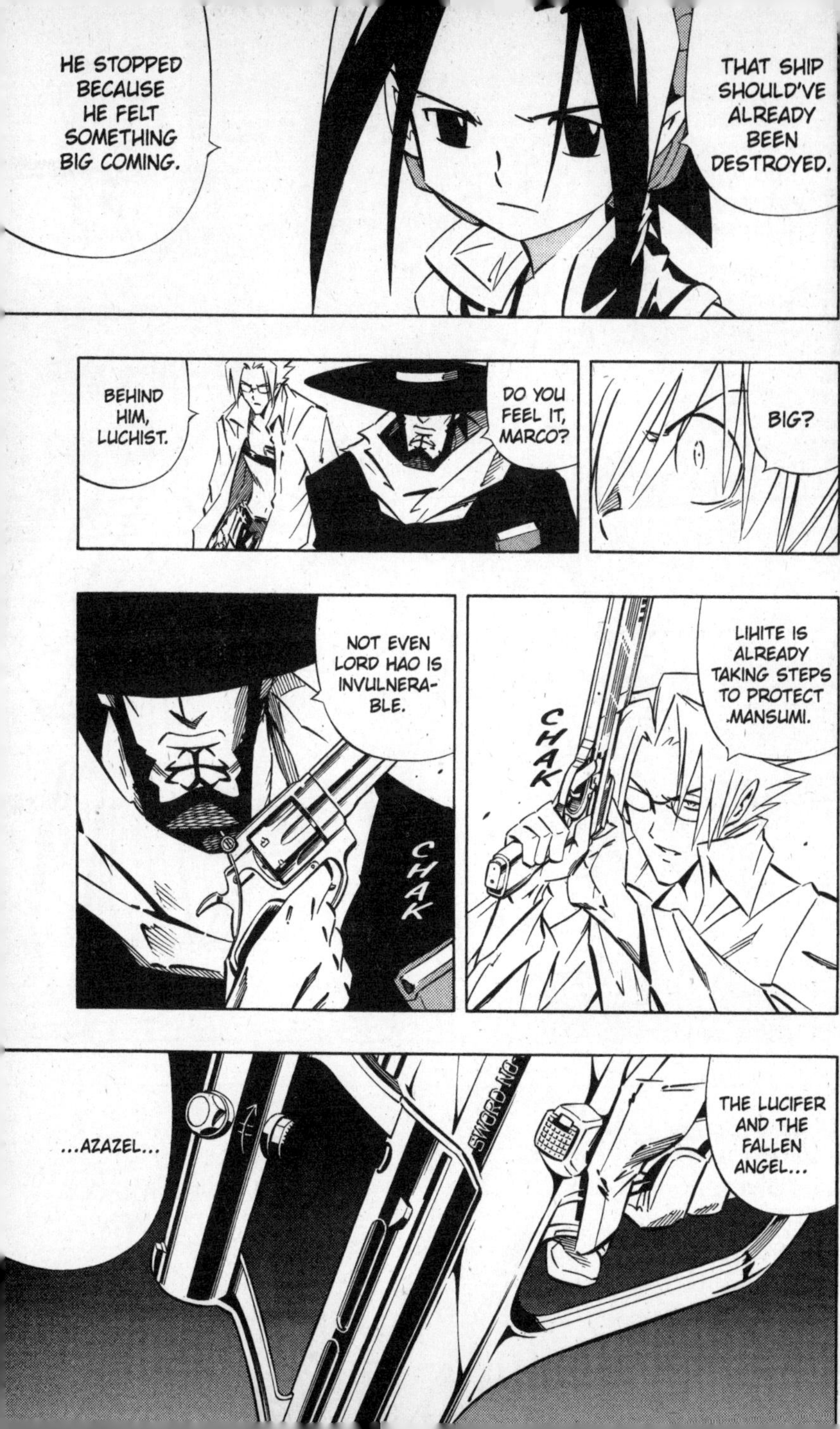
THAT SHIP SHOULD'VE ALREADY BEEN DESTROYED.
HE STOPPED BECAUSE HE FELT SOMETHING BIG COMING.
BIG?
DO YOU FEEL IT, MARCO?
BEHIND HIM, LUCHIST.
LIHITE IS ALREADY TAKING STEPS TO PROTECT MANSUMI.
CHAK
NOT EVEN LORD HAO IS INVULNERA-BLE.
CHAK
THE LUCIFER AND THE FALLEN ANGEL...
...AZAZEL...

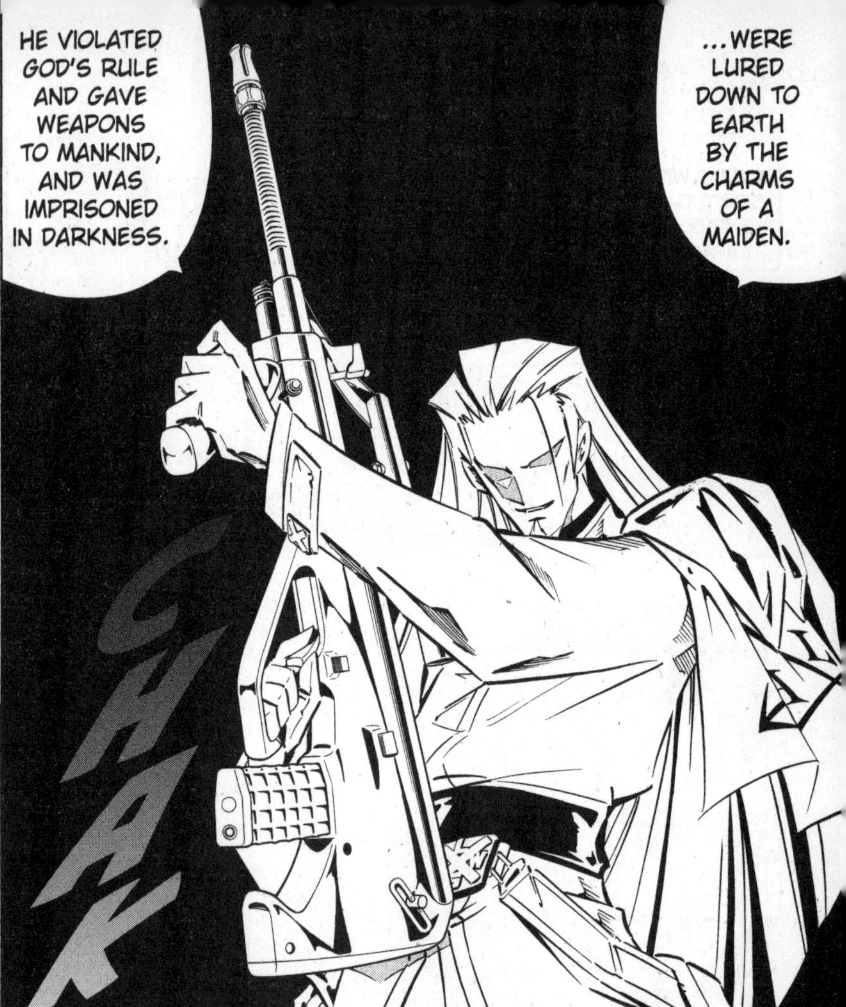
...WERE LURED DOWN TO EARTH BY THE CHARMS OF A MAIDEN.
HE VIOLATED GOD'S RULE AND GAVE WEAPONS TO MANKIND, AND WAS IMPRISONED IN DARKNESS.
CHAK

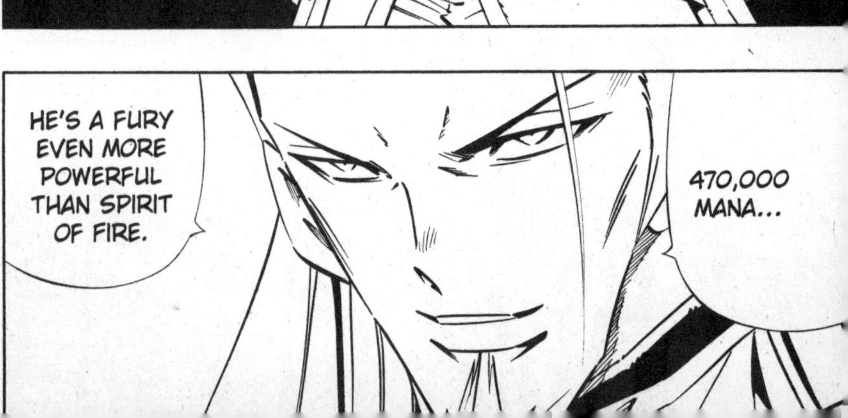
470,000 MANA...
HE'S A FURY EVEN MORE POWERFUL THAN SPIRIT OF FIRE.

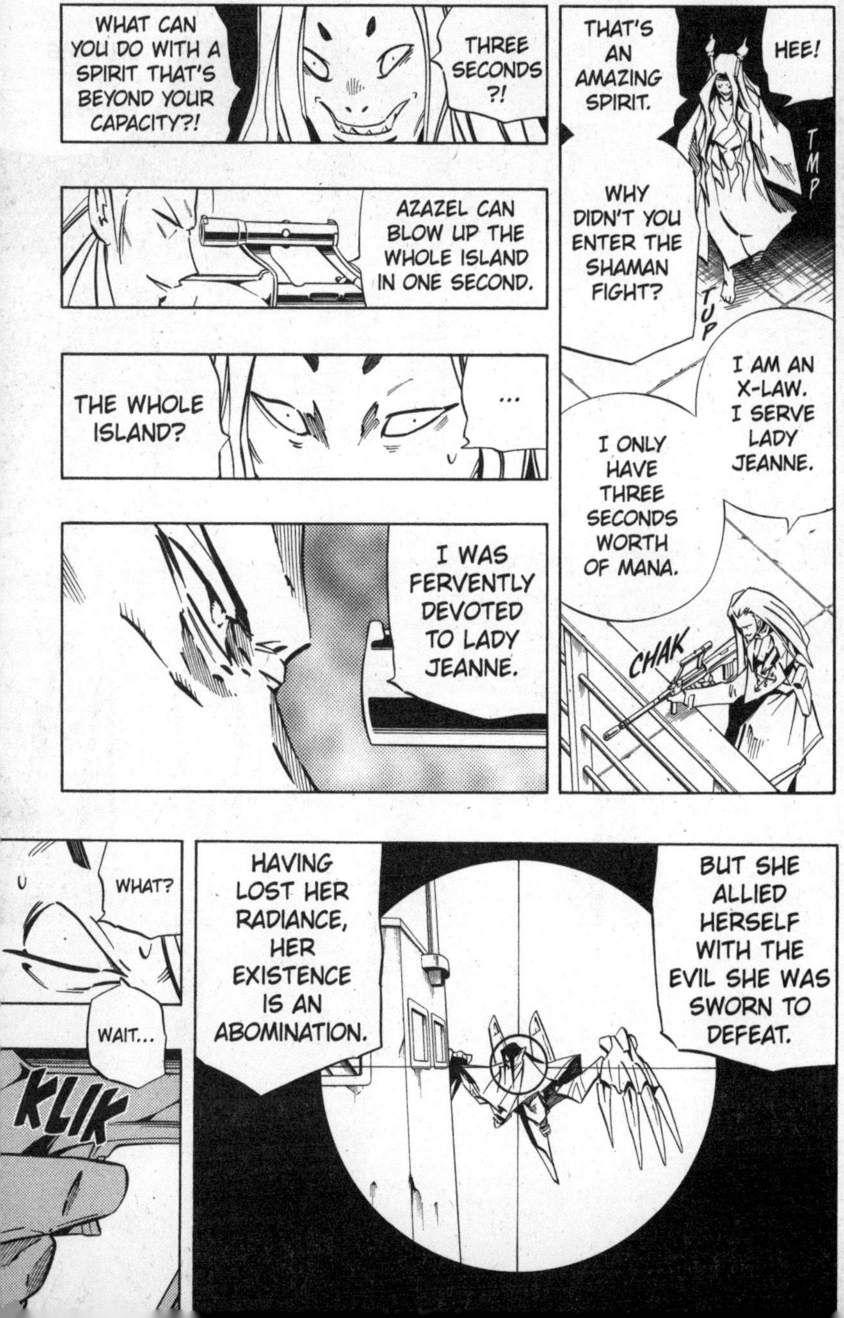
HEE!
THAT'S AN AMAZING SPIRIT.
TMP
WHY DIDN'T YOU ENTER THE SHAMAN FIGHT?
TUP
I AM AN X-LAW. I SERVE LADY JEANNE.
I ONLY HAVE THREE SECONDS WORTH OF MANA.
CHAK
THREE SECONDS?!
WHAT CAN YOU DO WITH A SPIRIT THAT'S BEYOND YOUR CAPACITY?!
AZAZEL CAN BLOW UP THE WHOLE ISLAND IN ONE SECOND.
...
THE WHOLE ISLAND?
I WAS FERVENTLY DEVOTED TO LADY JEANNE.
BUT SHE ALLIED HERSELF WITH THE EVIL SHE WAS SWORN TO DEFEAT.
HAVING LOST HER RADIANCE, HER EXISTENCE IS AN ABOMINATION.
WHAT?
WAIT...
KLIK

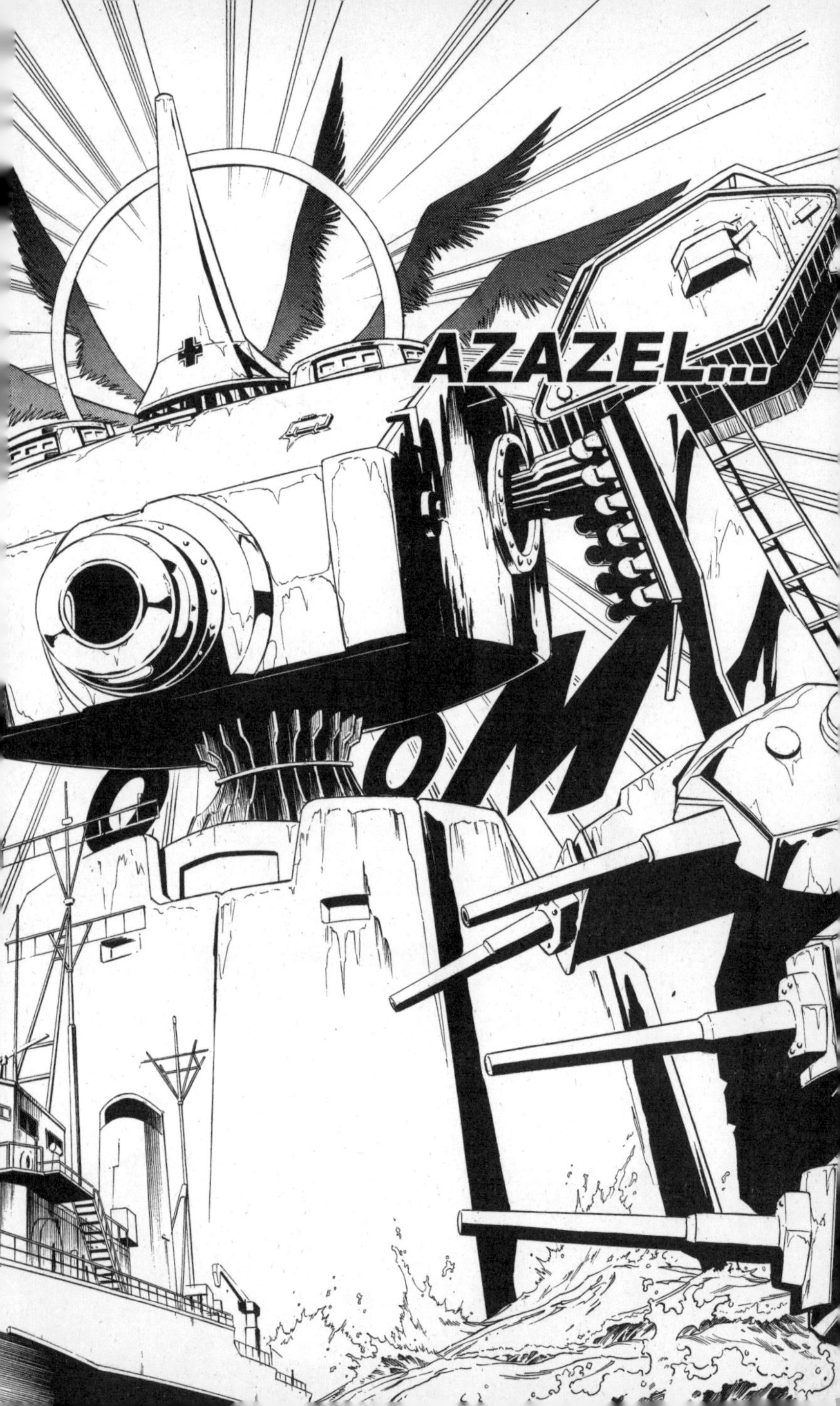
AZAZEL...

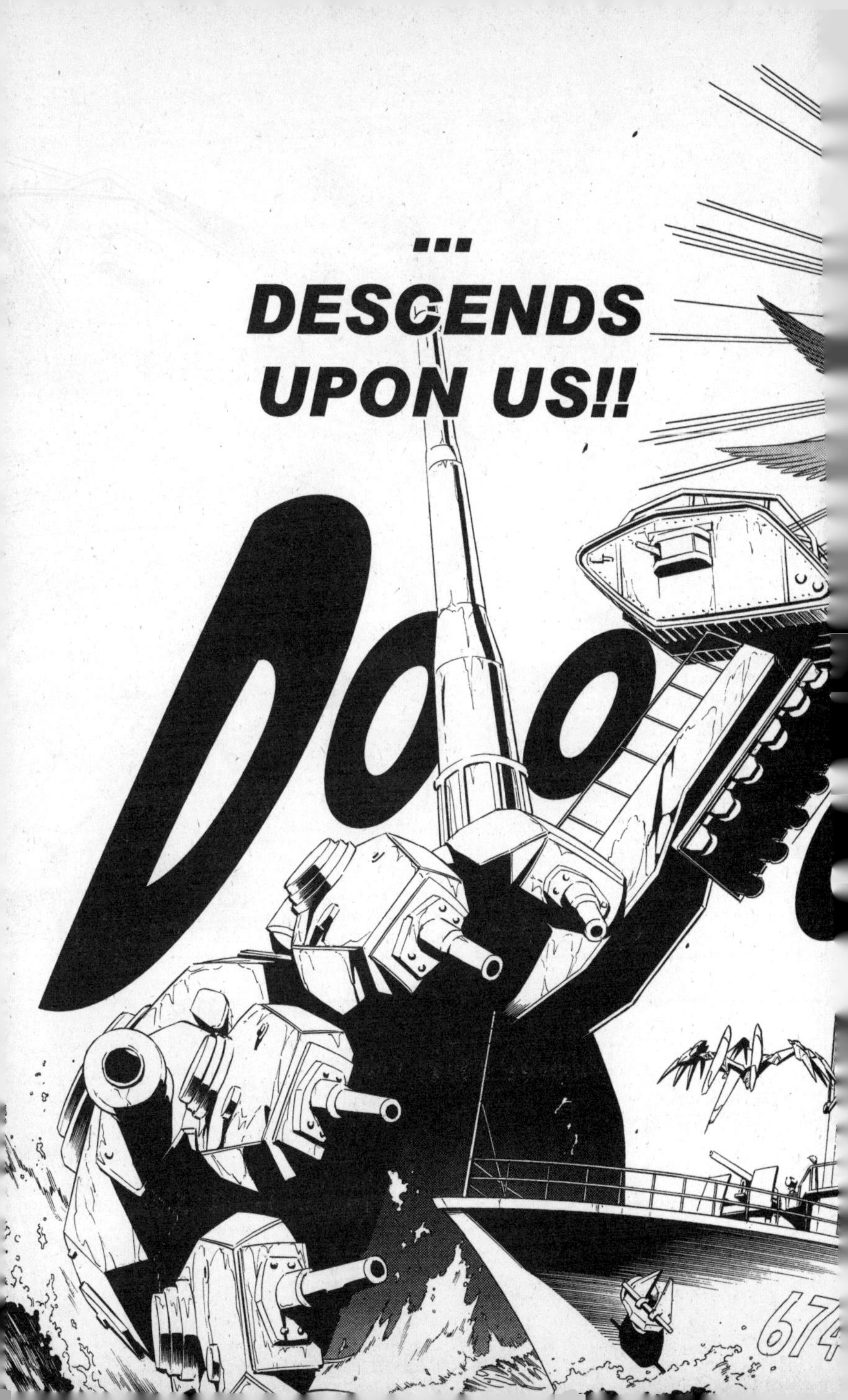
... DESCENDS UPON US!!
674

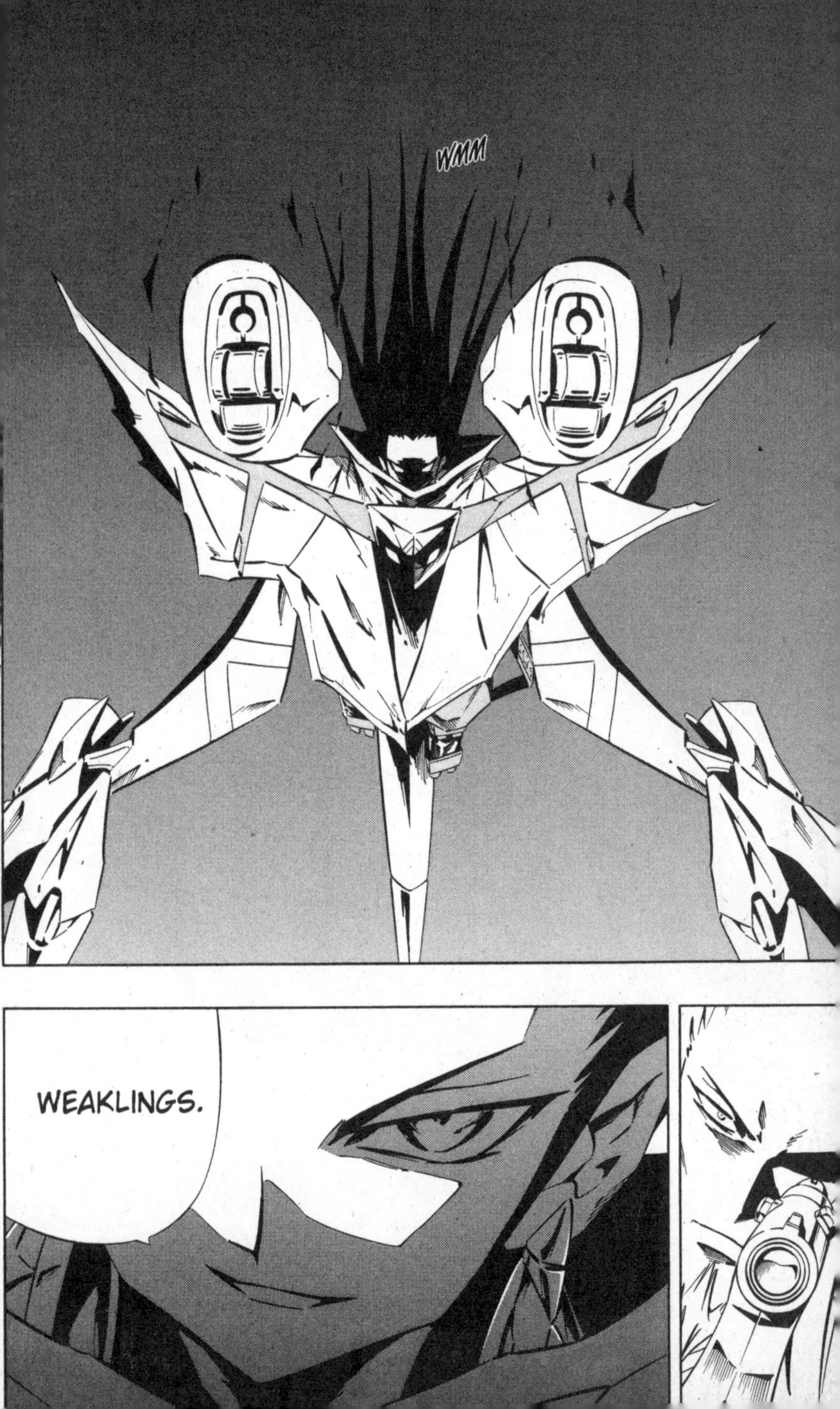
WMM
WEAKLINGS.

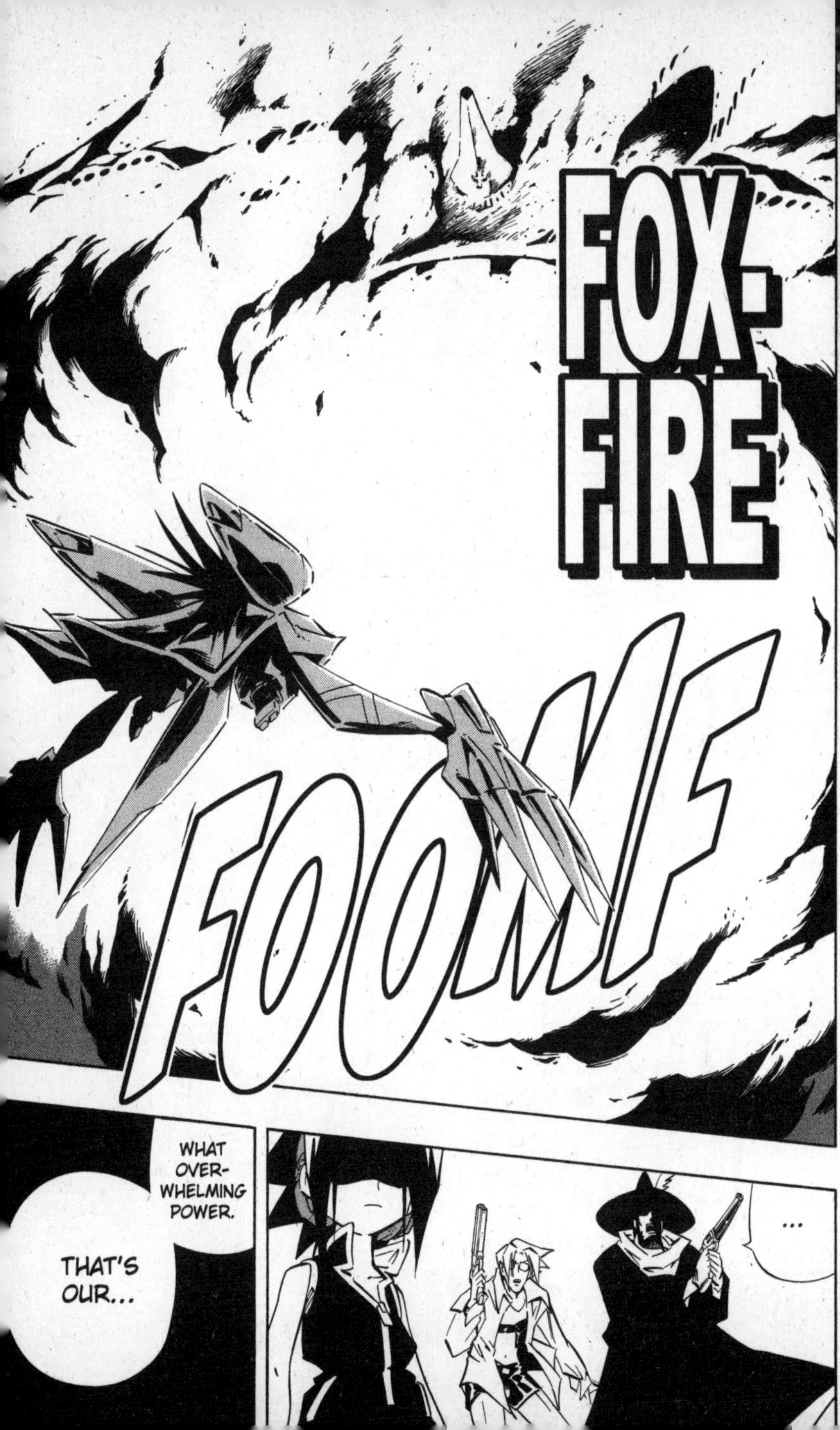
FOX-FIRE
FOOMF
...
WHAT OVER-WHELMING POWER.
THAT'S OUR...

SHAMAN KING CHARACTER FILE No.154

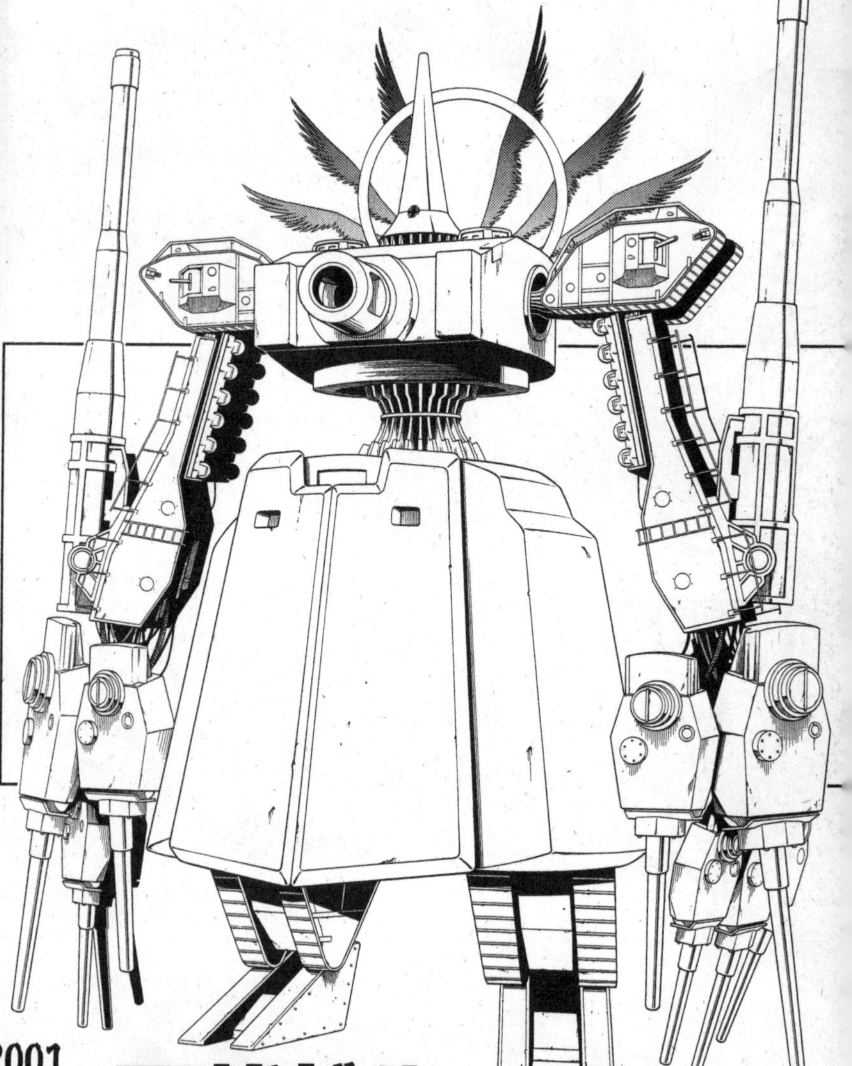

2001
(JAN)

アザゼル AZAZEL

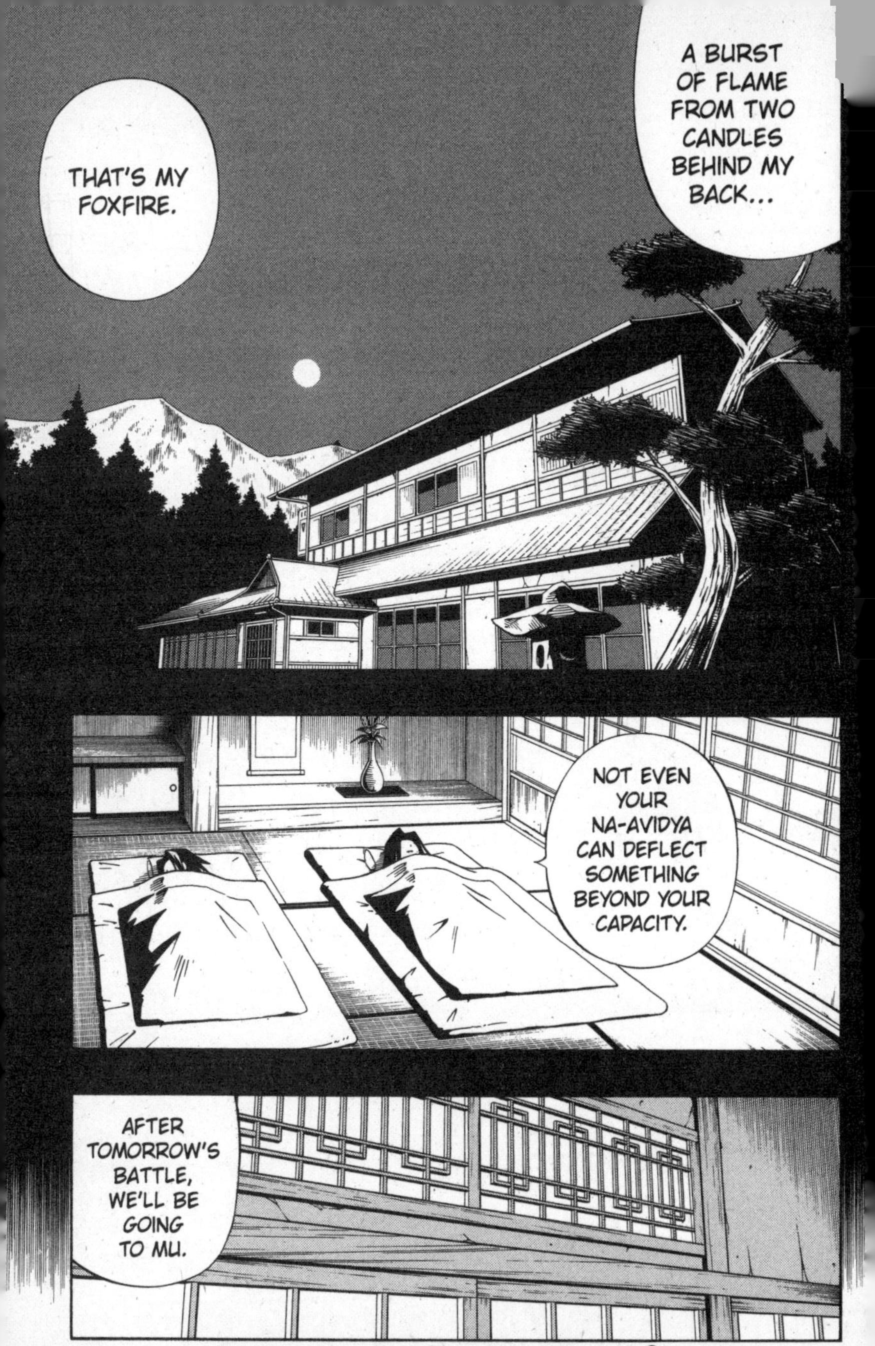
A BURST OF FLAME FROM TWO CANDLES BEHIND MY BACK...
THAT'S MY FOXFIRE.
NOT EVEN YOUR NA-AVIDYA CAN DEFLECT SOMETHING BEYOND YOUR CAPACITY.
AFTER TOMORROW'S BATTLE, WE'LL BE GOING TO MU.

Reincarnation 263: Teruko, the Voodoo Witch

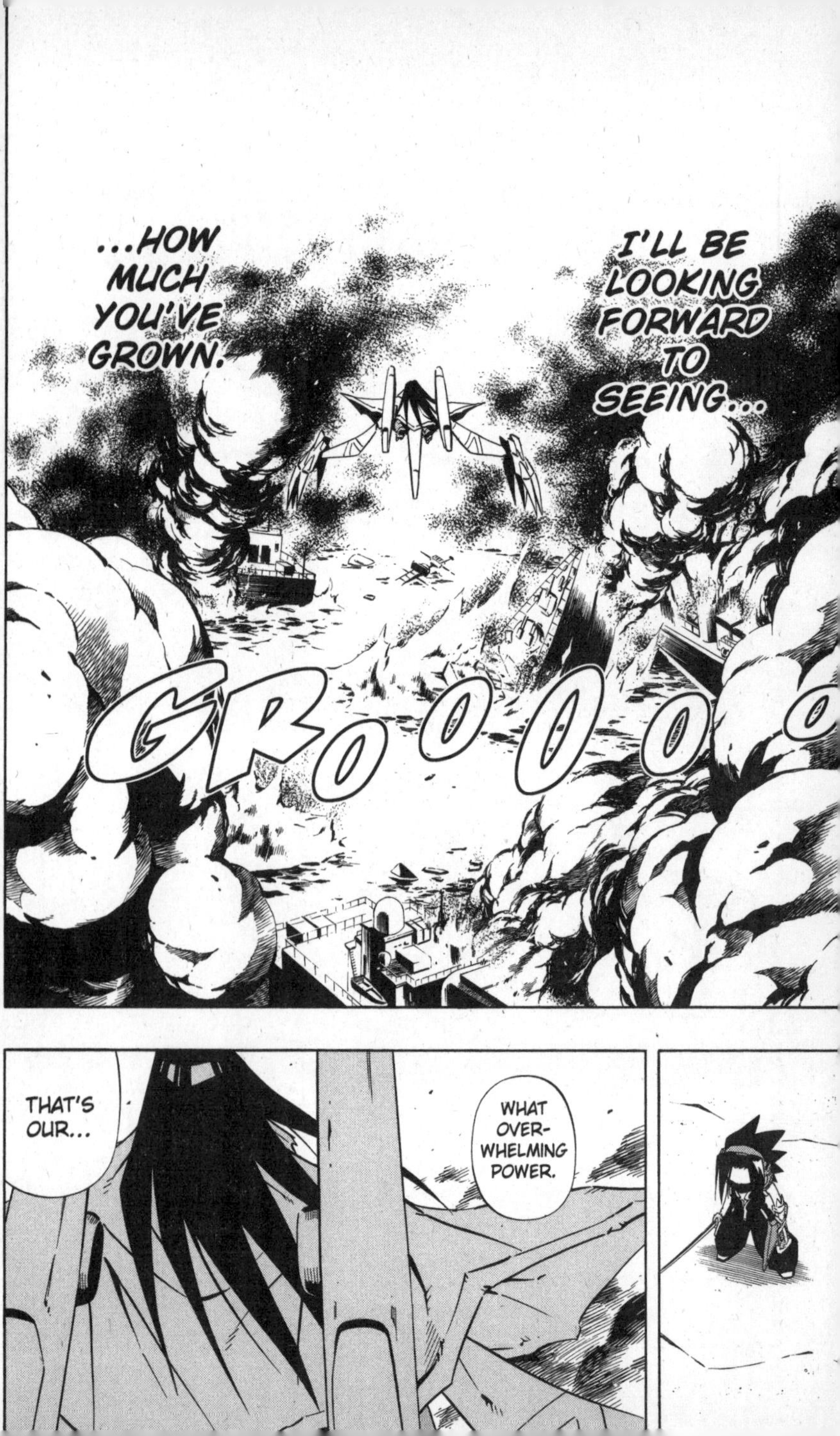
I'LL BE LOOKING FORWARD TO SEEING...
...HOW MUCH YOU'VE GROWN.
GROOOOO
WHAT OVER-WHELMING POWER.
THAT'S OUR...

Reincarnation 263: Teruko, the Voodoo Witch

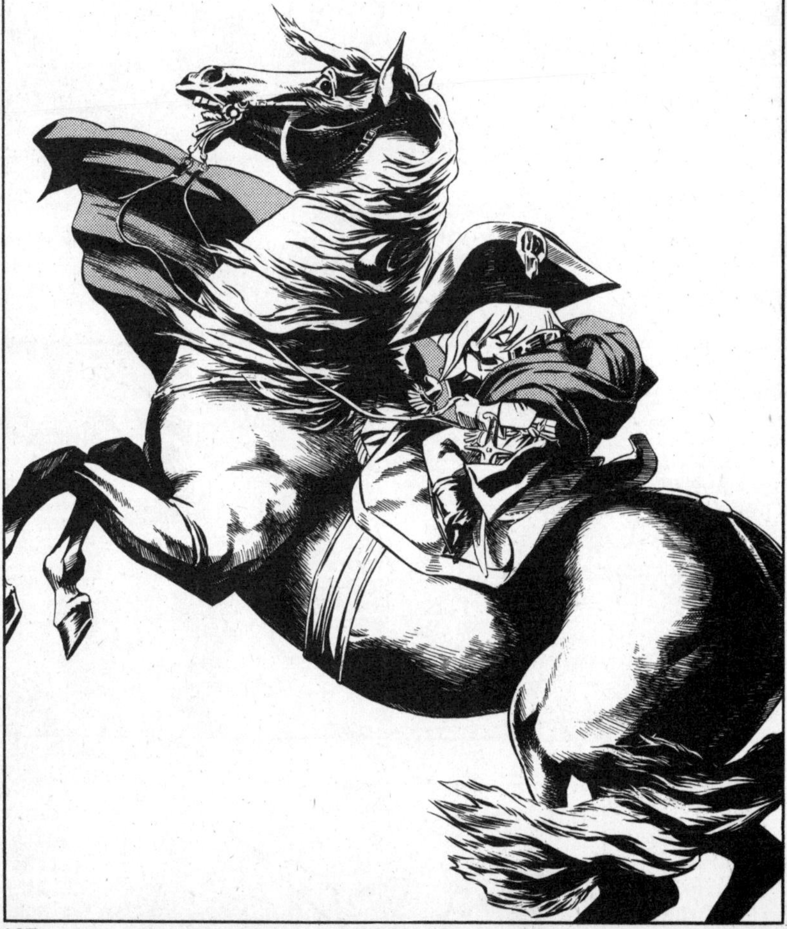

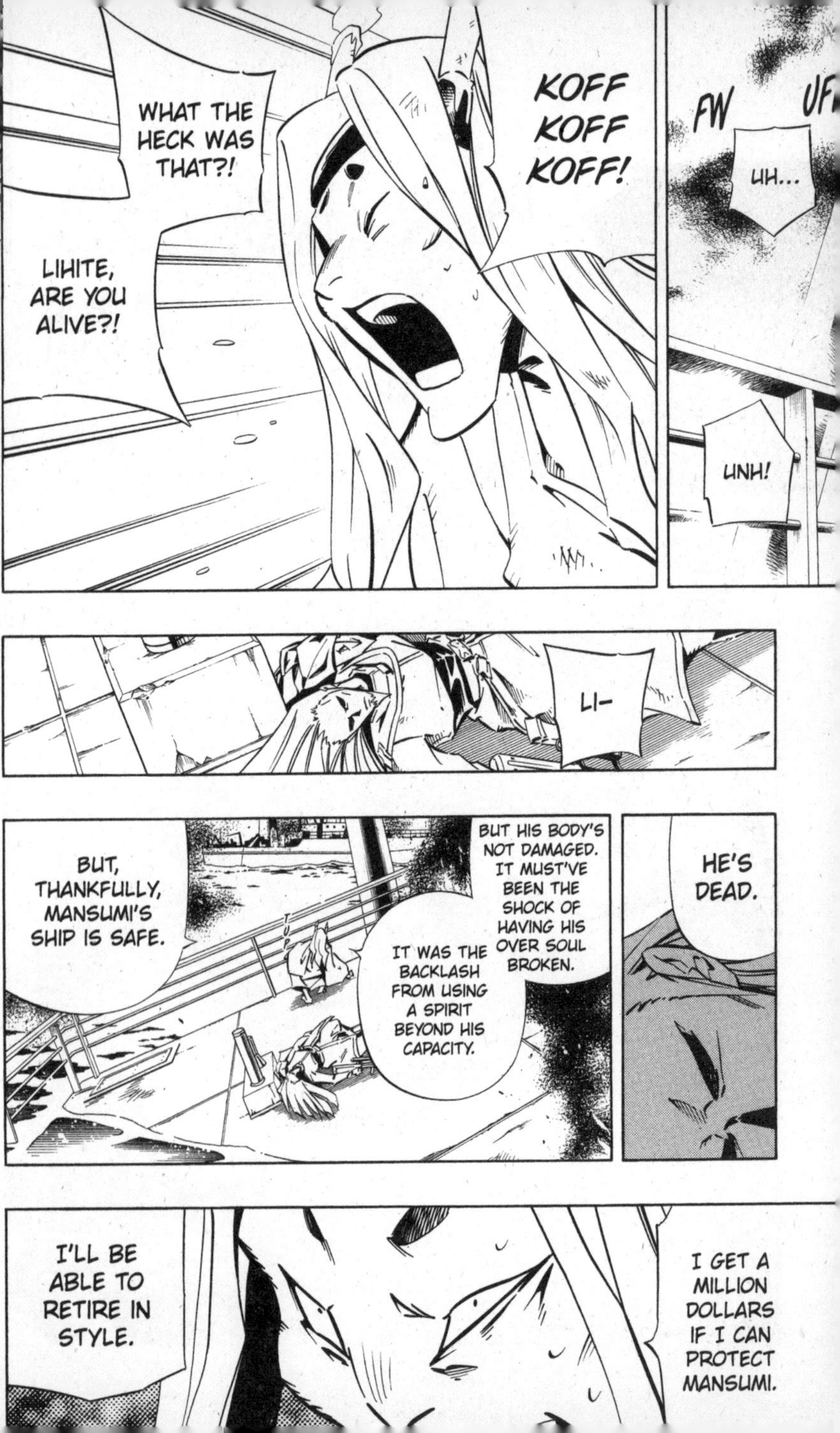
FW UF
UH...
UNH!
KOFF KOFF KOFF!
WHAT THE HECK WAS THAT?!
LIHITE, ARE YOU ALIVE?!
LI-
HE'S DEAD.
BUT HIS BODY'S NOT DAMAGED. IT MUST'VE BEEN THE SHOCK OF HAVING HIS OVER SOUL BROKEN.
IT WAS THE BACKLASH FROM USING A SPIRIT BEYOND HIS CAPACITY.
TUP
BUT, THANKFULLY, MANSUMI'S SHIP IS SAFE.
I GET A MILLION DOLLARS IF I CAN PROTECT MANSUMI.
I'LL BE ABLE TO RETIRE IN STYLE.

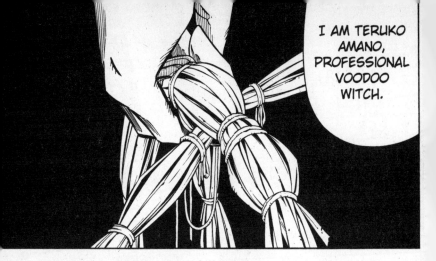

I AM TERUKO AMANO, PROFESSIONAL VOODOO WITCH.

THE GUY WITH GLASSES GAVE ME SOME HAIR FROM THE HOT SPRINGS. I PUT IT INSIDE THIS EFFIGY.

ALL I HAVE TO DO IS HAMMER A NAIL INTO IT, AND THE OWNER OF THE HAIR WILL GO STRAIGHT TO THE AFTERLIFE.

BUT I MADE A STUPID RULE THAT IT WOULDN'T HAVE ANY EFFECT IF ANYONE WAS WATCHING, SO I COULDN'T PARTICIPATE IN THE SHAMAN FIGHT.

BUT NOW MY TIME HAS FINALLY COME!

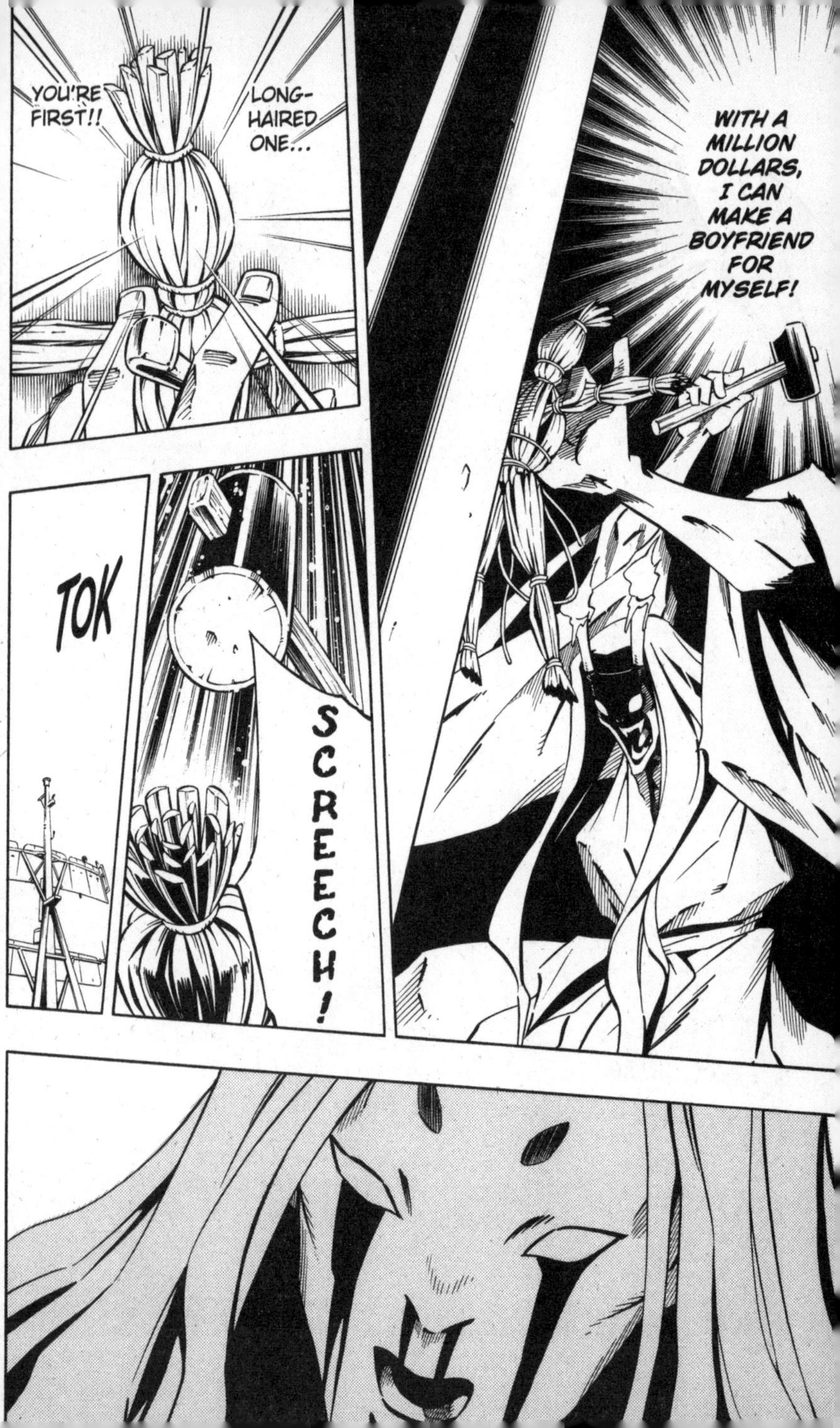
WITH A MILLION DOLLARS, I CAN MAKE A BOYFRIEND FOR MYSELF!
LONG-HAIRED ONE...
YOU'RE FIRST!!
SCREECH!
TOK

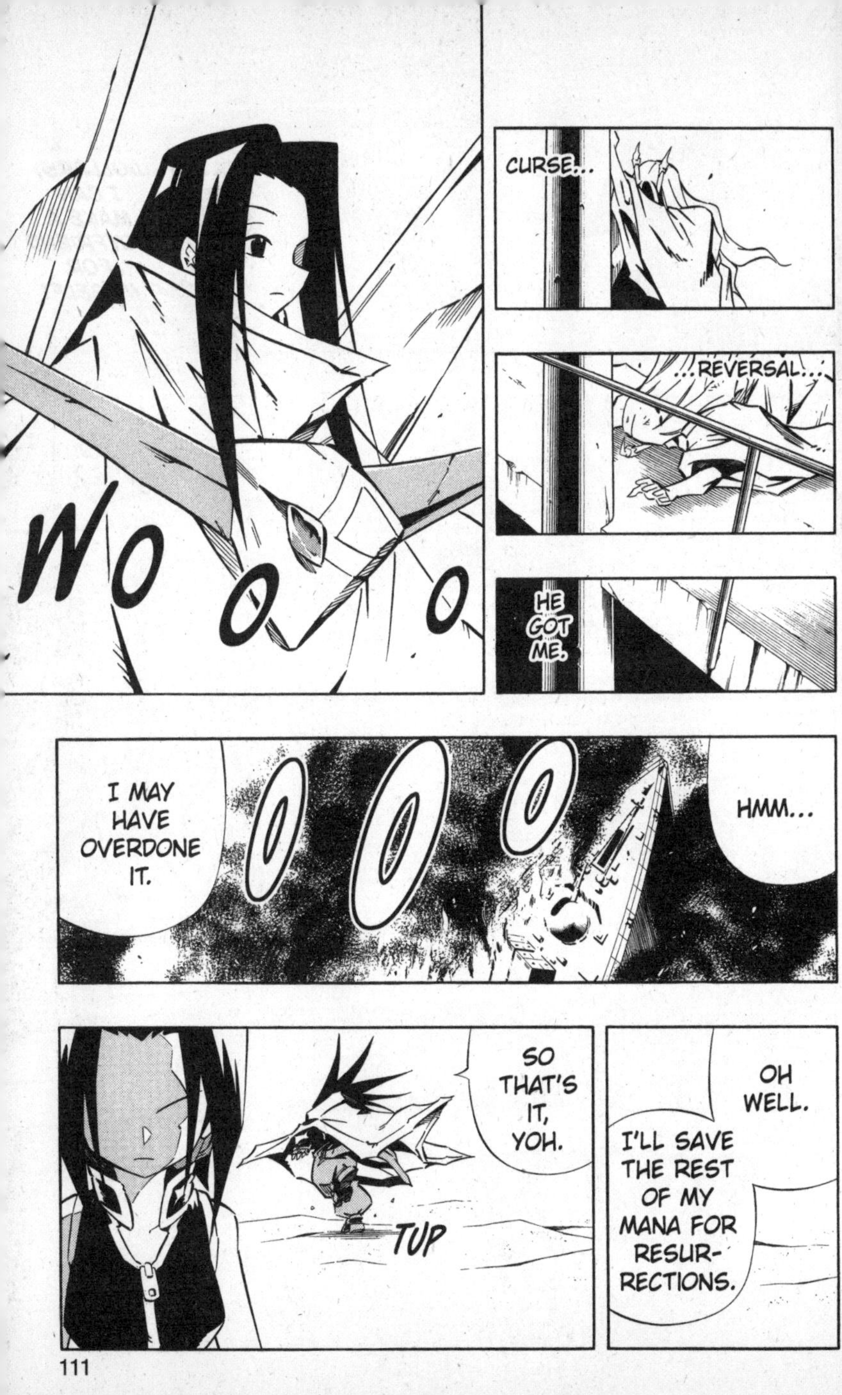
CURSE...
...REVERSAL...
HE GOT ME.
WOOO
HMM...
OOO
I MAY HAVE OVERDONE IT.
OH WELL.
I'LL SAVE THE REST OF MY MANA FOR RESURRECTIONS.
SO THAT'S IT, YOH.
TUP

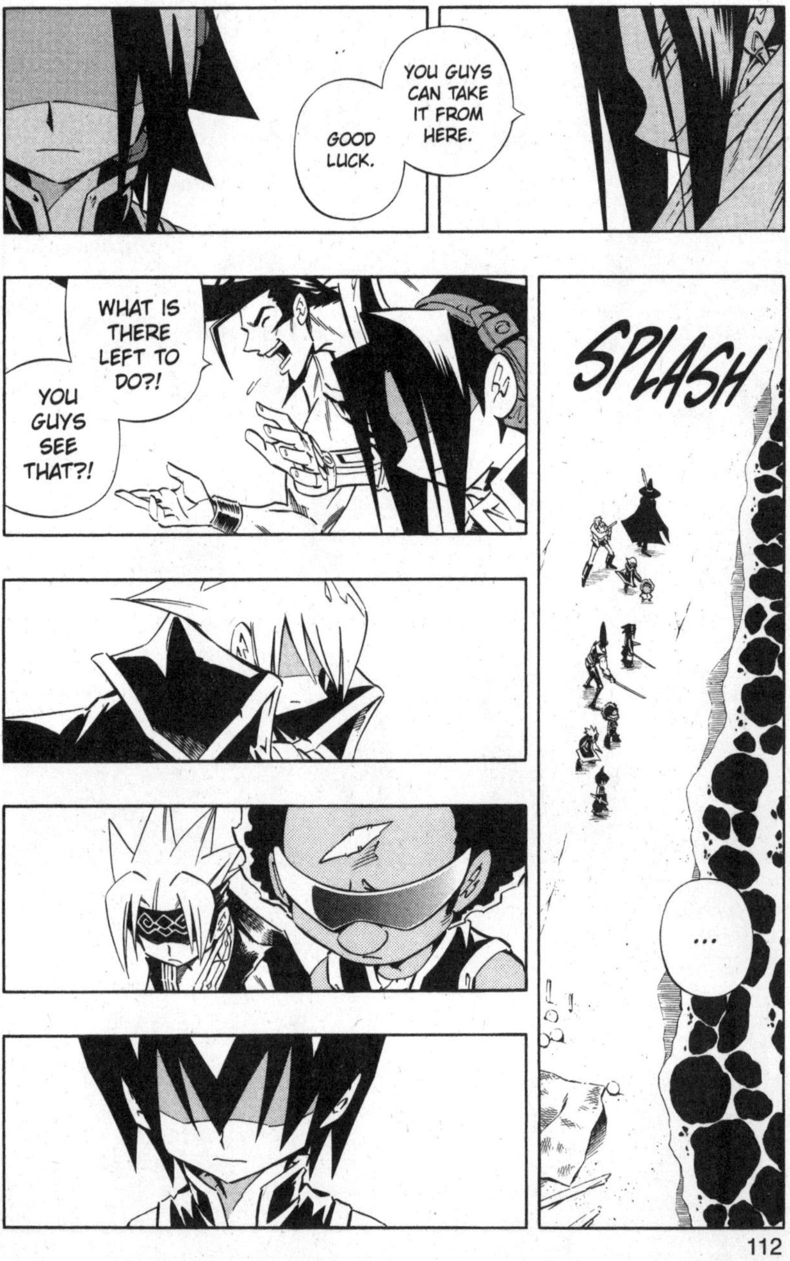
YOU GUYS CAN TAKE IT FROM HERE.
GOOD LUCK.
SPLASH
...
WHAT IS THERE LEFT TO DO?!
YOU GUYS SEE THAT?!

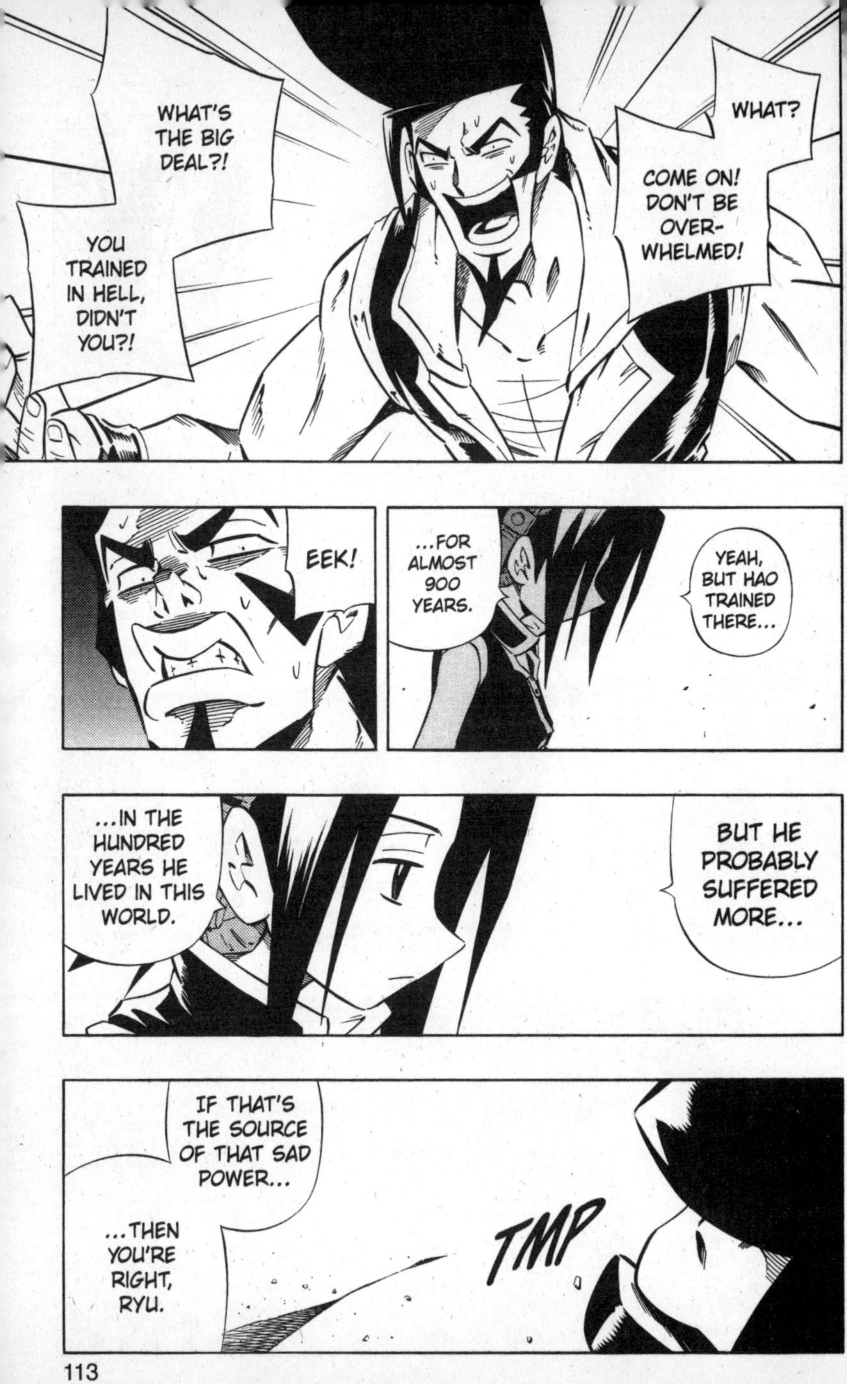
WHAT?
COME ON! DON'T BE OVER-WHELMED!
WHAT'S THE BIG DEAL?!
YOU TRAINED IN HELL, DIDN'T YOU?!
YEAH, BUT HAO TRAINED THERE...
...FOR ALMOST 900 YEARS.
EEK!
BUT HE PROBABLY SUFFERED MORE...
...IN THE HUNDRED YEARS HE LIVED IN THIS WORLD.
TMP
IF THAT'S THE SOURCE OF THAT SAD POWER...
...THEN YOU'RE RIGHT, RYU.

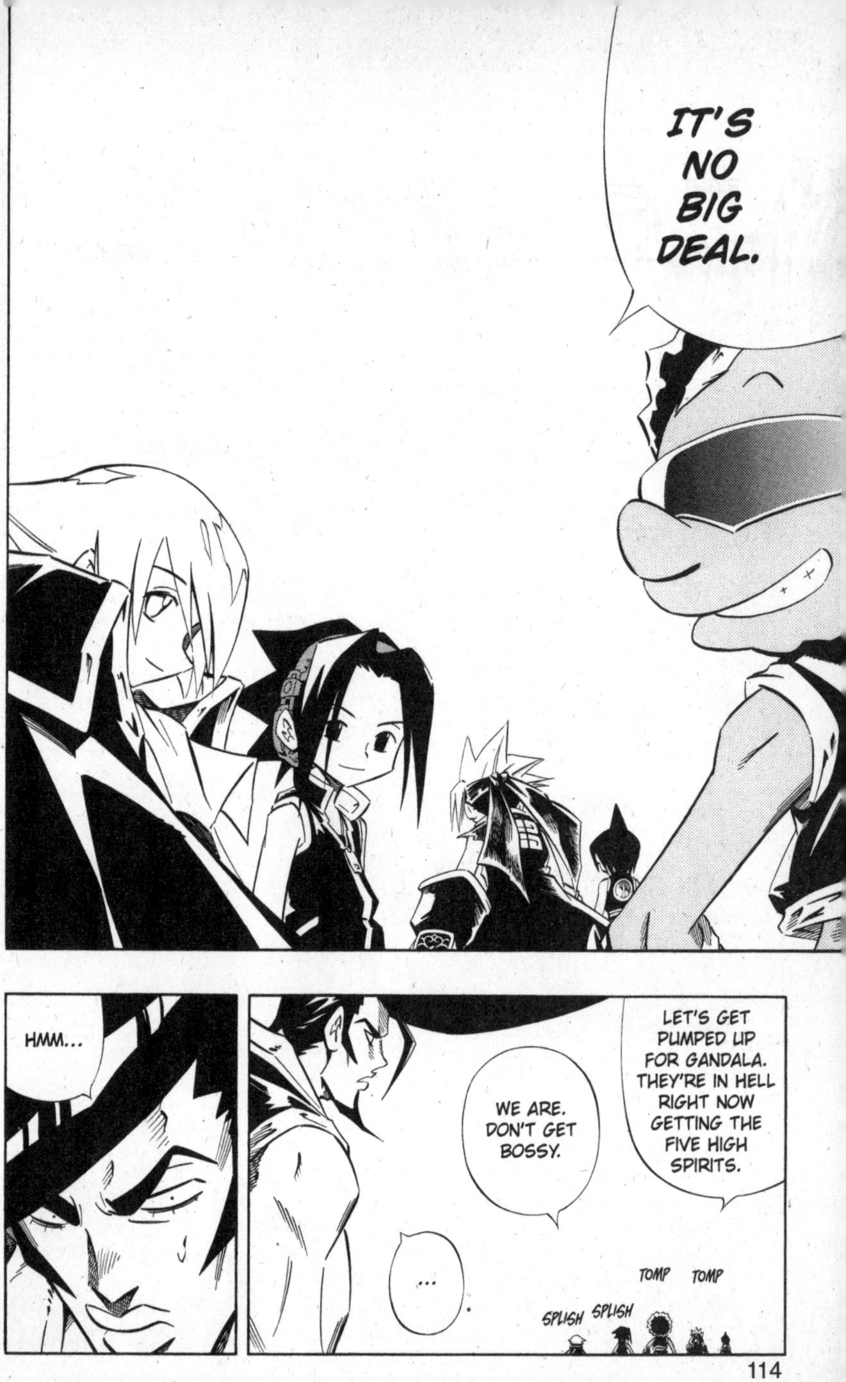
IT'S NO BIG DEAL.
LET'S GET PUMPED UP FOR GANDALA. THEY'RE IN HELL RIGHT NOW GETTING THE FIVE HIGH SPIRITS.
WE ARE. DON'T GET BOSSY.
...
TOMP TOMP
SPLISH SPLISH
HMM...

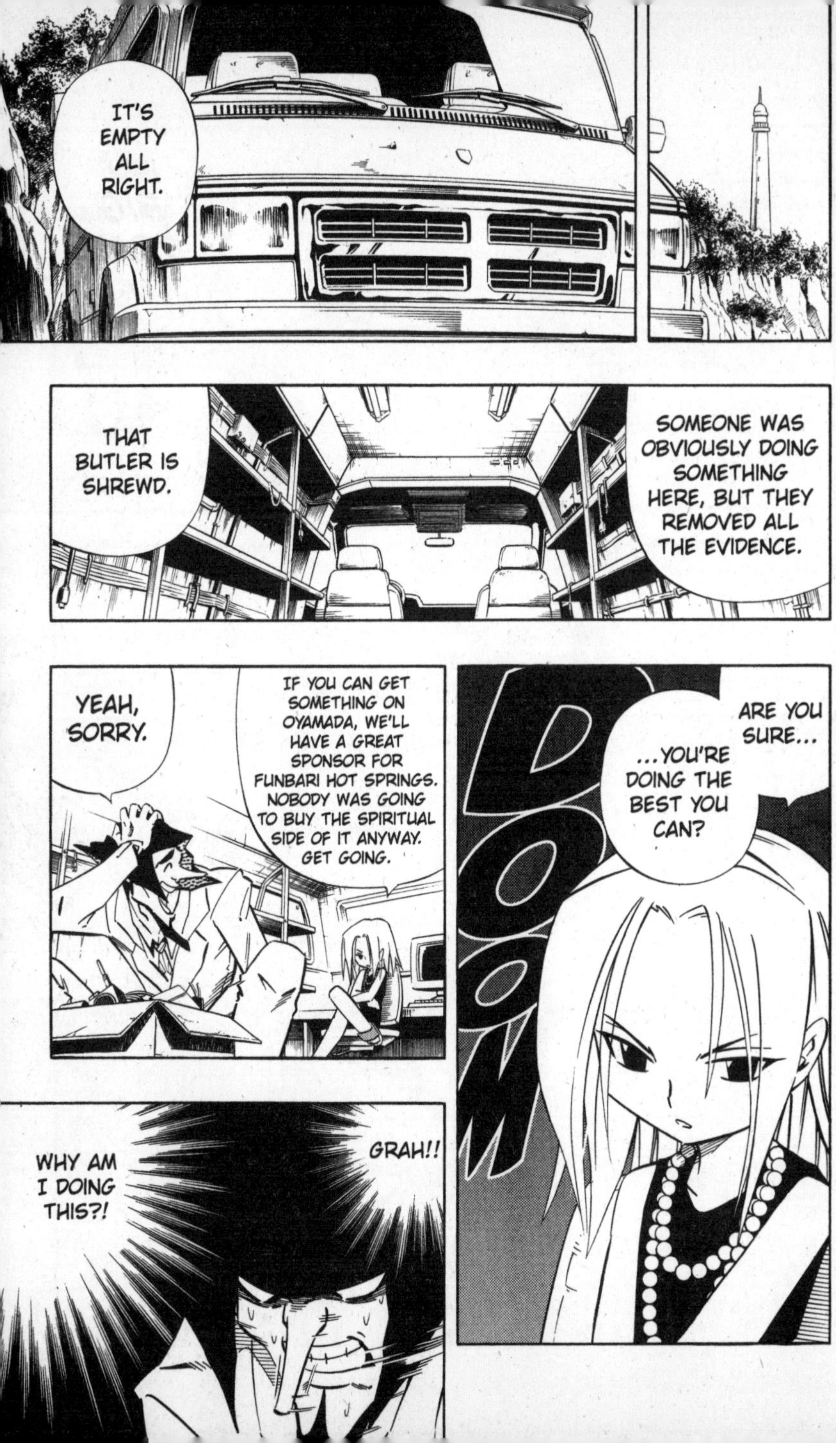
IT'S EMPTY ALL RIGHT.
SOMEONE WAS OBVIOUSLY DOING SOMETHING HERE, BUT THEY REMOVED ALL THE EVIDENCE.
THAT BUTLER IS SHREWD.
DOOOM
ARE YOU SURE...
...YOU'RE DOING THE BEST YOU CAN?
IF YOU CAN GET SOMETHING ON OYAMADA, WE'LL HAVE A GREAT SPONSOR FOR FUNBARI HOT SPRINGS. NOBODY WAS GOING TO BUY THE SPIRITUAL SIDE OF IT ANYWAY. GET GOING.
YEAH, SORRY.
GRAH!!
WHY AM I DOING THIS?!

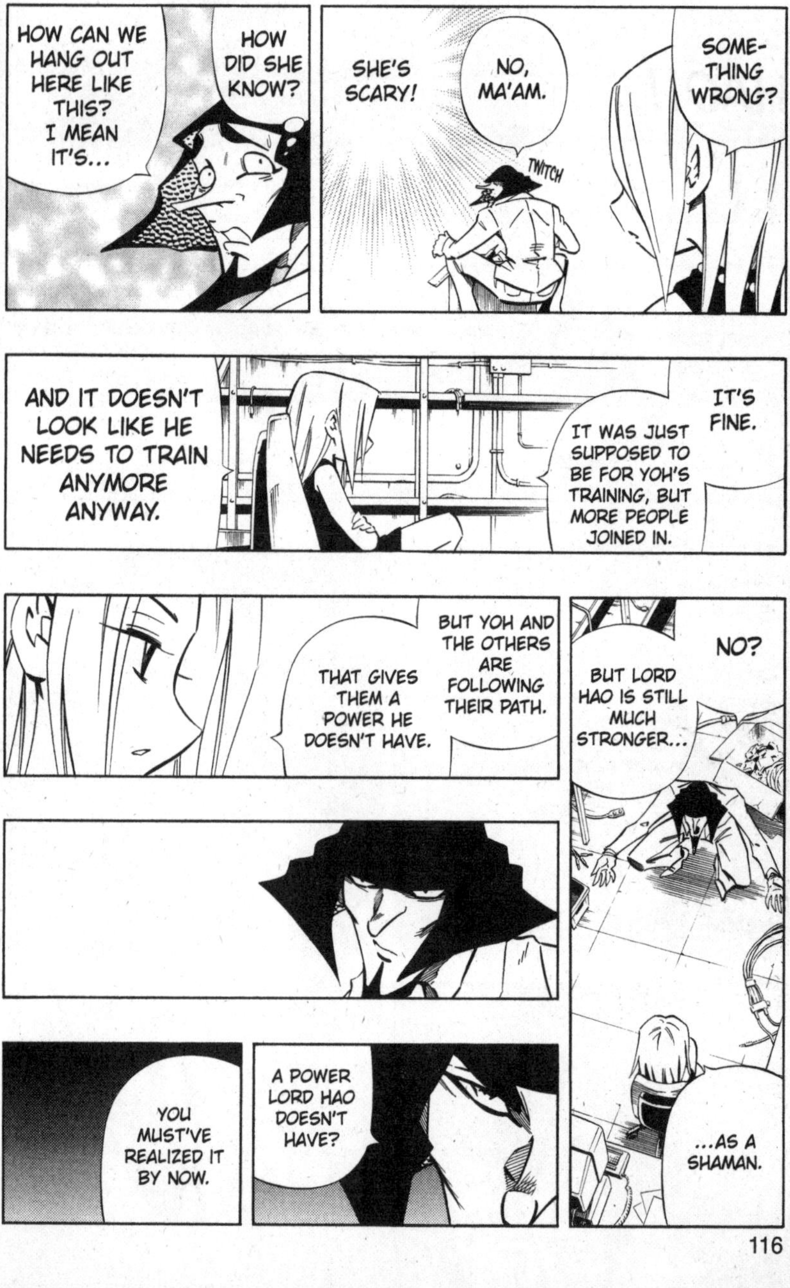
SOMETHING WRONG?
NO, MA'AM.
TWITCH
SHE'S SCARY!
HOW DID SHE KNOW?
HOW CAN WE HANG OUT HERE LIKE THIS? I MEAN IT'S...
IT'S FINE.
IT WAS JUST SUPPOSED TO BE FOR YOH'S TRAINING, BUT MORE PEOPLE JOINED IN.
AND IT DOESN'T LOOK LIKE HE NEEDS TO TRAIN ANYMORE ANYWAY.
NO?
BUT LORD HAO IS STILL MUCH STRONGER...
...AS A SHAMAN.
BUT YOH AND THE OTHERS ARE FOLLOWING THEIR PATH.
THAT GIVES THEM A POWER HE DOESN'T HAVE.
A POWER LORD HAO DOESN'T HAVE?
YOU MUST'VE REALIZED IT BY NOW.

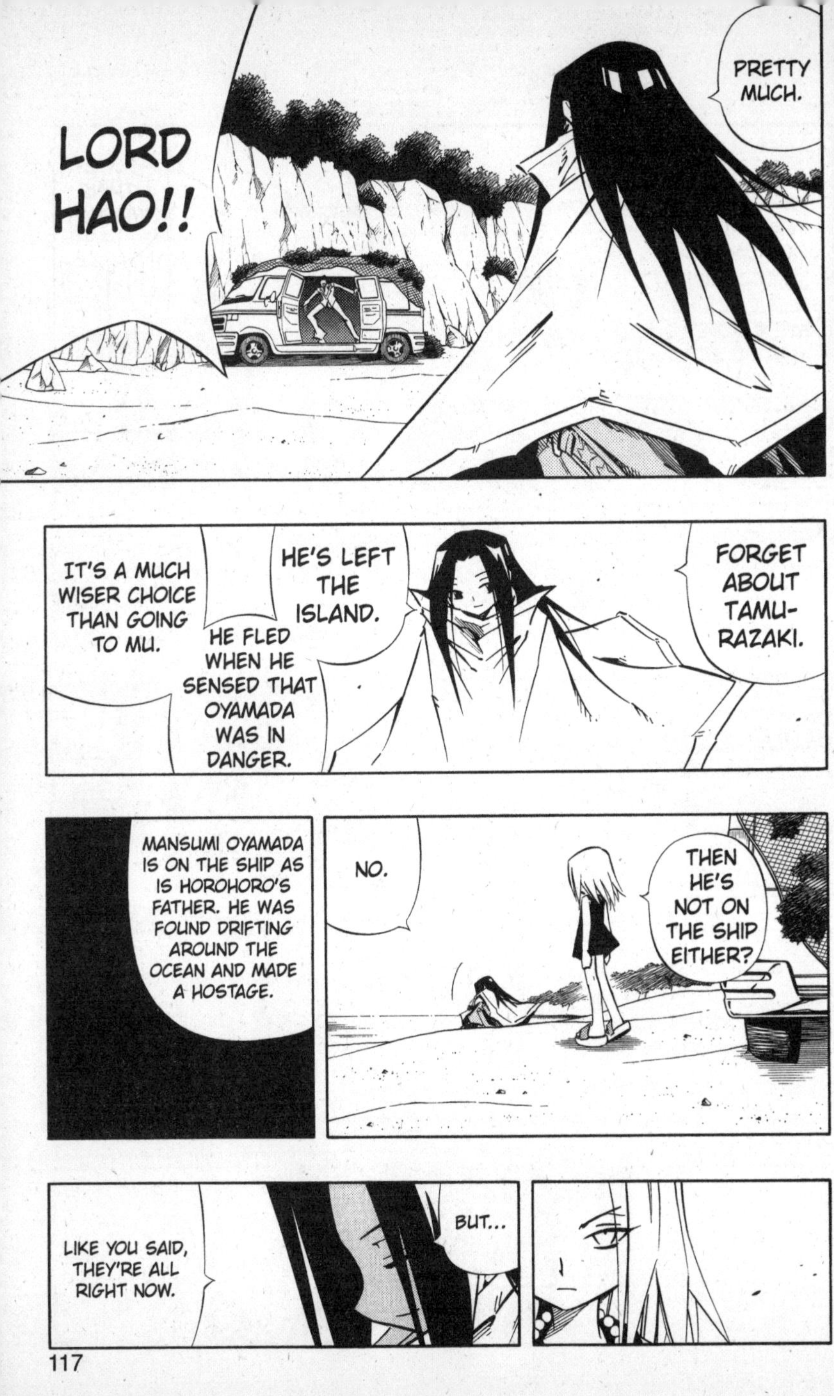
PRETTY MUCH.
LORD HAO!!
FORGET ABOUT TAMU-RAZAKI.
HE'S LEFT THE ISLAND.
HE FLED WHEN HE SENSED THAT OYAMADA WAS IN DANGER.
IT'S A MUCH WISER CHOICE THAN GOING TO MU.
THEN HE'S NOT ON THE SHIP EITHER?
NO.
MANSUMI OYAMADA IS ON THE SHIP AS IS HOROHORO'S FATHER. HE WAS FOUND DRIFTING AROUND THE OCEAN AND MADE A HOSTAGE.
BUT...
LIKE YOU SAID, THEY'RE ALL RIGHT NOW.

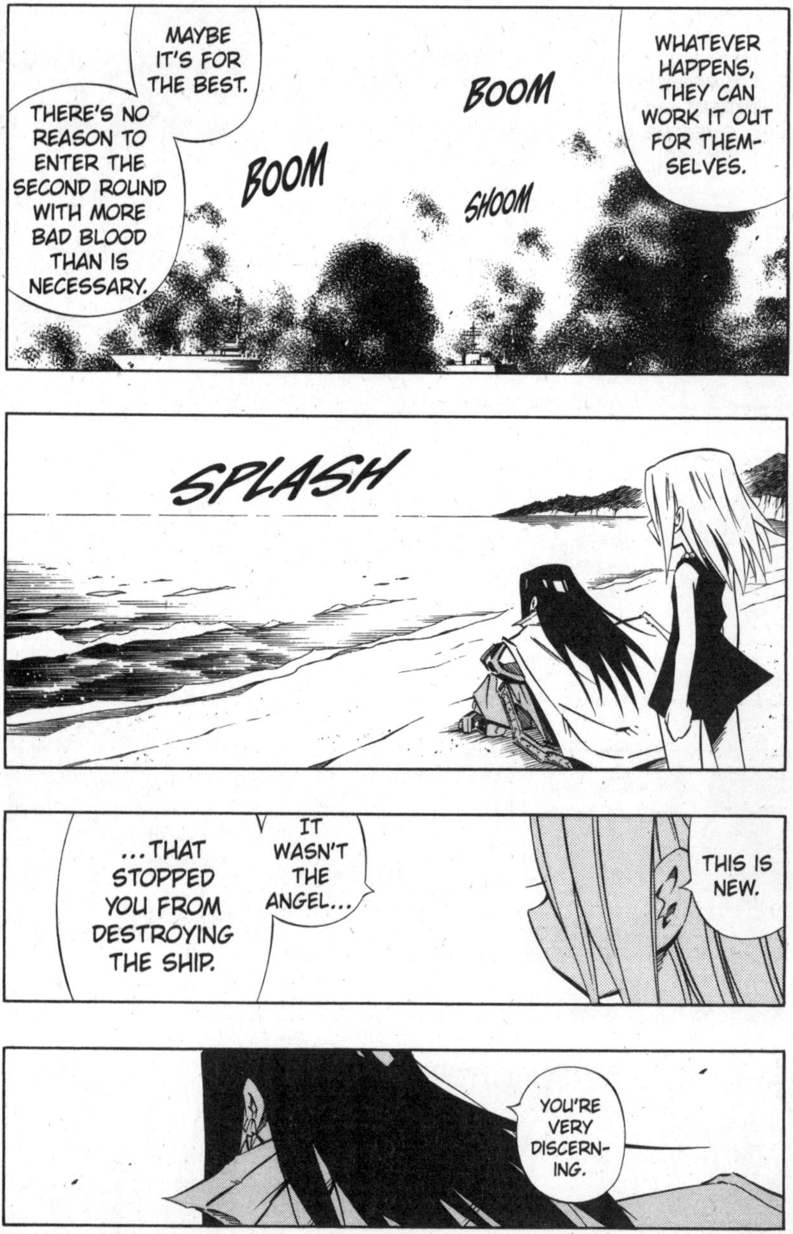
WHATEVER HAPPENS, THEY CAN WORK IT OUT FOR THEM-SELVES.
BOOM
SHOOM
BOOM
MAYBE IT'S FOR THE BEST.
THERE'S NO REASON TO ENTER THE SECOND ROUND WITH MORE BAD BLOOD THAN IS NECESSARY.
SPLASH
THIS IS NEW.
IT WASN'T THE ANGEL...
...THAT STOPPED YOU FROM DESTROYING THE SHIP.
YOU'RE VERY DISCERN-ING.

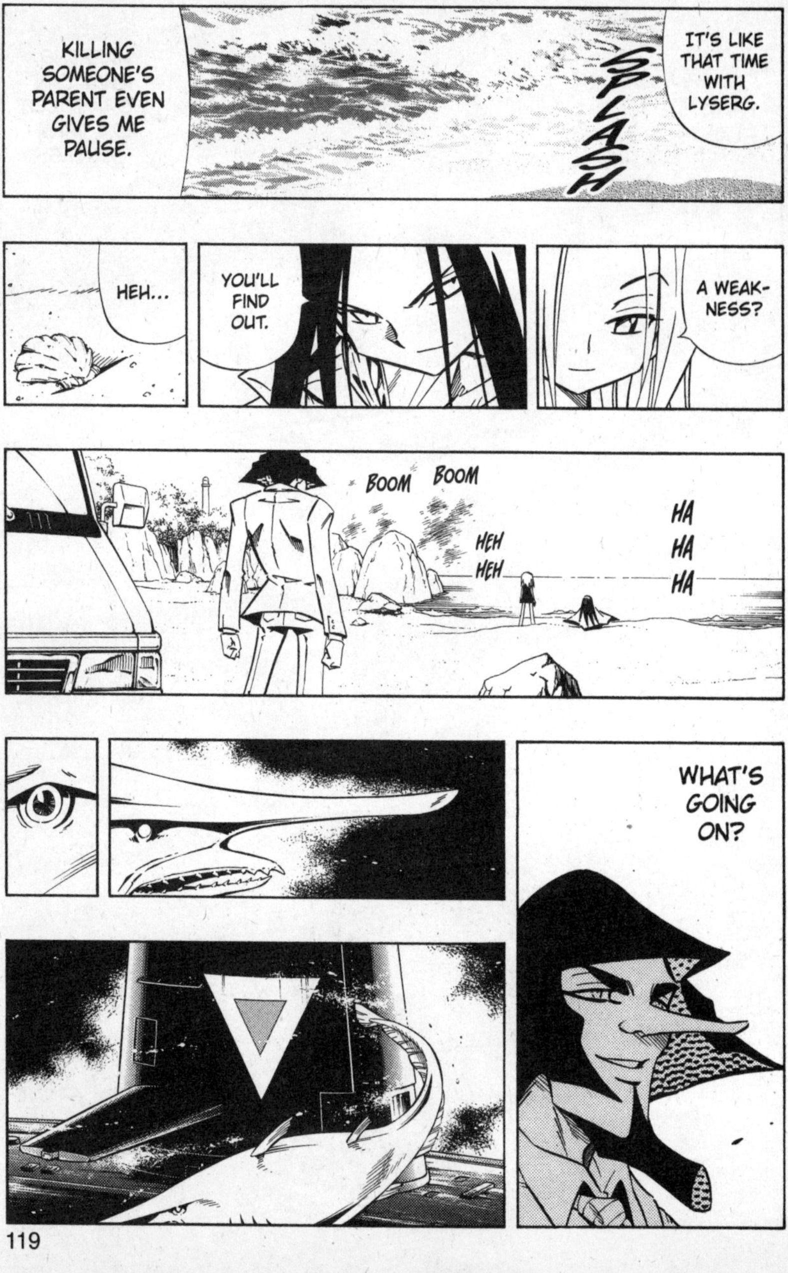
IT'S LIKE THAT TIME WITH LYSERG.
SPLASH
KILLING SOMEONE'S PARENT EVEN GIVES ME PAUSE.
A WEAK-NESS?
YOU'LL FIND OUT.
HEH...
HA HA HA
BOOM BOOM
HEH HEH
WHAT'S GOING ON?

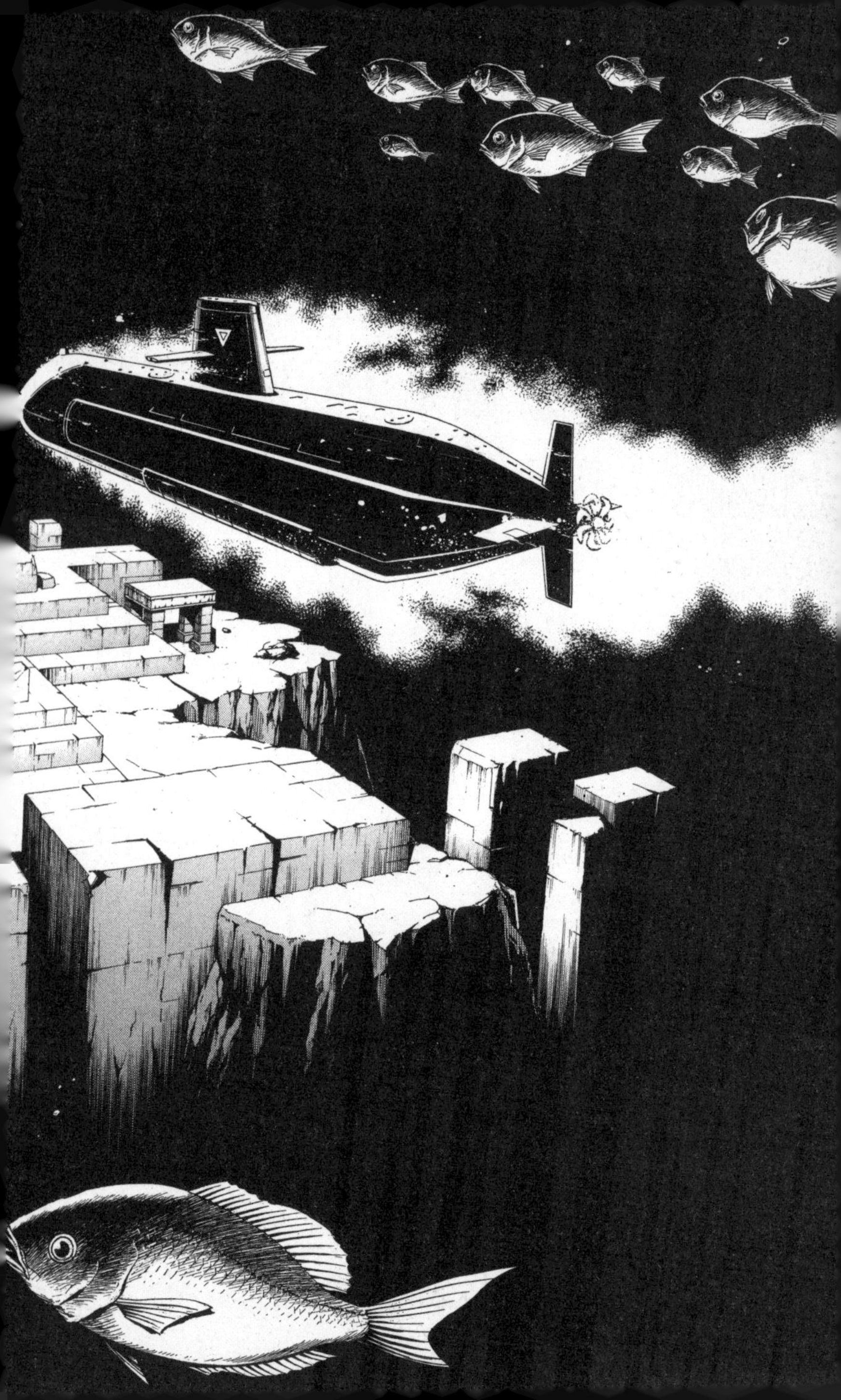

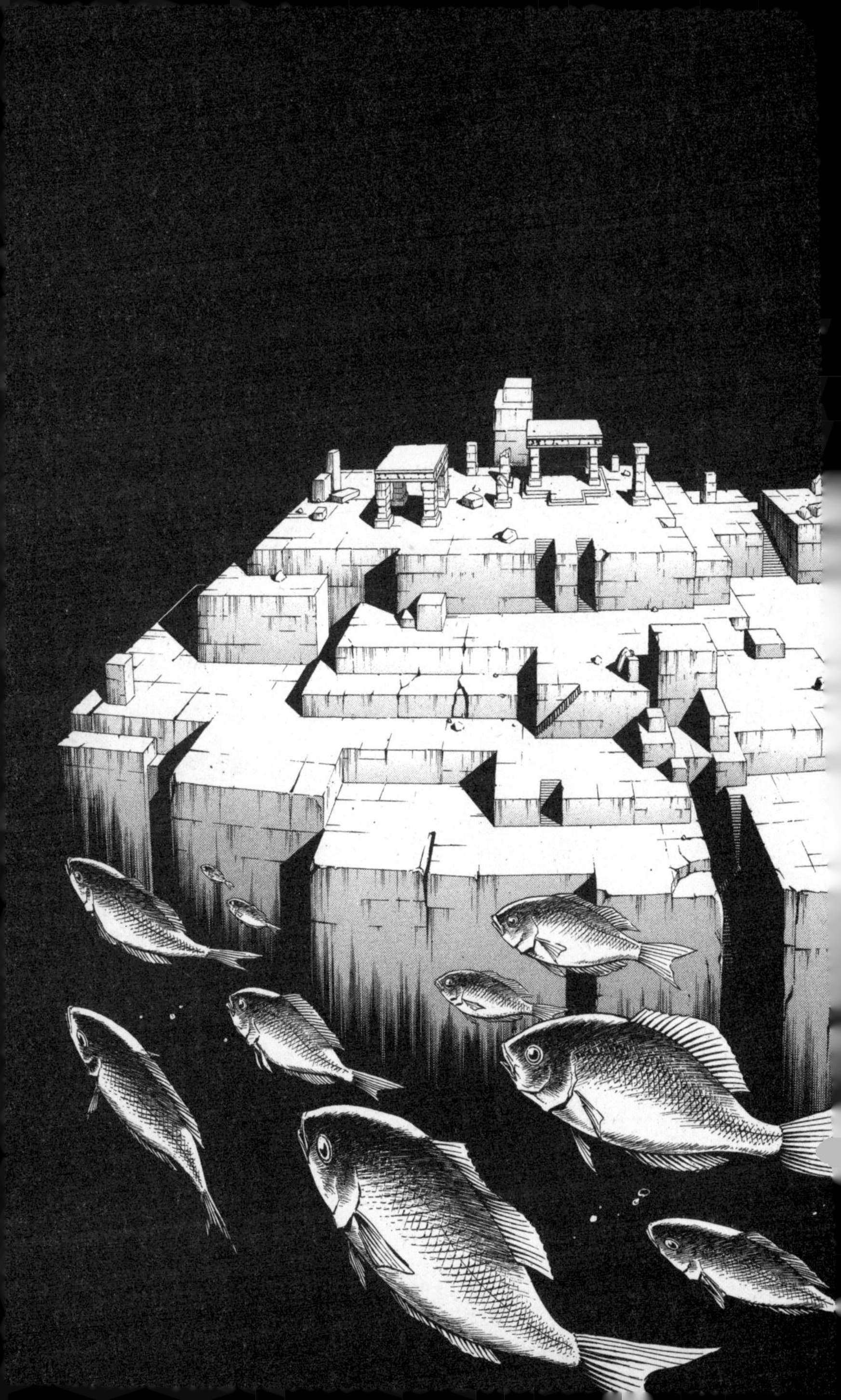

SHAMAN KING CHARACTER FILE No.155

天野輝子
TERUKO AMANO

2001
(JAN)

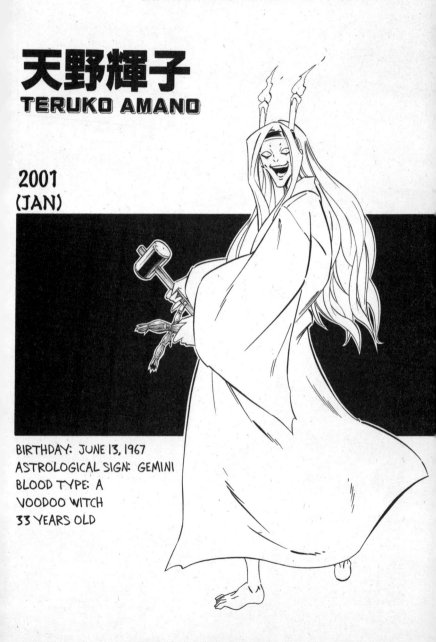

BIRTHDAY: JUNE 13, 1967
ASTROLOGICAL SIGN: GEMINI
BLOOD TYPE: A
VOODOO WITCH
33 YEARS OLD

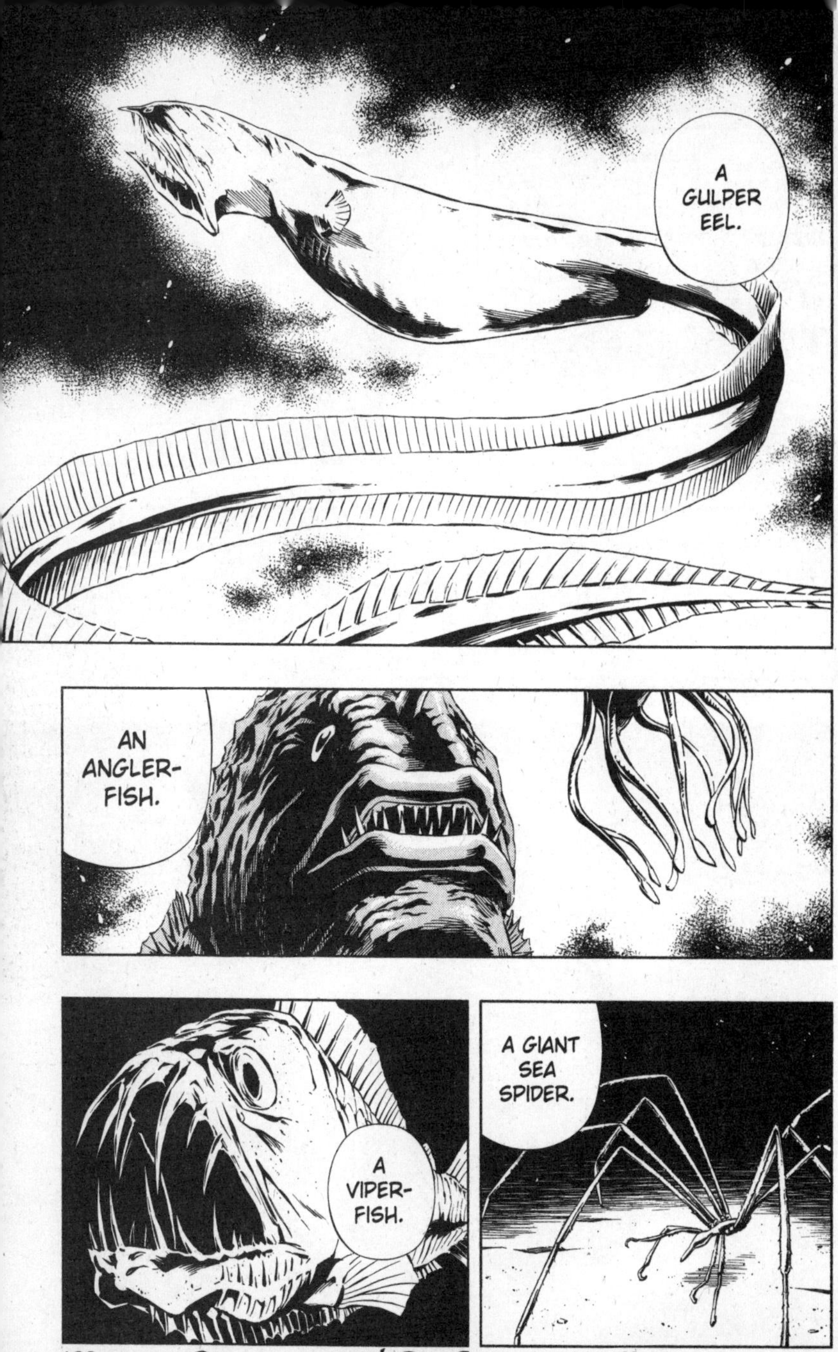
A GULPER EEL.
AN ANGLER-FISH.
A GIANT SEA SPIDER.
A VIPER-FISH.

Reincarnation 264: The Crowning of the King

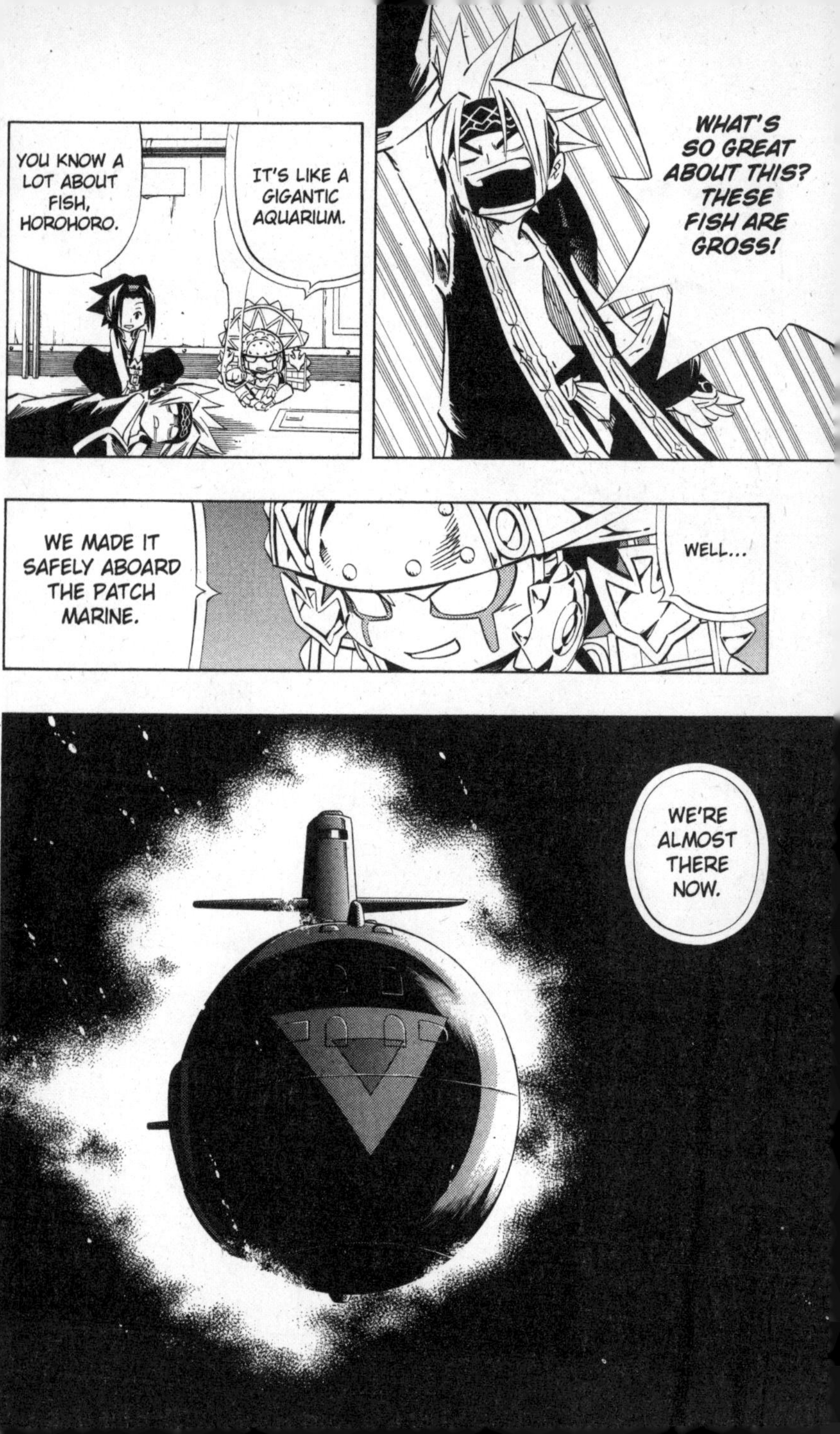
WHAT'S SO GREAT ABOUT THIS? THESE FISH ARE GROSS!
IT'S LIKE A GIGANTIC AQUARIUM.
YOU KNOW A LOT ABOUT FISH, HOROHORO.
WELL...
WE MADE IT SAFELY ABOARD THE PATCH MARINE.
WE'RE ALMOST THERE NOW.

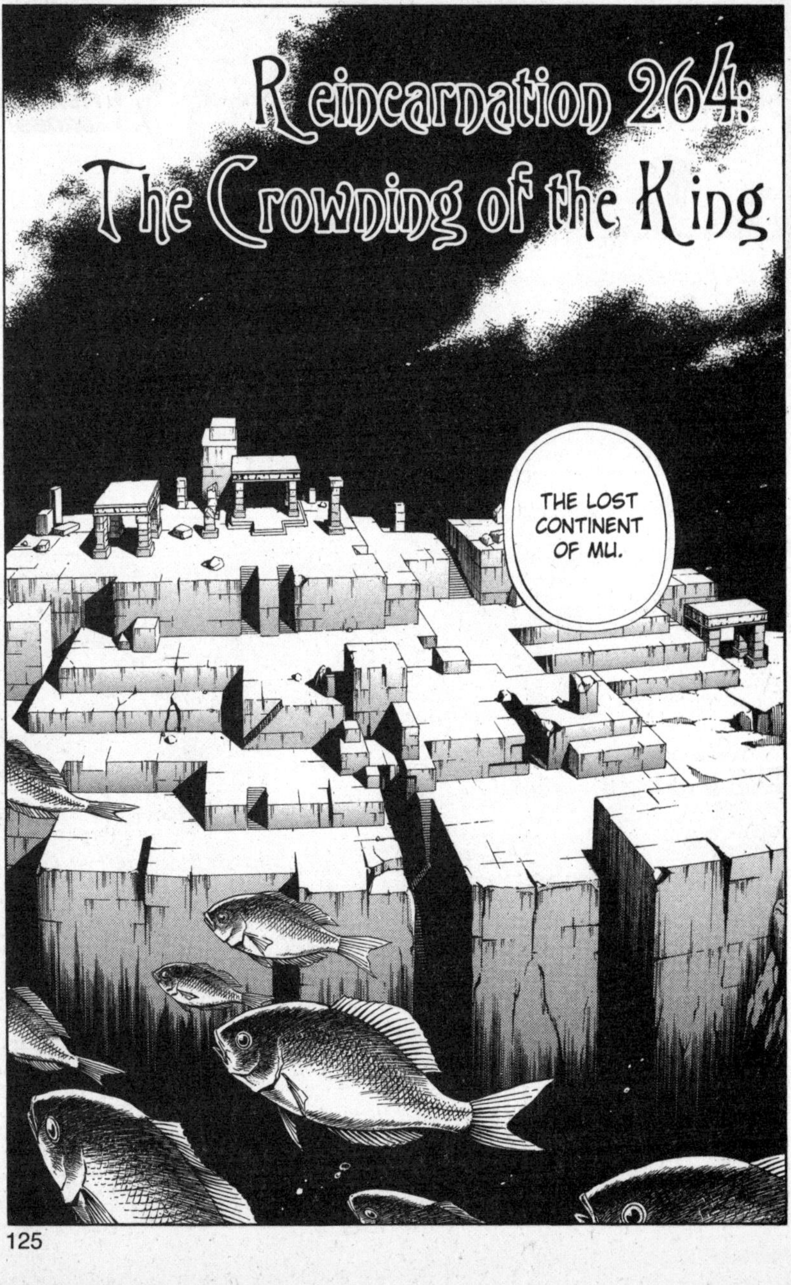
Reincarnation 264:
The Crowning of the King
THE LOST CONTINENT OF MU.

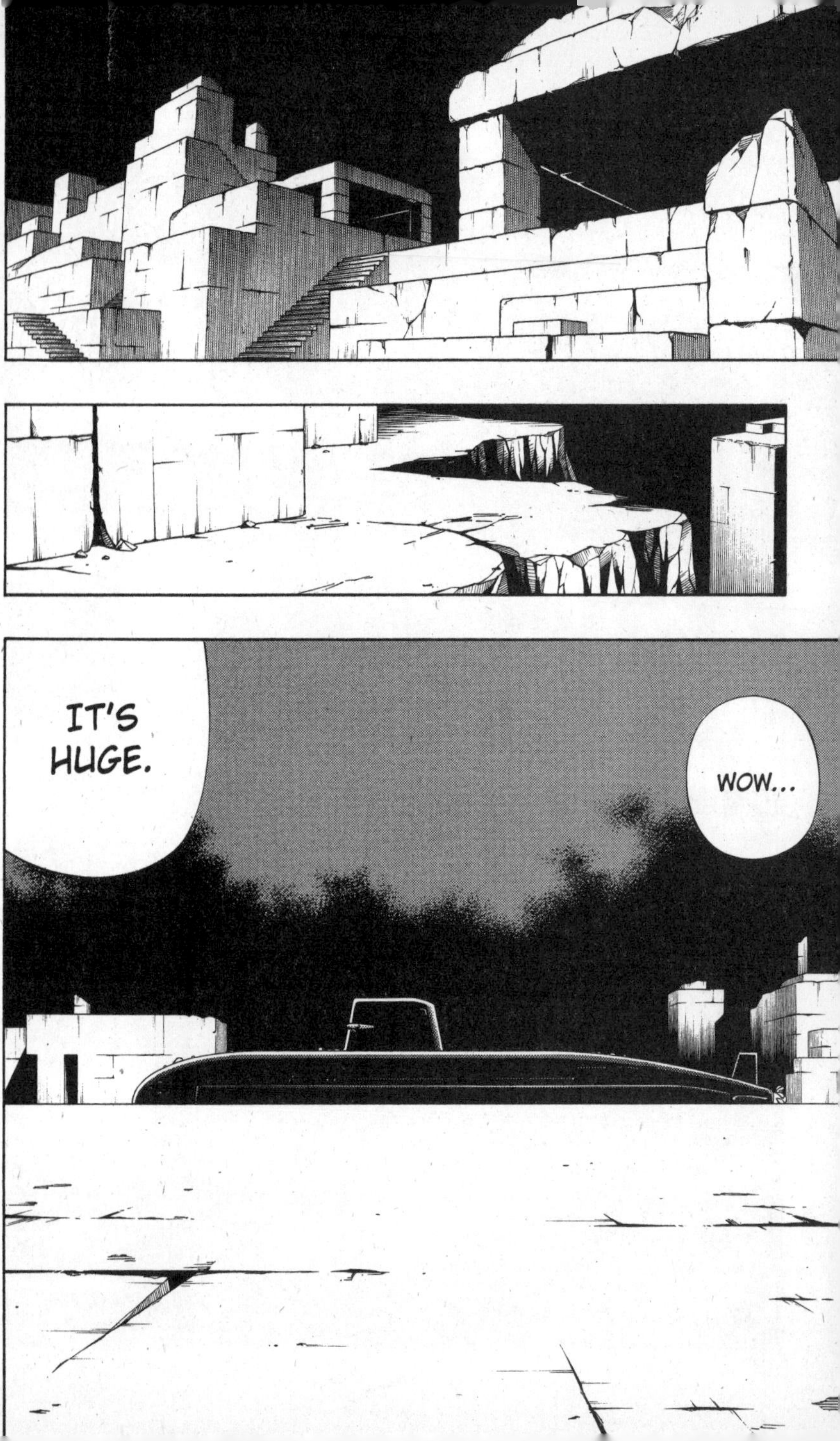
WOW...
IT'S HUGE.

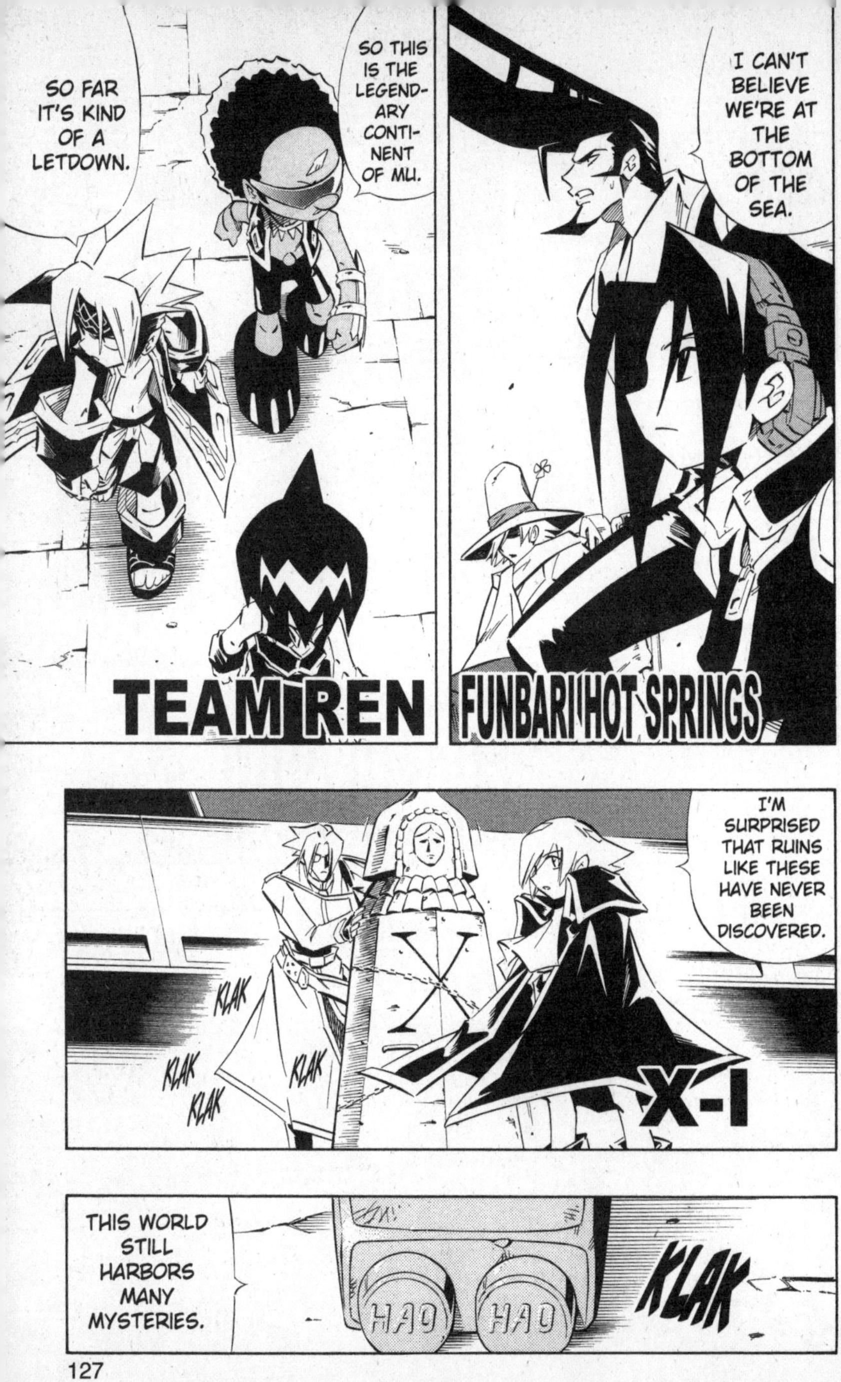
I CAN'T BELIEVE WE'RE AT THE BOTTOM OF THE SEA.
FUNBARI HOT SPRINGS
SO THIS IS THE LEGENDARY CONTINENT OF MU.
SO FAR IT'S KIND OF A LETDOWN.
TEAM REN
I'M SURPRISED THAT RUINS LIKE THESE HAVE NEVER BEEN DISCOVERED.
X-I
KLAK
KLAK
KLAK
KLAK
KLAK
HAO
HAO
THIS WORLD STILL HARBORS MANY MYSTERIES.

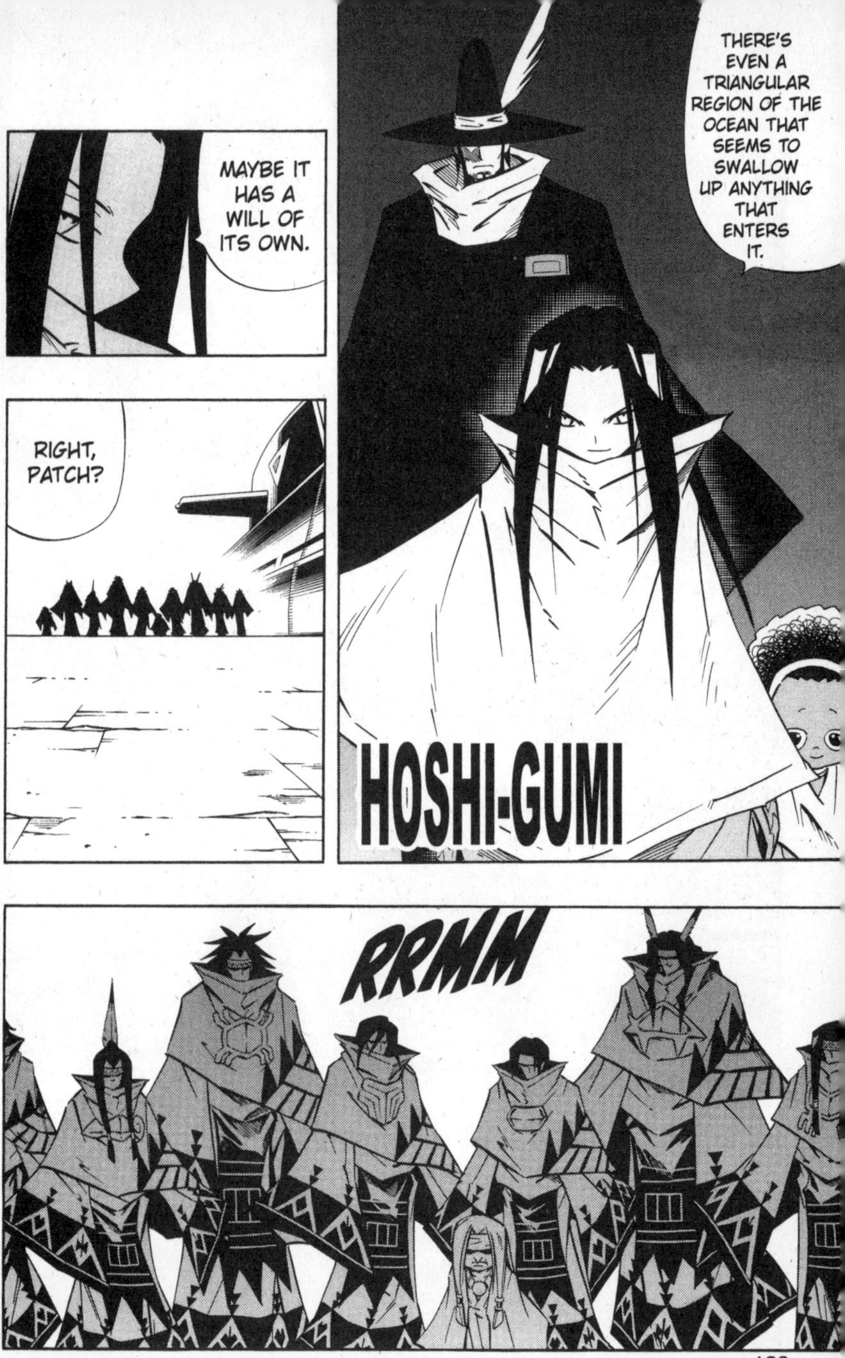
THERE'S EVEN A TRIANGULAR REGION OF THE OCEAN THAT SEEMS TO SWALLOW UP ANYTHING THAT ENTERS IT.
HOSHI-GUMI
MAYBE IT HAS A WILL OF ITS OWN.
RIGHT, PATCH?
RRMM

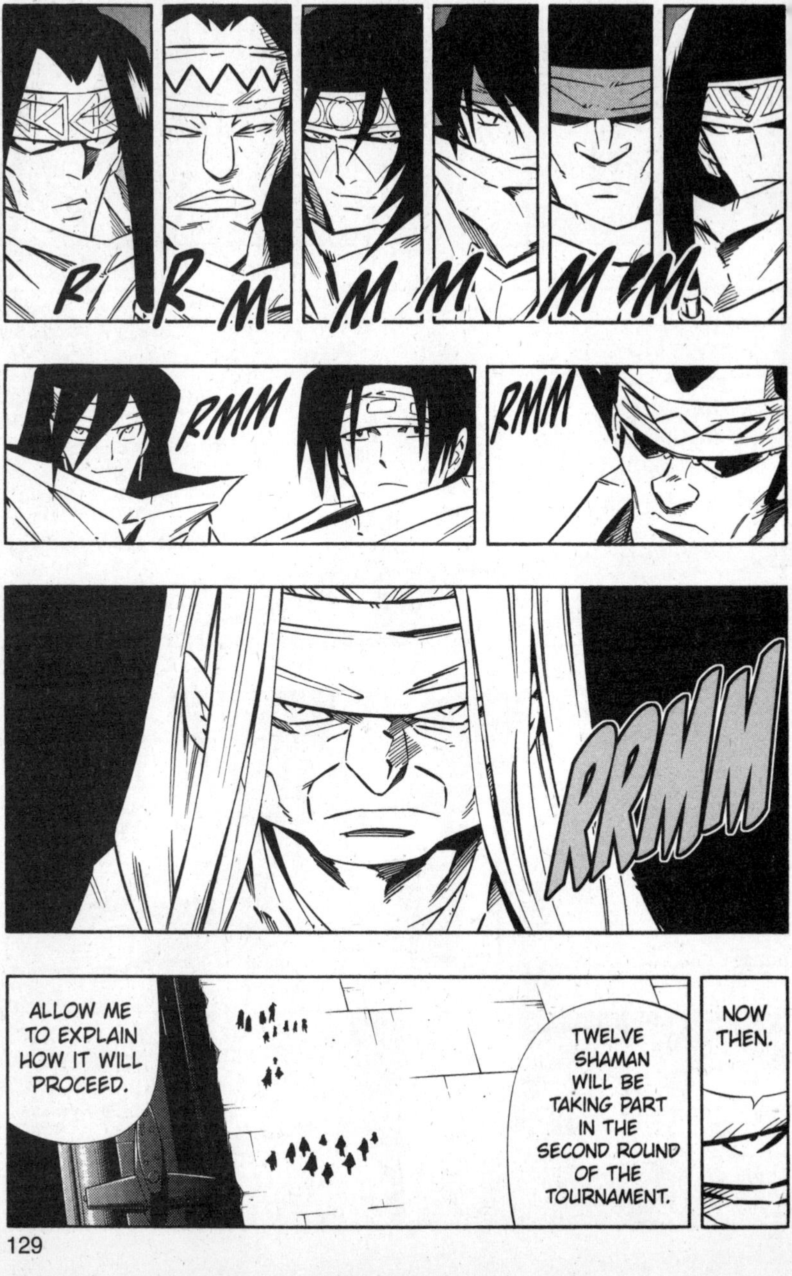
RRMMMMMMM
RMM
RMM
RRMM
NOW THEN.
TWELVE SHAMAN WILL BE TAKING PART IN THE SECOND ROUND OF THE TOURNAMENT.
ALLOW ME TO EXPLAIN HOW IT WILL PROCEED.

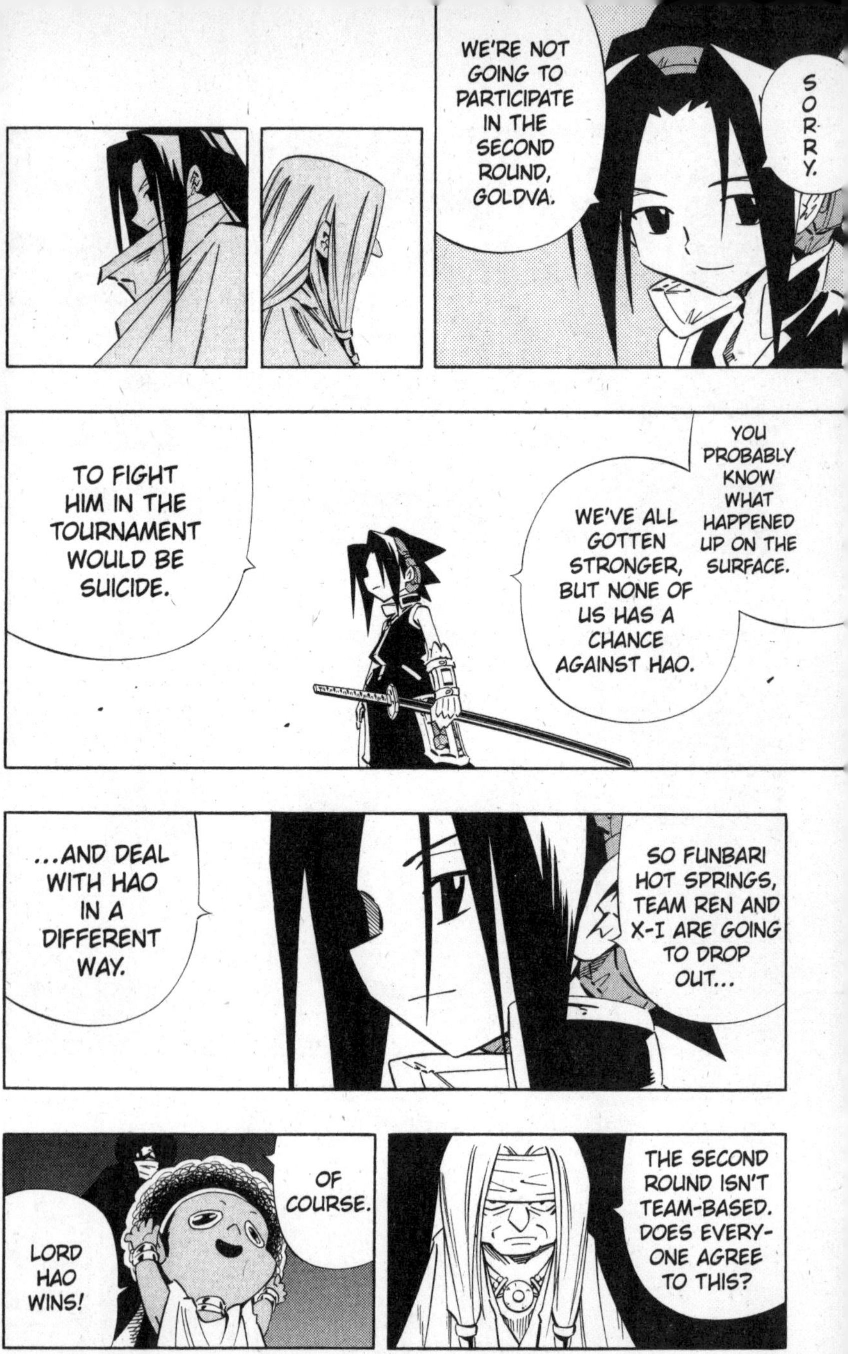
SORRY.
WE'RE NOT GOING TO PARTICIPATE IN THE SECOND ROUND, GOLDVA.
YOU PROBABLY KNOW WHAT HAPPENED UP ON THE SURFACE.
WE'VE ALL GOTTEN STRONGER, BUT NONE OF US HAS A CHANCE AGAINST HAO.
TO FIGHT HIM IN THE TOURNAMENT WOULD BE SUICIDE.
SO FUNBARI HOT SPRINGS, TEAM REN AND X-I ARE GOING TO DROP OUT...
...AND DEAL WITH HAO IN A DIFFERENT WAY.
THE SECOND ROUND ISN'T TEAM-BASED. DOES EVERY-ONE AGREE TO THIS?
OF COURSE.
LORD HAO WINS!

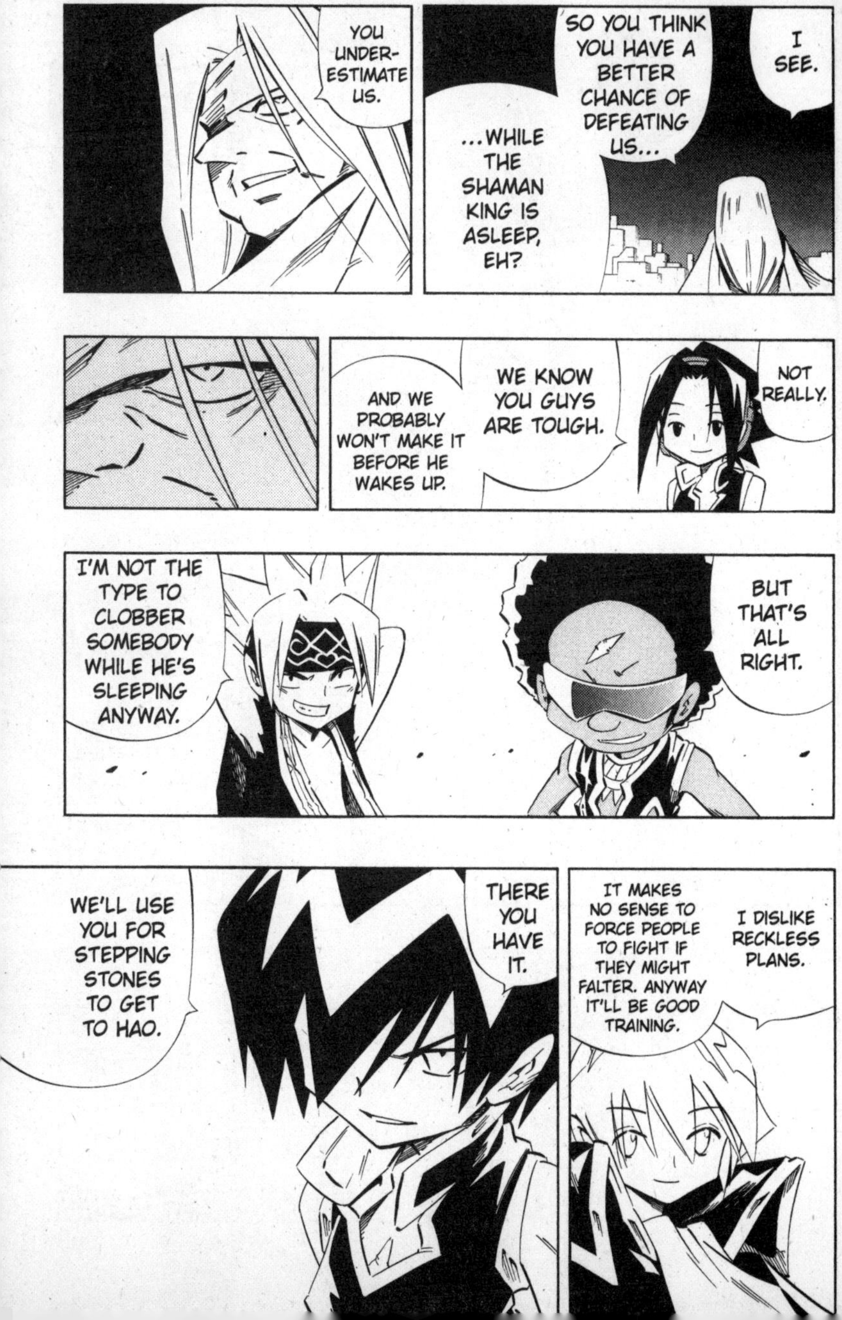
I SEE.
SO YOU THINK YOU HAVE A BETTER CHANCE OF DEFEATING US...
...WHILE THE SHAMAN KING IS ASLEEP, EH?
YOU UNDER-ESTIMATE US.
NOT REALLY.
WE KNOW YOU GUYS ARE TOUGH.
AND WE PROBABLY WON'T MAKE IT BEFORE HE WAKES UP.
BUT THAT'S ALL RIGHT.
I'M NOT THE TYPE TO CLOBBER SOMEBODY WHILE HE'S SLEEPING ANYWAY.
I DISLIKE RECKLESS PLANS.
IT MAKES NO SENSE TO FORCE PEOPLE TO FIGHT IF THEY MIGHT FALTER. ANYWAY IT'LL BE GOOD TRAINING.
THERE YOU HAVE IT.
WE'LL USE YOU FOR STEPPING STONES TO GET TO HAO.

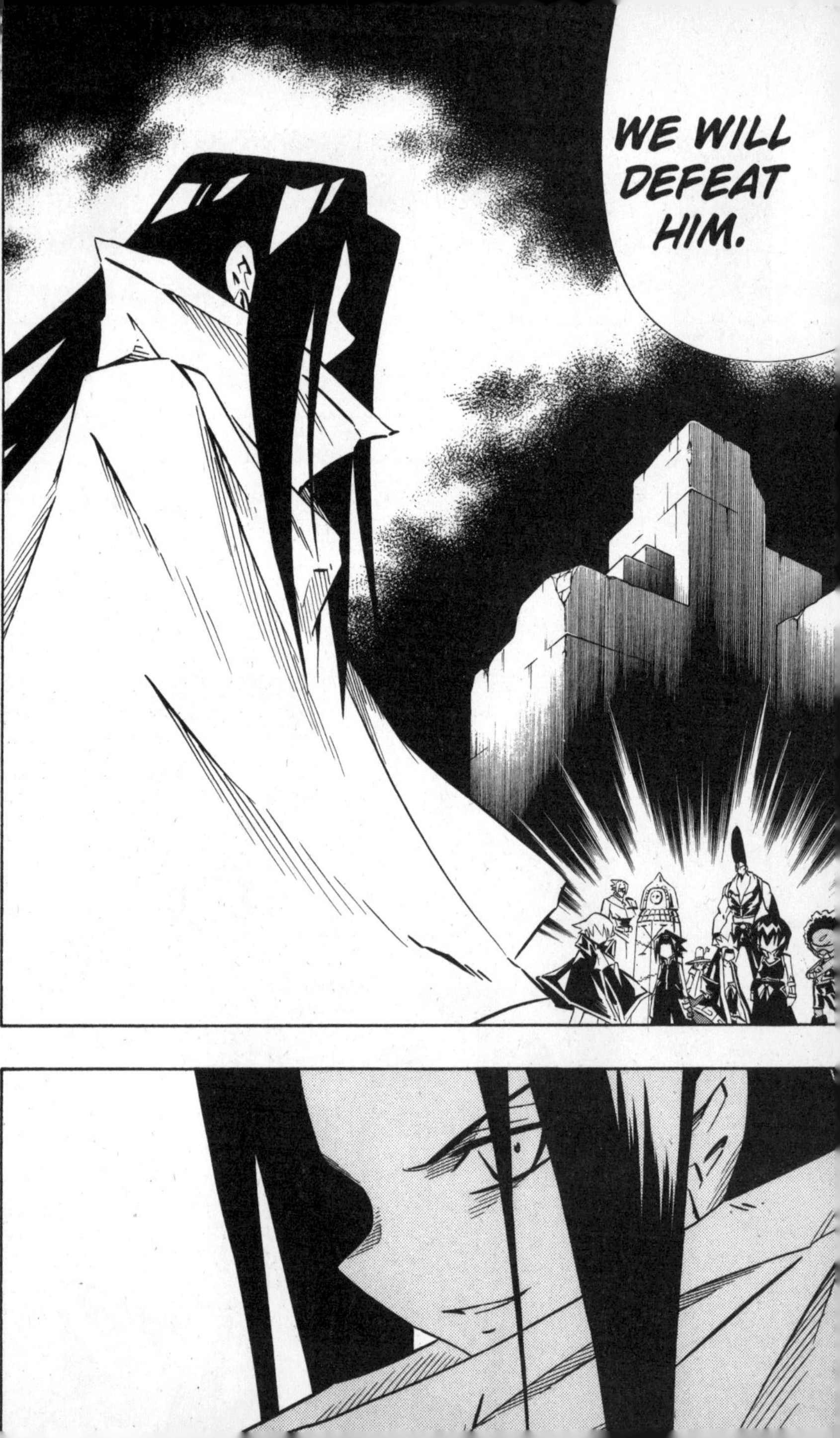
WE WILL DEFEAT HIM.

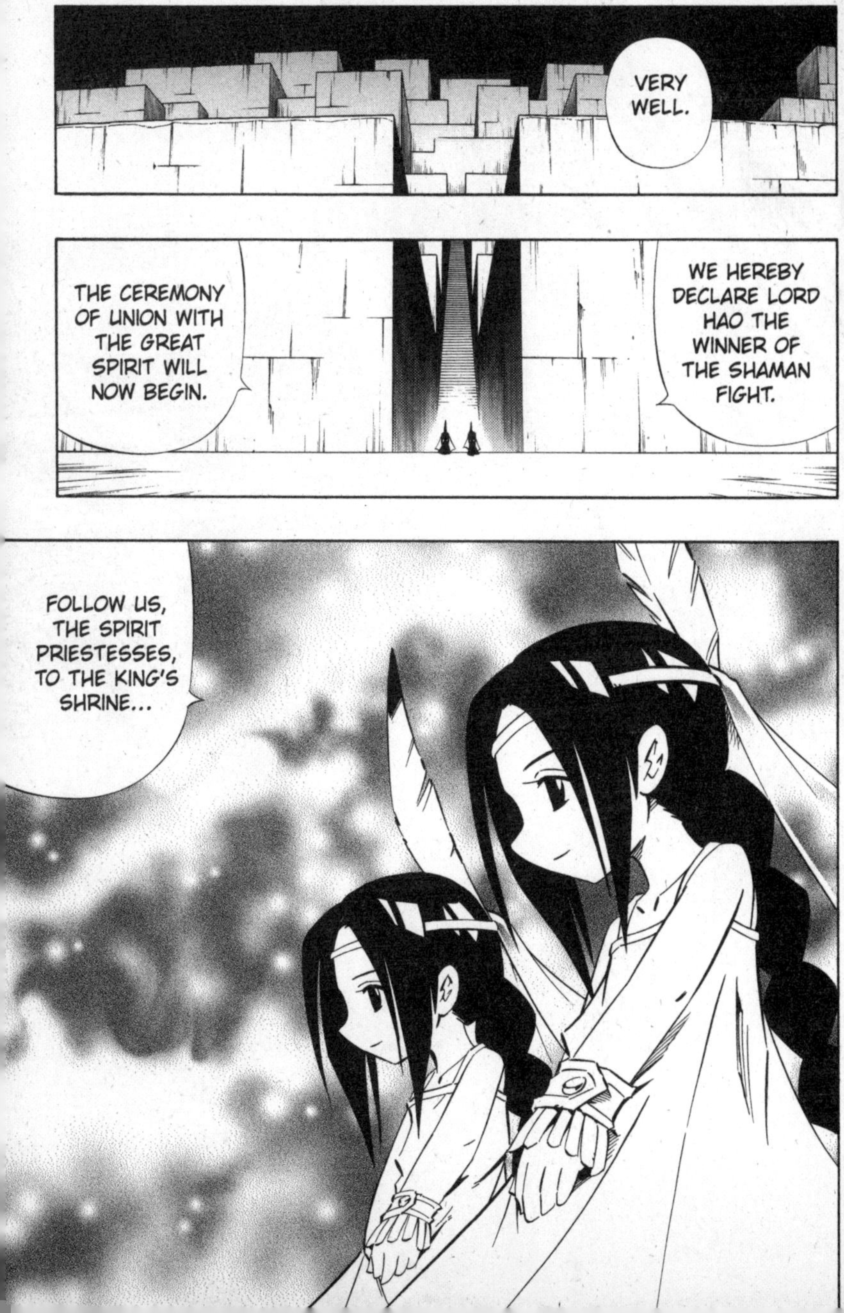
VERY WELL.
WE HEREBY DECLARE LORD HAO THE WINNER OF THE SHAMAN FIGHT.
THE CEREMONY OF UNION WITH THE GREAT SPIRIT WILL NOW BEGIN.
FOLLOW US, THE SPIRIT PRIESTESSES, TO THE KING'S SHRINE...

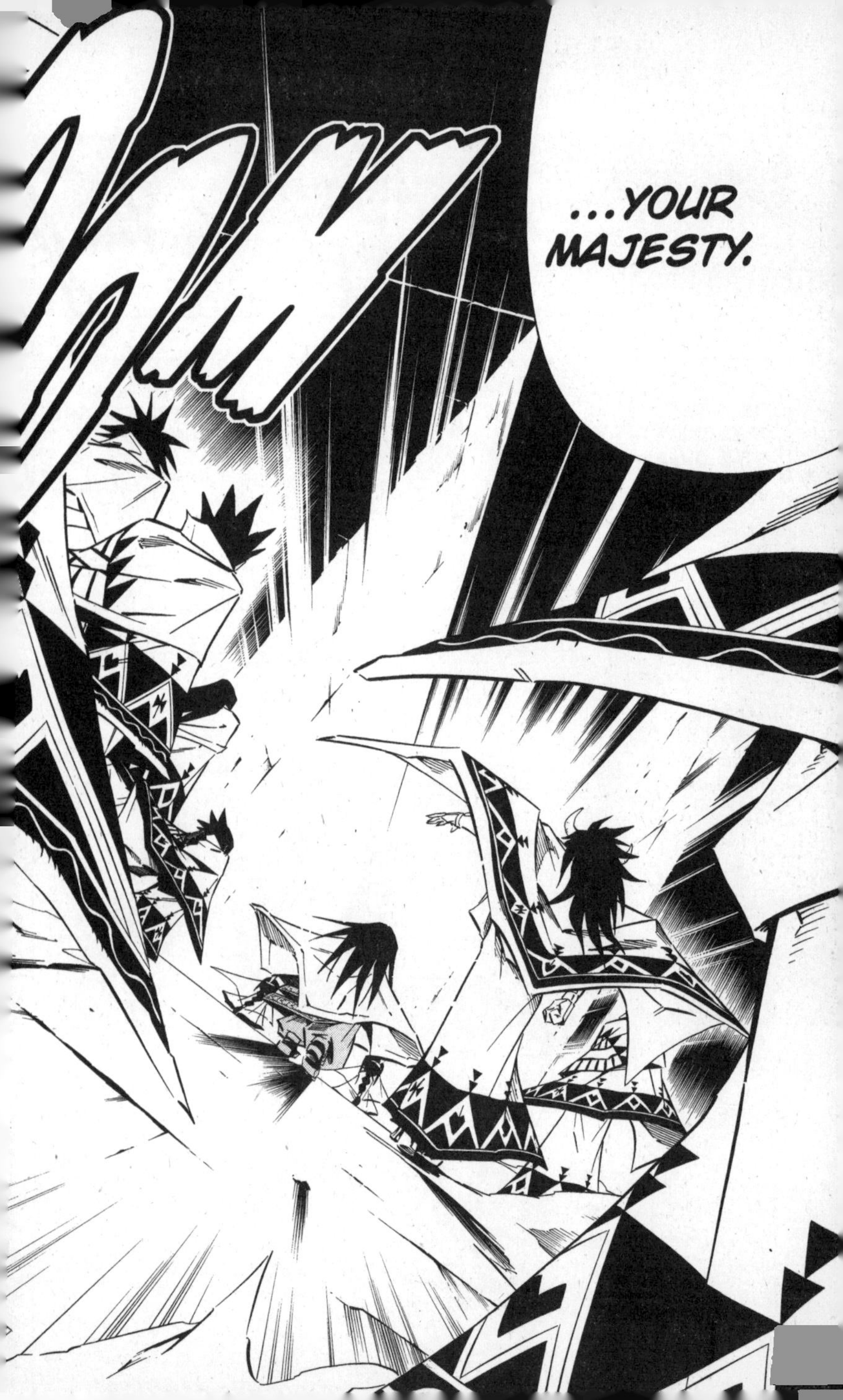
...YOUR MAJESTY.

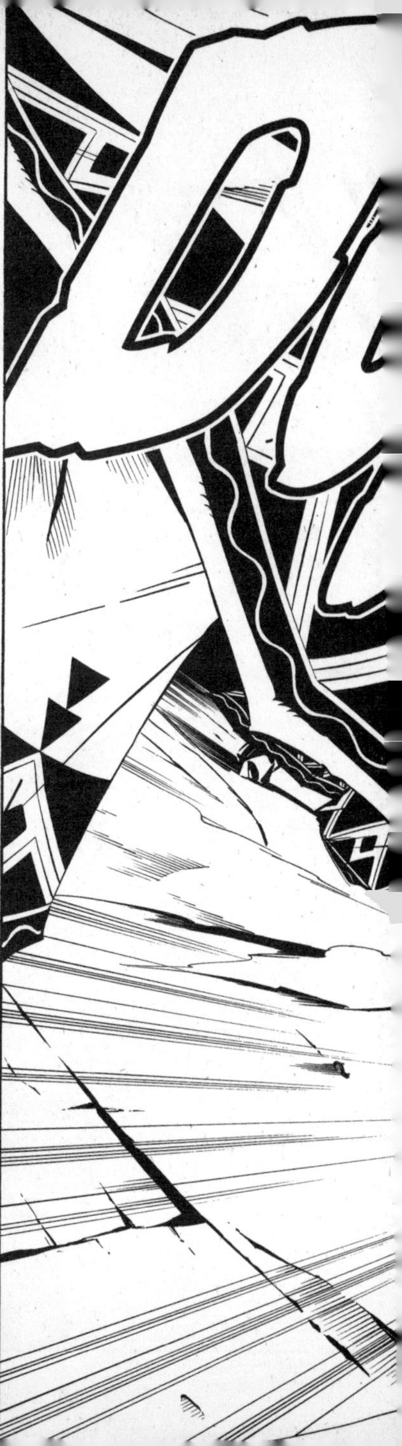

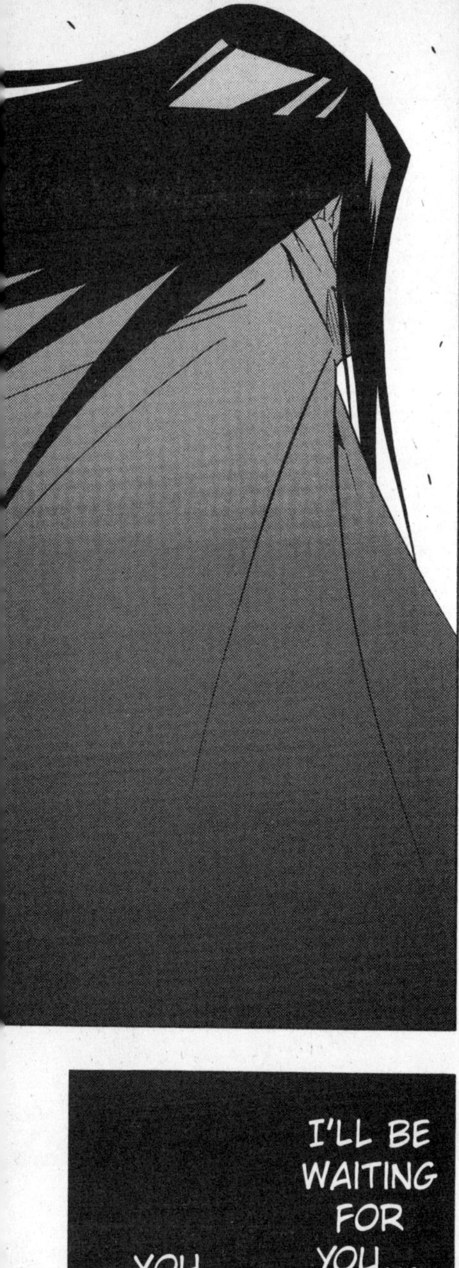
I'LL BE WAITING FOR YOU...
...YOH.

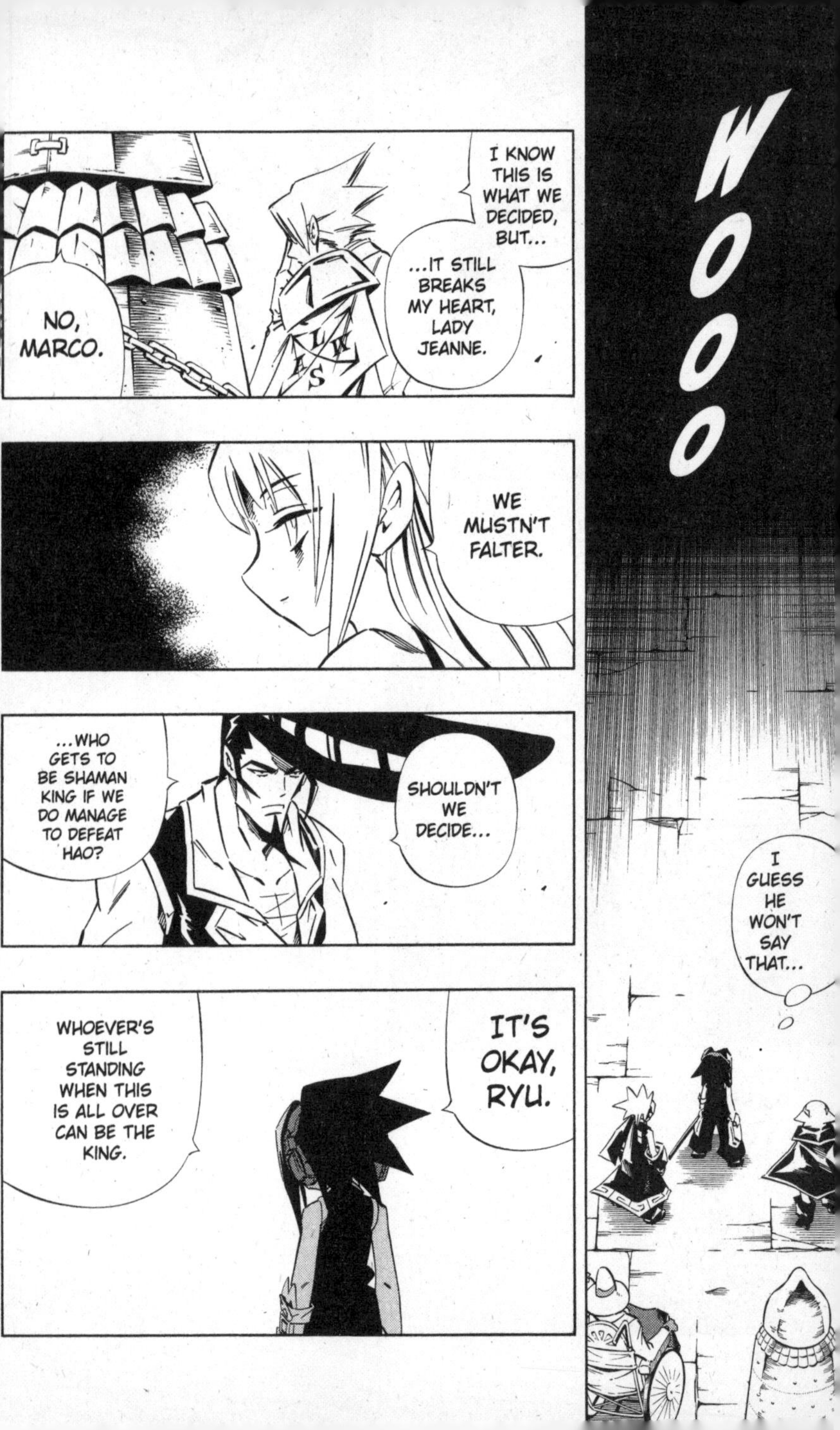
WOOOO
I GUESS HE WON'T SAY THAT...
I KNOW THIS IS WHAT WE DECIDED, BUT...
...IT STILL BREAKS MY HEART, LADY JEANNE.
NO, MARCO.
WE MUSTN'T FALTER.
SHOULDN'T WE DECIDE...
...WHO GETS TO BE SHAMAN KING IF WE DO MANAGE TO DEFEAT HAO?
IT'S OKAY, RYU.
WHOEVER'S STILL STANDING WHEN THIS IS ALL OVER CAN BE THE KING.

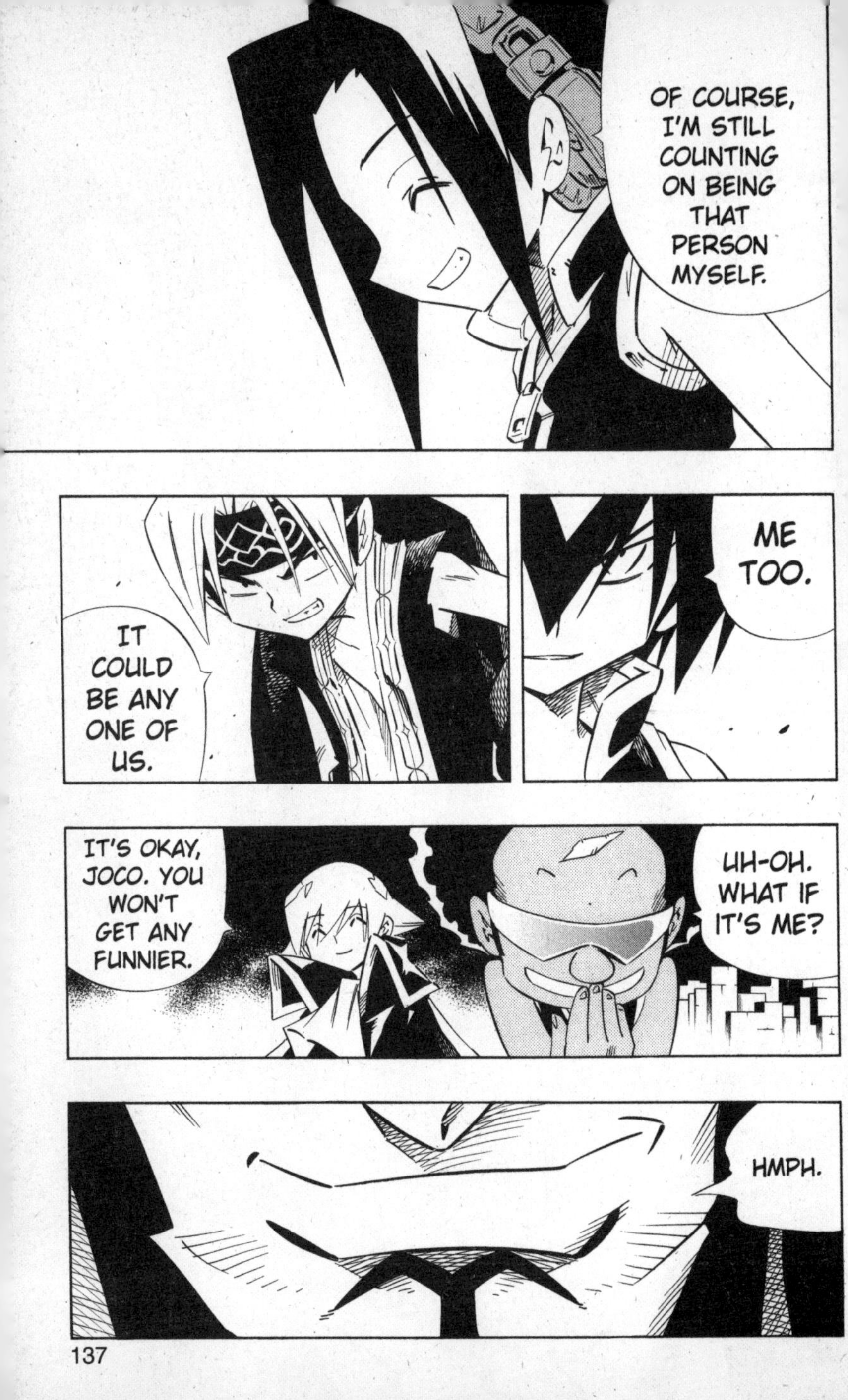
OF COURSE, I'M STILL COUNTING ON BEING THAT PERSON MYSELF.
ME TOO.
IT COULD BE ANY ONE OF US.
UH-OH. WHAT IF IT'S ME?
IT'S OKAY, JOCO. YOU WON'T GET ANY FUNNIER.
HMPH.

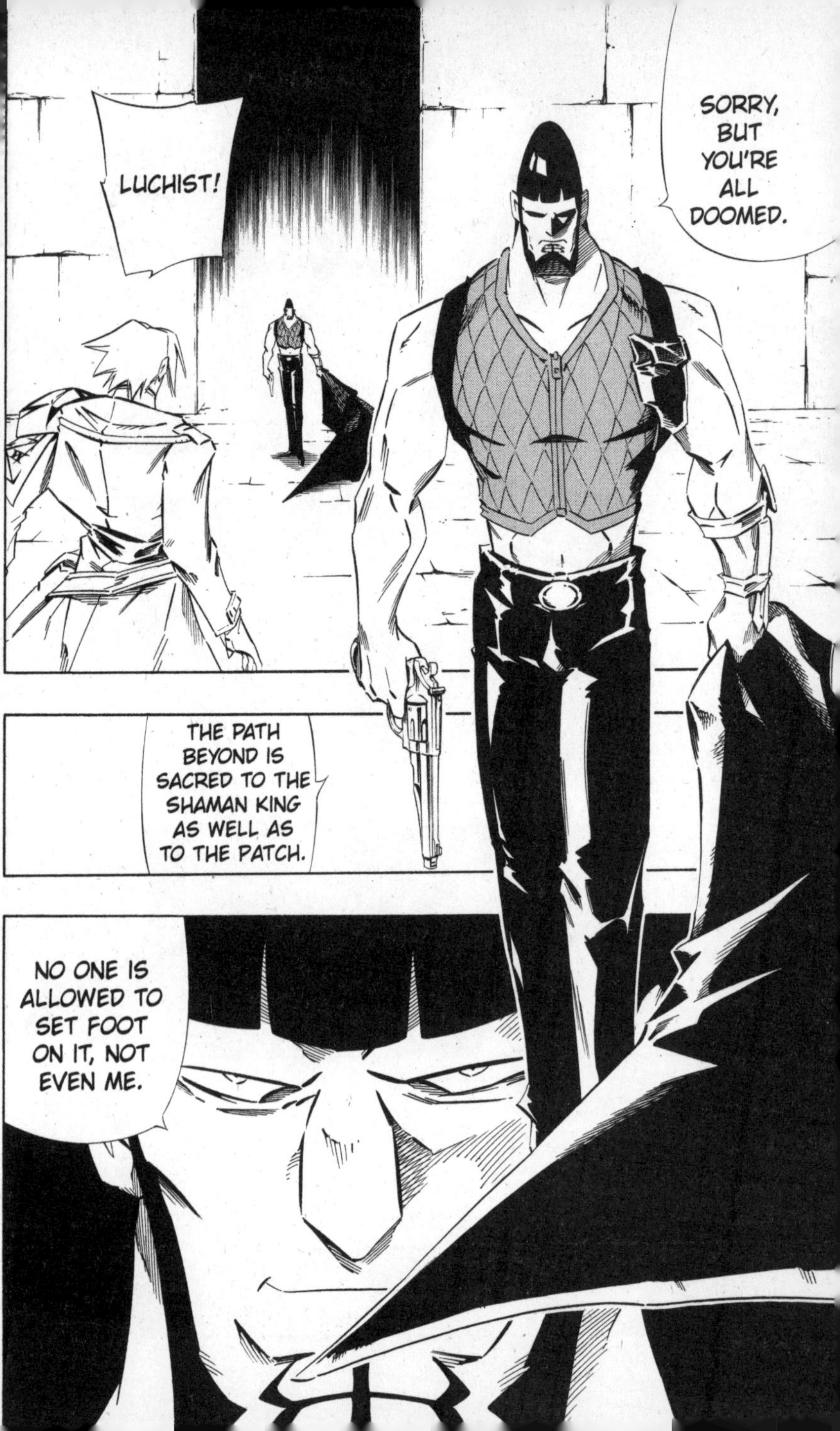
SORRY, BUT YOU'RE ALL DOOMED.
LUCHIST!
THE PATH BEYOND IS SACRED TO THE SHAMAN KING AS WELL AS TO THE PATCH.
NO ONE IS ALLOWED TO SET FOOT ON IT, NOT EVEN ME.

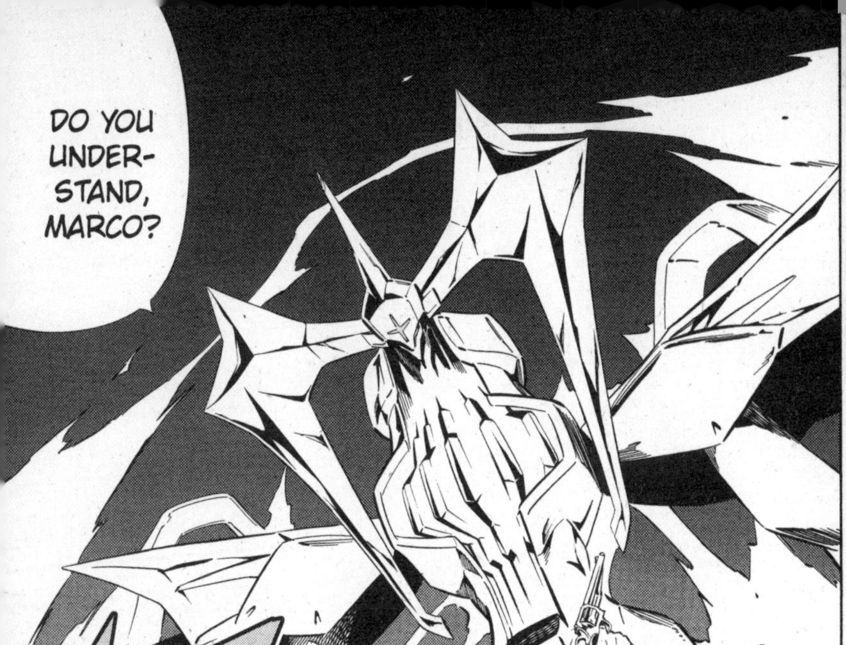
DO YOU UNDER-STAND, MARCO?

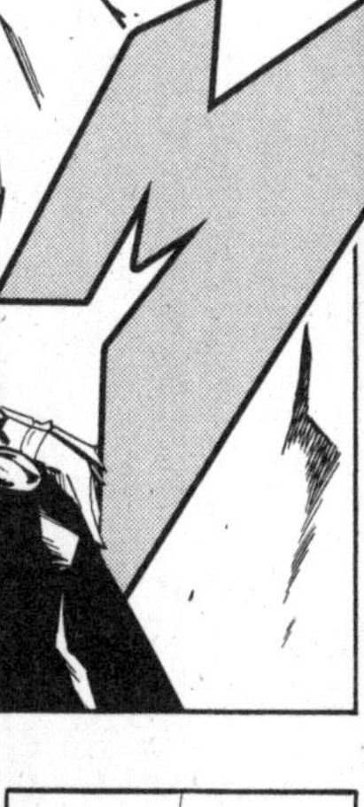
I CAN SEE YOU MEAN BUSINESS.

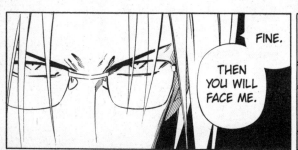

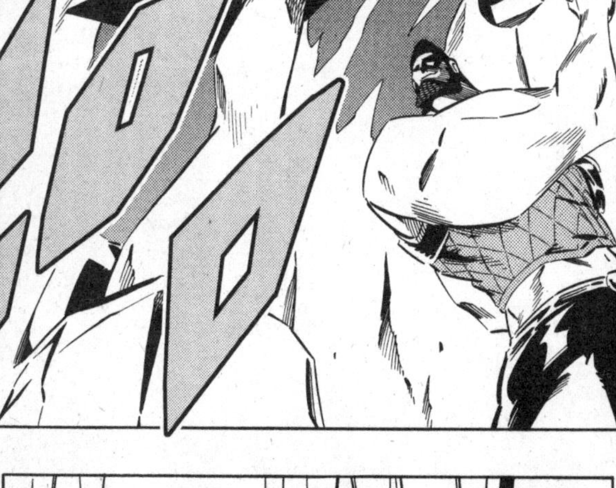
FINE.
THEN YOU WILL FACE ME.

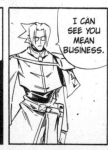

SHAMAN KING ITEM FILE No.79

2001
(JAN)

GWORD NO-00

ライハイト
ステアー

LIHITE
STEYR

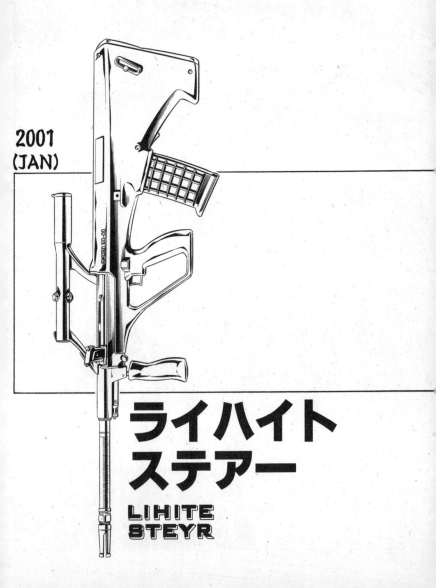

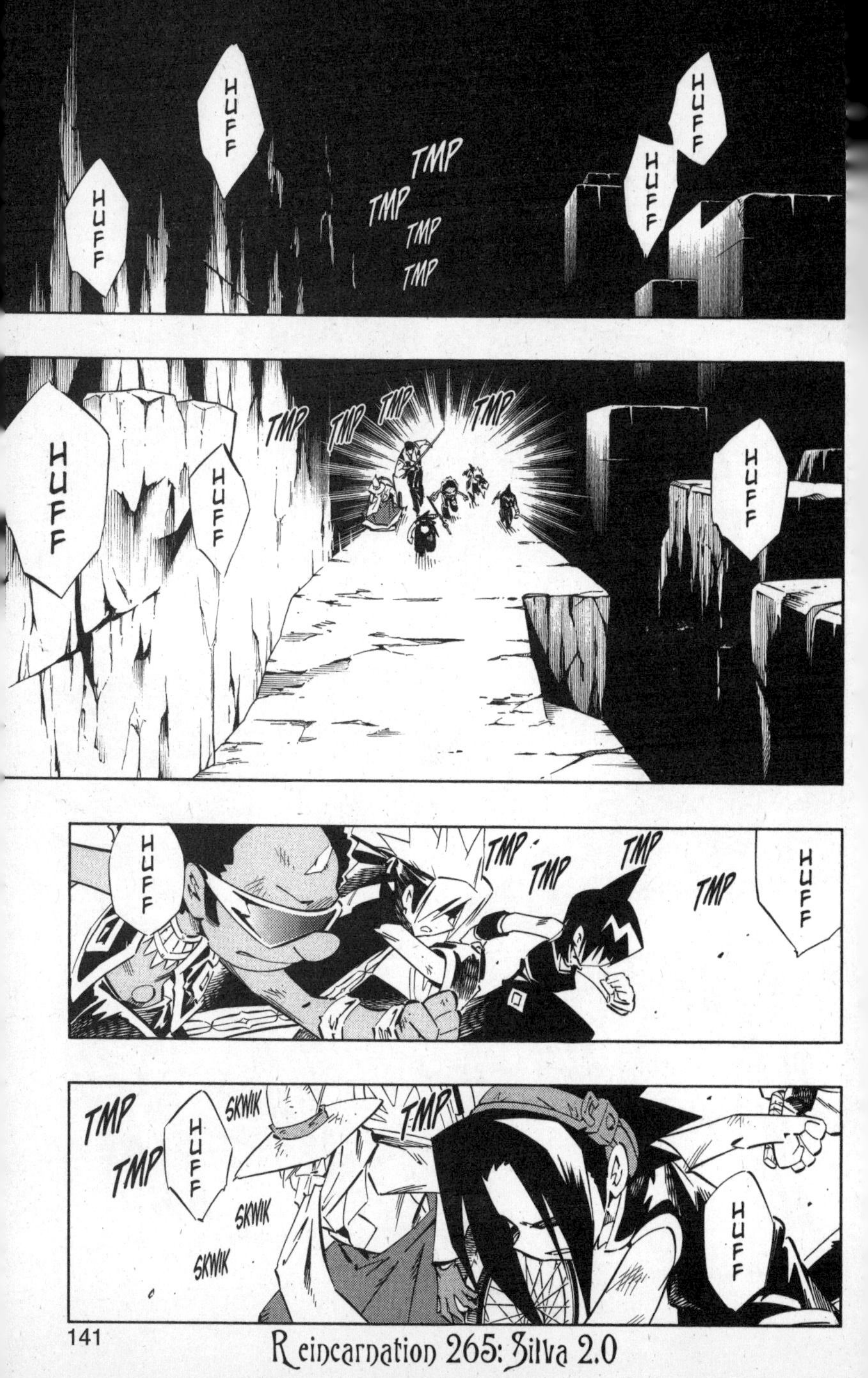
HUFF
HUFF
TMP
TMP
TMP
TMP
HUFF
HUFF
TMP
TMP
TMP
TMP
HUFF
HUFF
HUFF
HUFF
TMP
TMP
TMP
TMP
HUFF
HUFF
TMP
SKWIK
HUFF
TMP
TMP
SKWIK
SKWIK

Reincarnation 265: Silva 2.0

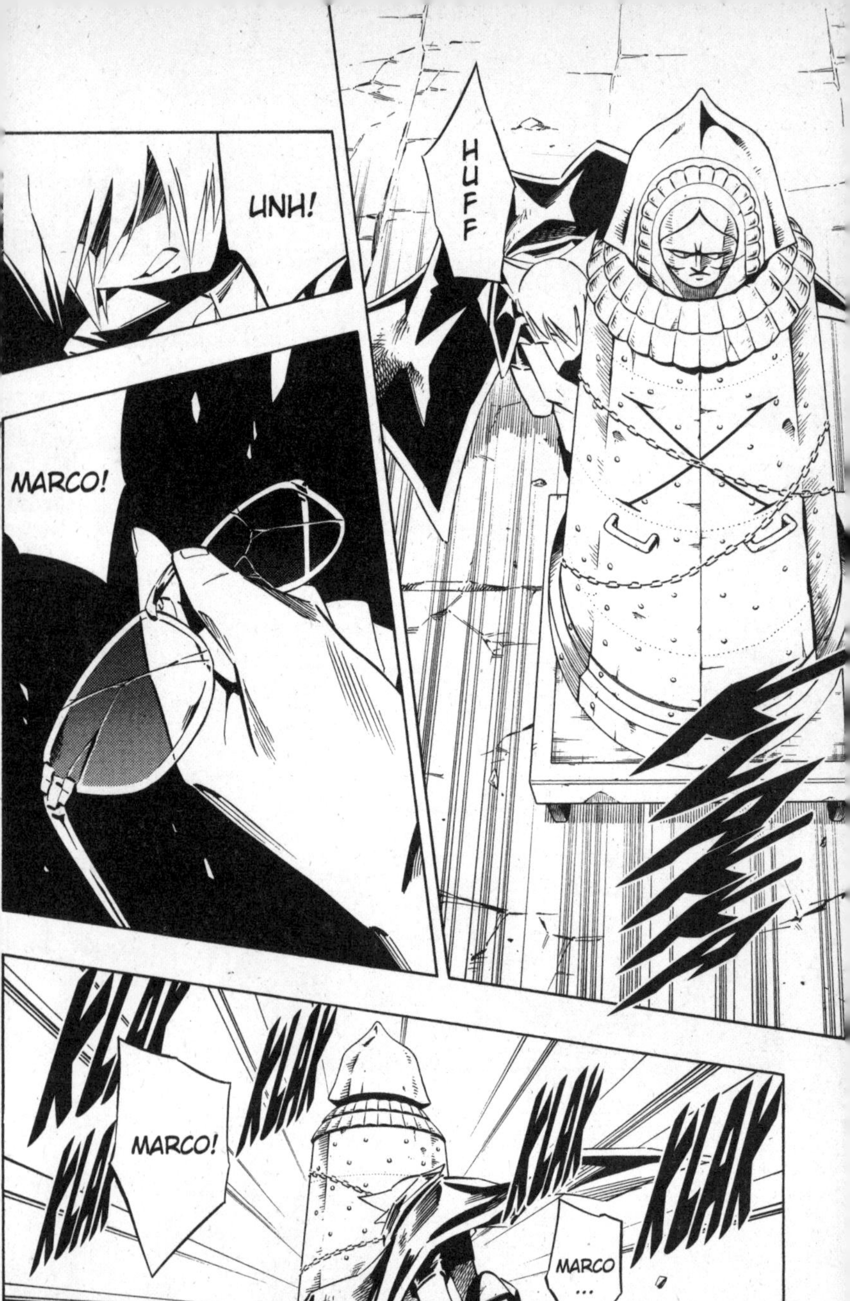
HUFF
UNH!
MARCO!
KLAK
KLAK
MARCO
...
MARCO!
KLAK
KLAK

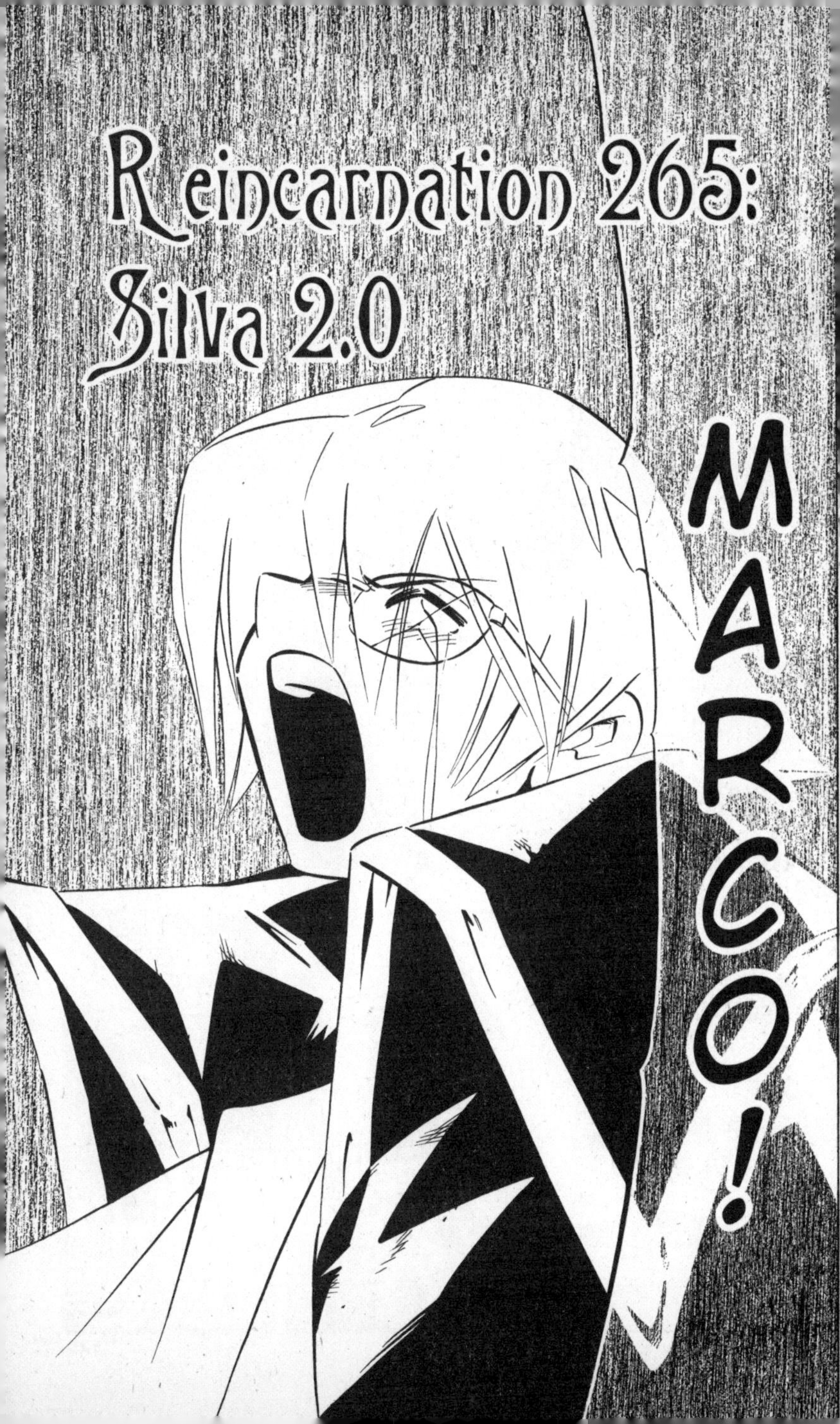
Reincarnation 265:
Silva 2.0
MARCO!

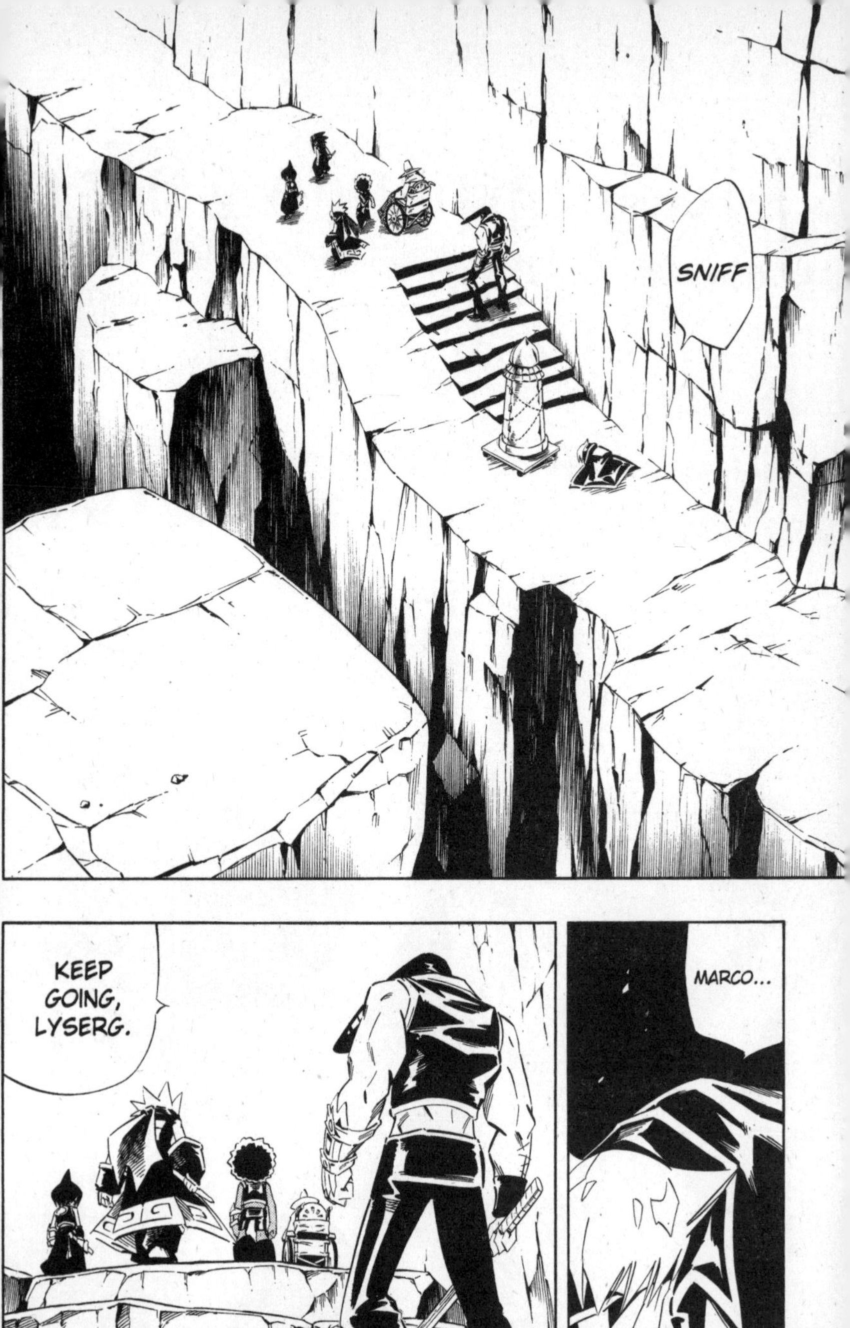
SNIFF
MARCO...
KEEP GOING, LYSERG.

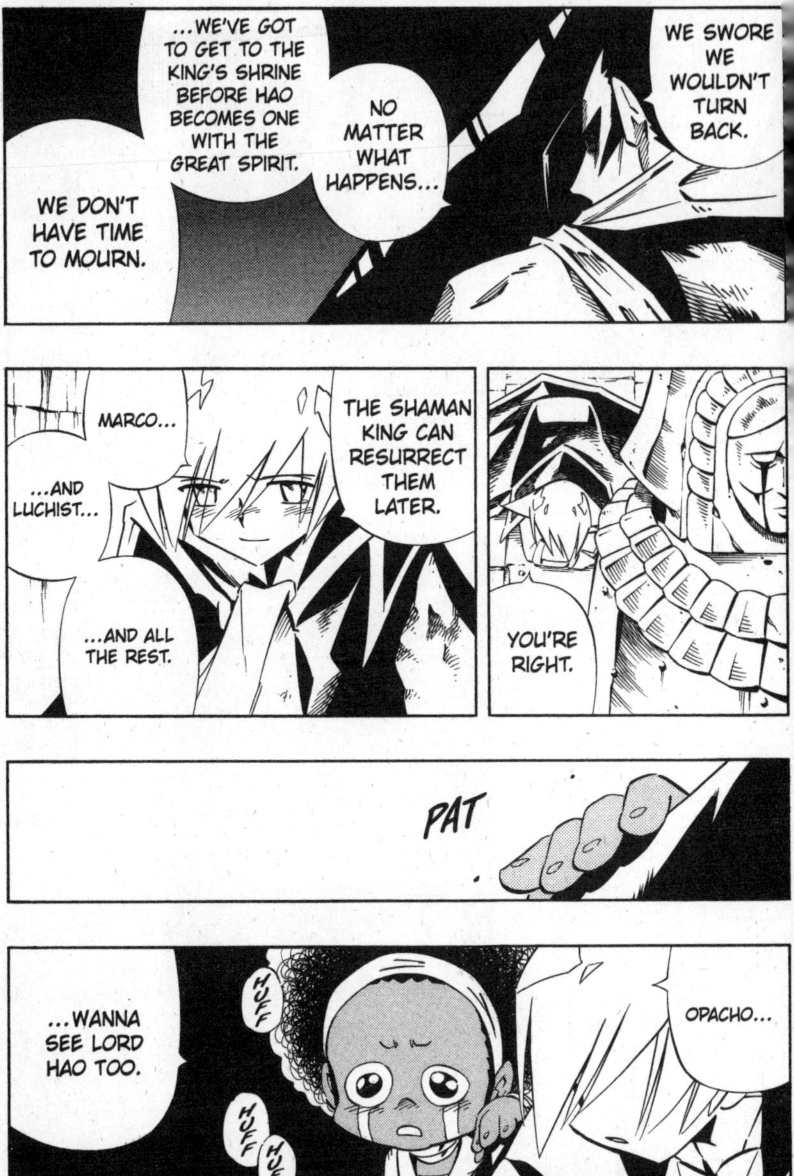
WE SWORE WE WOULDN'T TURN BACK.
NO MATTER WHAT HAPPENS...
...WE'VE GOT TO GET TO THE KING'S SHRINE BEFORE HAO BECOMES ONE WITH THE GREAT SPIRIT.
WE DON'T HAVE TIME TO MOURN.
YOU'RE RIGHT.
THE SHAMAN KING CAN RESURRECT THEM LATER.
MARCO...
...AND LUCHIST...
...AND ALL THE REST.
PAT
OPACHO...
HUFF
HUFF
HUFF
...WANNA SEE LORD HAO TOO.

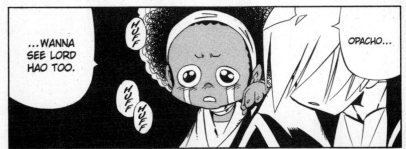

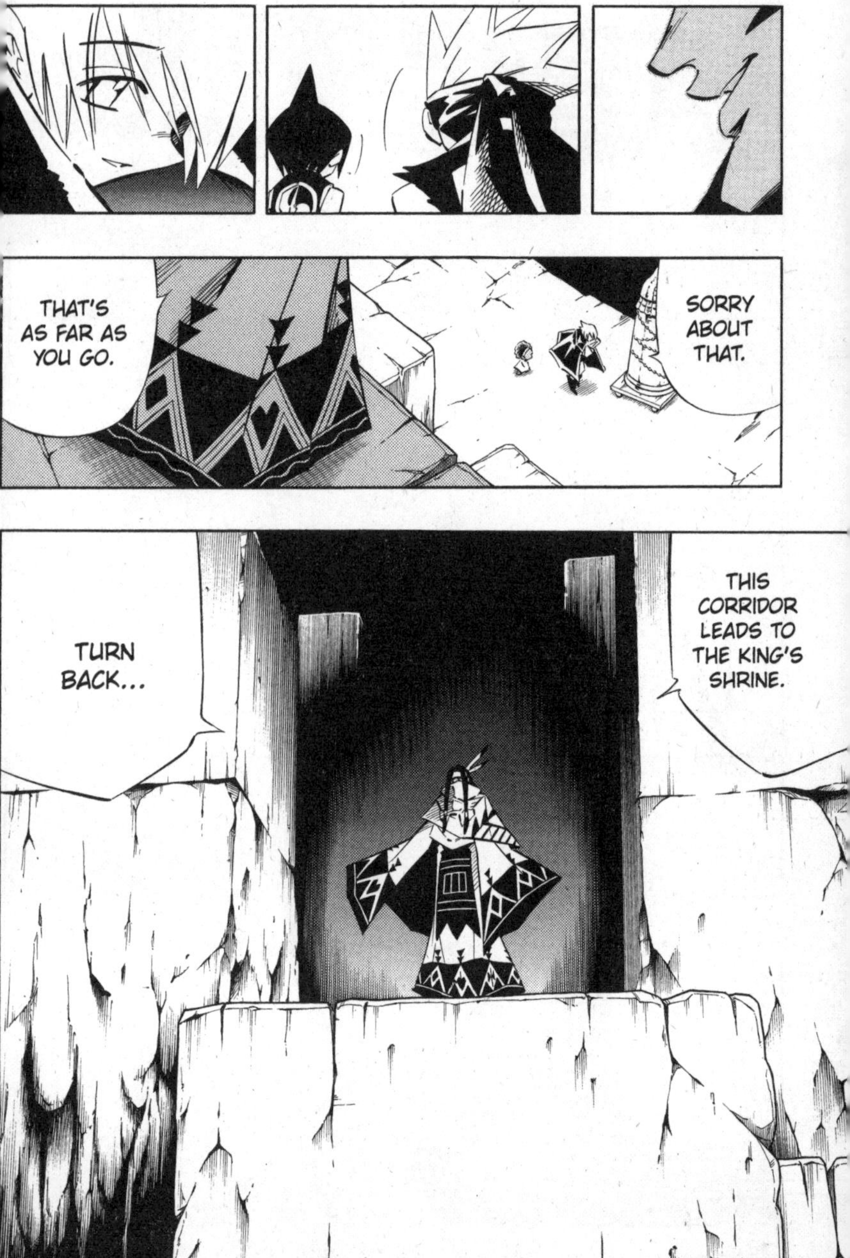
SORRY ABOUT THAT.
THAT'S AS FAR AS YOU GO.
THIS CORRIDOR LEADS TO THE KING'S SHRINE.
TURN BACK...

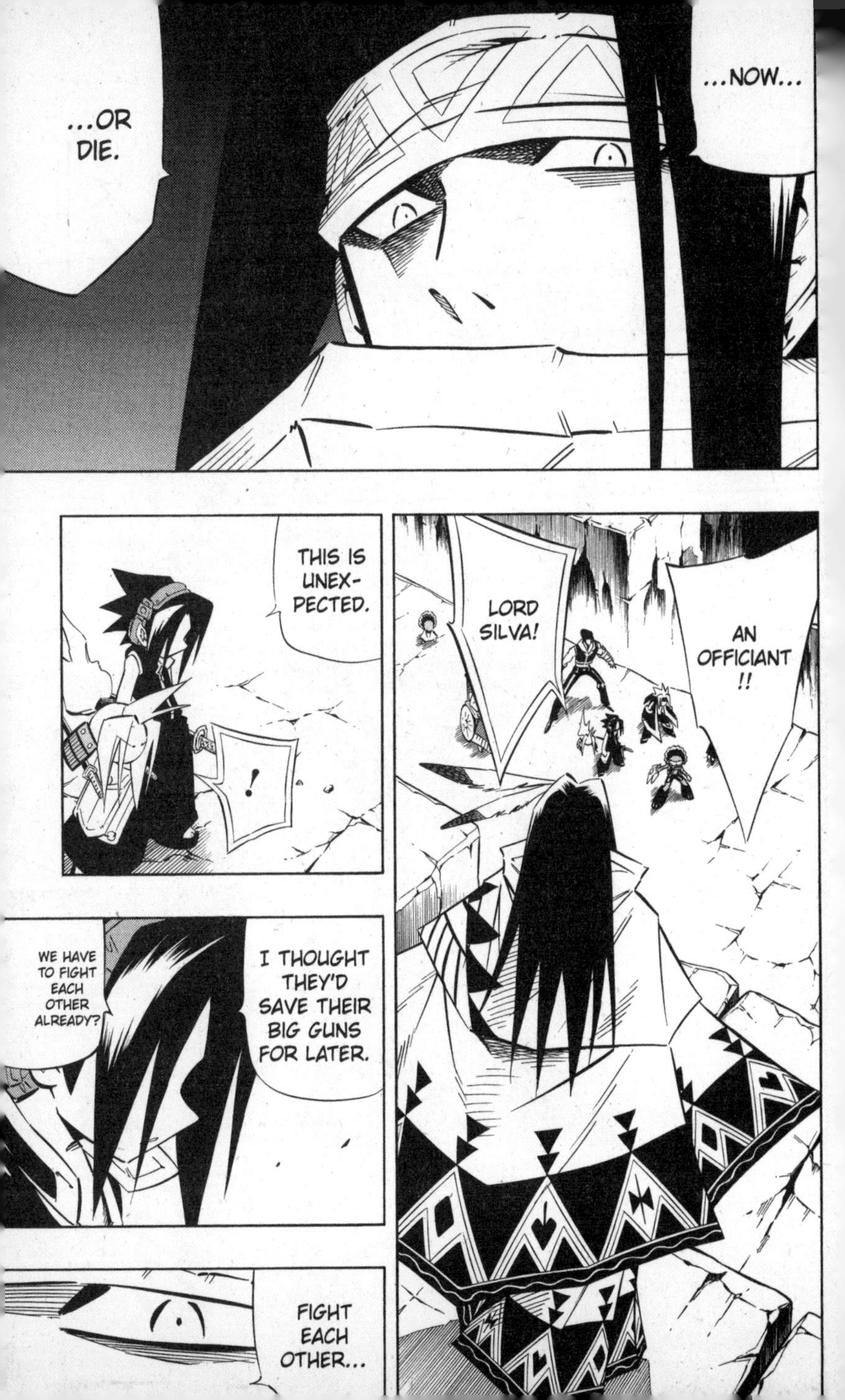
...NOW...
...OR DIE.
AN OFFICIANT!!
LORD SILVA!
THIS IS UNEX-PECTED.
!
I THOUGHT THEY'D SAVE THEIR BIG GUNS FOR LATER.
WE HAVE TO FIGHT EACH OTHER ALREADY?
FIGHT EACH OTHER...

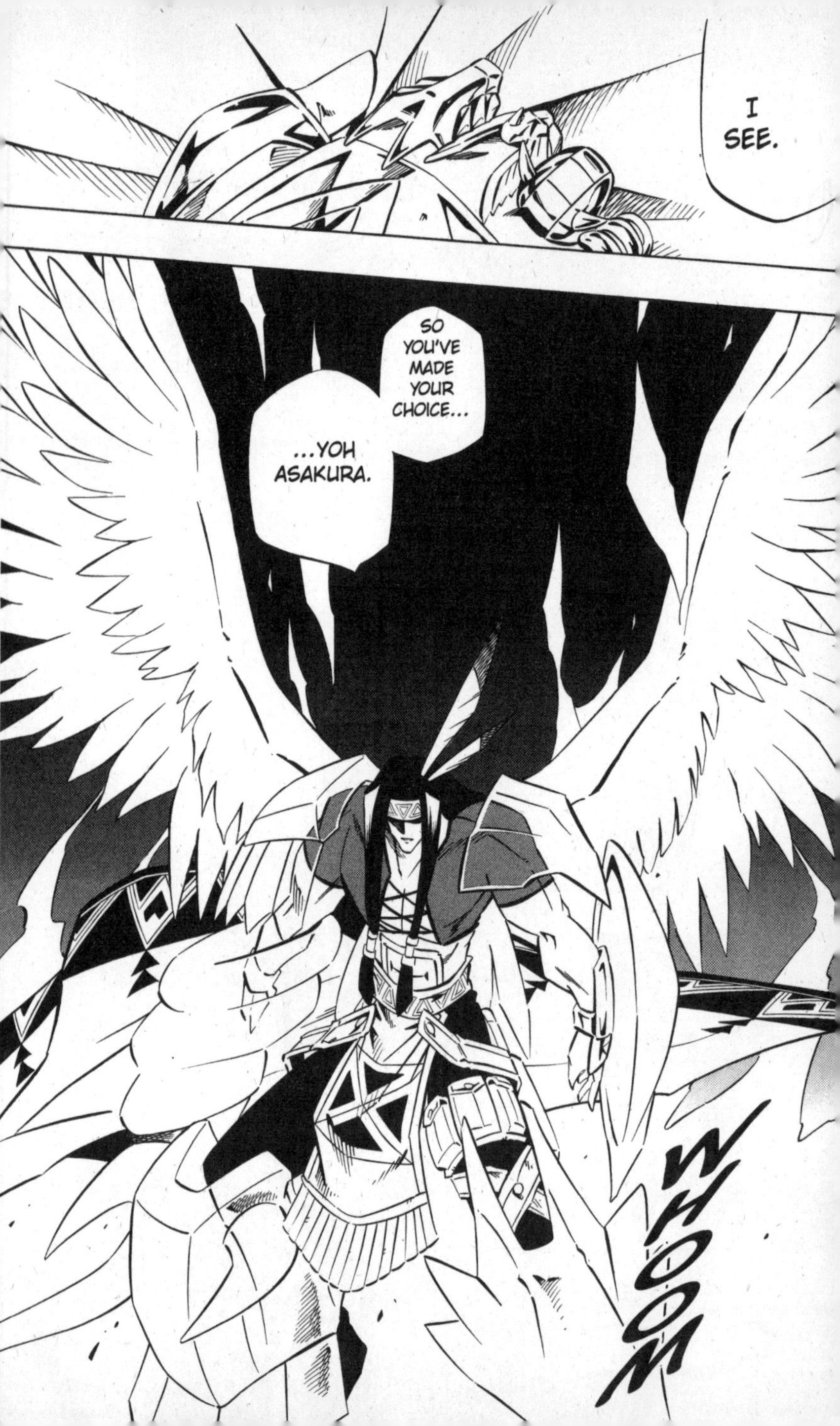
I SEE.
SO YOU'VE MADE YOUR CHOICE...
...YOH ASAKURA.
WHOOOM

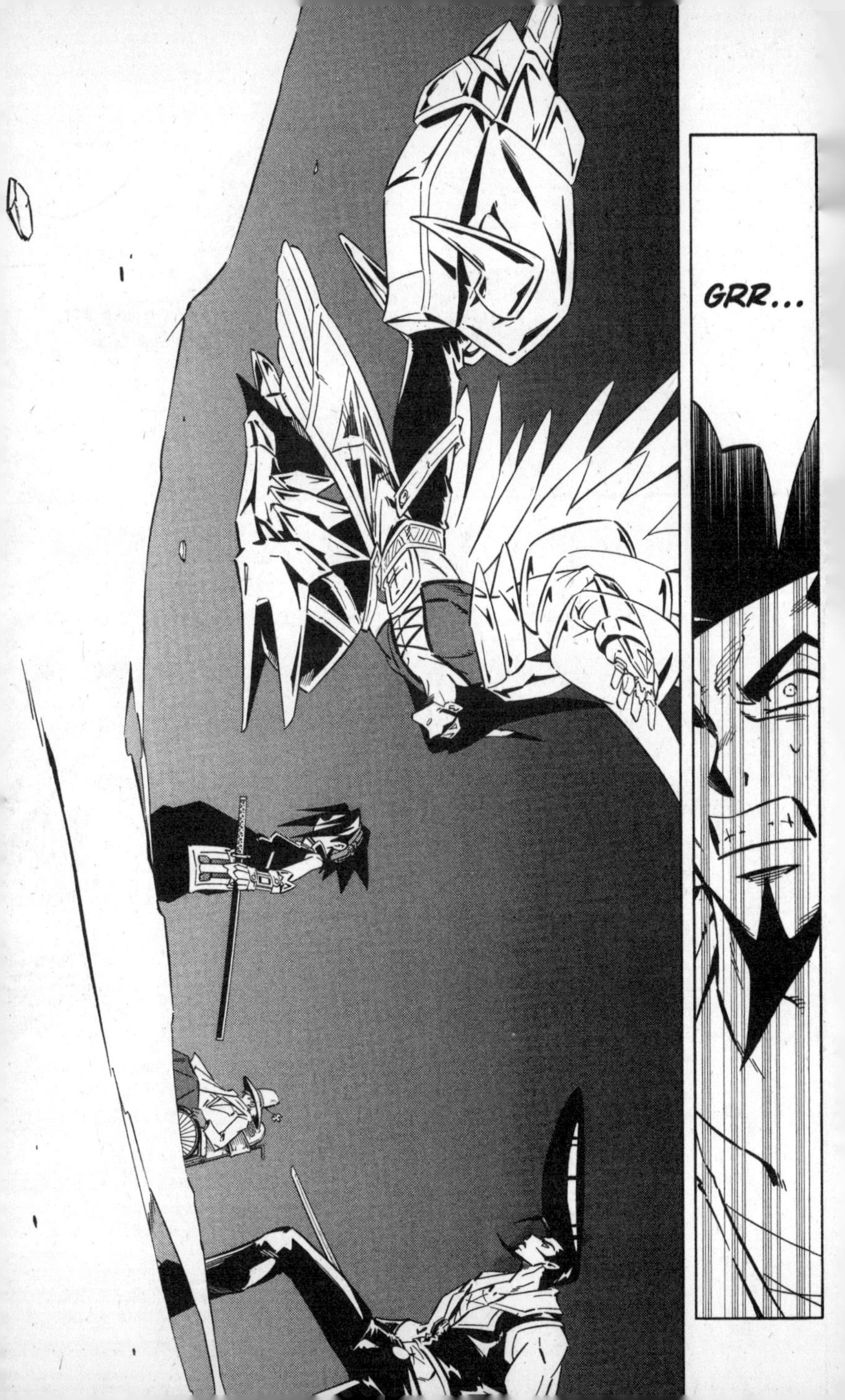
GRR...

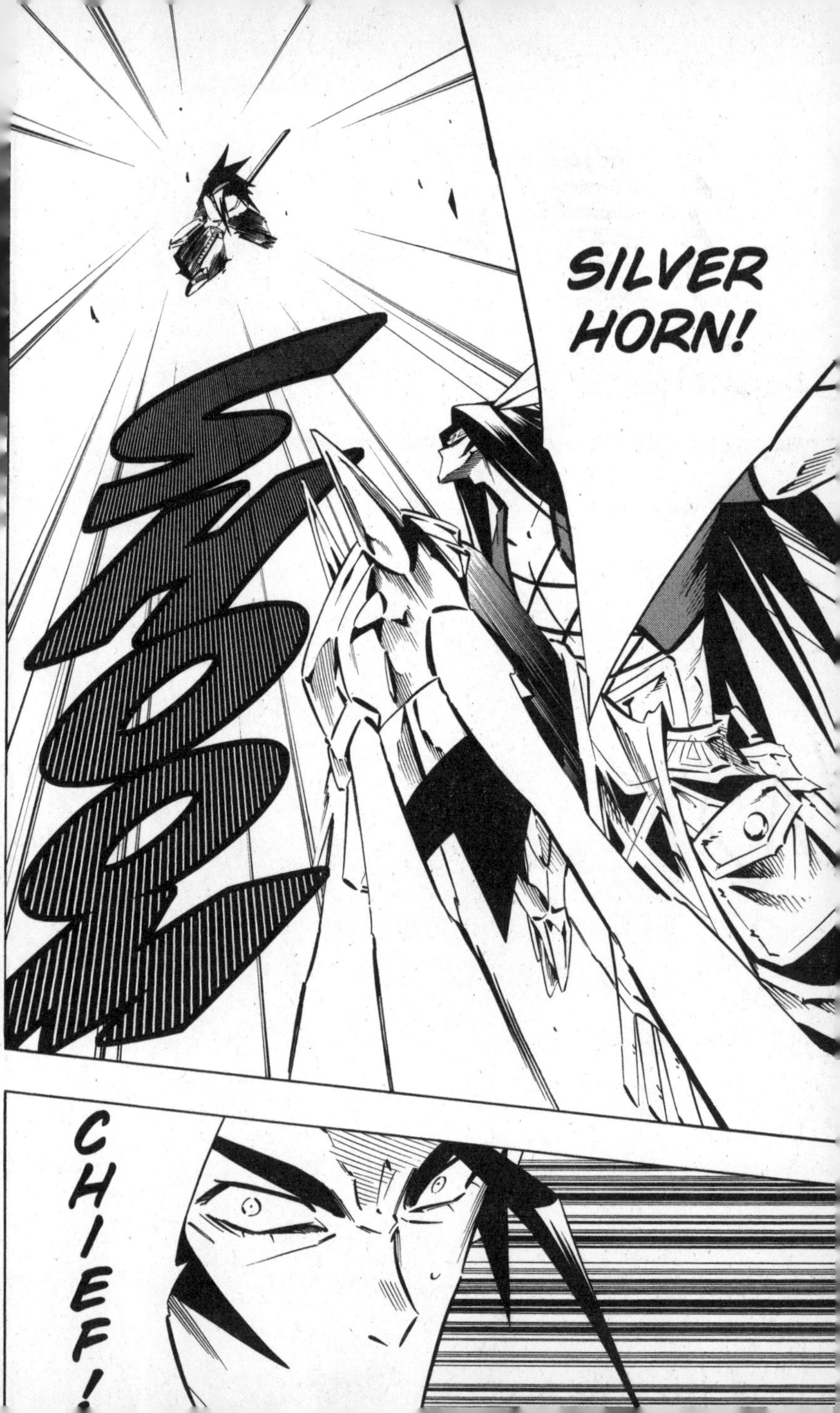
SILVER HORN!
CHIEF!

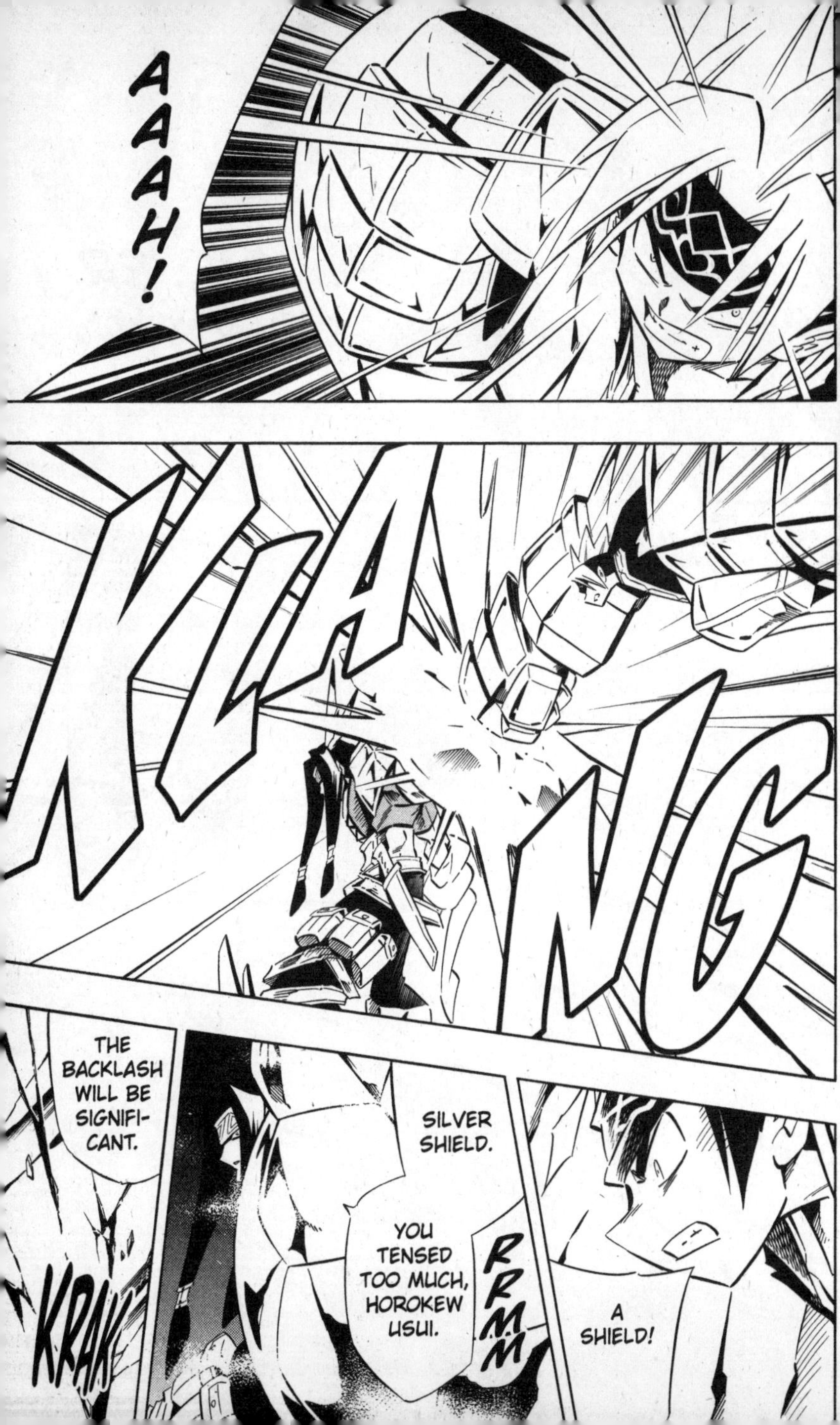
AAAH!
KLANG
A SHIELD!
SILVER SHIELD.
RRMM
YOU TENSED TOO MUCH, HOROKEW USUI.
THE BACKLASH WILL BE SIGNIFICANT.
KRAK

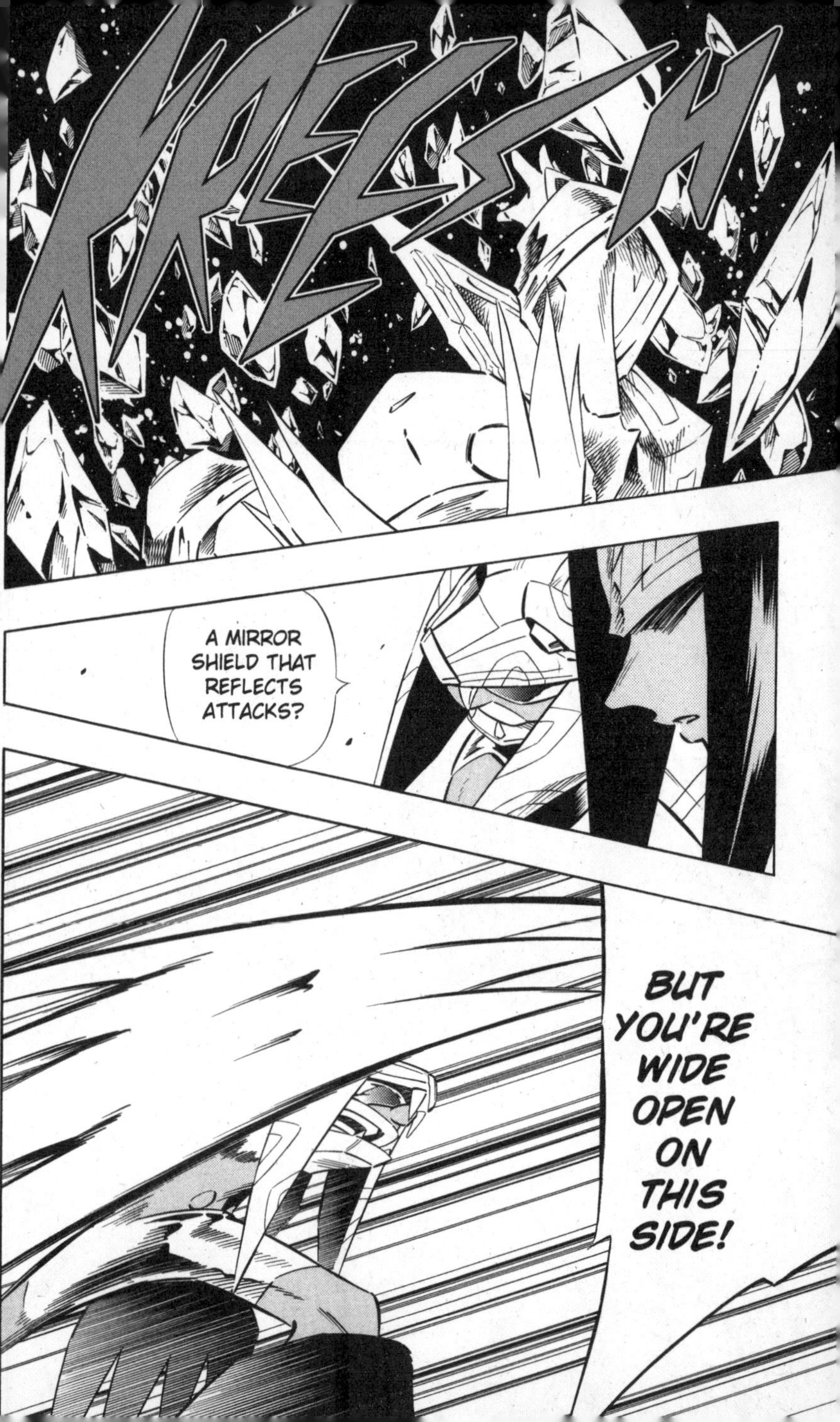
A MIRROR SHIELD THAT REFLECTS ATTACKS?
BUT YOU'RE WIDE OPEN ON THIS SIDE!

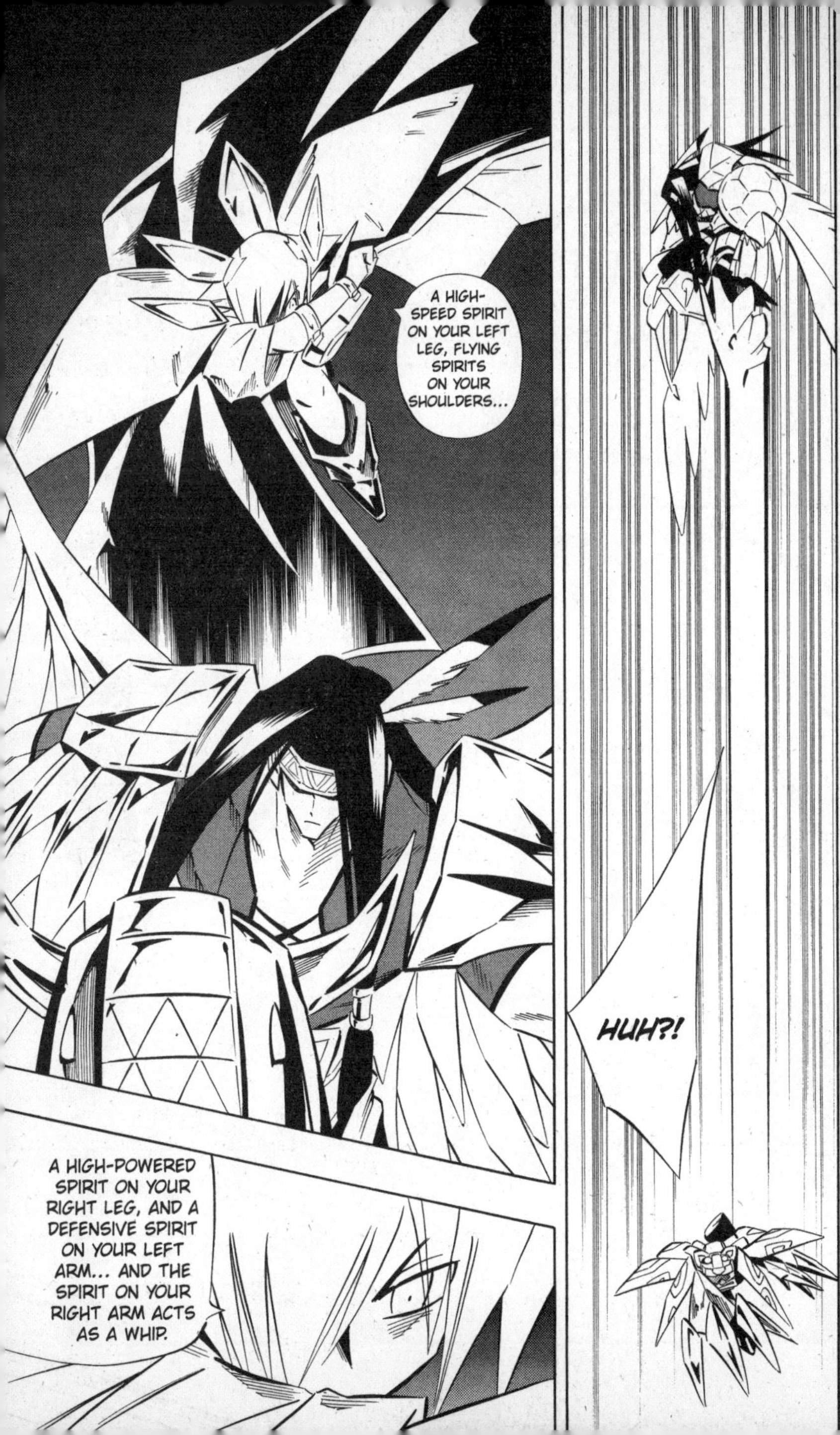
HUH?!
A HIGH-SPEED SPIRIT ON YOUR LEFT LEG, FLYING SPIRITS ON YOUR SHOULDERS...
A HIGH-POWERED SPIRIT ON YOUR RIGHT LEG, AND A DEFENSIVE SPIRIT ON YOUR LEFT ARM... AND THE SPIRIT ON YOUR RIGHT ARM ACTS AS A WHIP.

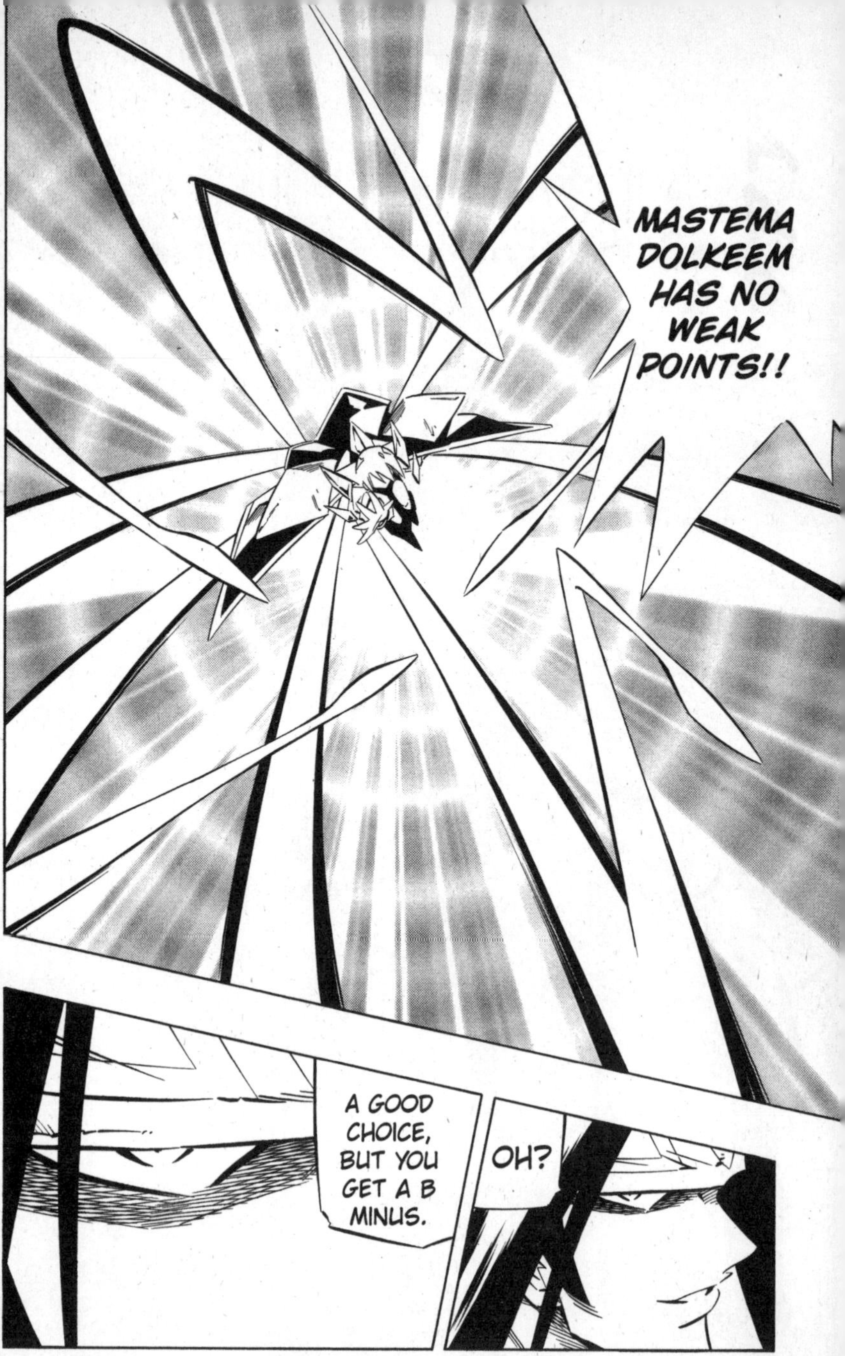
MASTEMA DOLKEEM HAS NO WEAK POINTS!!
OH?
A GOOD CHOICE, BUT YOU GET A B MINUS.

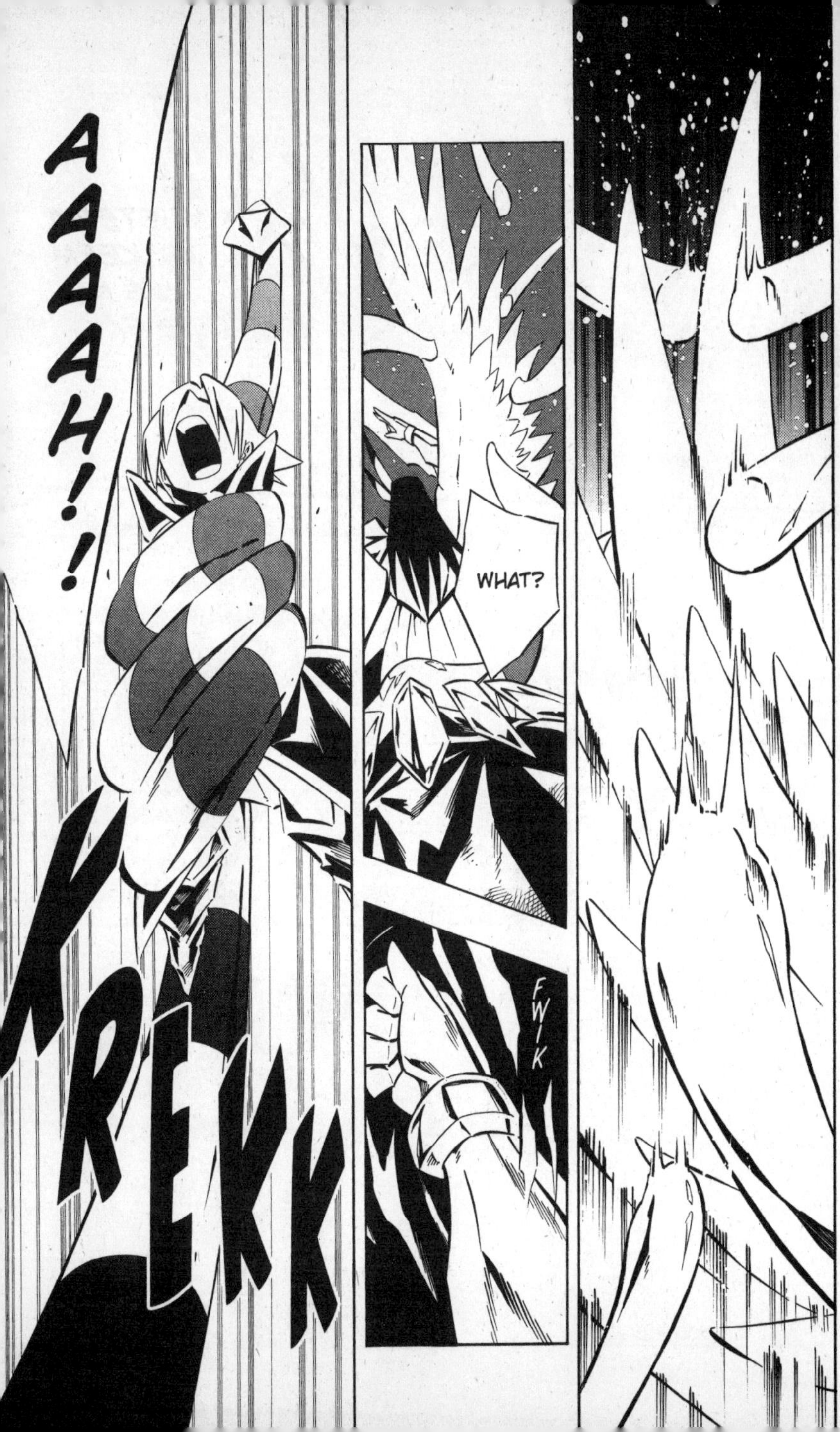
WHAT?
FWIK
AAAAH!!
KREKK

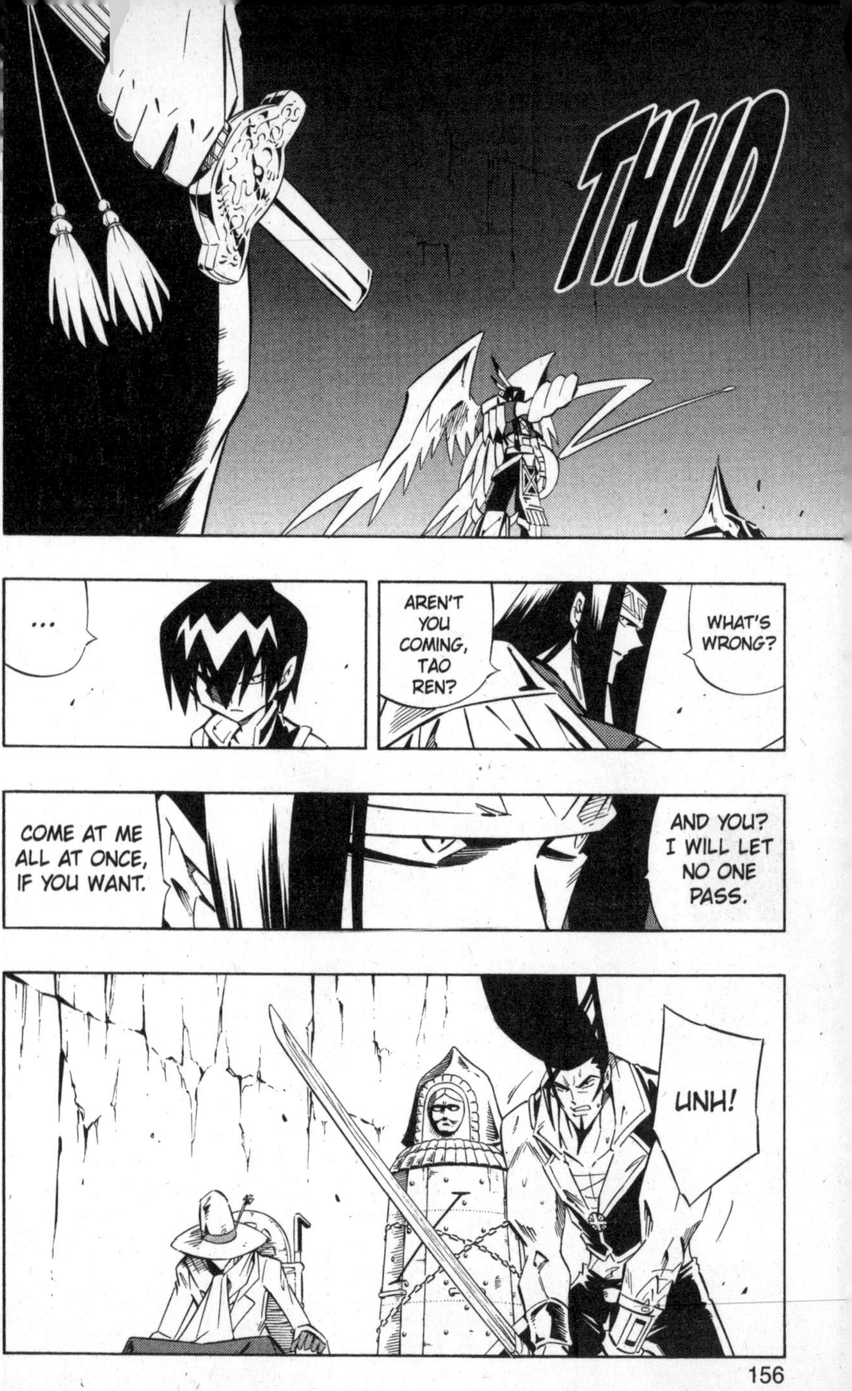
THUD
WHAT'S WRONG?
AREN'T YOU COMING, TAO REN?
...
AND YOU? I WILL LET NO ONE PASS.
COME AT ME ALL AT ONCE, IF YOU WANT.
UNH!

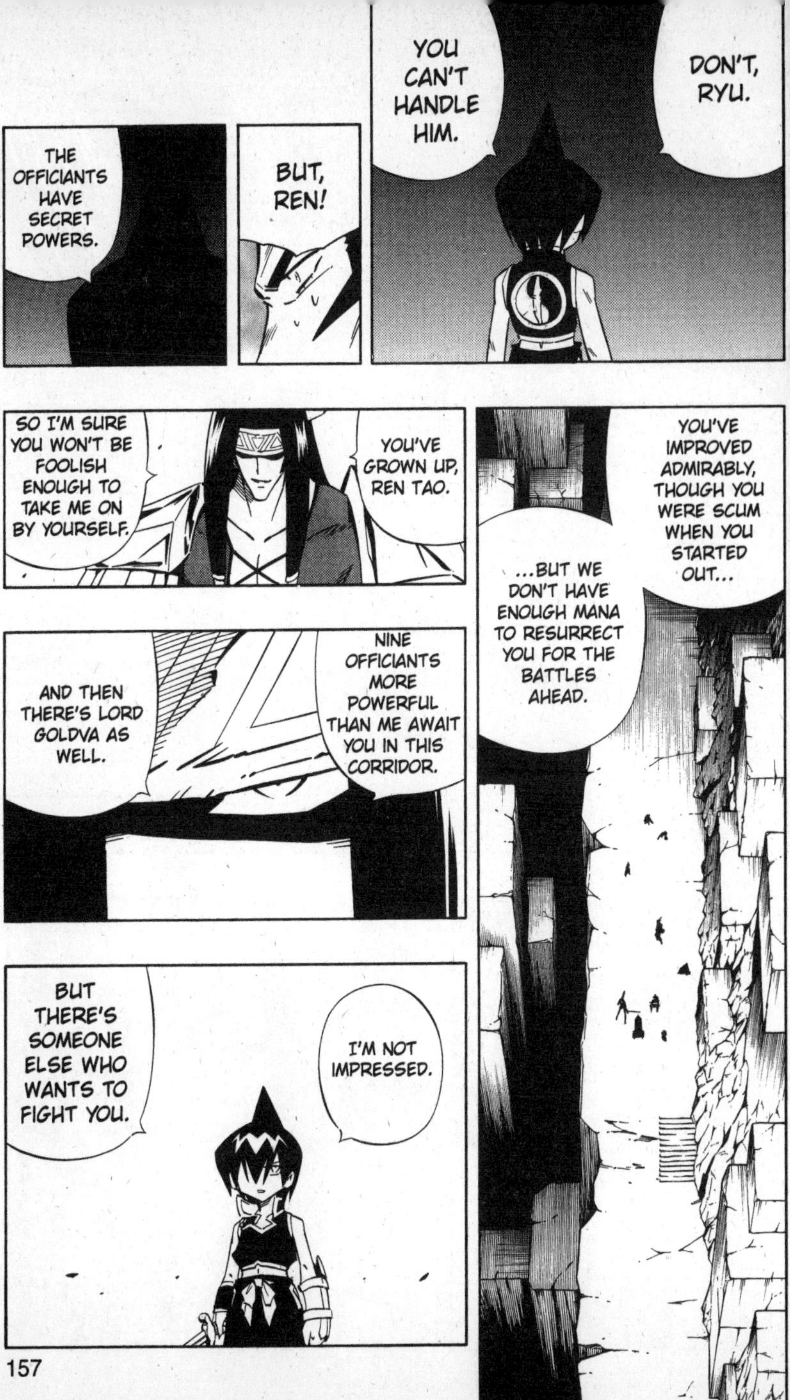
DON'T, RYU.
YOU CAN'T HANDLE HIM.
BUT, REN!
THE OFFICIANTS HAVE SECRET POWERS.
YOU'VE IMPROVED ADMIRABLY, THOUGH YOU WERE SCUM WHEN YOU STARTED OUT...
...BUT WE DON'T HAVE ENOUGH MANA TO RESURRECT YOU FOR THE BATTLES AHEAD.
YOU'VE GROWN UP, REN TAO.
SO I'M SURE YOU WON'T BE FOOLISH ENOUGH TO TAKE ME ON BY YOURSELF.
NINE OFFICIANTS MORE POWERFUL THAN ME AWAIT YOU IN THIS CORRIDOR.
AND THEN THERE'S LORD GOLDVA AS WELL.
I'M NOT IMPRESSED.
BUT THERE'S SOMEONE ELSE WHO WANTS TO FIGHT YOU.

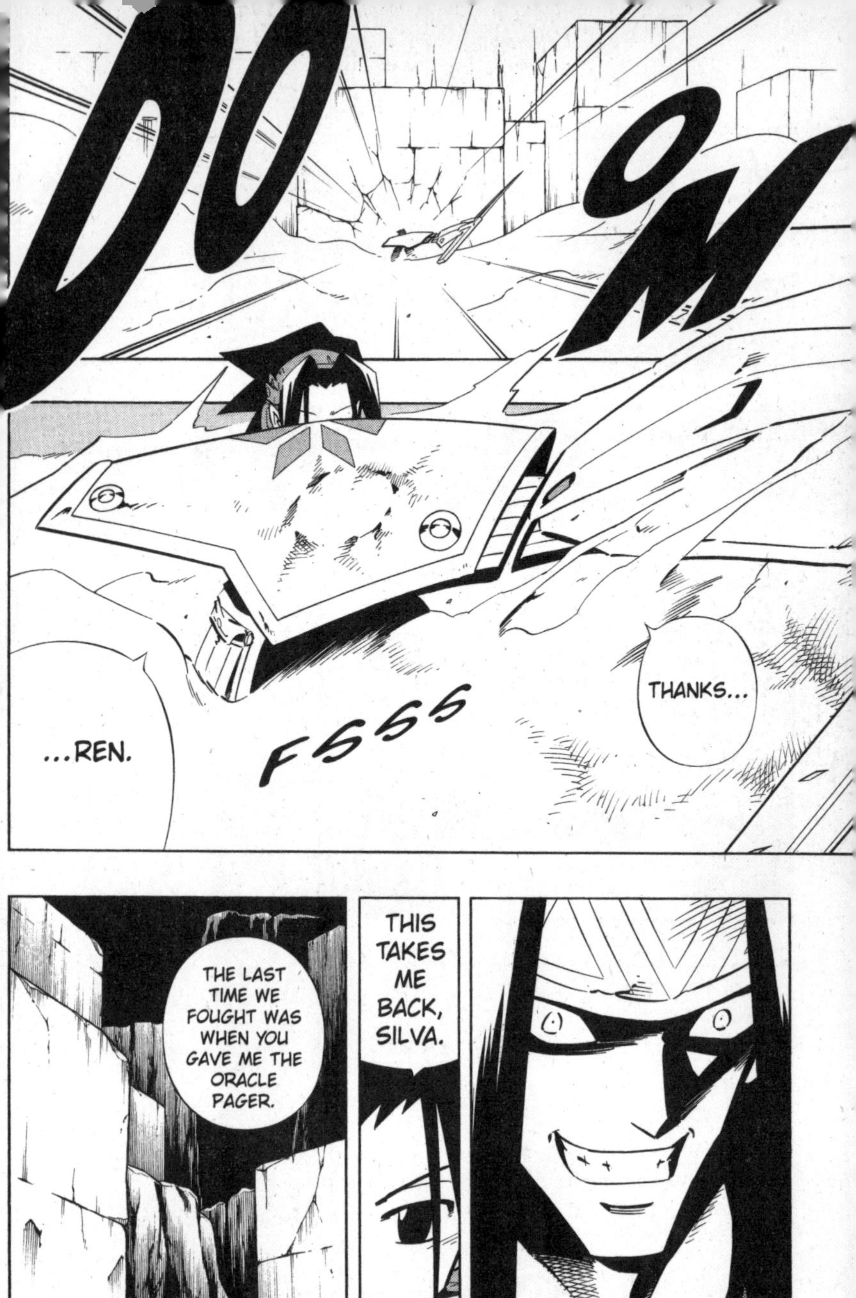
DOOM
THANKS...
FSSS
...REN.
THIS TAKES ME BACK, SILVA.
THE LAST TIME WE FOUGHT WAS WHEN YOU GAVE ME THE ORACLE PAGER.

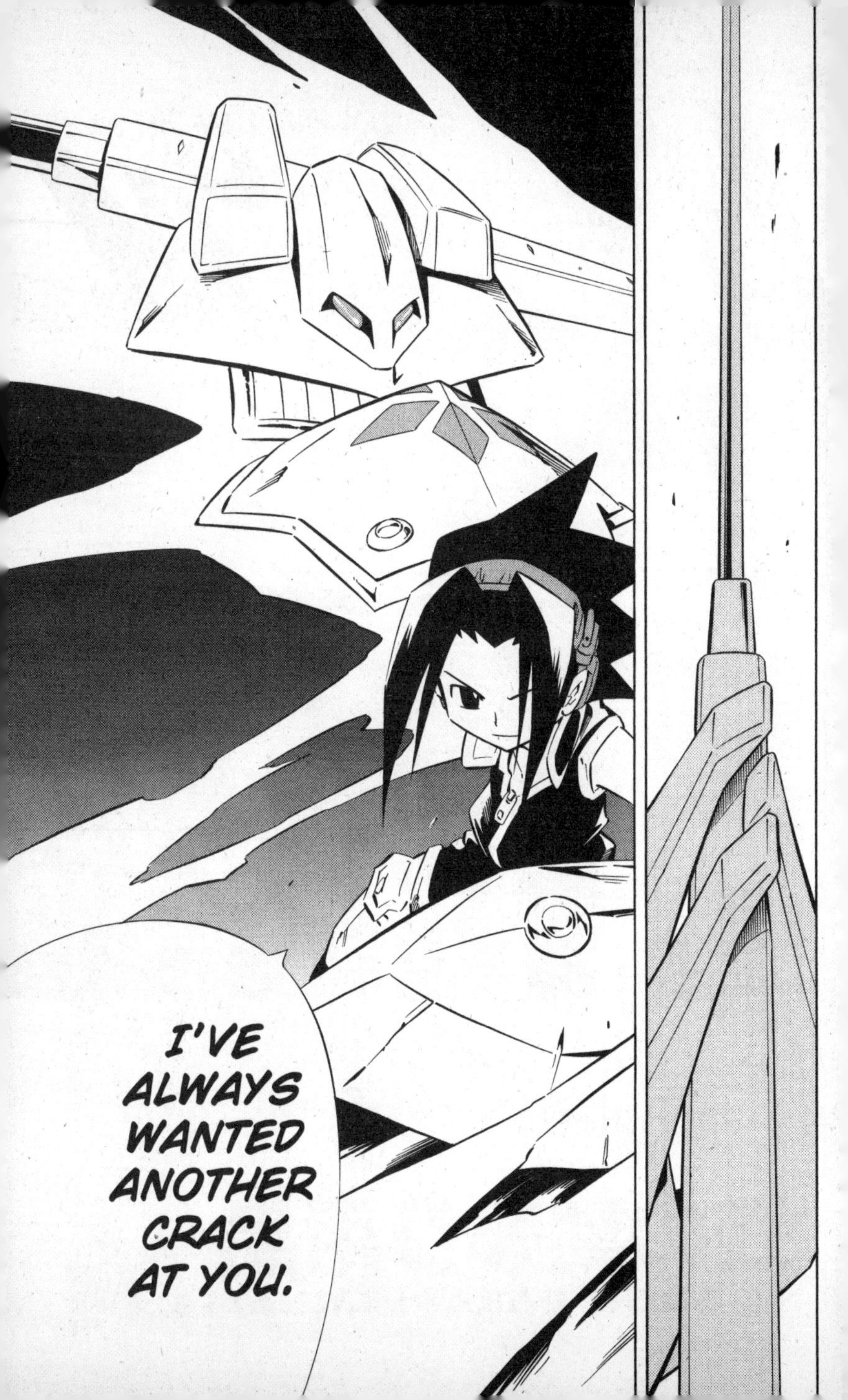
I'VE ALWAYS WANTED ANOTHER CRACK AT YOU.

SHAMAN KING ITEM FILE No.80

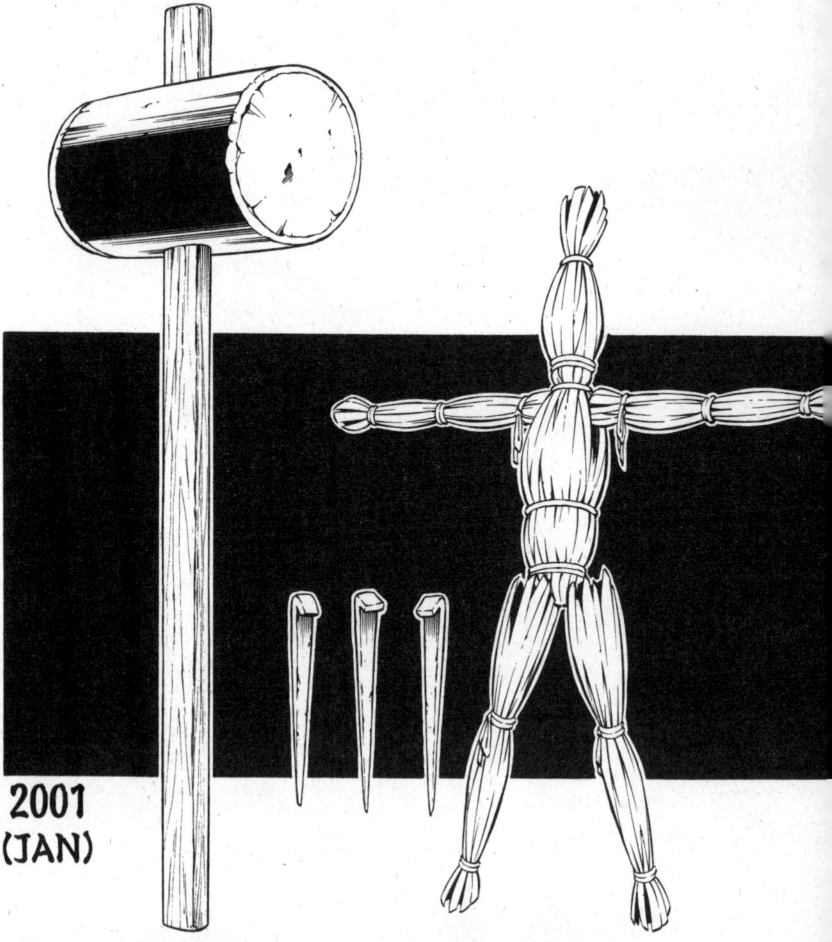

2001
(JAN)

丑(うし)の刻参(こくまい)り用品(ようひん)

VOODOO PARAPHERNALIA

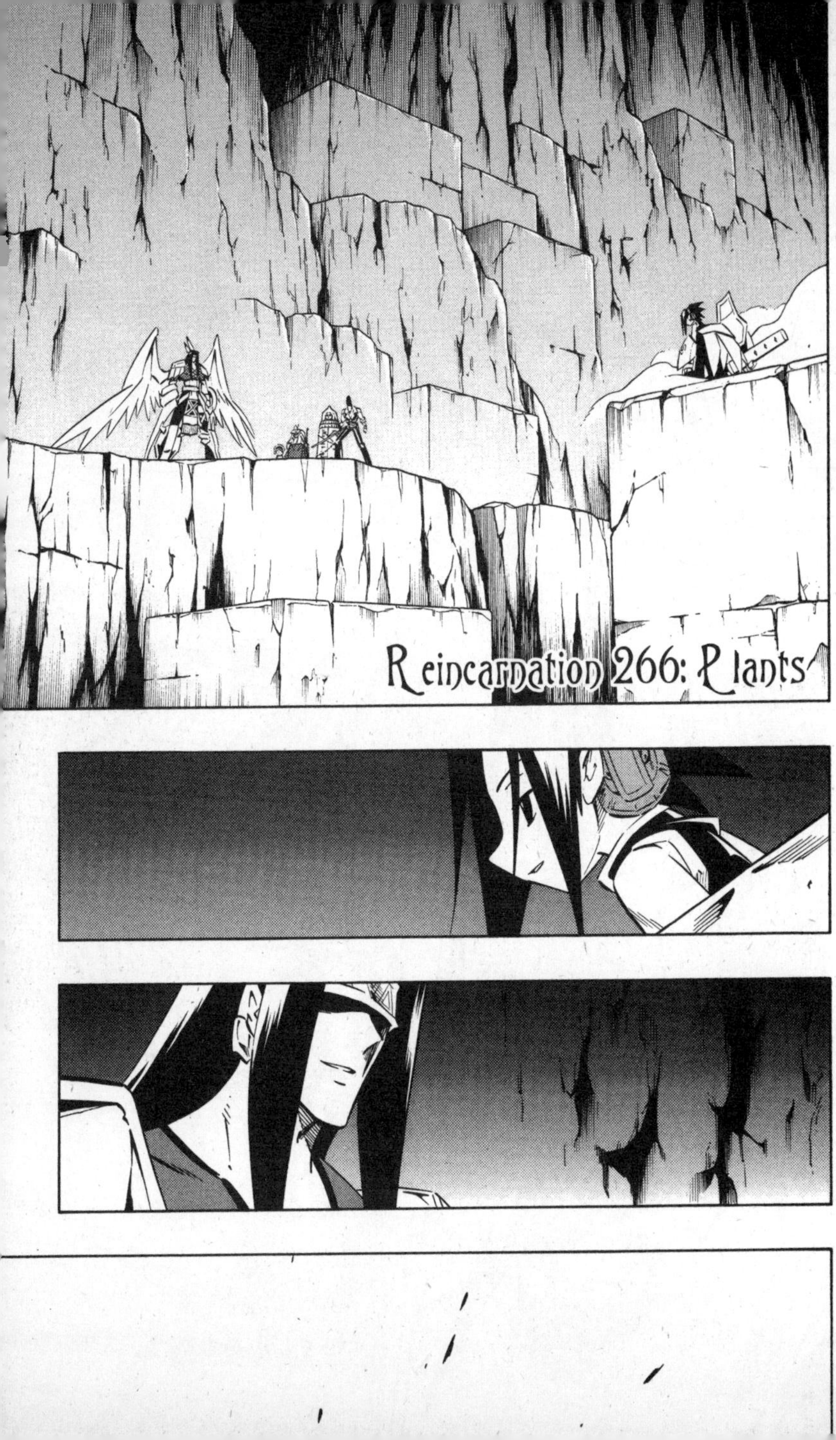
Reincarnation 266: Plants

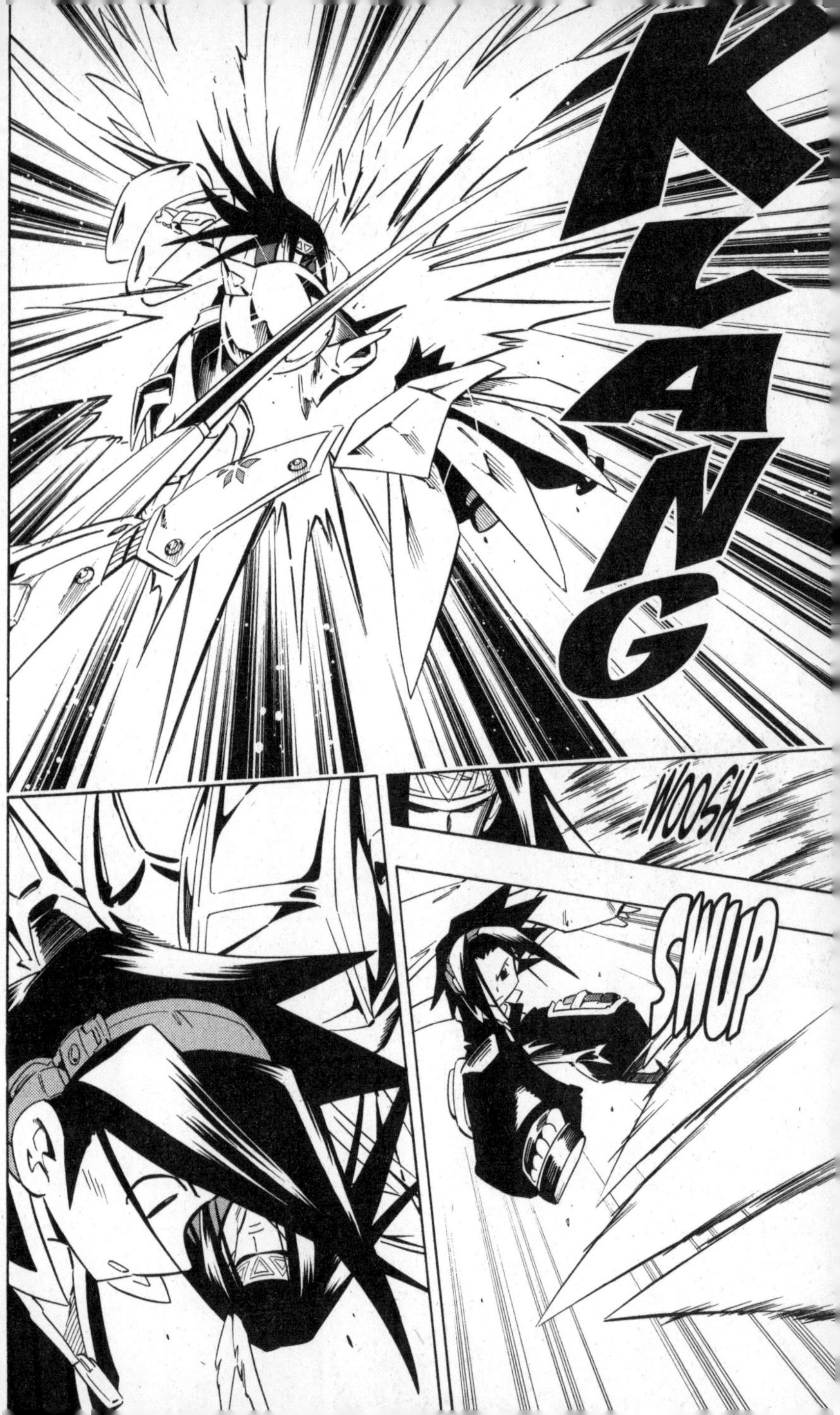
KANG
WOOSH
SWUP

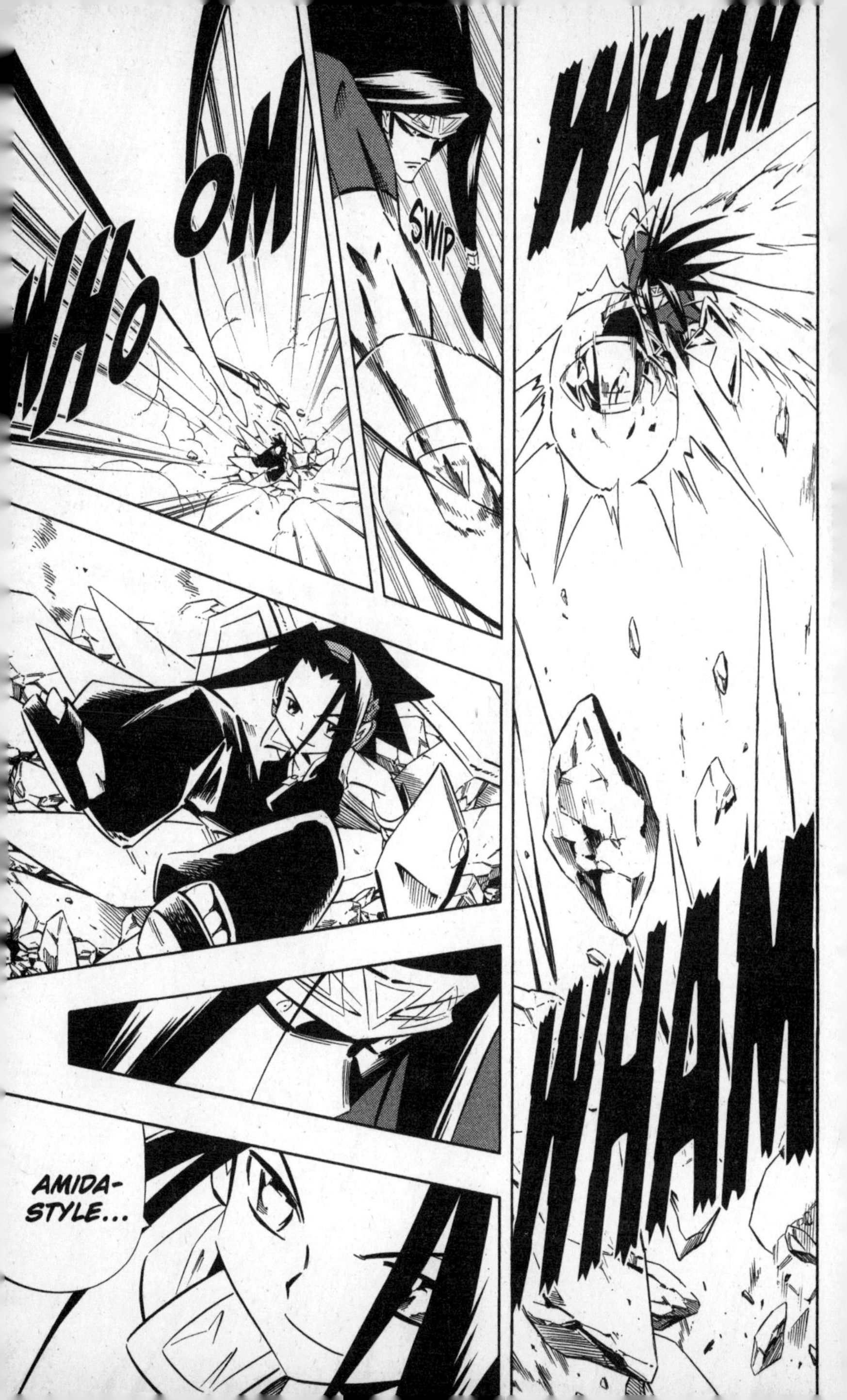
WHAM
WHAM
SWIP
WHOOM
AMIDA-
STYLE...

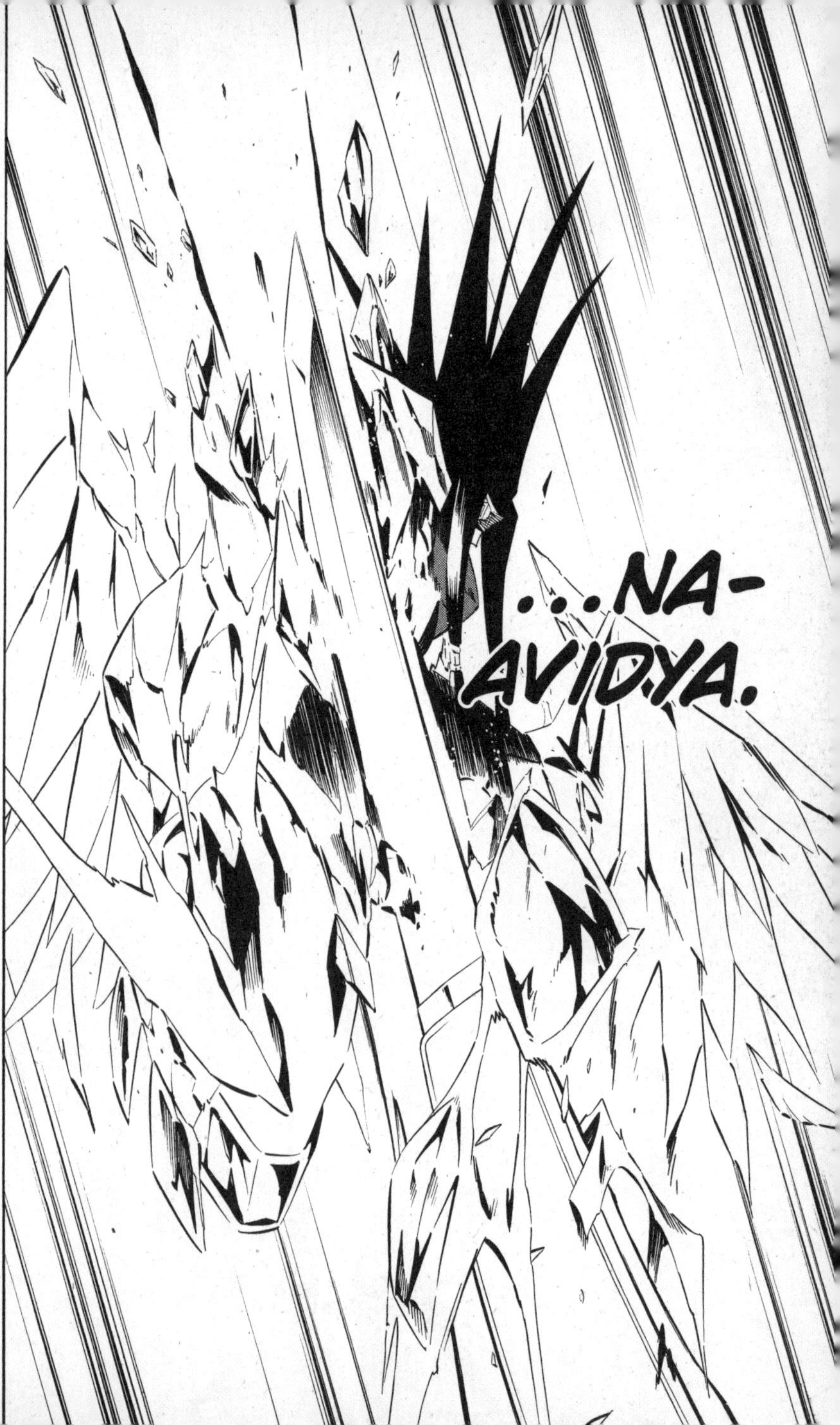
...NA-
AVIDYA.

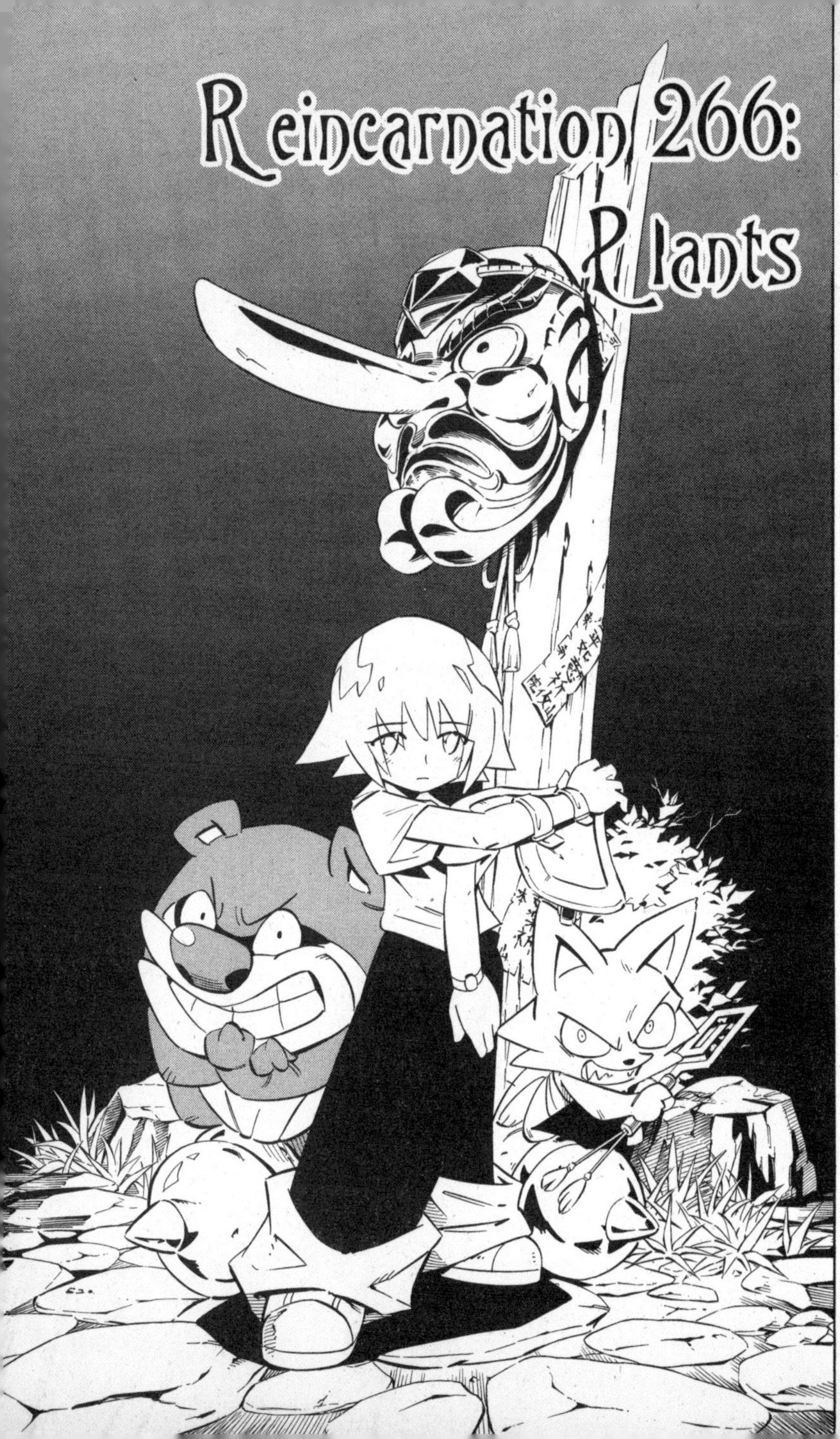
Reincarnation 266:
Plants

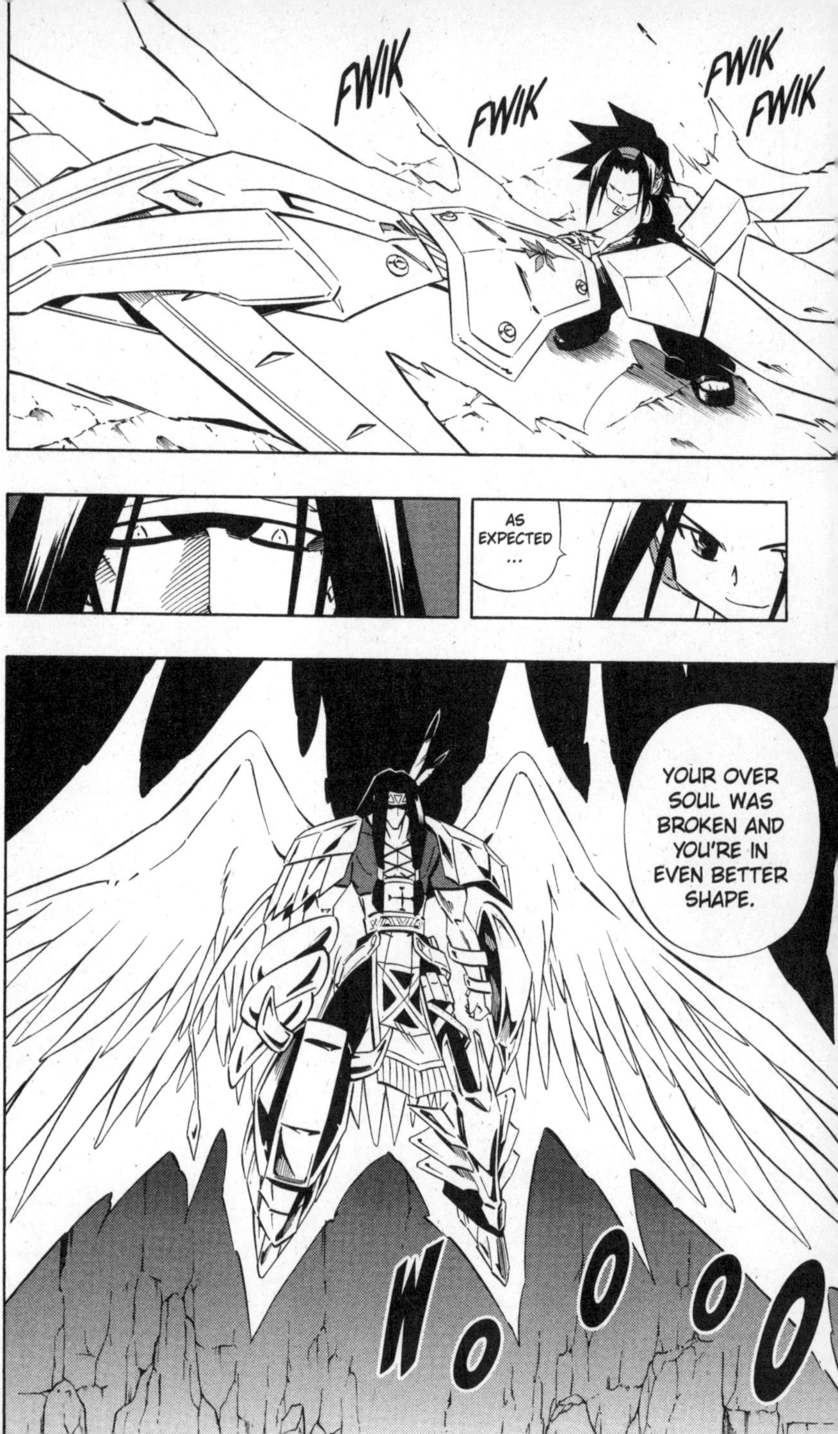
FWIK
FWIK
FWIK
FWIK
AS EXPECTED ...
YOUR OVER SOUL WAS BROKEN AND YOU'RE IN EVEN BETTER SHAPE.
WOOOO

...IS WHAT WE'RE UP AGAINST.

THIS...

GULP

WE DON'T HAVE ENOUGH MANA TO RESURRECT YOU FOR THE BATTLES AHEAD.

I WASN'T SINGLING YOU OUT.

...A BURDEN.

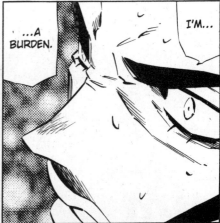

I'M...

167

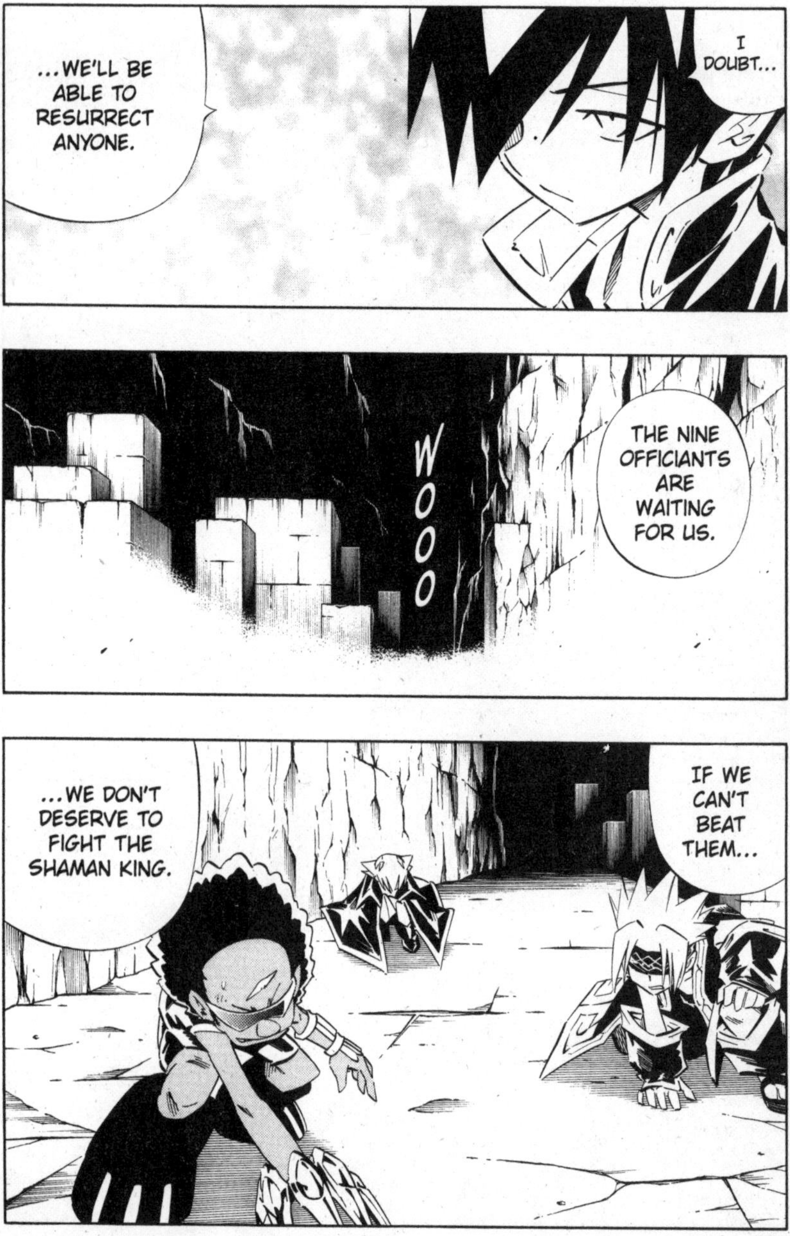
I DOUBT...
...WE'LL BE ABLE TO RESURRECT ANYONE.
THE NINE OFFICIANTS ARE WAITING FOR US.
WOOO
IF WE CAN'T BEAT THEM...
...WE DON'T DESERVE TO FIGHT THE SHAMAN KING.

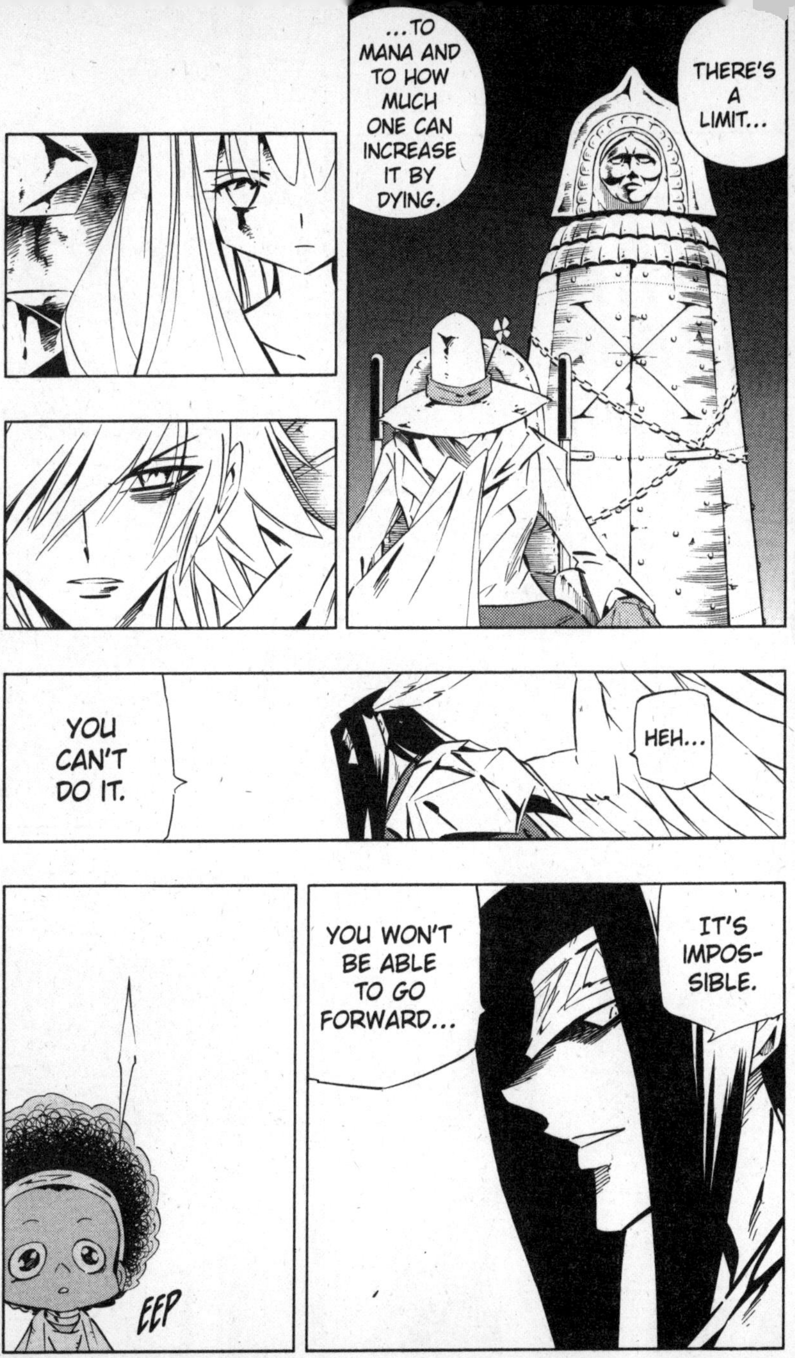
THERE'S A LIMIT...
...TO MANA AND TO HOW MUCH ONE CAN INCREASE IT BY DYING.
HEH...
YOU CAN'T DO IT.
IT'S IMPOS-SIBLE.
YOU WON'T BE ABLE TO GO FORWARD...
EEP

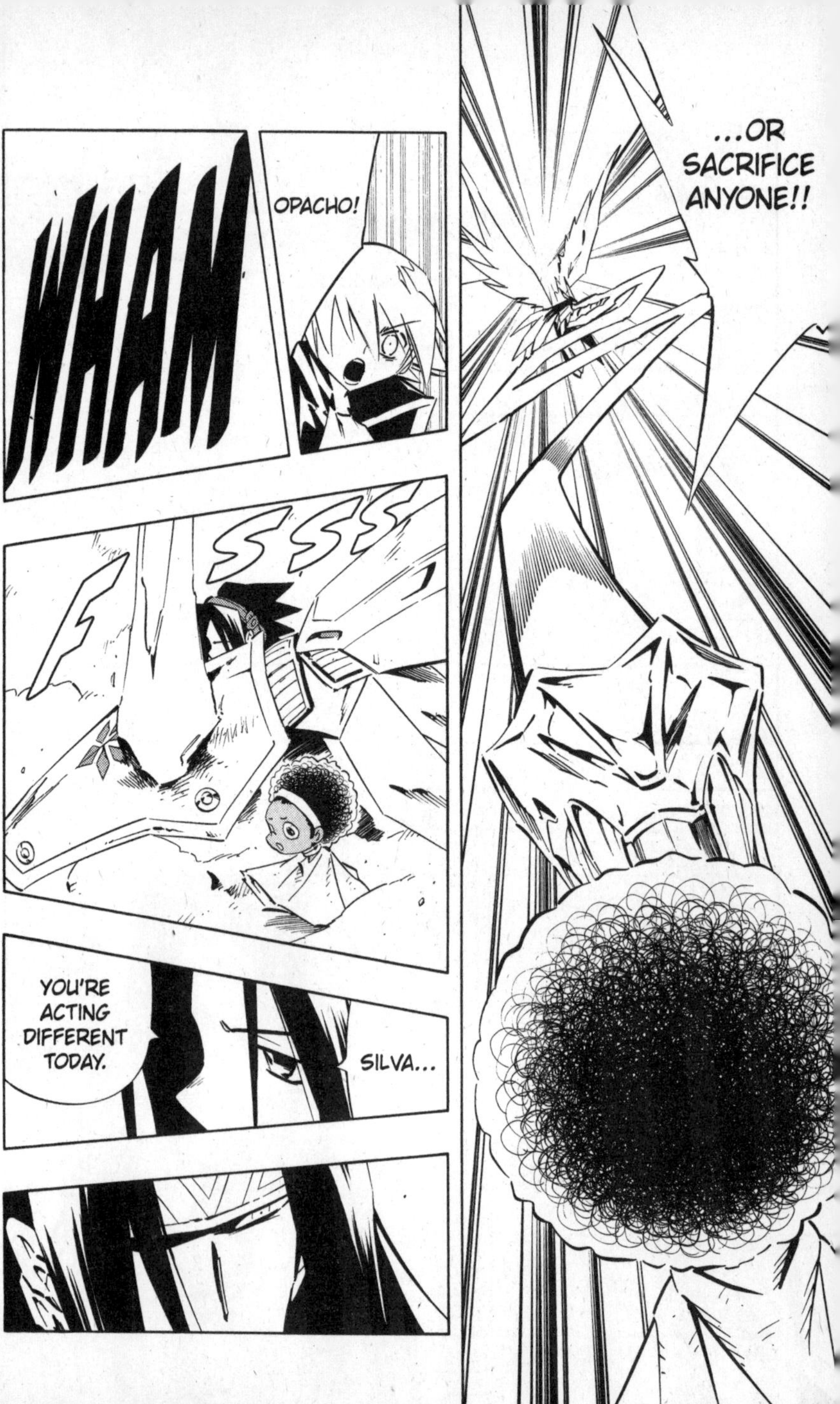
...OR SACRIFICE ANYONE!!
OPACHO!
WHAM
SSSS
SILVA...
YOU'RE ACTING DIFFERENT TODAY.

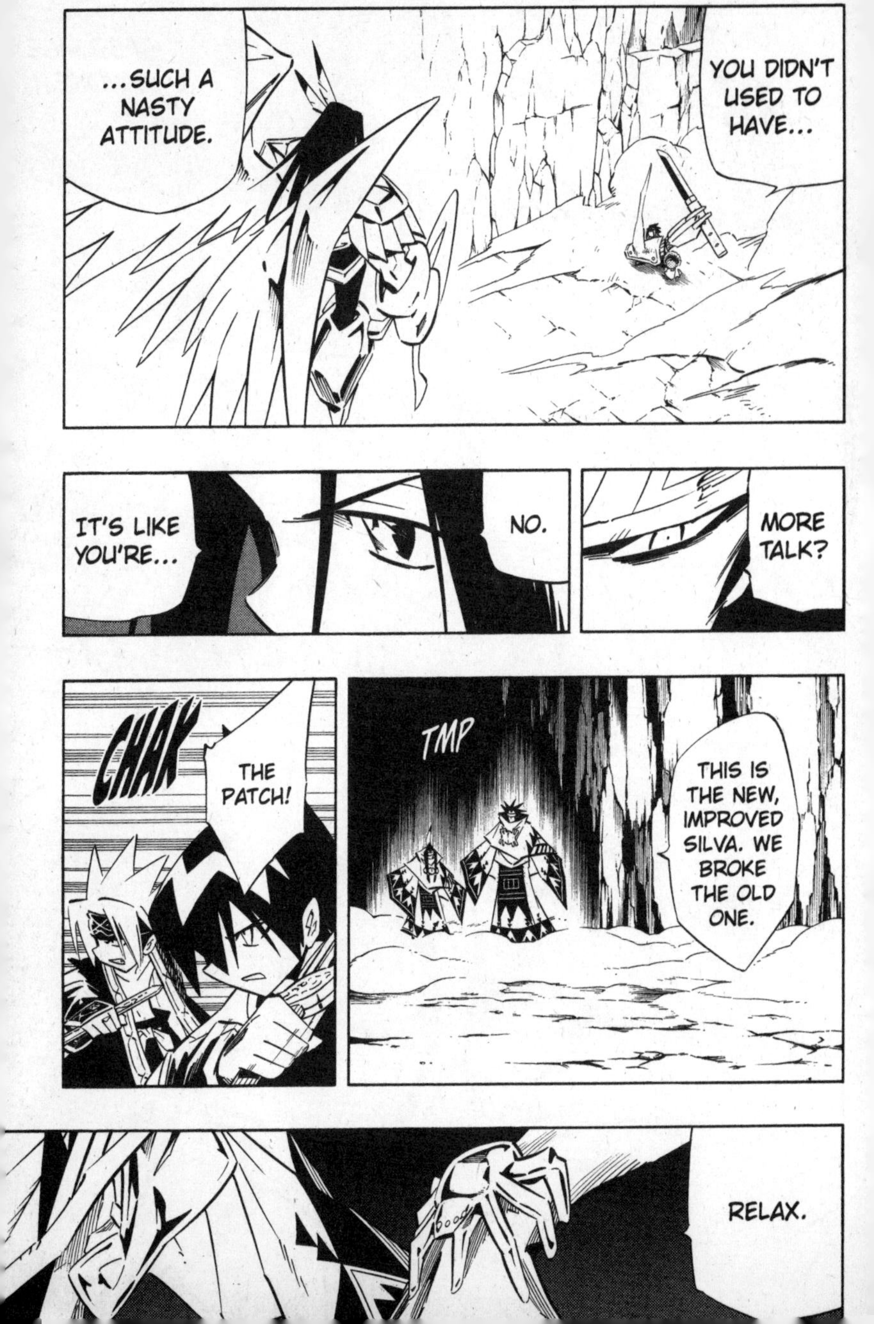
YOU DIDN'T USED TO HAVE...
...SUCH A NASTY ATTITUDE.
MORE TALK?
NO.
IT'S LIKE YOU'RE...
TMP
THIS IS THE NEW, IMPROVED SILVA. WE BROKE THE OLD ONE.
THE PATCH!
CHAK
RELAX.

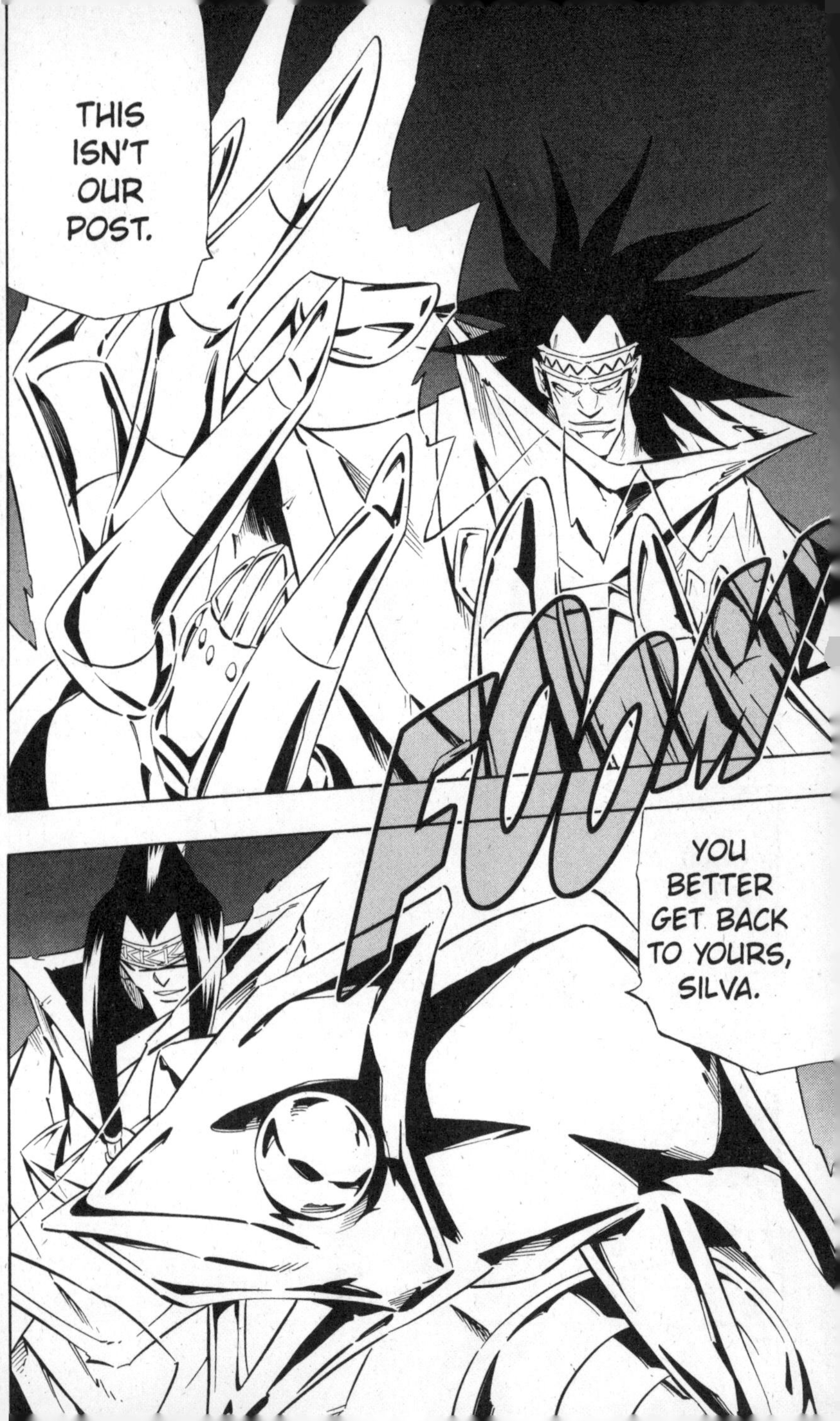
THIS ISN'T OUR POST.
FOOOM
YOU BETTER GET BACK TO YOURS, SILVA.

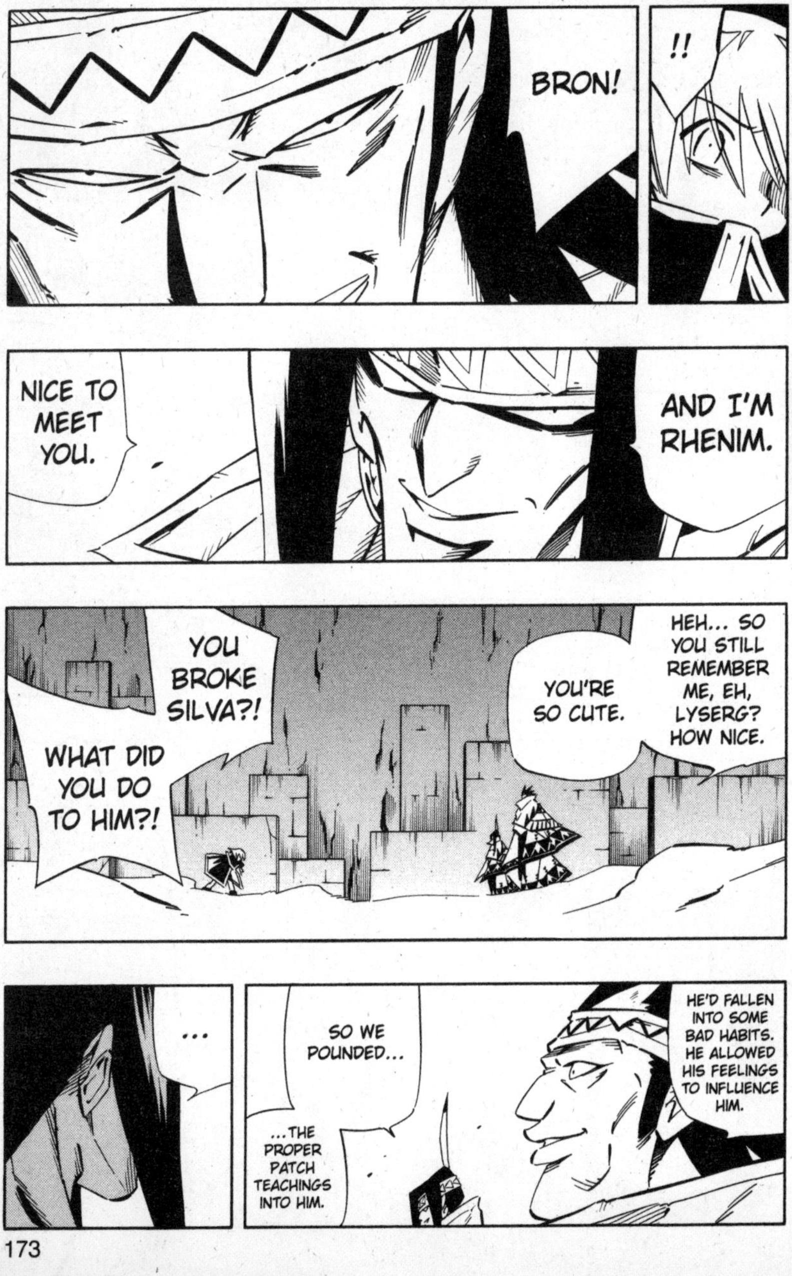
!!
BRON!
AND I'M RHENIM.
NICE TO MEET YOU.
HEH... SO YOU STILL REMEMBER ME, EH, LYSERG? HOW NICE.
YOU'RE SO CUTE.
YOU BROKE SILVA?!
WHAT DID YOU DO TO HIM?!
HE'D FALLEN INTO SOME BAD HABITS. HE ALLOWED HIS FEELINGS TO INFLUENCE HIM.
SO WE POUNDED...
...THE PROPER PATCH TEACHINGS INTO HIM.
...

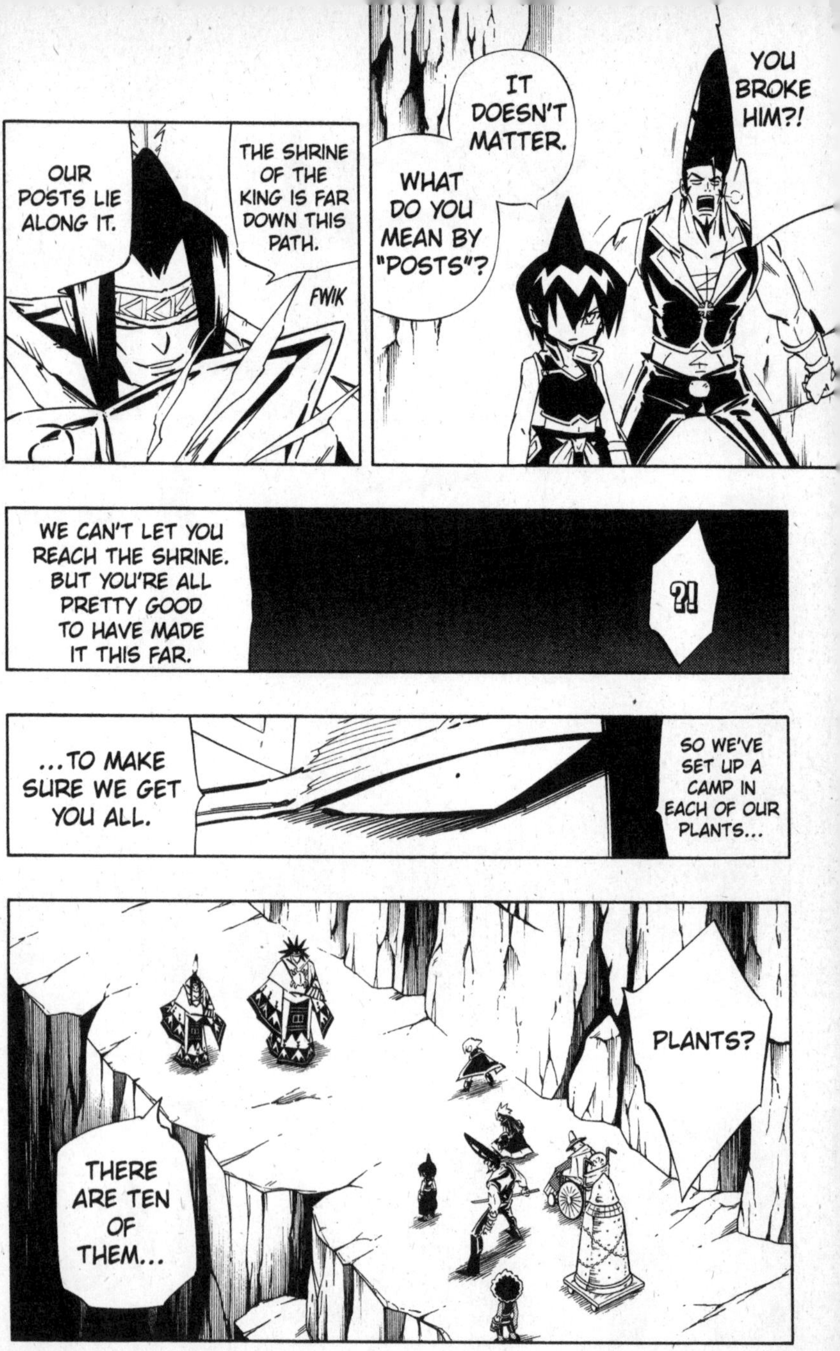
YOU BROKE HIM?!
IT DOESN'T MATTER.
WHAT DO YOU MEAN BY "POSTS"?
THE SHRINE OF THE KING IS FAR DOWN THIS PATH.
FWIK
OUR POSTS LIE ALONG IT.
?!
WE CAN'T LET YOU REACH THE SHRINE. BUT YOU'RE ALL PRETTY GOOD TO HAVE MADE IT THIS FAR.
SO WE'VE SET UP A CAMP IN EACH OF OUR PLANTS...
...TO MAKE SURE WE GET YOU ALL.
PLANTS?
THERE ARE TEN OF THEM...

DESERT...
VOLCANO ...
LAKE...
GORGE...
HIGH-LANDS ...
CAVE...
FOREST ...
OCEAN...
GLACIER ...
AND OUTER SPACE-ONE FOR EACH OFFICIANT.

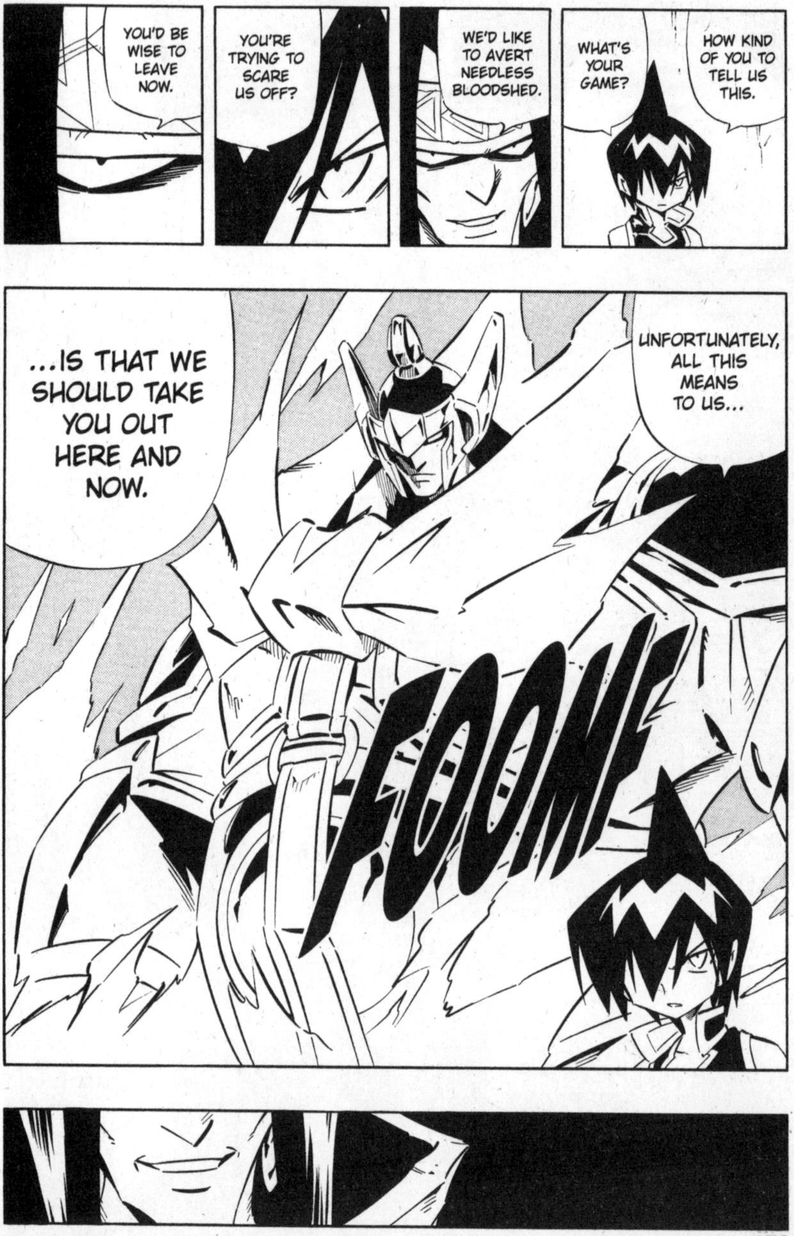
HOW KIND OF YOU TO TELL US THIS.
WHAT'S YOUR GAME?
WE'D LIKE TO AVERT NEEDLESS BLOODSHED.
YOU'RE TRYING TO SCARE US OFF?
YOU'D BE WISE TO LEAVE NOW.
UNFORTUNATELY, ALL THIS MEANS TO US...
...IS THAT WE SHOULD TAKE YOU OUT HERE AND NOW.
FOOM!

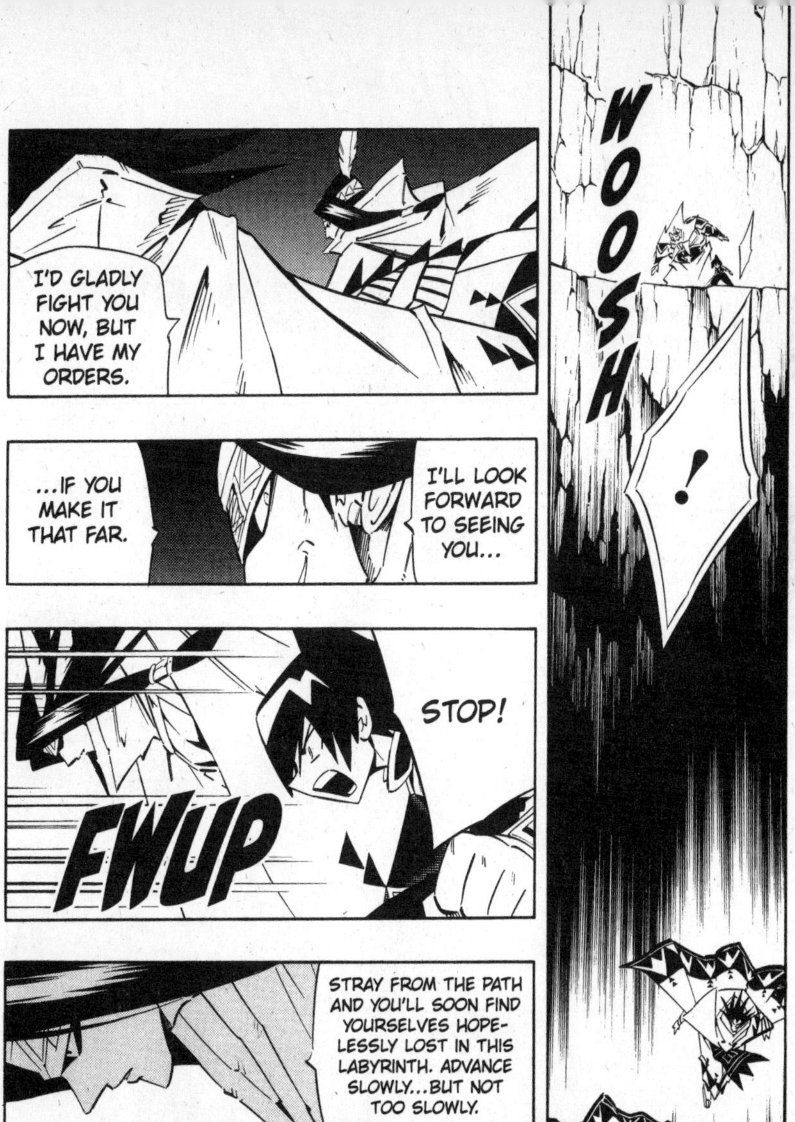
WOOSH
!
I'D GLADLY FIGHT YOU NOW, BUT I HAVE MY ORDERS.
I'LL LOOK FORWARD TO SEEING YOU...
...IF YOU MAKE IT THAT FAR.
STOP!
FWUP
STRAY FROM THE PATH AND YOU'LL SOON FIND YOURSELVES HOPE-LESSLY LOST IN THIS LABYRINTH. ADVANCE SLOWLY...BUT NOT TOO SLOWLY.

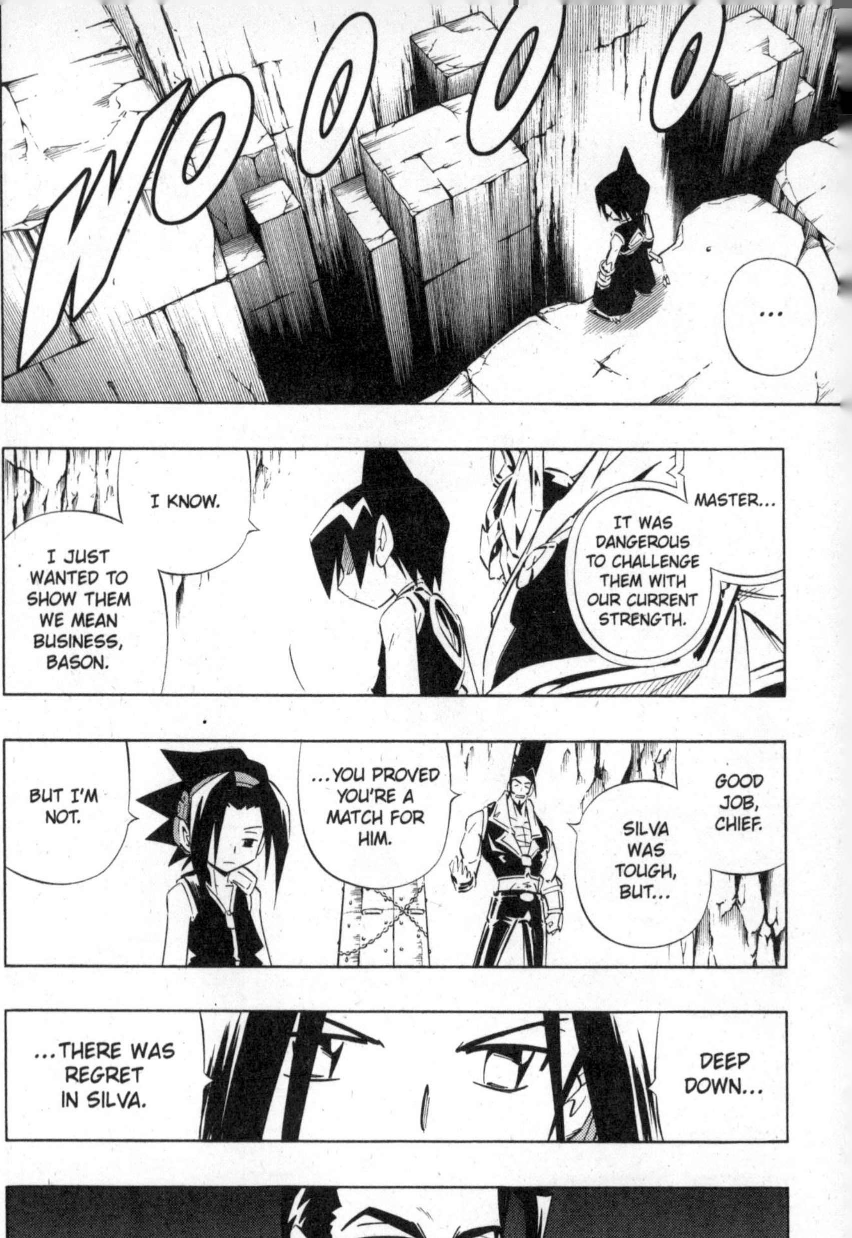
WOOOOO
...
MASTER...
IT WAS DANGEROUS TO CHALLENGE THEM WITH OUR CURRENT STRENGTH.
I KNOW.
I JUST WANTED TO SHOW THEM WE MEAN BUSINESS, BASON.
GOOD JOB, CHIEF.
SILVA WAS TOUGH, BUT...
...YOU PROVED YOU'RE A MATCH FOR HIM.
BUT I'M NOT.
DEEP DOWN...
...THERE WAS REGRET IN SILVA.

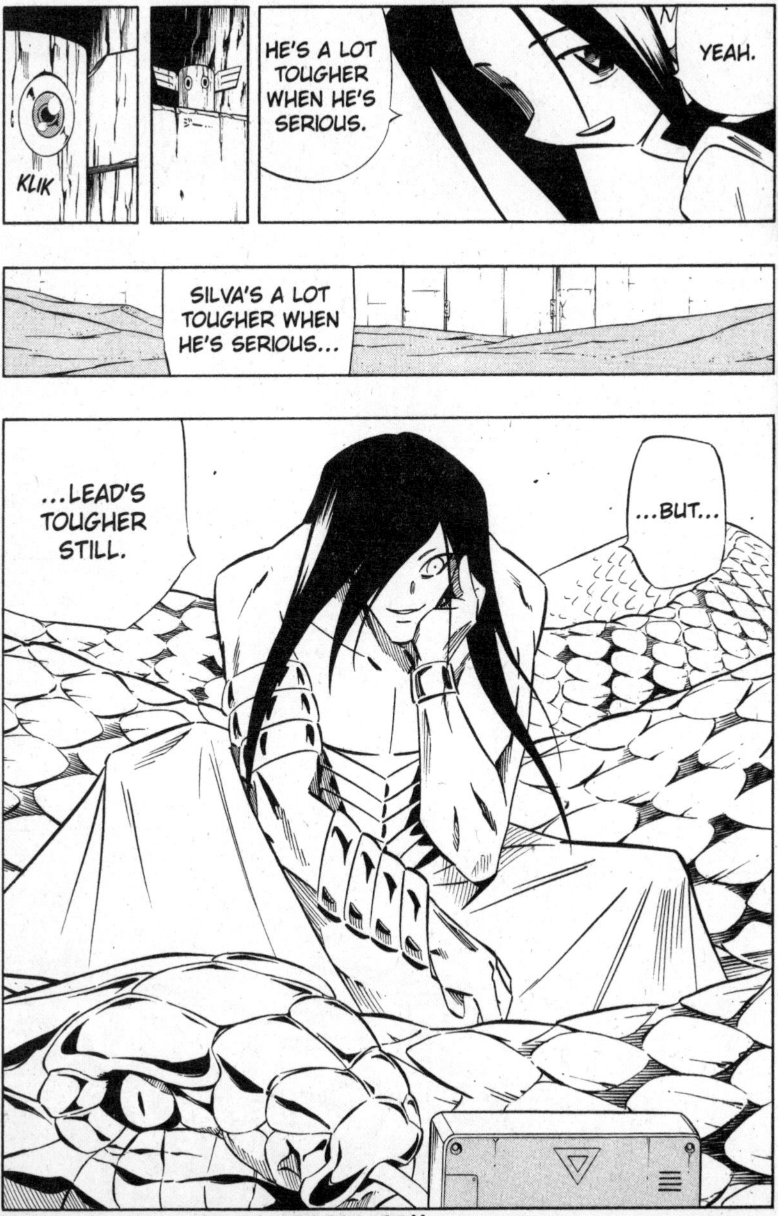
YEAH.
HE'S A LOT TOUGHER WHEN HE'S SERIOUS.
KLIK
SILVA'S A LOT TOUGHER WHEN HE'S SERIOUS...
...BUT...
...LEAD'S TOUGHER STILL.

TO BE CONTINUED!!

Shaman King

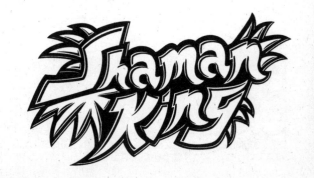

FUNBARI POEM:
THE BLOOM OF YOUTH

MICKEY'S WORLD

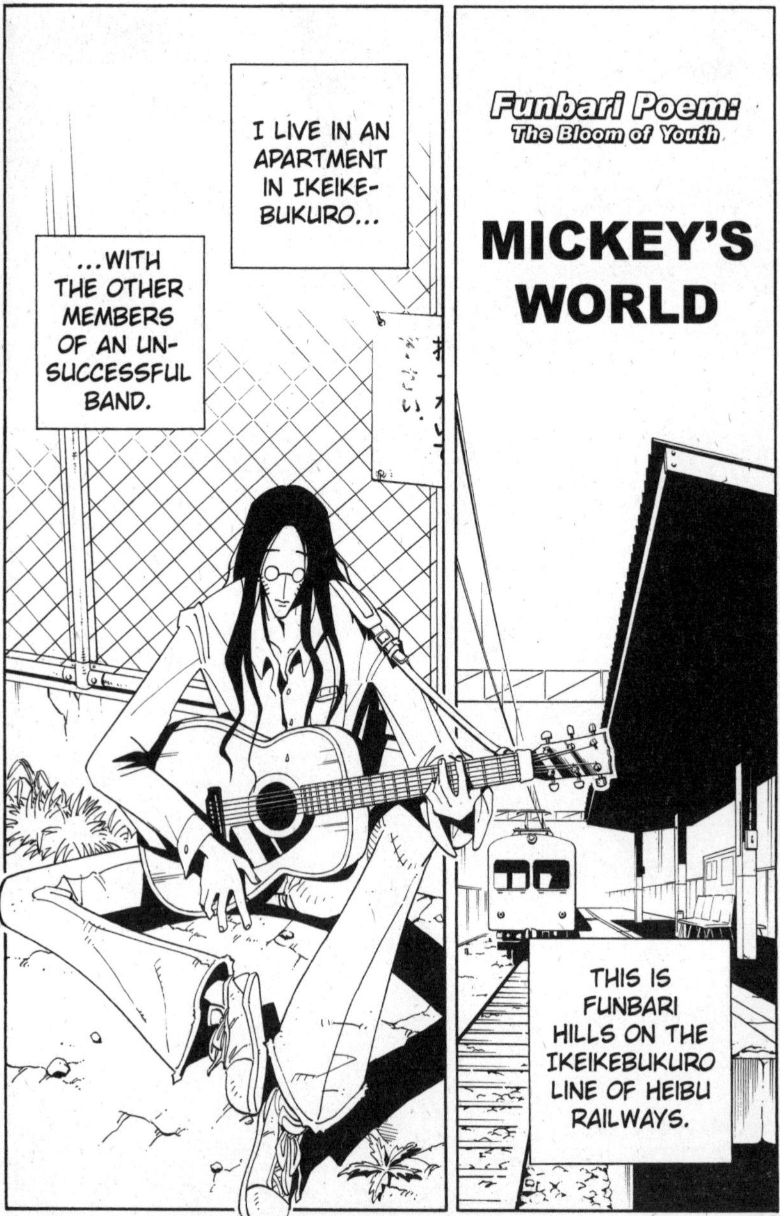
Funbari Poem:
The Bloom of Youth
MICKEY'S WORLD
THIS IS FUNBARI HILLS ON THE IKEIKEBUKURO LINE OF HEIBU RAILWAYS.
I LIVE IN AN APARTMENT IN IKEIKE-BUKURO...
...WITH THE OTHER MEMBERS OF AN UN-SUCCESSFUL BAND.

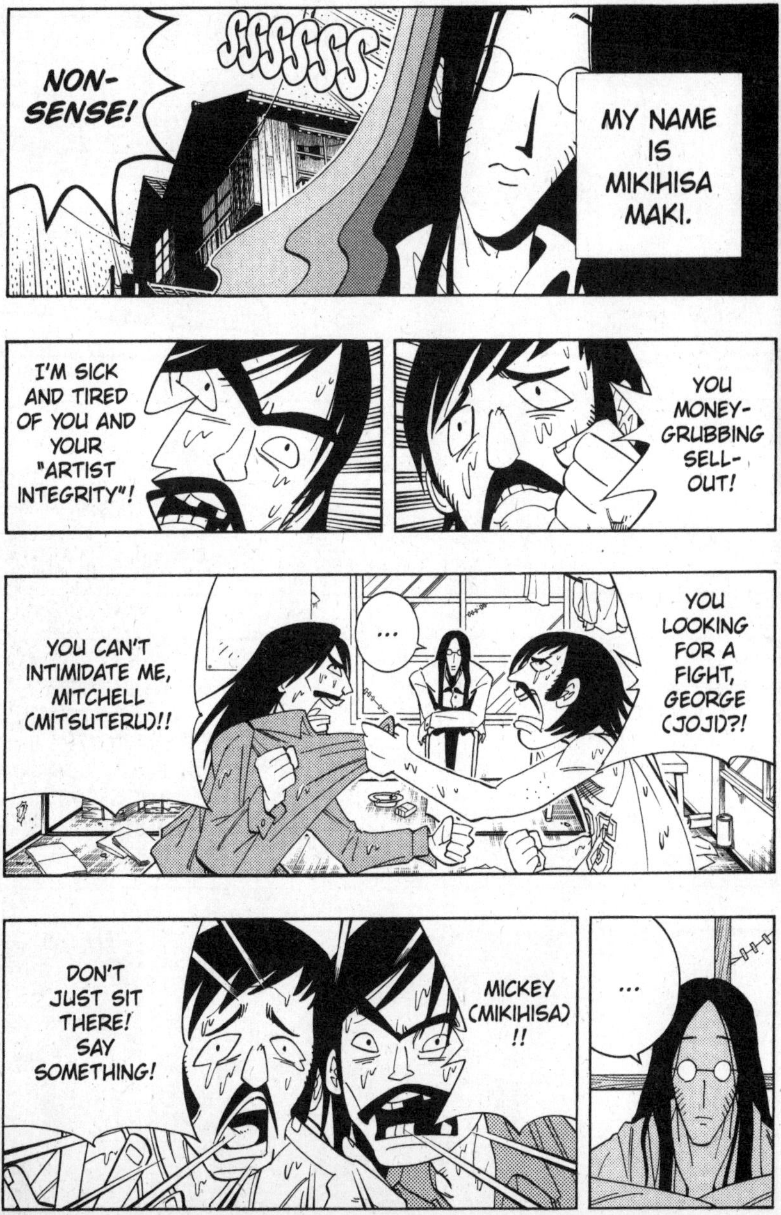
MY NAME IS MIKIHISA MAKI.
SSSSSS
NON-SENSE!
YOU MONEY-GRUBBING SELL-OUT!
I'M SICK AND TIRED OF YOU AND YOUR "ARTIST INTEGRITY"!
YOU LOOKING FOR A FIGHT, GEORGE (JOJI)?!
...
YOU CAN'T INTIMIDATE ME, MITCHELL (MITSUTERU)!!
...
MICKEY (MIKIHISA) !!
DON'T JUST SIT THERE! SAY SOMETHING!

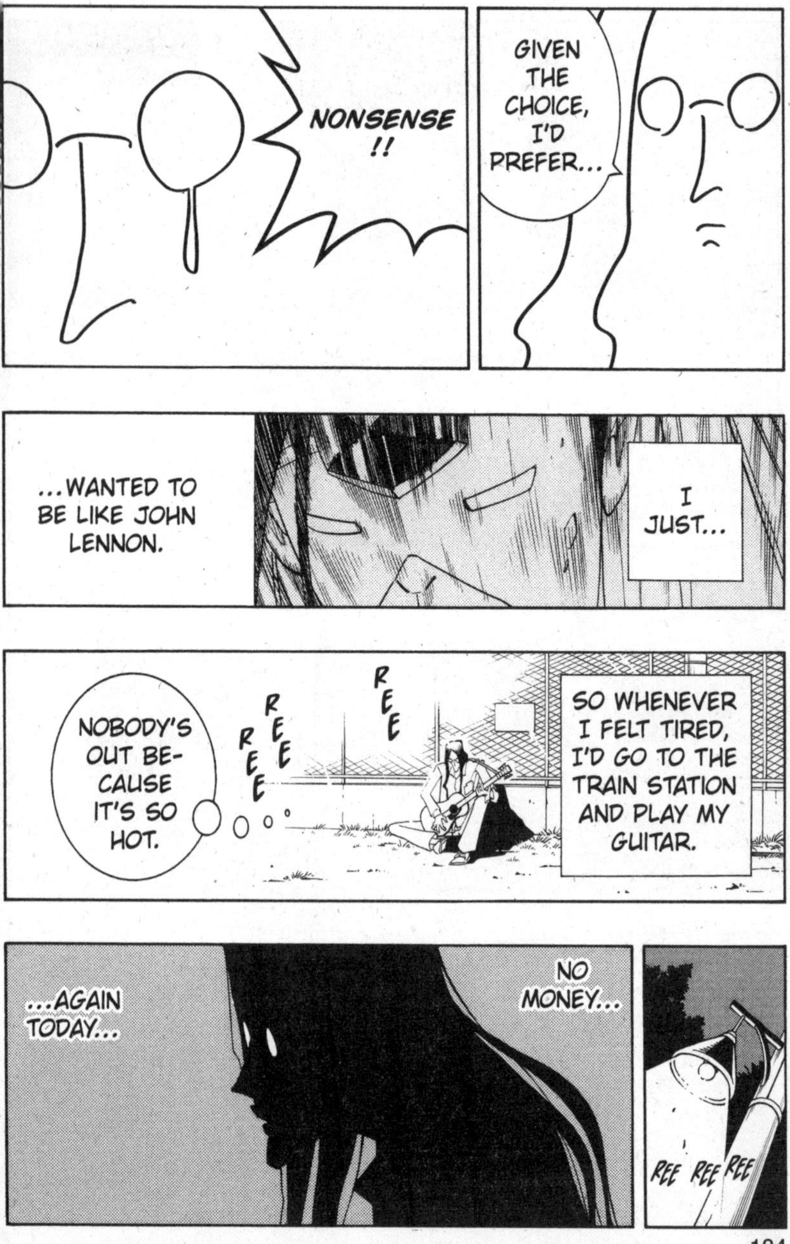
GIVEN THE CHOICE, I'D PREFER...
NONSENSE !!
I JUST...
...WANTED TO BE LIKE JOHN LENNON.
SO WHENEVER I FELT TIRED, I'D GO TO THE TRAIN STATION AND PLAY MY GUITAR.
REE
REE
REE
NOBODY'S OUT BE-CAUSE IT'S SO HOT.
REE REE REE
NO MONEY...
...AGAIN TODAY...

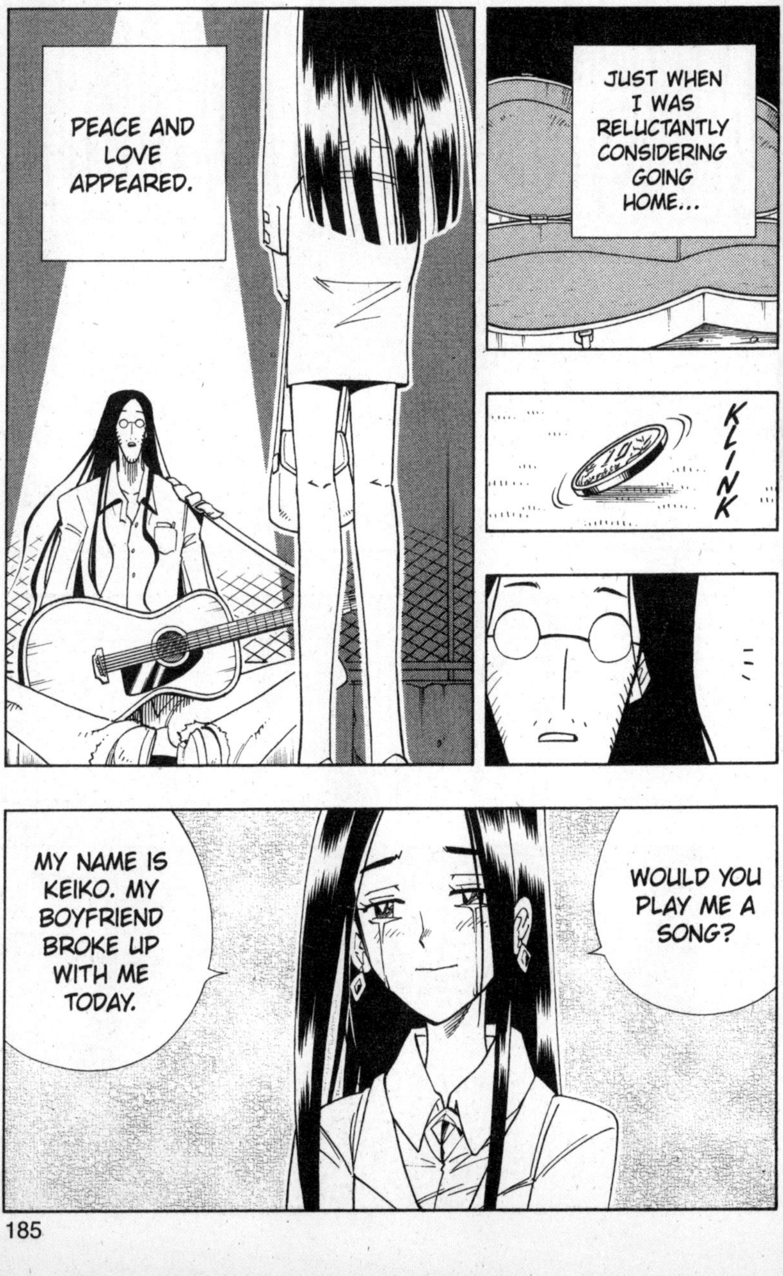
JUST WHEN I WAS RELUCTANTLY CONSIDERING GOING HOME...
KLINK
PEACE AND LOVE APPEARED.
MY NAME IS KEIKO. MY BOYFRIEND BROKE UP WITH ME TODAY.
WOULD YOU PLAY ME A SONG?

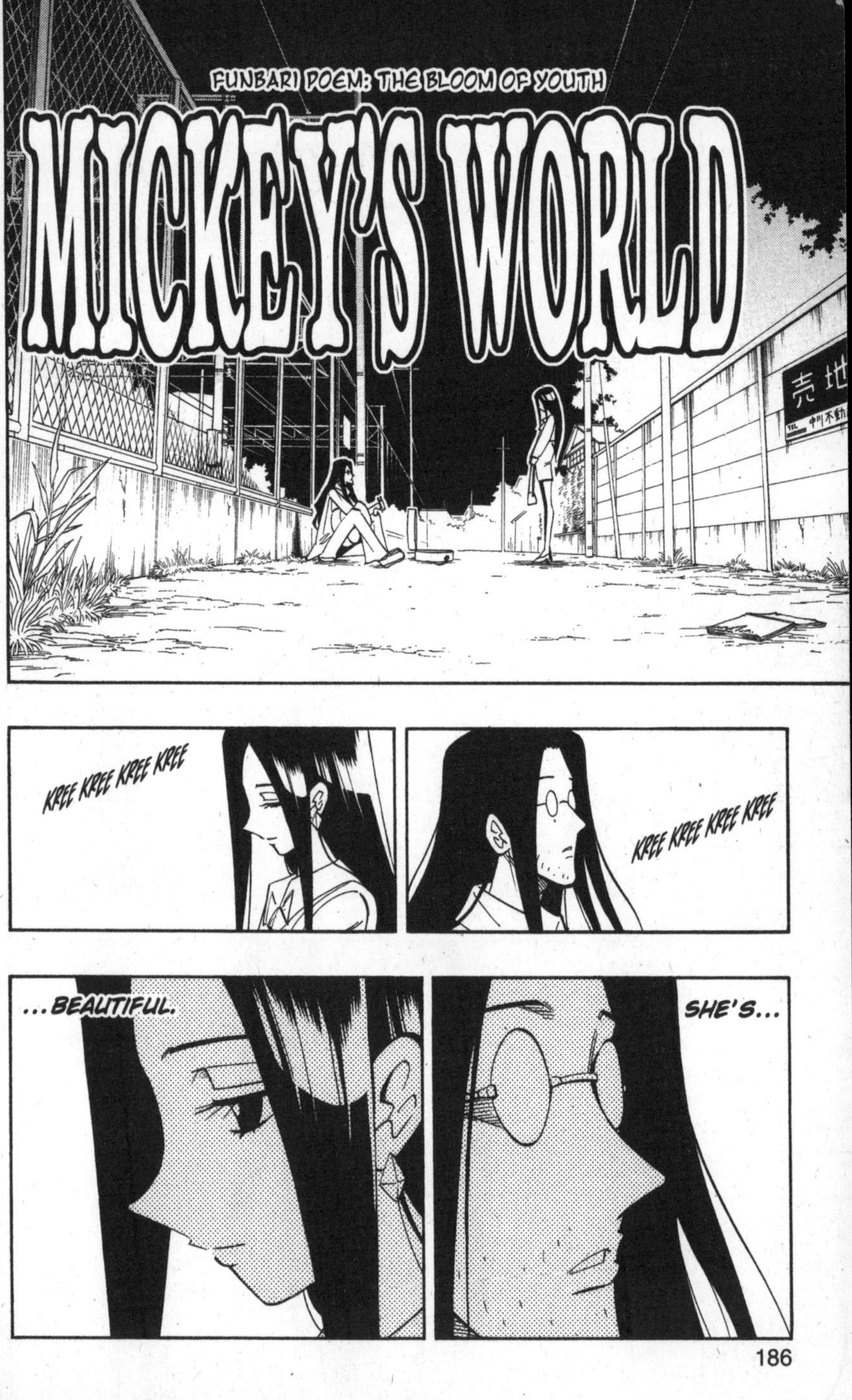
FUNBARI POEM: THE BLOOM OF YOUTH
MICKEY'S WORLD
売地
KREE KREE KREE KREE
KREE KREE KREE KREE
SHE'S...
...BEAUTIFUL.

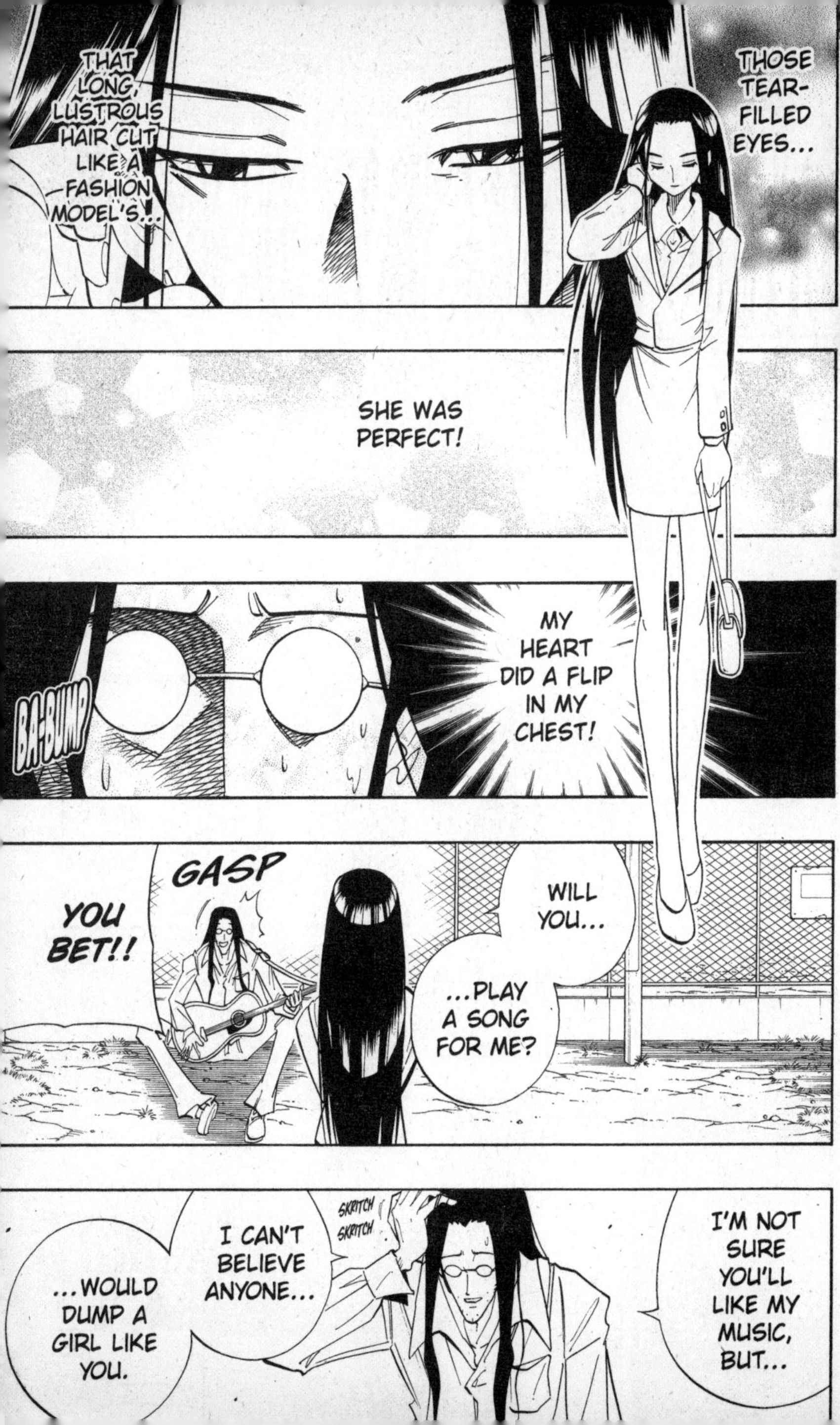
THOSE TEAR-FILLED EYES...
THAT LONG, LUSTROUS HAIR CUT LIKE A FASHION MODEL'S...
SHE WAS PERFECT!
MY HEART DID A FLIP IN MY CHEST!
BA-BUMP
WILL YOU...
...PLAY A SONG FOR ME?
GASP
YOU BET!!
I'M NOT SURE YOU'LL LIKE MY MUSIC, BUT...
SKRITCH SKRITCH
I CAN'T BELIEVE ANYONE...
...WOULD DUMP A GIRL LIKE YOU.

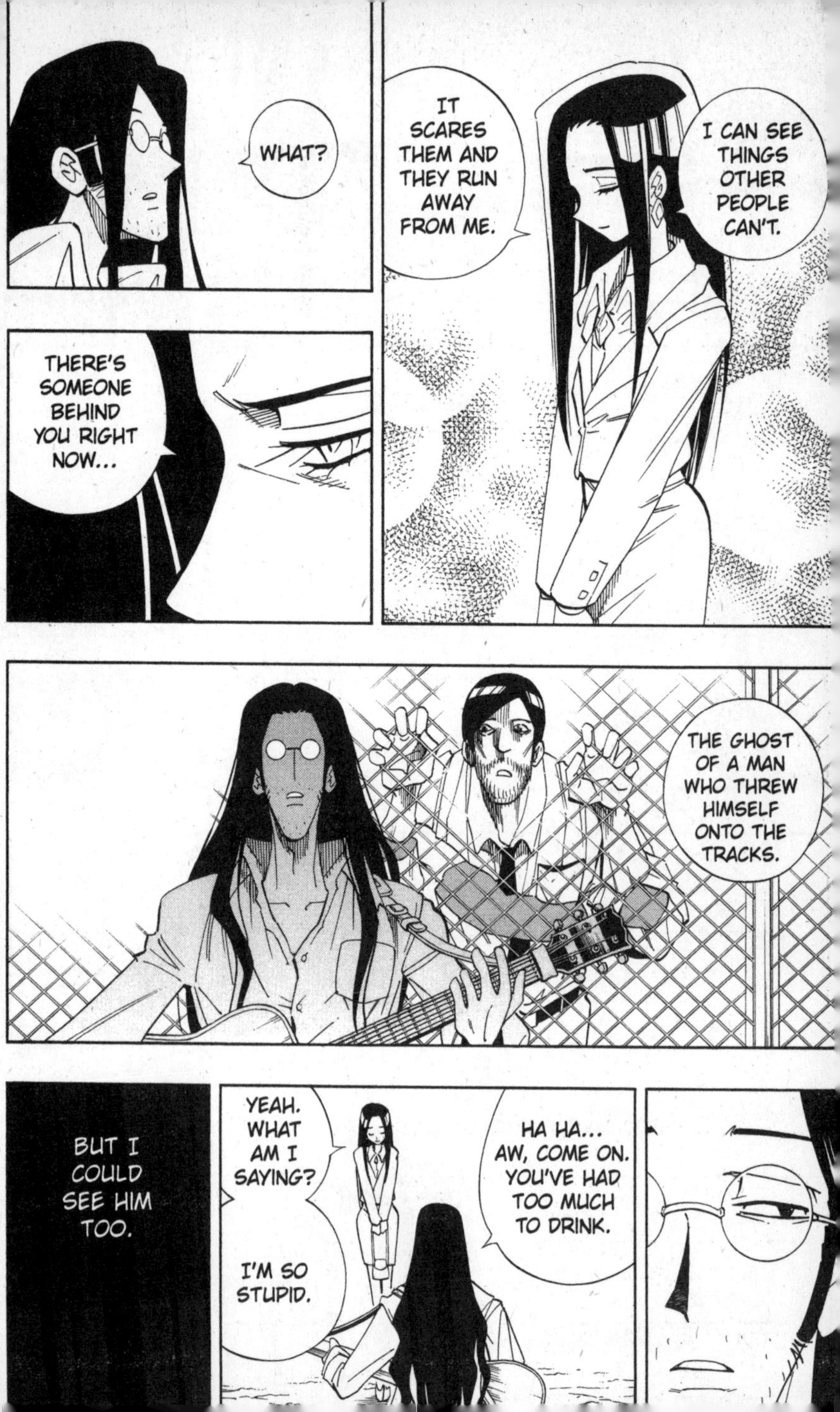
I CAN SEE THINGS OTHER PEOPLE CAN'T.
IT SCARES THEM AND THEY RUN AWAY FROM ME.
WHAT?
THERE'S SOMEONE BEHIND YOU RIGHT NOW...
THE GHOST OF A MAN WHO THREW HIMSELF ONTO THE TRACKS.
HA HA... AW, COME ON. YOU'VE HAD TOO MUCH TO DRINK.
YEAH. WHAT AM I SAYING?
I'M SO STUPID.
BUT I COULD SEE HIM TOO.

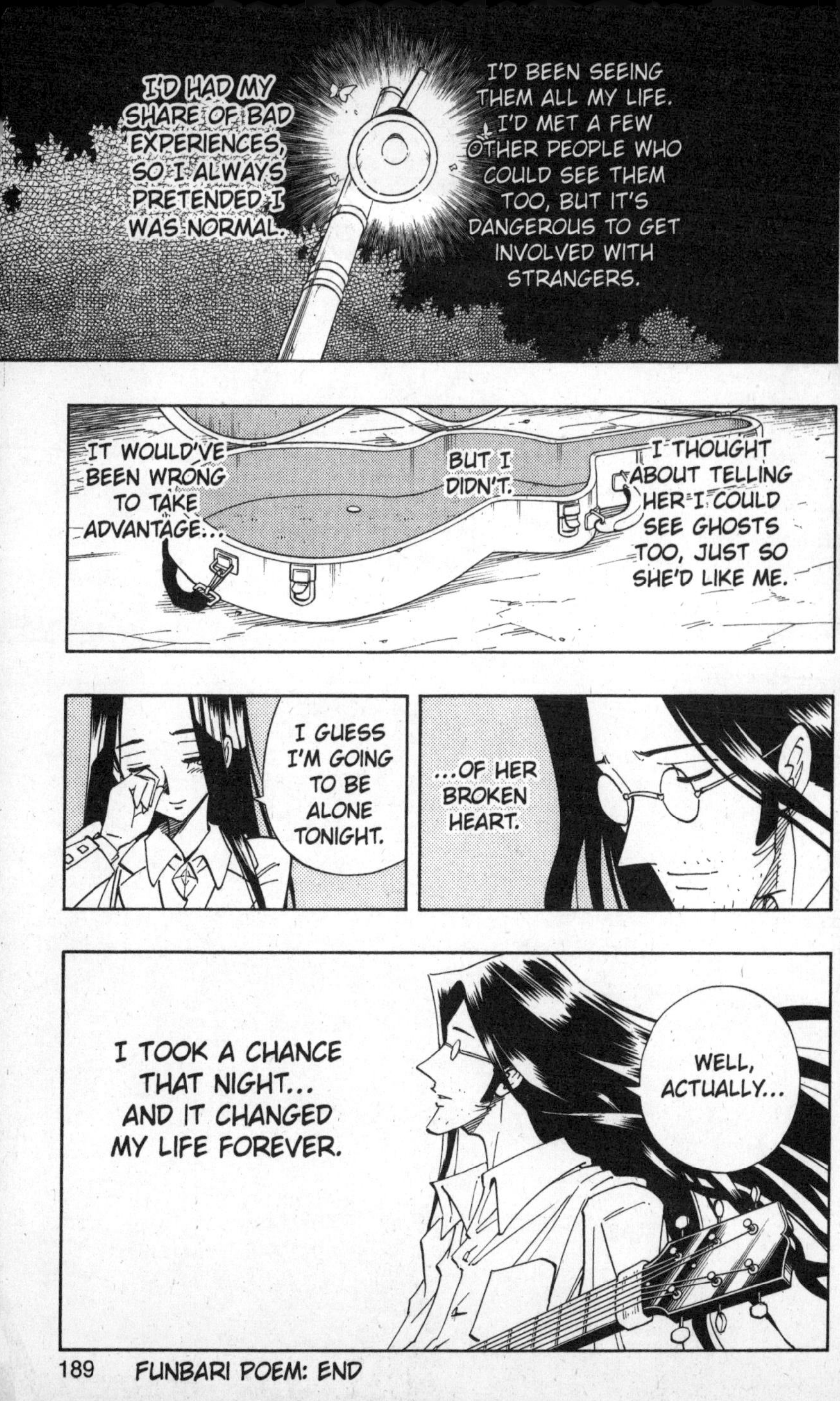
I'D BEEN SEEING THEM ALL MY LIFE. I'D MET A FEW OTHER PEOPLE WHO COULD SEE THEM TOO, BUT IT'S DANGEROUS TO GET INVOLVED WITH STRANGERS.
I'D HAD MY SHARE OF BAD EXPERIENCES, SO I ALWAYS PRETENDED I WAS NORMAL.
I THOUGHT ABOUT TELLING HER I COULD SEE GHOSTS TOO, JUST SO SHE'D LIKE ME.
BUT I DIDN'T.
IT WOULD'VE BEEN WRONG TO TAKE ADVANTAGE...
...OF HER BROKEN HEART.
I GUESS I'M GOING TO BE ALONE TONIGHT.
WELL, ACTUALLY...
I TOOK A CHANCE THAT NIGHT... AND IT CHANGED MY LIFE FOREVER.

 FUNBARI POEM: END

IN THE NEXT VOLUME...

In successive order, Yoh and his crew find themselves pitted against a snake spirit, a spider spirit and an owl spirit. Each freaky adversary presents a puzzle more complex than the one preceding it. And to complicate matters further, Yoh has only fifteen hours to get it done.

AVAILABLE NOVEMBER 2010!